Technical Writing

D0580052

The Graphics of Communication

Fifth Edition

The Graphics of Communication

Typography
Layout
Design
Production

Russell N. Baird
Ohio University

The Late
Arthur T. Turnbull
Ohio University

Duncan McDonald
University of Oregon

Holt, Rinehart and Winston
New York   Chicago   San Francisco   Philadelphia
Montreal   Toronto   London   Sydney
Tokyo   Mexico City   Rio de Janeiro   Madrid

To ATT

Acquisitions Editor: Lucy Rosendahl
Senior Project Editor: Lester A. Sheinis
Senior Production Manager: Nancy Myers
Senior Design Supervisor: Louis Scardino

Library of Congress Cataloging-in-Publication Data

Baird, Russell N.
  The graphics of communication.

  Rev. ed. of: The graphics of communication /
Arthur T. Turnbull.
  Bibliography: p.
  Includes index.
  1. Printing, Practical.   2. Graphic arts.
I. Turnbull, Arthur T.   II. McDonald, Duncan.
III. Turnbull, Arthur T. Graphics of communication.
IV. Title.
Z244.B17   1987   686.2′24   86–18386

ISBN 0-03-071646-2

Address correspondence to:
383 Madison Avenue
New York, NY 10017
All rights reserved
Printed in the United States of America
Published simultaneously in Canada
7 8 9 0   039 9 8 7 6 5 4 3 2 1

Holt, Rinehart and Winston
The Dryden Press
Saunders College Publishing

Preface

Preparation of this fifth edition of *The Graphics of Communication* was begun just twenty years after the publication of the first edition. In that twenty years a technological revolution has occurred, affecting every aspect of print media production. One need only recall that in 1964 hand setting of type was the only production laboratory activity taking place in graphic arts courses of schools of journalism to appreciate the scope of that revolution.

Our preface for the fourth edition spoke with enthusiasm and sheer amazement of the "totally new technology now involved in word processing and mass communication. With the computer at its center, an explosion of technological innovations has burst upon us more quickly and with far greater force than we previously had imagined could be possible."

What was startling and innovative then has now become commonplace. Our tasks for this edition therefore were to reorder the presentation of material to put subject matter in better perspective and more logical sequence; to take into account the greater emphasis on images in the presentation of messages; to change emphases to take into account technological change; to update and increase illustrations explaining textual material; and, above all, to make this a better teaching aid.

A new introductory chapter sets the framework for the new order of presentation; an added chapter on qualitative aspects of picture editing puts production aspects of illustrations in the supportive role they properly play; two chapters of detail about computer systems have been condensed into a less technical chapter accommodating the widespread familiarity with personal computers that has developed since the last edition; and illustrations have been replaced or added as necessary throughout. The chapters on design, color, processes, and photo scaling have been totally reconstructed to make them more effective, and many other chapters have been substantially changed with the same goal in mind.

Even with all the changes, much of the basic approach taken in the previous editions has been carried over into this one. The death of Professor A. T. Turnbull, as preparations for this edition got underway, was a great loss to his colleagues and to students who have benefited from his teaching and writing for several decades. Much of the valuable information carried over to this edition represents a contribution he continues to make.

Professor Duncan McDonald of the University of Oregon agreed to share authorship for this and succeeding editions and took primary responsibility for Chapters 2, 3, 4, 8, 11, 16, and 17. Responsibility for the remaining chapters rests with Professor Baird.

As was the case with previous editions, a debt of gratitude is due to the editors, publishers, artists, and production persons who contributed to this edition. Many of the illustrations added to this edition come from newspapers, magazines, printers, equipment manufacturers, and others associated with graphics-related industries who contributed to this edition. Although credit is given wherever such material appears in the text, we wish to add our special thanks here for these valuable contributions.

We wish to acknowledge the following reviewers: Ray Laakaniemi, Bowling Green State University; Ken Metzler, University of Oregon; Linda Schamber, Syracuse University; Robert Taylor, University of Wisconsin-Madison; and Birgit Wassmuth, University of Missouri. We would also like to thank photographers Greg Blackman, Stanley Forman, Ralph Kliesch, Rosanne Olson, Patrick Sullivan, and Betty Udesen for their contributions. Assistance from Robert Vereen, John Hammond, and the staff of *DIY Retailing* magazine, as well as Ralph Brem of the *Pittsburgh Press*, Gus Hartoonian of the *Chicago Tribune*, and Maureen Decker of the Allentown (Pa.) *Morning Call* was far beyond that normally given by professionals cooperating with an educational project. Credit is also due Professor Bob Richardson of Ohio University for consultation and advice regarding illustrations and to artist John Goodwin who drew many of the charts and diagrams used throughout. And, as is always the case with a project such as this, special thanks for assistance and support must go to family members, in this case to Jane and Vanessa McDonald and Jane and Tate Baird. The assistance of all of the above in the preparation of this edition is hereby gratefully acknowledged, but for any faults that remain, full responsibility is shared by the authors.

RNB
DMcD

Contents

1

The Graphics of Communication: An Introduction

Graphics, *the visual aspects of written communication,* have emerged as basic foundation blocks for effective communication in a society that is becoming increasingly reliant on technology and communication for solving day-to-day problems.

Trying to imagine our modern world without printed communication is like trying to imagine a desert without sand or an ocean without water. Virtually everything we do is geared to printed communication. Our scientific discoveries are recorded and passed along to others in printed journals. Religious faiths are nurtured and carried from generation to generation through printing. The information required in a democratic society is distributed to mass audiences via brochures, advertising leaflets, billboards and other media as well as the ever-present newspapers, magazines and books. Printed forms, many of them marvelous examples of the need for printed messages to transmit complex information clearly, feed the tax mills and keep government in operation. We move from place to place with the assistance of printed maps, create new structures based on printed plans and separate toothpaste from hair cream and poisons from medicines by way of printed packages. We know one-way streets from two-way thoroughfares, men's rooms from women's and exits from entrances through printed signs. Indeed, virtually all modern human activities rely in some way on our ability to communicate with visual means.

Communication, Not Art

Although most discussions of printing and related activities refer to the industry as *graphic arts,* the choice of the phrase *Graphics of Communication* as a title for this book is deliberate. Although creating visual works of *art* is an interesting and valuable activity that can be the source of great *self-satisfaction,* it is not our concern here. Graphic art is excluded here to permit concentration on the study of communication, of effective techniques for relaying information from a source to an intended audience. Self-satisfaction can only be a secondary, not a primary goal.

Communication of any kind seems to be difficult enough without the complications which arise from the introduction of printed *media* into the process. When the warden in a prison movie mutters, "What we have here is a failure to communicate," and then moves to physical violence to make his point, he is joining others in all walks of life who have voiced the same complaint. Failures of marriages, business firms, educational processes and most other human endeavors, including international relationships, are often laid to a failure to communicate.

The communication model in Figure 1-1 makes the process look simple enough. Direct interpersonal communication is simple to model with its source, message, receiver and feedback route, and obviously offers the best opportunity for effective communication. Even so, human frailties in source and receiver and vagaries in the message can slow or block the process. Interference with communication (noise) is at work in every stage. When the third party, a medium to carry the message, is necessary (because the receiver is too distant or in a greater mass than can be reached in person), new sources of noise are introduced. These new obstacles and challenges are the subjects of this book.

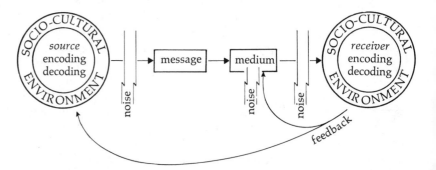

1-1 The communication model.

Graphic Noise in Communication

The ultimate in graphic noise would be the presentation of a message in black ink on black paper; the visual presentation would be illegible and would block communication as effectively as the roar of motorcycles outside an open window overpowers a speaker in a classroom. Such an obvious graphic fault may—and should—seem ridiculous, but there are others not so readily noticeable to laymen that should seem equally ridiculous for the graphic communicator. Some such flaws, however, can be detected so often in visual messages as to seem common and routine.

Here are just a few examples of graphics getting in the way of communication:

Dark ink on a dark background may not stop the communication, but it certainly slows it down.

Some large type, turned on its side and run from top to bottom, may not be as "noisy" in the communication process as type that is upside down, but it is nonetheless causing interference because of its form. Lines of type can be so long as to make reading difficult, and type size obviously can be inadequate for mass readers or certain age groups.

A heading can be too small to attract attention and miss its mark completely. Or it may be placed over a strong illustration that grabs readers and moves them along into the rest of the message, causing the heading to be ignored.

Color can either aid communication or get in its way. A drawing of a purple Easter bunny over a column of type can make it virtually impossible for the reader to get the type's message.

Complicated subjects, loaded with numbers beyond human capacity to comprehend, when presented only in words and figures can meet instant rejection by intended receivers. When illustrated with good graphs and charts, however, they may increase interest and comprehension sufficiently to get the message across.

Design of a visual message, too, can be so cluttered and confusing as to interfere with communication. Even the selection of a printing method for moving the message can interfere: Some methods do well with pictures and poorly with words, or vice versa. Professionals working with graphics, therefore, are concerned with the principles of good design, the selection and effective use of typography, color, photos and other illustrations, and the use of appropriate technology to accomplish their goals. These subjects are all explored in depth in later chapters.

Goals of Graphic Presentation

The desire for efficient communication in print leads us to four logical goals for each such communication:

1. capture the attention of the desired audience
2. guide the audience through the message without injecting graphic noise and perhaps add to the effectiveness of the message
3. leave some lasting impression
4. use appropriate technology to deliver the message efficiently and economically.

To achieve the first three of these goals we obviously have these things to work with: large and small type, photos and other illustrations, and the necessary technology to deliver them well. This listing, however, omits one element, and that omission points to two important underlying principles of graphic presentation. The element is *white space,* the starting element in design. Actually, it is the white space that one "sees" when viewing a printed medium. Seeing involves light entering the eyes and registering an image. Those who work with film in darkrooms know that a camera, recording a black on white image, receives only the white space. Consequently the film is exposed where light strikes it, but remains perfectly clear and unexposed where the image is black. The camera has seen the white space around the black headline, not the headline itself.

Although it may seem to be belaboring theoretical trivia to say we see only the white space, the principle does drive home the importance of white space in design for print. To realize that *white space can destroy design as effectively or more so than black space* is essential for the novice. Secondly, the earlier example of black on black being illegible can be expanded to include red on red, white on white, and any other presentation lacking contrast. *Without contrast there is no design;* all is lost. No meaningful message can be conveyed. It is wise to remember that many words, too, get their meaning from contrasts: large from small, tall from short, wet from dry, and so on.

These two principles are especially evident as we try to achieve the first goal: to capture the attention of the reader. They also prevail, however, as we try to deliver the details of the message without letting graphic presentation interfere with the message delivery. Each printed message, whether it is an ad trying to get readers to return a coupon, or a news article delivering information, cannot leave the desired impression if we do not adhere to these principles.

Like so many things in life, graphics decisions are also tied directly to costs and consequently to technology. Reaching mass audiences can be expensive and technically difficult, but increasingly sophisticated technology has opened up new doors while increasing the complexity of decision making in this aspect of printed communication.

Scope of the Industry

Sophisticated technology has brought us computers, satellites, microwave relays, electronic scanners, and related devices that can record words and illustrations in seconds, transmit the information to distant points, and produce the images for mass distribution in very little time.

Figures showing the size of the printing/publishing industry spawned by this technology and public demand are staggering. It is the largest category of the 20 major manufacturing groups for which the government keeps records. Nearly 50,000 plants employing more than a million persons produce about $76 billion in goods annually. And we all know it is difficult to find a town or county without some sort of printing establishment.

These plants turn out about 1740 daily newspapers, 8000 weeklies, and 11,000 magazines, according to U.S. Standard Industrial Classification listings. About 45,000 books are published annually, and catalogs, directories, newsletters, greeting cards, labels, legal documents, advertising and public relations brochures, shoppers, maps, music and assorted other items are produced in a never-ending flow.

Staggering though they are, these figures do not include, in a broad sense, much of what must be considered printing. For example, commercial organizations produce, often in their own duplicating departments, internal periodicals that escape any tallying. Government agencies, hospitals, colleges, school systems, and other groups also operate internal printing departments. And the flood of home computers with their own printers has taken a form of printing into countless homes in all parts of the country.

Citizens of the United States and most countries in the Western world are being flooded with the printed word, and to keep from drowning they must discard much of what they receive without even reading it. The term "junk mail" that is applied to unsolicited promotional materials is symbolic of an attitude approaching contempt for printed messages. Bombarded from all sides with great volumes of printed matter, readers view such material with indifference or even ridicule and disrespect. But that has not always been the case.

Early Attempts

In the years when the clergy struggled to preserve their views by recording their teachings through hand lettering, the importance of a message was immediately enhanced when it could be said that "It is written." Words in print carried an instant authority that often could be missing from oral utterances.

This special importance attached to written communication was then well deserved, and it prevailed through centuries of struggle to improve communication technology. One of the most remarkable developments of human civilization was the alphabet, the basis for our printed language. Although it is often placed in the context of "simple as your ABCs," the alphabet's symbols form a visual code enabling formation of words and sentences to carry meaning of both concrete and abstract subjects from one human to another. Without such a code, printed communication, as we know it, could not exist.

Johann Gutenberg and Movable Type

With the invention by Johann Gutenberg of movable type and a system of pressing raised, ink-bearing metal letters against paper to mass produce writing, modern printing was born in the middle of the fifteenth century. Gutenberg's letterpress printing, with its hand composition of type, prevailed for centuries without significant improvements. More than five hundred years later, the great editor of the *New York Tribune,* Horace Greeley, laboriously picked each metal letter from a drawer to reproduce such great journalism as his editorials urging President Lincoln to free the slaves and the unemployed of New York to "Go West, young man." Making lines flush to the right as well as the left (called justification) involved placing thin pieces of metal between words. And then there was the boring process of returning each piece of type to its proper bin, from which it would be drawn and used again and again until its printing face was so worn as to make it almost illegible.

Linotypes and Photoengravings

One can imagine the impact of a series of improvements developed in the United States near the close of the nineteenth century. The burgeoning popularity of newspapers arising from cheap prices (the Penny Press) and sensational content (yellow journalism) created demand for millions of copies on a daily basis, an impossibility with Gutenberg-era technology. Hand typesetting and lever presses were too slow to satisfy the ever-increasing demand of a growing population. Emphasis on research and development by publishers quickly brought satisfactory results. A keyboard operated machine called a Linotype permitted an operator to set full lines of type as a solid slug of lead with lines automatically justified. Instead of requiring each letter to be returned to its bin, the Linotype made it possible to discard lines of type into a melting pot to be molded into type again. This carefree distribution of type also meant that worn-out letters were a thing of the past; each line was freshly cast from new metal.

The reproduction of photographs in print seemed to signal the ultimate step in the evolution of printing. Readers of the *New York Graphic* in 1880 were the first to see a printed reproduction of a photo, made possible by what is called the *halftone* process. The blending of tones in a photo (referred to as *continuous tone*) had seemed to defy creation of a metal plate with a raised printed surface that would produce all the tones. An optical illusion created by dots of ink on paper proved to be the solution. With the halftone process the original continuous tone photo was rephotographed through a screen, thus breaking the image into dots on a film negative. Exposure of light through this negative onto a light-sensitized sheet of metal created a dotted image on the metal. With these dots coated with an acid-resistant substance, an acid bath removed the metal around the dots, allowing them to stand in relief. The varying size and closeness of these dots formed a relief image to carry the continuous tones to paper without too much loss of quality.

Stereotyping and Fast Presses

Faster printing presses, using curved lead cylinders as the raised surface to carry ink to paper, rounded out the turn-of-the-century developments. *Stereotyping,* a process for creating these cylinders by first pressing a mold of the type faces and the halftone plates and then injecting molten lead against the mold, was the basis for these faster presses.

Now, about one century later, technological developments have taken printing from a factory-like environment to office or home-like settings. Written communication starts anywhere and goes anywhere. Its pervasiveness, as noted earlier, has tended to breed massive reader indifference.

Importance of Graphics

This reader indifference has produced a selectivity which in turn has increased the importance of the form or graphics of a visual message. It is obvious that, unless the graphic presentation of a message attracts the attention of prospective readers, printed material will not be read. Consequently, large portions of today's printed material are doomed to an instant wastebasket fate. Some hits the circular file in spite of extravagant display; some is discarded because the presentation is too subdued. On the other hand, one need only watch high school athletes explore their local newspaper the day following a game to know that some material is read in spite of its form rather than because of it. Ignoring shouting graphics on the front page telling of world problems, skillfully designed ads on other pages telling of rare bargains, and the main headlines of the sports page telling of the Super Bowl, these young athletes find their way to a small item describing their own activities of the night before. A basic lesson in graphics of communication can be learned here: *Importance of form in presentation varies inversely with the interest of the reader.* Hence, magazine publishers promoting circulation by sending unwanted solicitations to homes know they must employ every possible device to get the readers' attention. Sports scores, telephone numbers, and classified ads with higher reader interest can be presented in the most prosaic fashion; they will still be read.

It should be noted, however, that *all* written communication is intended to be read, and intense interest on the part of recipients cannot be an excuse for not giving a message at least adequate visual treatment. For example, doctors reading their journals with an interest born of necessity may not want or need graphics gymnastics, but they can rightfully insist on form that contributes to, rather than impedes, their assimilation of the information. It is the responsibility of anyone working with graphics to present *every* message in a visual form that helps and does not hinder reception of the message.

Vocational Opportunities

Figures showing the size of the printing/publishing industry suggest but do not fully reveal the breadth of opportunity for careers that use the skills and information presented in later chapters of this book. In some cases, establishing the form of printed communications is the primary area of responsibility for a person in the workplace, but often it is ancillary to other communication responsibilities. Here is a quick review of some of these kinds of activity.

Production Plants

In the 50,000 printing plants throughout the country there are departments staffed by men and women whose role it is to plan and design brochures, posters, small magazines, forms, and other printed matter for customers without skilled personnel of their own to accomplish such tasks. These individuals are often trained in art and design and spend all their time with related tasks in departments called Art or Design. Others, however, are engaged in sales or customer service and use their knowledge of design and production in that setting. Their primary training often is in production, backed up by some design skills.

Newspapers

The term *editor* in a newspaper office usually indicates that the person has some responsibility in graphics and production. Departmental editors, usually selected for their skills in newsgathering and personnel administration, often put together their own pages. Copy editors, the skilled wordsmiths on the staff, must work in a direct way with the production department. A trend to establish separate graphics departments staffed with design experts and artists has been accelerating as a result of an increased emphasis on appearance by newspapers.

Advertising

With its obvious need for emphasis on graphics, advertising provides us with the most sophisticated use of all aspects of printing design. More research, more time, and more skill are invested in the preparation of advertising messages than any other. The emphasis on design in advertising, plus the great breadth of the field, make this the most fertile area for those who have the talents and knowledge required. Within advertising there are three divisions of activity having a need for graphics specialists.

Perhaps best known and most glamorous are the *advertising agencies,* organizations of specialists in all phases of mass communication which offer services to clients for a percentage of the client's budget. Artists and production experts provide some of the most valuable services that an agency may offer its clients. Preparation of all kinds of printed ads—magazine, newspaper, direct mail, and billboard—requires the services of the most talented and best-trained personnel available. Intense competition among agencies forces more effort in and attention to the fine points of graphic design. In selling not only the product, but also their services to their clients, agencies also provide some of the best examples of preliminary materials as well as the final ads.

Advertising departments of department stores, mail-order firms, product manufacturers and other businesses also provide career opportunities for graphics specialists. Mail-order catalogs, brochures, newspaper ads, and other printed materials are often prepared by the advertising or marketing departments of business organizations. Some of these are also excellent examples of the best possible graphic presentation.

Print media, such as newspapers and magazines, also will have advertising departments. In these departments the major emphasis may be on selling space, but in selling space to businesses that have no ad departments of their own, design and production specifications become the responsibility of the medium's department. Newspaper ad salesmen, for example, usually find it necessary to lay out ads in final detail for their customers before they can sell the space.

Magazines

Most consumer-oriented magazines show through their staffing that appearance of their product is of top importance. Headed by a top staff executive, usually called an *art director,* the art or graphics departments play a major role in developing each issue. One can appreciate their influence by examining the attractive, functional, appealing page designs that are typical of such magazines. Excellent training in art and design and special creative talents are essential for those who work in these departments. The tremendous competition and reader inertia that must be overcome to sell single copies on newsstands and yearly subscriptions make appearance of the product absolutely vital.

The greatest number of magazines, however, are in what we call the *public relations* and *specialized business* categories. Public relations magazines, often called house organs, are produced by companies or other organizations to maintain and improve favorable relations with various publics, such as employees or customers. Specialized business magazines are those produced by magazine publishers to help readers in different businesses, occupations, or professions. These magazines, directed toward very specific audiences that are often small in number, have a minimal (or no) staff of graphics specialists. A typical specialized business magazine would have one or two graphic specialists; a typical PR magazine probably would have none.

It is the public relations magazine editors, probably more than any others, who must have good design and production proficiency to complement their editing skills.

Books

Book publishers rely on editors, production specialists, and artists on their own staffs, supplemented by freelance designers, to make their products attractive and functional. By their very nature, books are expected to demonstrate meticulous attention to the fine points of typographic design as well as the accuracy of their subject matter.

Public Relations

Agencies similar to advertising agencies (and often combined with them) offer total public relations services for their clients, including the preparation of printed material. Brochures, posters, newsletters, magazines, and assorted promotional materials may be designed by the agencies. Many business firms, however, have their own public relations departments to take care of these activities. In either case, the expertise of artists and production specialists is required.

In-House Printing

Mushrooming technology has made the production of printed materials possible for all kinds of organizations and institutions. Hospitals, schools, universities, manufacturers, and even advertising and public relations agencies, now have their own printing departments, which usually have grown out of mimeographing departments of old. These departments often require not only tradespeople, but production specialists and managers who must have broad design and production backgrounds.

Systems Managers

Computerization of all phases of word processing and printing production has led to the development of new career specialties. Systems that incorporate all of technology's potential for efficient communication can be complicated. Such systems usually are much broader in scope than merely the preparation of printed material, often including data processing and telecommunication as well. Knowledge that can provide a basis for selection of appropriate systems and the ensuing management of such systems has become a valuable commodity as the need for systems managers has arisen in newspaper, magazine, and other media offices, as well as in other large corporations.

Blending Creativity and Technology

Everyone who works with graphics is involved in the constant blending of creativity with technology. The process of getting words and pictures into print proceeds through three successive stages:

1. planning
2. copy preparation and
3. production

This is true whatever the material: newspapers, magazines, books, advertisements, brochures, or other miscellaneous matter. In general, it seems that creativity prevails in the former stages and technology takes over in the latter. In reality the two are intertwined throughout the whole process.

Most people, if asked, "Which of the three stages makes the most creative demands?" would say, "The second stage." And why shouldn't they? After all, it is in this stage that the words and pictures are prepared and a drawing, called a *layout,* is made of their formal arrangement (see Figure 1-2). And we generally credit writers and artists with high levels of creativity.

But consider: If you are talking with someone and you want to make a point, a plan of what you are about to say must precede your statement. If you don't know ahead of time—for however brief a period—what you are about to say, how can you say it? If you were asked to letter or draw a capital letter alphabet, you would have to have in your brain neural codes: first, to tell you what the letters look like; second, their order; and third, to direct your muscular activity in putting them on paper as visual symbols.

Planning Stage

The most significant creative activity, in other words, comes in the planning stage. The organization of content and form is decided at this time, before the words are written and the pictures are made, or before they are combined together in a layout. The process of deciding such matters is called *visualizing.* Both writer and designer should be involved in this process.

ArKo 12-Cup
Coffee Maker
Factory Rebate

$32.95
-10.00

$22⁹⁵

Brews 3-12 Cups

1-2 This layout, a production blueprint, shows picture and type positions. The headlines are lettered, and parallel lines indicate the placement of lines of smaller type.

Visualizing is primarily a thinking process. The ideas to be communicated are given to the writer and designer and together they plan how the finished material will appear to the reader. Different possible arrangements of visual images are "seen in the mind's eye," until the one that most effectively conveys the ideas is selected. Although visualizing is not a layout exercise, the designer may "doodle" miniature sketches to aid the thinking process. Figure 1-3 shows two such sketches that preceded the layout shown in Figure 1-2.

Technology also enters at this point because the designer must make decisions in the planning stage that primarily concern the printing and production techniques involved in the third stage. These techniques are complicated, and in order to utilize them to the fullest, the designer must have a sound working knowledge of their limitations and capacities. Only in this way can the designer discharge these two major responsibilities:

1. present a visually effective message
2. control the costs

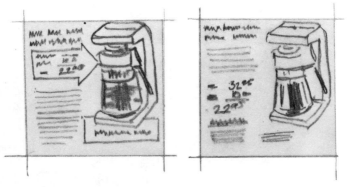

1-3 These are experimental miniatures that preceded the layout. The one on the right was developed into the layout.

Preparation Stage

Once plans for the printed materials have been set, three functions must be carried out:

1. Words must be prepared.
2. Pictures—if to be used—must be prepared.
3. A layout must be prepared.

All of these tasks must be completed, although there is no set order in which they must be done. The order depends on the types of printed material. In the book field, for example, the finished manuscript and pictures are sometimes turned over to the designer before a layout or design is begun.

In the newspaper and magazine fields the designer faces somewhat unique conditions. The format of these publications is continued from issue to issue. *Format* means such things as size, shape, width of columns, typefaces to be used and relative amounts of words and pictures. These determinants of overall appearance are decided upon in the planning stage for most other printed materials. Because of these preset conditions of format, we treat newspapers and magazines separately in later chapters.

The design of advertisements and direct literature usually offers the designer a freer hand. In these cases each printed unit "starts from scratch." The three stages are more in evidence for each ad and for each piece of direct literature, since none of them has a predetermined format. Some direct literature in the form of folders is unique in that it is three dimensional, as opposed to ads or publication pages, which are two-dimensional. Folders are large sheets folded down to one size. Special design problems that are common to folders are also discussed in a separate chapter.

Design Principles

Regardless of the type of literature—book, magazine, newspaper, advertisement or direct—the principles of effective design are unchanging.

1-4 Copy preparation must be geared to the final product through planning. Here Tim Martin, an editor at the *Pittsburgh Press*, follows format as he executes a page plan to make certain photos and words fit their assigned positions. (Photo by Greg Blackman)

Because the designer has a freer hand in designing advertisements, we discuss these principles first with specific attention focused on advertisements, then as they apply to specific media.

A great deal of information in print is presented using words alone. This does not imply that formal arrangement is thereby deserted. A strictly verbal printed message may be pleasing or unpleasing to the eye. The principles involved in using type alone are considered in the chapters dealing with typography.

Copy Preparation

Early on in his or her career, the person whose work involves getting visual images into print faces two particularly vexing problems:

1. fitting the number of words to the allotted space on the layout
2. fitting pictures to the allotted space on the layout

As this person gains experience, these problems become easier to solve, but they must be solved in the preparation stage, before production (see Figure 1-4). If the pictures or the words do not fit, either the layout must be changed or the number of words or sizes of pictures must be altered. In either case, considerable cost can be involved. How such problems are handled is covered in chapters dealing with preparation for print of words and illustrations.

Production Stage

In the production stage the visual images—words and pictures—are arranged together according to the layout and are printed (see Figure 1-5). In the planning stage the designer had to incorporate into the plan information about the production methods to be used. The designer would then have to follow through, working closely with production persons, to assure that his or her "job" would turn out as visualized. The designer's task would parallel that of an architect's being on the construction site to see that the building that the architect planned, and for which he or she drew blueprints, would turn out as visualized.

The designer must have specific knowledge in these production areas:

1. printing processes
2. type composition
3. selection of paper or other printing surface
4. paper folding, binding and finishing

These subjects are all explored in appropriate chapters later in this book, but should be put into context here.

Printing Processes

There are a number of different printing processes. The selection of the method best suited to the job at hand has as much to do with the designer's proper discharge of his or her responsibilities as any other factor. A decision in this area has a marked effect on all other areas of production and even in the preparation of words and pictures, as we shall see.

The designer is used to working with images on paper. Words are composed on paper. Paintings and drawings are done on paper; even

1-5   Even large presses such as this have size and shape limitations that must be adhered to as pages are planned.

the layout is prepared on paper. Photos generally appear on paper, although they may be in the form of transparencies (much like color slides). In any event, transparencies can be imagined as being on paper.

The finished printed piece will be made up of these same images appearing again on paper, or possibly some other surface in one, two or more colors. To make printing possible, some sort of image carrier, called a *printing plate,* is needed. When it has been placed on a printing press and inked with the proper color, the printing plate transfers the images it carries to the printing surface.

At least this is the case with the three processes that are most widely used in mass communication. There are additional processes, but in every case printing requires separating the image area from the non-image area.

Type Composition

The processes and techniques involved in converting written words into type as they will appear to the reader are termed *type composition* or *typesetting.* The primary considerations facing the designer in this area are:

1. legibility of the typeface
2. design possibilities
3. composition method

Type Legibility

Because language is the primary means of human communication, legibility of the face or faces selected is of greatest concern. The term *typeface* refers to the design style of the characters of an alphabet. There are literally thousands of different typefaces, and some are more easily read than others.

Design Possibilities

When a number of words are composed together, they take up a portion of the layout space. The area they occupy will take on a shape, a tone and a texture. This depends principally on the typeface, size of the type, length of the lines of type, wordspacing (space between words), letterspacing (space between letters) and linespacing (space between lines).

Remember—shape, tone and texture are part of the designer's resources. This means that the shapes formed by areas of type composition can be arranged to interact with the shapes of picture elements to deliver a visually effective message.

These same factors—typestyle, size, line length, wordspacing, letterspacing and linespacing—also affect legibility. A certain copy area shape, tone or texture may be desirable, but if a trade-off is necessary, it should always favor legibility.

Selecting the Composition Method

For centuries, the process of getting words into type remained relatively unchanged. After the writer finished the copy, it was edited and marked with typesetting instructions and then sent to the compositor, who probably worked for a printer. The compositor might also have worked for a "type house" (a company that set the type and forwarded it to the printer) or in a newspaper composing room.

A wedding of photography and computer technology gave birth to new typesetting methods in the mid-twentieth century. These methods made it possible to set type by exposing one character after another on photographic paper or film at incredible speeds. Before three decades had passed, *phototypesetting* had become the principal means of type composition. A refinement of phototypesetting, the computer generation of alphanumeric symbols that are formed on photopaper via the scan lines of a television screen (cathode ray tube), has made full-page typesetting almost instantaneous.

One of the most significant changes brought about by the growth of phototypesetting has been the effect on the role of the writer, particularly in the newspaper and magazine fields. No longer does the writer type out words on a typewriter. Rather, the writer now operates keys on a typewriterlike keyboard and words appear on a televisionlike screen. The machine of which the keyboard and screen are a part is called a VDT (video display terminal). Assisted by a computer control, the writer or an editor can change the copy in any way desired by using the proper command keys. Once finished, the copy can then be sent from VDT to a computer memory.

At the time the copy is written, instructions are also written on the VDT and sent along with the copy to the computer concerning such matters as typeface; line length; letter, line and word spacing; and so on. The computerized typesetter adapts the writer's copy to these requirements. Thus, in effect, the writer is also the typesetter.

What was traditionally the preparation assignment—writing the words—has become a broader assignment: preparation/composition. As we stated earlier, these developments are most notable in the publishing fields. However, increasing numbers of businesses and organizations that have printing needs are assuming the composition functions and are installing phototypesetting equipment.

This means that the writer of today, whether he or she works as a reporter or magazine writer, as an advertising-promotion writer, or as a publicity–public relations writer, should not only know how to write but should know typography and electronic word processing as well. The new processes stand ready to make the writer a typographer.

Composition in the editorial office, and "in-house" composition (done in the offices of other businesses and organizations requiring printed materials) make sense. Phototypesetting equipment is modern in styling, befitting the writer's setting in office surroundings, and is less bulky and industrial-looking than the metal type-producing equipment used by the traditional printer.

But of greatest importance is the fact that phototypesetting puts typography directly in the hands of users, increasing creative possibilities and reducing problems.

Selection of Paper

Printing can be done on surfaces other than paper and the choice of surface is based on the selection of the printing process. However, our major concern in this text is with the use of paper in printing. The designer can select from a wide range of kinds and colors of paper. Choosing the right paper for the job involves many factors, factors that are discussed in later chapters.

Paper Folding, Binding and Finishing

Even after paper has passed through a printing press and has received the printed images, production is still not complete. Final processing requires converting large single sheets into separate pieces as they will be seen by the reader. The large sheets must be folded and bound to become sections (signatures) of books or booklets, which are then trimmed (cut) on three sides. If the final printed piece is to be in the form of single sheets, these must be cut from the press sheet; if the piece is to be in the form of folders, these must be cut from the press sheet and then properly folded.

Web printing (printing from rolls of paper) also involves, at least in part, *folding, binding* and *finishing* on the press. This is particularly true in the case of newspapers, magazines, and books.

Finishing involves a number of special treatments that will be discussed along with folding and binding.

CHECKLIST: **Some Points to Remember**

1. Graphics are the visual aspects (form) of written or printed communication.
2. Printed media should be designed to communicate their messages; self-satisfaction of the designer with his or her work of art is not sufficient.
3. Graphic noise (interference) stems from faults in presentation that can prevent or severely hamper successful communication.
4. White space is as important as type and illustrations in graphic design.
5. Contrast is the source of all meaning; therefore all graphic elements in a design should stand out enough to be recognized.
6. Goals of graphic communication are:
   (1) to attract attention,
   (2) to help receiver get the message, and
   (3) to create some final impression or action.
7. Printing/publishing is the largest category of the 20 manufacturing groups in the U.S. Standard Industrial Classification list.
8. Importance of graphics varies inversely with the interest of the readers, but in no case should form interfere with function.
9. Creative and technological aspects of mass communication must blend together through the three stages of preparation of materials for printing:
   (1) planning,
   (2) copy preparation, and
   (3) production or manufacture.
10. Visualizing, a thinking process, must precede actual design of printed matter.

2

Effective Communication— by Design

Graphics can enhance or hinder mass communications. Whether your visual message succeeds or fails is truly a matter of *design*.

Here we use the word design in a deliberately ambiguous manner because for graphic communicators it has two definite and interlocking meanings. In an artistic sense, it means the look and feel of the final printed communication. In a more organizational sense, it means the deliberate plan followed to produce the final product. The attractive and successful presentation of a message (a good design) is the result of a plan that includes attention to all aspects of preparation of printed materials that will be discussed in later chapters.

In this chapter, however, we set forth a vocabulary and rationale for design in its artistic sense so remaining chapters can be put into a design-related framework.

Functions of Design

Design is best defined according to its functions in printed communications. These include:

—creating a clear, orderly flow of graphic elements;
—attracting the intended audience with proper focus and stimulating presentation;
—reflecting production needs through a design system that considers available processes and personnel; and
—supporting content rather than overwhelming it.

From the point of view of graphic communications, you should consider design a form of *packaging.* Your design should attract and intrigue viewers; it should draw them to the content so they can receive the full message; it should have a lasting effect so that the message can be retained.

Good design has both aesthetic and business implications. An artistic, tasteful presentation of graphic elements looks attractive and sophisticated. It can also be economically successful if the audience responds to it as intended. This was demonstrated at a daily newspaper in Florida when the paper hired a graduate of the Rhode Island School of Design to become its editorial art director. Using what he called the "practical application of the art aesthetic," the director redesigned the newspaper. Result: a 15 percent increase in newsstand and rack sales—an important test for the "look" of a product.

It is important to realize, however, that what appears to be poor design may work well for a particular message and audience. The so-called "circus" makeup—a noisy, jumbled presentation of mixed typography, crowded spacing and outlandish art (the kind of ad you may see for a bargain basement sale)—is a good example of this principle. Such an example may be an exaggerated instance of the old design axiom that "form follows function."

Focusing on your audience and trying to determine what manner of presentation will elicit the best response are key ingredients in the design challenge. Look at Figures 2-1 and 2-2 and evaluate how the designs and messages fared. In 2-1, a simple design of copy block, headlines and pictures made up of letters and numbers creates a direct, well-focused message for people in the advertising agency business. It is easy to read, if the subject of the message interests you. In Figure 2-2, you see a busy, cluttered design that juggles typography and is stingy with white space. However, if you've ever suffered the anguish of a wet basement, you'd probably read every word of this advertisement. Having been softened up by the nightmare of mildew and wet basement walls, you probably were ready to be attracted to a no-nonsense, chock-full-of-information ad. A *Vanity Fair* or avant-garde approach probably wouldn't have worked well with the intended audience.

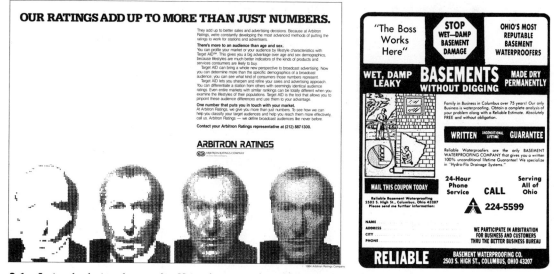

2-1   A simple design that works. Using letters and numbers to create faces shows that this company's ratings "deliver" people. (Courtesy Arbitron Ratings Co.)

2-2   Cluttered design, effective content. This presentation is much less abstract than Figure 2-1, but its concrete approach reaches a willing audience. (Courtesy Reliable Basement Waterproofing Company)

Keeping these examples in mind, let's examine some terms that will help you understand the language of design and the principles that govern it.

Language of Design

There are certain parallels between verbal and visual language. Although the use of symbols and abstractions makes visual language less logical than its verbal component, a syntax of design does exist; understanding it can help elicit the hoped-for response from the viewer. In design, the most important vocabulary consists of *space*, the *point*, the *line*, *shape*, *texture* and *tone*.

Space

Consider space the canvas of the designer. It is the area of your message, the boundaries of the viewer's perception of that message. Space has been called many things: *negative* if it is in the background of the design; *positive* if it is dominant, in the foreground or in the center of attention; *crowded* if the space seems uncomfortably occupied; *open* if the space seems free and unrestricted.

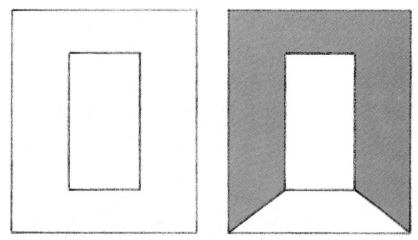

2-3   Monotony of shape and tone results in a lack of dimension.

2-4   Greater depth is achieved with only minor changes.

Remember that in printed designs, all space is two-dimensional. There is only length and width; however, good design can give the impression of depth and volume. Understanding space and its relationship to shape and tone will help you use space to best advantage. Lack of shape variety and tone keeps a design within its two basic dimensions, as in Figure 2-3. With no shading of tone and repetition of shape, the example looks flat. In Figure 2-4, using some shading and narrowing shapes create an illusion of depth.

Closure as a Key to Good Design

Understanding what to do with space is a major challenge in design. The key to the proper use of space, however, is the understanding and the use of *closure*—a term used in various disciplines to denote recognition and understanding of symbols and images. Typography and spacing can help us understand this concept. Take, for example, the term "Rent To Own" that might be used in business advertising. In Figure 2-5, normal spacing and reasonable type selection help the viewer "close" the image. The symbols (letters) form understandable words. In Figure 2-6, awkward spacing causes the letters to fly away without proper recognition. Insertion of dots or "bullets" can help close the image and improve recognition (Figure 2-7). And even when there is no spacing between words, shading and contrast can give the illusion of word spacing (Figure 2-8).

In the same way, proper use of space in layout can help message recognition. It is vital that all design elements—copy, headline, art and white space—can be "closed" to form an understandable image.

2-5 "Normal" presentation produces quick closure.

RENT TO OWN

2-6 Flyaway letters fight closure.

RENTTOOWN

2-7 Typographical devices can help close image.

RENT·TO·OWN

2-8 Variations in tone can change entire presentation.

Point

Like the focal target of a photograph, the point is a position in space that holds the primary attention of the viewer. It signals a start, an end or an area of primary focus for the eye. The point can be an area of highlight or harsh contrast in a design; it can be a dominant shape or sharp outline; it can even be a large capital letter that begins the text in a layout (Figure 2-9).

Line

Like the point, the line can be real or imaginary. It is real enough when it delineates shape, as in a simple line drawing or in the letters of the alphabet. It can be imaginary when it is used to show direction, movement and emphasis in a design. Guiding the eye to positions where important information can be found is a key goal in all design.

Figures 2-10 and 2-11 show how lines create movement, show direction and illustrate emphasis. When the lines are vertical, they create a sense of convergence at an imaginary point somewhere above the top of the image. Variance in line thickness also creates a variety of weight or emphasis. In the horizontal mode, greater movement can be detected. In this design, the thick line near the top breaks a long plane and gives a sense of depth—helping to change the sense of direction. (Note: Al-

2-9 Common device in magazine layout, the large initial letter, signals beginning *point* in design.

though the image looks abstract, it is actually a photograph of a stand of alder trees, with the camera held in a horizontal position and moved upward during a long exposure time. In this case, movement helped create lines.)

In the Lees Carpet ad, Figure 2-12, imaginary grid lines divide the space into three components, as Figure 2-13 indicates. Note that the vertical line separating *Out* and *In* draws the reader to the dominant shape of ad copy on the right, while the tag line "Lees the Newsmaker" breaks the vertical to pull the entire design back together.

A more vivid use of lines is seen in Figure 2-14. A long, dark field (of inland passage water) is broken by the textured line of the wake of a cruise ship. That line moves from the top of the layout, where copy begins, and directs the viewer to the copy below. Seen narrowly, that line looks like an exclamation mark against a plain background. It has given movement, direction and emphasis to the message.

Shape

Lines articulate shapes, which in turn help define the function and dimension of space. With the proper tone or perspective a shape can create depth. Through its size or exaggeration of proportion, it implies importance and impact.

Most designs utilize three basic shapes: four-sided (quadrilateral), triangle and circle. In the photograph of the peaceful bay in Figure 2-15,

2-10 Vertical lines show movement, convergence and weight.

2-11 Horizontal lines show even greater movement and depth.

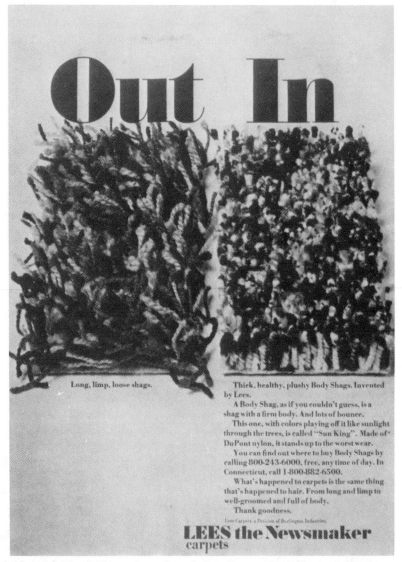

2-12 and 2-13   Grids produce clean design. Text and graphics are placed in three grids, with bottom grid anchoring presentation. (Courtesy Lees Carpets; agency: Doyle-Dane-Bernbach)

the design has two triangles and three quadrilaterals, as sketched in Figure 2-16. The peaks of the triangles point sideways to the horizon line of the bay, creating a sense of depth and perspective for the long quadrilaterals of the water and the sky. Just as a photographer searches long

this grid has heavier
weight (more art, copy).
It leads the reader
down to name of advertiser.

this narrow grid breaks up
the two long verticals by
"reaching" into left-hand
grid with advertiser name.

and hard for the proper design and emphasis in an image, so does the
designer consider typography, art and open space in creating a layout.
    Examine any modern advertisement, an opening two-page spread
of a magazine article, or newspaper layout today and you probably will

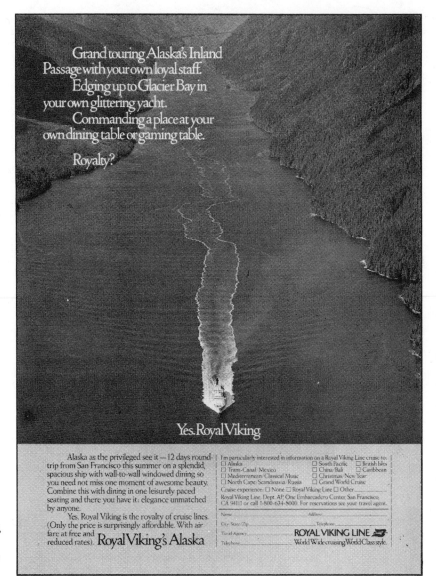

2-14 Lines create movement and contrast, taking reader to copy anchoring page. (Courtesy The Marschalk Company)

see the use of *modular design*—the use of quadrilateral shapes to define white space, type and art. Indeed, a typical newspaper front page could easily look like the design in Figure 2-17. Research has shown that readers identify with "blocks" of information, as it helps them with the *closure* of that information. Even in the IBM ad of Figure 2-18, with its odd black and white shapes representing tire tread, the design is basically four rectangles: white space as the background field, the tire line as an overlay, the type as an insert, and the IBM logo.

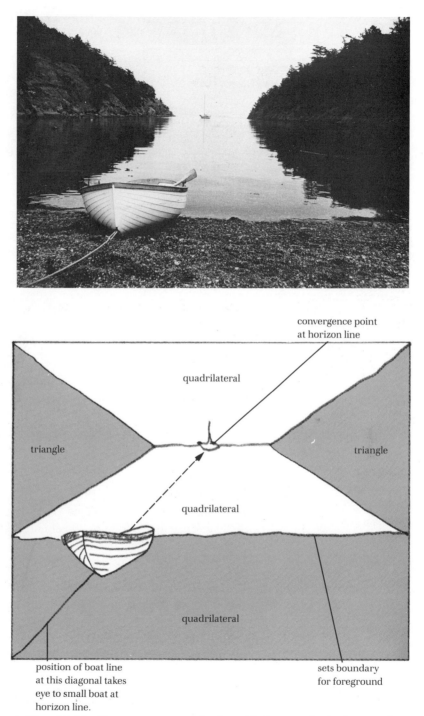

2-15 and 2-16 Shapes suggest emphasis and balance, as both photograph and interpretative sketch show. (Photography courtesy of Duncan McDonald)

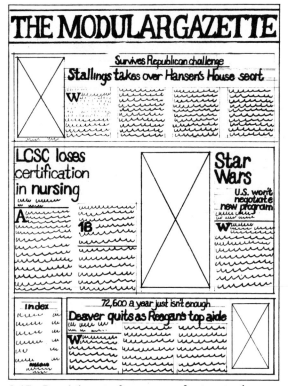

Direct Sales Tire Company of Colorado tracks sales of its retail stores in six states with a System/38 computer from IBM. There are as many ways to use IBM Small Systems as there are businesses. Learn how one can help you become more productive. Call us at 1 800 IBM-2468, ext. 54.

2-17   Rough layout of newspaper front page shows modular influence.

2-18   Seemingly irregular shapes are actually encased in a modular grid. (Courtesy International Business Machines Corp. Agency: Doyle-Dane-Bernbach; art director: Amy Levitan)

Texture

Any surface structure can be "felt" visually. With our eyes, we can sense the pattern on a design. Crosshatching and the other use of lines in Figure 2-19 create a sense of shadows on the childrens' faces. Texture thus can be another way to give dimension to space.

Tone

The range of light values—from textureless white to deep black—constitutes tone. Tones can be dull, as in a middle gray or flat brown, or they can be bright and vivacious, as in an area of highlight or shiny yellows and greens. Tone is also referred to as gradation; when you think of tonality, you should think of scale. Is the tone high or low? Flat or sharp? Does it fit the mood of the design or run counter to it?

All of these terms constitute an important vocabulary. Speaking the same language is critical when working with designers, printers and graphic arts specialists. These terms also help us understand the prin-

2-19 Simple shading techniques create texture and improved tone. (Courtesy American Newspaper Publishers Association Foundation)

ciples of design, which guide the visual component of effective communication.

Principles of Design

Style, whether it refers to writing or fashion, is a description of expression. If we say we don't like a writer's style, we might mean that his or her expression lacks originality, is ostentatious or lacks flow. In short, the writer's manner of presentation fails, and the message is not absorbed.

Design depends heavily on style for effectiveness of meaning. In this section we examine some standards of style, or design principles. These include contrast, balance, rhythm and harmony. It would be convenient to say these principles are listed in order of importance. They're not, because they're interactive. One design principle should support another; when they don't, they continue to interact, causing confusion and disarray. Some quick examples help point this out.

The nervous excitation that takes place in the brain becomes a part of the visual design when we look at it. A simple do-it-yourself experiment will make this clear. Draw two parallel lines on a piece of paper, $\frac{3}{4}$ inch apart and $2\frac{1}{2}$ inches long. Put a dot midway of their length and their distance apart. Draw straight lines fanning out from the dot as in Figure 2-20. Be sure these lines extend an inch or so beyond your parallel lines.

Now look at the drawing by tilting your head to the left or the right. Your parallel lines no longer look straight; they appear bowed. Are they really?

2-20 What the eyes see excites the brain.

2-21   *Left:* The two rectangles seem to belong together. *Right:* Interaction with other elements seems to pull the same two rectangles apart.

Look at Figure 2-21. The two dark rectangles are $\frac{3}{8}$ inch apart. They seem to belong together. Now look at the same rectangles on the right. This time, the same pair is joined by another rectangle on each side, but at a distance of only $\frac{1}{8}$ inch. The original two rectangles no longer seem to belong together. What happened?

The various layout elements interact. We feel these changes and call them *attractions.* Attraction refers to the "pull" of these energy effects we project into the image. It is thus possible to attract the eye. But attraction is not the same as attention.

Attention comes after attraction—maybe only a few milliseconds after, but *after.* Attention involves assigning meaning to what attracts. Perhaps an ad is merely intended to remind. The product is shown in large size, the verbal message is minimal, and the meaning is quickly attached. This is the typical task of the poster or billboard.

On the other hand, some ads must do more of a selling job. Before the reader can develop a sound concept—that is, discover its meaning—he or she must learn its defining features. More points of attraction must be placed in the message. More attention is necessary, and the reader must be held longer to learn the concepts involved.

Contrast

In any form of communication, some materials or ideas are stressed more than others. The selection of this stress or focus is perhaps the most important part of the pre-visualization of design.

In design, to contrast means to set off one element against the other, to show differences in size, shape, tone, texture, and direction as well as in concepts.

In Figure 2-22, there is low contrast where the sizes of design elements are relatively the same; contrast improves—and so does attraction—when size difference is emphasized. The same is true for shape differences, as seen in Figure 2-23.

Tonal accents, too, can improve the attractiveness of design. Look again at Figure 2-15, the photograph of the dinghy in the bay. Not only is there strong contrast between the white boat, greyish water and dark gravel and hills but there is also a substantial difference in textures. Contrast also emphasizes the small sailboat at anchor in the bay, while the horizontal flow of the lines from the hills and the vertical lines of the water and sky give great contrast—and attraction—in direction.

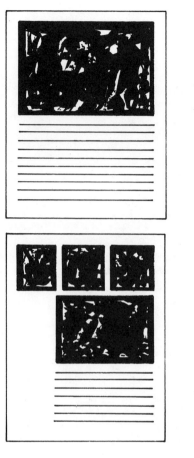
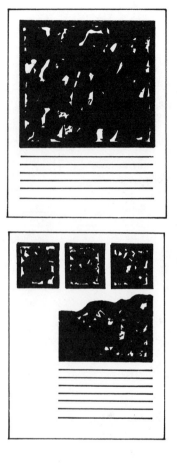

2-22 Monotony of text and graphic size at *left* shows improvement in contrast on *right* when illustration size becomes more dominant.

2-23 *Left:* Monotony of shapes. *Right:* One irregular shape improves contrast and attraction of design.

Balance

Balance exists when design elements are placed with a sense of equilibrium and proportion. To understand proper balance, remember the function of the point: to be the area of primary focus. The point is also a fulcrum of sorts, an axis or seesaw that supports various elements and tries to keep them in balance. In design, the point can be the optical center, where a "gravitational pull" keeps design elements from flying out into space. Figures 2-24 and 2-25 show how this balance can be spoiled or attained. Look at the narrow vertical "alley" to the left of the physical center in 2-25, and you can detect the axis that holds design elements in balance. No such axis exists in 2-24, and it is this lack of optical center that causes such disarray.

Balance and proportion are not synonymous with symmetry, which implies an equal division of design elements on both sides of the dividing plane. Balance and proportion try to achieve a less stilted equilibrium to attract the viewer.

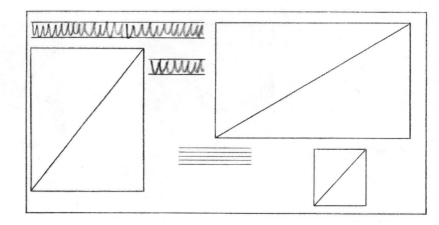

2-24 Failure to hold design elements together can be blamed on poor balance.

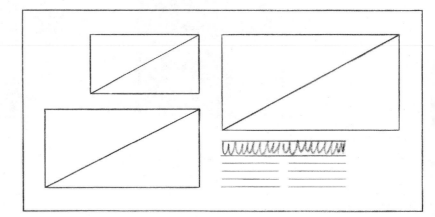

2-25 An example of effective, informal balance.

Rhythm

Rhythm is achieved through orderly repetition of such elements as line, shape, tone and texture. The eye identifies this rhythm and follows its pattern of movement.

Reading produces a sense of movement, even in the most prosaic and formally balanced presentation. The eye moves left to right, top to bottom. However, because the entire message is presented at the same time (unlike in TV or radio), the reader is free to look at any given area at any given time. Good design attempts to discourage this, and use of rhythm tries to direct the reader to a more productive pattern of movement. Another look at Figure 2-14 shows how rhythm is achieved through effective use of contrast and lines. The reverse (white) type is placed over the dark area of the forested hills in the upper left. The wake (line) of the cruise ship moves us from the type, down the water, to the name of the company and to its coupon information. Through the use of rhythm, nothing is left to chance; the reader will view this in a predictable, effective way. Manipulation of elements—the essential grammar of design—is the means of eye movement control. The sought-after standard is: Does this design carry the eye in the direction required by the content?

Harmony

We mentioned previously that design principles interact. The principle of harmony, which is responsible for a sense of order and unity, helps design elements relate to one another to provide a sense of coherence. Without harmony, the visual message cannot register a single, overall impression. With harmony, a sense of clarity exists. Look again at Figures 2-24 and 2-25 and see how a lack of unity in 2-24 spreads the focus unnecessarily. In the same way, clutter and imbalance hurt the message in Figure 2-26. The message is important, and the text can be persuasive, but crowded layout and poor picture selection can turn away viewers. A good example of harmonious composition is found in Figure 2-25. What elements do you see there that support good design principles?

Creating Effective Design

It is one thing to understand the vocabulary of design and another to articulate those words with fluency. In the abstract, it may seem easy to comprehend basic design principles, but the reality of creating clean, effective design is a difficult challenge. Meeting it is a matter of understanding how to get the reader to absorb the message. Understanding traits or tendencies of the reader is an important part of this challenge. We have already discussed how elements of design are interrelated; these will receive more discussion in Chapters 8, 14, and 15. A brief discussion of how eye movement can affect your design plans follows.

Eye Movement

The designer may devote considerable time to individual parts of his or her effort, but the reader tends to scan the total layout for an overall impression. After that, assuming that points of attraction will create attention, the designer may devote some time to details.

Thus it becomes important to consider eye-movement tendencies of the reader as he or she scans a page or a spread. These tendencies have been revealed through lab experiments using a specialized eye camera, with the following conclusions:

1. The eye tends, after leaving the initial fixation, to move to the *left and upward.*
2. The exploratory coverage of the space is from this point in a *clockwise direction.*

2-26 Strong message, weak balance. Lack of unity and clarity pits design against content.
(Courtesy Ziff-Davis Publishing Co.)

3. The eye prefers *horizontal movement.*
4. The *left* position is preferred to the right, and the *top* position is preferred to the bottom. Thus, the four quadrants of a space might be given communication values from 1 to 4 in descending order, as shown in Figure 2-27.

Figure 2-28 illustrates what we have said about eye-movement tendencies. Point 1 represents the intitial fixation, usually at the *optical* cen-

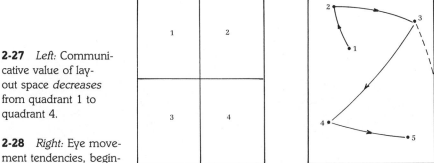

2-27 *Left:* Communicative value of layout space *decreases* from quadrant 1 to quadrant 4.

2-28 *Right:* Eye movement tendencies, beginning at point 1.

ter. The clockwise path from 2 to 3 is exploratory. Conceivably, the eye may leave the space at 4 and move to something else.

The fact that these have been labeled "tendencies" means that the eye will not always follow this path. The designer can influence eye direction by proper placement of elements. However, if the eye is drawn to points 4 and 5, it is important that they involve content of interest to the reader.

If you analyze a number of ads in different printed media, you will note that some are primarily illustrative with very little verbal copy, whereas others are structured to highlight copy.

Copy should tend to be longer when the product is of exceptional interest because it is new or offers new features, when the need is more immediate, or when the product is technical in nature. An advertiser who is trying to solicit orders or to persuade nonusers of a product's merits also is likely to use longer copy. Copy is often shorter if the ad is a reminder, primarily reaffirming favorable attitudes, or if the product is of such low interest that a splashier, more illustrative design is needed.

Admittedly, these ideas are oversimplified. Their purpose is to point out that the designer must consider the nature of the message and reader interests before he or she begins work.

Putting It All Together

Now that we know the elements of the designer's vocabulary, let us see how the designer puts them all together to form a visual plan or blueprint. If the finished work is to be an advertisement, the plan will be called a *layout;* if it is a page in a newspaper or magazine, it is called a *page dummy.*

In this discussion on composition, we concentrate on layouts. Advertisers have been more effective in researching the effects of composition than have printers or publishers. This success is probably the result of the high cost of advertising space and the rough competition for attention that advertisers face. Examples of newspaper and magazine designs are found in Chapters 14 and 15.

Once the strategy of the message has been discussed and decided, the designer can consider arrangement of the four components of printed communication:

1. body type
2. display type
3. illustrations
4. white space

The results of this arrangement should be a unified entity that reflects good design principles. For example, white space should interact with the other components to provide good focus, contrast and balance.

In most designs, white space is most advantageously used when it dwells to the outside of the layout. If too much of it appears in the center, it scatters the other components around, hurting the simplicity and unity of the presentation.

The first step in the laying-out or ordering process is *visualization,* which lets the designer consider the "look" of a design before it is actually on paper. In visualization, the designer must consider:

1. the ideas (content) and symbols (verbal and graphic) to be represented
2. the number of design elements to be used
3. the relative importance of information
4. the order of presentation

These decisions are influenced by the kind of product being advertised, the nature of the consumer and the degree of existing consumer interest.

Preparing the Layout

There are three kinds of layout, classified according to the care in drawing them: the *miniature* or *thumbnail,* often used to aid visualization; the *rough;* and the *comprehensive.*

The Miniature. Miniatures are advantageous because they can be done quickly and efficiently. Working on a full-scale layout while testing ideas would expend precious time and energy, instead of discarding weak or mediocre efforts. Working on miniatures also begets new ideas. In this scale, this work is much like copy editing—changes can be made easily, with the polishing and tightening becoming apparent in the final version.

The Rough. The miniature selected as best is redrawn as a rough, which is a full-sized layout (Figure 2-29). Several drafts of a rough may be needed to take care of revisions. The "final" rough bears a close

2-29   Rough layout allows designer to work quickly and get feedback from client without too much investment in artwork.

resemblance to the finished ad. Headlines are letttered in to approximate their printed form. The position of the elements is precise enough to allow the compositor to work from a rough in making up the ad in the print shop.

Designing the rough is simplified by using proper equipment. The best paper is a transparent bond known as layout paper, although a tough tracing paper will do. A T-square and triangle ensure accuracy. Also needed are three pencil types—2H for light lines, 2B for heavier ones, and a 6B for broader strokes. A sandpaper pad is useful for shaping heads to fit the kind of stroke you need. If working in color, wide-tipped felt pens are handy for laying down colors in larger areas.

The Comprehensive. The so-called *comp* (Figure 2-30) is very exact, done to show how the layout will look in print. It is very helpful to show to clients who may have difficulty visualizing what the designer can easily see in the rough. Illustrations imitate their finished look and headlines are precisely lettered in, although occasionally they may even

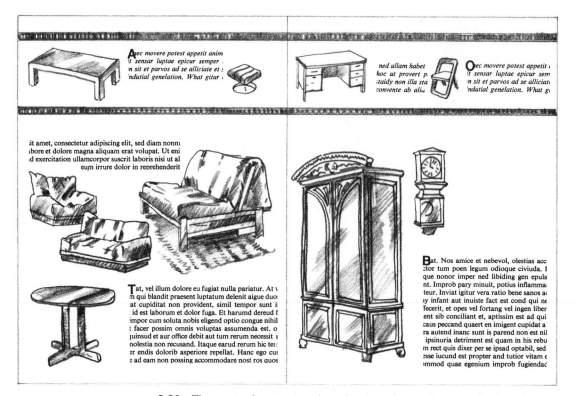

2-30 The comprehensive is only a client's nod away from the final production process. (Courtesy Mary Fish Advertising and Marketing)

be typeset for the benefit of the client. Body type (text) is ruled in to show amount and position. The *comp,* however, is not the *finished* design for mechanical reproduction. The final step in this process is to have all elements typeset, engraved and drawn in for printing.

As you proceed through the rest of this book, keep in mind the principles of good design. Consider them as you examine the pros and cons of various printing processes. Think about design as you examine the elements of typography. In *all* aspects of production, remember the tools of good design. If your design elements interact well, if your layout has balance and harmony, if you design with the message and viewer in mind, you will have put graphics to its most valuable use.

3

Type and Typesetting

Typography—the design, manufacture and use of *type*—has an exciting and artistic history that reaches to the core of civilization's development of mass communication. As you read the type that makes up this book, you are scanning descendants of symbols that have been molded in clay, carved in wood, cast in metal, exposed on film—and that are now generated by computer memory. That we are no longer dependent on wall drawings and hand-copied manuscripts is a testament to systems that have successfully mass-produced these symbols, providing us with the foundation for mass media.

Today, we have visual proof of this revolution. In the last 100 years there has been rapid movement from hot-metal linecasting to photo-typesetting to digital generation of type. (See Figure 3-1.)

Although many cite Gutenberg's development of movable, reusable metal type in the fifteenth century as the catalyst for the spread of information, there is ample evidence that similar developments were present in Korea, China and Japan as early as the ninth century. However, as these developments gained force in Europe, it is not surprising that some

3-1 Less than 100 years separate hot-metal typesetting on the Linotype and screen-displayed, computer-generated type.

early commercial type would look like the laborious hand lettering of medieval manuscripts. Figure 3-2 shows a "Text" type, referred to long ago as Black Letter, Gothic or Old English. What followed were movements to create type designs (faces) that were different from old-style penmanship. These were more readable faces, and they proudly carried the names of their designers—people like John *Baskerville*, Giambattista *Bodoni*, William *Caslon*, Claude *Garamond* and Frederic *Goudy*. (See examples, Figure 3-3.) More recent faces like *Melior*, *Optima* and *Univers* (Figure 3-4) show how far designs have progressed since the use of Old English.

Today we can choose from thousands of different typefaces. Special publications discuss and analyze typographical design. It is an embarrassment of riches for the graphic designer, who nonetheless realizes that choosing *appropriate* typefaces is an important factor in good design and effective communication.

Old English
abcdefghijklmnopqrstuvwxyz
ABCDEFGHIJKLMNOPQRSTUVWXYZ

3-2 A hard-to-read Text or "Black Letter" face.

Baskerville   **Goudy**

3-3 Examples of traditional faces.

Optima   Univers

3-4 Examples of more recent faces.

3-5 Spaces between and within letters are important to the recognition of the form and meaning of both letters and words.

To the designer, type is more than black marks on paper. These marks break the white of the paper into various shapes, as shown in Figure 3-5. Thus, the spaces between letters, words and lines of type contribute to type recognition. In addition, when a large number of words are composed, they form shapes of texture and tone that, when incorporated into a layout, interact with other elements.

To utilize such subtleties to the greatest advantage, it becomes important that the designer have a knowledge of typefaces, the mechanics of composition and the terminology involved in typography. This chapter involves a discussion of these matters.

Typesetting Terminology

This section introduces the reader to the terminology involved in getting words into print. The terms for the most part cover both phototypesetting and traditional metal typesetting; there are some exceptions and they are noted.

Typeface Terminology

"Typeface" refers to the visual symbol seen on the printed page. These symbols collectively are called *characters,* and they include letters, numerals, punctuation marks, and other assorted symbols such as dollar signs ($), cents signs (¢), ampersands (&), fractions and so on.

Capital letters are called *uppercase;* small letters are called *lowercase.* They are generally abbreviated to *u.c.* (or *uc*) or *caps* or *c* and *l.c.* (or *lc*), respectively. Normally text is composed as *c/lc (caps/lc)* or *u/lc.*

Other terms refer to the "look" of characters in print:

x-height: The depth of lowercase center body letters such as *a, r, i, c,* and so on; actually based on the letter *x.*
ascender: The part of lowercase letters extending above the x-height.
descender: The part of lowercase letters extending below the x-height.
baseline: The line on which center body and capital letters rest.
counter: White space within a letter.
hairline: The thin stroke of a letter.
serif: The finishing stroke at the end of a main stroke of a letter.

Figure 3-6 shows a letter and a word with these terms identified. Figure 3-7 shows a different style of typeface—called *sans serif*—one of the many faces that do not have serifs or varying width strokes.

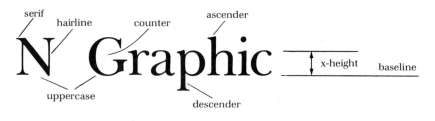

3-6 Type terms.

3-7 Not all typefaces have serifs and varying strokes. This face is of the *Sans Serif* group.

Graphic

Typeface Classification

For some time after the invention of printing, printers found one style of typeface in one size sufficient for their purposes. With the passing of time came an ever increasing demand for additional designs and sizes to add variety to printed materials. As the expanding craft spread across Europe, design changes reflecting the different cultures were made by a sort of natural evolution.

In Italy, for example, letterforms were designed and cast that resembled the graceful characters in manuscripts prepared by Italian scribes. The basic *roman* form has undergone so many mutations that today there are literally hundreds of roman style faces that have been subtly individualized. The typeface in Figure 3-6 falls within the category or set of roman letterforms.

Other sets are composed of individualized letterforms. The sans serif face in Figure 3-7 is an example. Literally thousands of faces are available in the various sets. Often the differences are quite subtle and two or more faces that closely resemble each other may have different names because they are supplied by different producers.

Obviously the designer should be able to identify typefaces. But to learn to recognize all, or any substantial number of them, would be a monumental task. To facilitate recognition, the designer or typographer should learn how type is organized. Once the designer understands the system, he or she will be better able to locate the face that meets his or her need.

Type is organized into

1. groups or styles
2. families
3. fonts and
4. series

Type Groups

Type groups or styles are based on two considerations: historical development of the various faces within each category or set and their

ḤARṖ ꞇO REAṖ

3-8   All-caps Text composition is difficult to read.

structural form. These groups include text, old style roman, modern roman, square serif, sans serif, script/cursive and novelty.

Text Faces

As Figure 3-8 shows, the text design resembles the calligraphy of the German monks of Gutenberg's time. Faces in this group are difficult to read when they are run in all uppercase (caps) or when they are composed in several lines. When used in the Gutenberg-published Bible, the text face was very large and meant to be read aloud. Today, these are usually seen on wedding or graduation announcements, documents and diplomas and religious materials.

Old Style Roman. Designers in Italy, France and Germany began to break away from the difficult-to-read text faces by creating new forms that were lighter and more elegant. They showed variation in strokes and dramatic serifs but retained angles similar to typical pen strokes. These variations in thickness of stroke and interesting serifs are features that make old style roman faces legible, especially for textual matter. Two excellent examples of this group are Caslon and Garamond. Note how similar they are (Figure 3-9).

Caslon
abcdefghijklmnopqrstuvwxyz
ABCDEFGHIJKLMNOPQRSTUVWXYZ

Garamond
abcdefghijklmnopqrstuvwxyz
ABCDEFGHIJKLMNOPQRSTUVWXYZ

3-9   Two of the best-known Old Style faces are Caslon and Garamond.

ABCDEFGHIJKLMNOPQRSTUVWXYZ&
ABCDEFGHIJKLMNOPQRSTUVWXYZ&
abcdefghijklmnopqrstuvwxyz

3-10 The Bodoni face heralded the beginning of the Modern Roman type designs.

Modern Roman. Although *modern* suggests newness, the first modern roman face was designed more than two centuries ago by Firmin Didot of France. Both he and Bodoni were influenced by the Englishman Baskerville, who designed what many typographers call a *transitional* face between old style and modern. Bodoni, however, is most often cited as the first modern face (Figure 3-10). As you can see, the most distinguishing characteristic of modern roman is the straight, thin and unbracketed serif.

Square Serif. It isn't surprising that on the way to a cleaner, more functional face without stroke variations (called block type at one stage) that serifs would be squared for a heavier, bolder look. Clarendon, designed in 1845, is a good example (Figure 3-11). Note the difference, however, in the more modern "slab" serifs, such as Stymie and Beton Extra Bold (Figure 3-12).

Sans Serif. Sometimes referred to as gothic or grotesque, the *sans (without) serif* is a modern, functional type that was influenced by the German Bauhaus design movement of the 1920s. Generally speaking, sans serif faces have uniform strokes, as seen in Futura (Figure 3-13). But compare that with another face in this group, Optima, also seen in Figure 3-13. One of the early uses for faces in this group was for poster advertising, where the clean, lean look lent itself well to large sizes. This

abcdefghijklmnopqrstuvwxyz
ABCDEFGHIJKLMNOPQRSTUVW
XYZ

3-11 Clarendon, one of the earliest Square Serif faces.

Stymie **Beton Extra Bold**

3-12 The Square or "Slab" Serif group is still popular today, as the extensive use of these faces demonstrates.

Futura   Optima

3-13   Futura, one of the oldest Sans Serif faces, compared with a recent face, Optima.

type was often made of wood. Today, there are many varieties of sans serif faces—almost as many as roman. While sans serif still seems to be preferred for display or headline type, there is increasing use of certain faces for body type. Optima is an example of this dual usage. (More on the legibility and readability of roman and sans serif faces in Chapter 4.)

Script/Cursive. Although members of this group emulate handwriting, their style is not like elaborate manuscript lettering of the text faces. Script letters *appear* to be joined, but cursives do not. These are special-purpose faces, used primarily for announcements, invitations, letterheads, etc. Commercial Script and Coronet (Figure 3-14) are examples of this group.

Novelty. This group cannot be so precisely defined. These faces create a sense of mood, time or decoration. Invariably, they are used as display matter. Examples are Broadway, Calypso and Rustic (Figure 3-15).

Type Families
In our discussion of groups, we mentioned type designs such as Bodoni, Caslon, Futura, Stymie and so on. How the design *elements* or *parts* of the face are styled sets one *family* apart from the other within the same design. So, the Bodoni design will have great variations within its type. But because they are all related, these are all members of the Bodoni "family."

ABCDEFGHIJKLMNOPQRSTUVWXYZ&
abcdefghijklmnopqrstuvwxyz

ABCEFGHIJKLMNOPQRSTUVWXYZ&
abcdefghijklmnopqrstuvwxyz

3-14   Coronet is a good example of the Cursive group. Commercial Script represents the Script group; note how its letters appear to be joined.

BROADWAY   CALYPSO   RUSTIC

3-15   Broadway, Calypso and Rustic are examples of Novelty faces.

Family Variations. Within a given family there may be a number of variations, sometimes referred to as *branches,* involving width, weight and posture. However, regardless of these branches, the basic family design characteristics may remain.

Width variations refer to the *condensing* of type, a sort of narrowing of the letterforms, and *extension,* a sort of widening of them. Such treatments are referred to as *condensed* or *extended.*

Some typestyles are designed with thinner or thicker strokes than are found in the normal face. Such variations include *light, semibold* (or *demibold*), *bold* and *extrabold.* Bold, or *boldface,* often written *bf,* is the most common of the weight variations.

The normal typestyle is often referred to as *normal* or *fullface,* which means no variation in either weight or width. Typefaces that are slanted to the right are referred to as *italic* in contrast to the normal, upright posture, which is referred to as *roman.* Because the word "roman" also refers to a type group, this seems to be a sort of inconsistency, as there would be a roman Caslon as well as a roman Futura; the latter belongs to the sans serif and not the roman group. Trade practice dictates that roman is assumed unless typesetting specifications state otherwise.

Some families are available with a number of variations, as shown in Figure 3-16. However, the majority come only as roman, italic and bold. A few faces offer such variations as shaded, shadowed and outlined letterforms. These typestyles are not usually thought of as family variations; instead, they may be classified as novelty.

Type Fonts

A *font* consists of the letters, numerals, punctuation marks and other symbols that constitute a branch of a family in one size. By *branch* we refer to a variation in the family, such as bold or italic. The different kinds and the total number of characters per font differ among the various phototypesetting machines as well as among metal composition machines. For example, some fonts may have small caps, written *sc,* in addition to standard size uppercase letters. Such a font is shown in Figure 3-17.

3-16 Variations in the Helvetica family. The term *Helvetica* alone refers to the normal or fullface version of the face.

Helvetica Light
Helvetica Light Italic
Helvetica
Helvetica Italic
Helvetica Bold
Helvetica Bold Italic
Helvetica Condensed
Helvetica Bold Condensed
Helvetica Bold Condensed Italic

3-17 A font of type (Baskerville), which includes caps and lower case in both roman and italic variations and small caps.

ABCDEFGHIJKLMNOPQRSTUVWXYZ
ABCDEFGHIJKLMNOPQRSTUVWXYZ
abcdefghijklmnopqrstuvwxyz

ABCDEFGHIJKLMNOPQRSTUVWXYZ
abcdefghijklmnopqrstuvwxyz

* © § † ℗ ‡ ® ¶ ™ @ ¢ ☞ ⊗
○
● • ○ ■ □ ★
+ − × = ÷

3-18 A phototypesetting pi font.

Special Characters

There are times when special characters not available in standard fonts are needed. Such symbols are called *pi characters* or *sorts* (usually a metal typesetting term) and may be available in special phototypesetting fonts called *pi fonts*. An example is shown in Figure 3-18. In metal composition, which involves casting type from molds, the machine operator will often hand-insert the molds for these pi characters in the line of assembled molds before casting the type.

In both phototypesetting and metal typesetting, most machines can compose from more than one font. Thus, it is possible to call for characters from two or more fonts, one of which might contain pi symbols.

Type Series

The range in sizes in a family branch available for composition is called a *series.*

Type and Typesetting Measurements

Several specialized units of measurement are widely used in graphic communication. Principal among them are the *point, pica, em, unit* and *agate line.* The *inch* is also used, usually only for paper and page size and the dimensions of pictures.

Type size is measured in *points,* and *line length* (its measurement horizontally) is measured in *picas.* There are six picas to an inch and twelve points to a pica; thus there are 72 points to the inch. For example, a column of type set on a 24-pica "measure" is four inches wide.

Early type was identified by name rather than by size. What we call nine-point (abbreviated pt.) today was once called Bourgeois; 36-pt. was Double Great Primer. But 100 years ago, the United States adopted a variant of the point system invented by Fournier of France, and it remains the standard today.

The Point

Type sizes generally range from tiny 4-pt. to 72-pt., although some machines are capable of producing sizes as large as 144-pt. With computer-generated type and phototypesetting, any size is possible. Figure 3-19 shows the most common sizes of *body type*—which is used for textual

4 pts.	Type
6 pts.	Type
8 pts.	Type
9 pts.	Type
10 pts.	Type
11 pts.	Type
12 pts.	Type
13 pts.	Type

3-19 The common range of body type sizes, set here in Century Schoolbook.

matter. This is set in a modern roman face called Century Schoolbook. Ten and 11-pt. seem to be the most readable for large amounts of text matter.

Type sizes 14-pt. and larger are called *display type sizes.* The most-frequently used are shown for size comparison in Figure 3-20, which is set in Univers, a sans serif face.

With just a little experience working with type, many people can eyeball its approximate size. To be sure, however, measure the type from the top of the ascender (refer to Figure 3-6) to the bottom of the descender to get point size. A *printer's rule,* which is gauged in points, picas and inches, is the best device for measurement. You may not always come up with an exact point size because a small amount of space is usually added above ascenders and below descenders so that lines of type will not touch. Another measurement problem occurs when

14 pts.	Type
18 pts.	Type
24 pts.	Type
30 pts.	Type
36 pts.	Type
42 pts.	Type
48 pts.	Type
60 pts.	Type
72 pts.	Type

3-20 The common range of display type sizes, set here in Univers.

Bodoni **Ultra Bodoni**

3-21 Both these members of the Bodoni type family have the same point size (24), but the extended nature of Ultra Bodoni makes it look larger.

Accurate copyfitting will save you many head-

3-22 A line measure of 21 picas (3½ inches wide), set in 12-pt. Palatino.

type is photographically altered; this may be done when making negatives of page pasteups before platemaking.

An example of the visual tricks type can play is seen in Figure 3-21. Indeed, the Ultra Bodoni face is thicker (more extended), but it is the same 24-pt. type size as the plainer member of its family.

The Pica

One pica equals 12 points; a half equals six. Thus, a line measure of 21 picas is $3\frac{1}{2}$ inches across (21 divided by 6). When you calculate how typeset copy will fit into an assigned space, it is important to know the height (point size) of the type and its measure (picas). Note the measure in Figure 3-22. Copyfitting is discussed in Chapter 5.

The Em

The em is a special measure used for paragraph indentation and for spacing. It is a *square* of the type size being set; thus, *a 10-pt. em is 10 points wide as well as high.* In traditional metal typesetting, the em is a square, blank body.

The Unit

The *unit* is a fraction of the width of an em. The number of units per em varies from one phototypesetting machine to another, although the 18-unit count is most common. Phototypefaces are designed with each character being allotted a certain number of units; see Figure 3-23. The character does not quite fill the width of its allotted units; the slight extra space is needed so that composed characters do not touch. The width of the various characters is called *set* or *set width,* and this dimension may vary from family to family. That is, an *x* may be 9 set or 9 units in one family and 10 set or 10 units in another.

Applying the Unit System

A knowledge of the unit system and how to apply it in phototypesetting offers the designer a number of advantages that are not generally

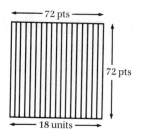

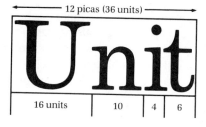

3-23 Unit distribution on a phototypesetting em. The word *Unit* is set in 72-pt. type.

available in metal composition. The designer can call for either an increase or decrease of spacing between letters—called *letterspacing*—and for either an increase or a decrease of spacing between words—called *wordspacing*. These advantages result:

1. The legibility can be improved.
2. The tone of a block of copy can be altered.
3. Tightening both letterspacing and wordspacing will permit getting more copy into a given space.

Type composed without spacing alteration is said to have *normal letterspacing*. It is possible, however, to call for *loose letterspacing* (or *loose set*) or *tight letterspacing* (or *tight set*), or even very loose or very tight.

3-24 *Opposite page. Left column:* The sample paragraph at top is set in a Roman face with *normal* letterspacing and wordspacing. In order below, it is set with the following letterspacing and wordspacing: $+\frac{1}{2}$, $+1$, $-\frac{1}{2}$, -1. Composition is 10-point with 2-point leading (linespacing). *Right column:* The sample paragraph at top is set in a condensed Sans Serif face with *normal* letterspacing and wordspacing. In order below, it is set with the following letterspacing and wordspacing: $+\frac{1}{2}$, $+1$, $-\frac{1}{2}$, -1. Composition is same as the left column, but note how condensed faces can be set tighter than regular faces.

Line length or measure is referred to as being so many picas or as so many picas and points long. Thus "15.6" would mean a measure of 15 picas and 6 points or 15½ picas. Lines of justified type are usually a whole number of picas long or a whole number and one-half.

Line length or measure is referred to as being so many picas or as so many picas and points long. Thus "15.6" would mean a measure of 15 picas and 6 points or 15½ picas. Lines of justified type are usually a whole number of picas long or a whole number and one-half.

Line length or measure is referred to as being so many picas or as so many picas and points long. Thus "15.6" would mean a measure of 15 picas and 6 points or 15½ picas. Lines of justified type are usually a whole number of picas long or a whole number and one-half.

Line length or measure is referred to as being so many picas or as so many picas and points long. Thus "15.6" would mean a measure of 15 picas and 6 points or 15½ picas. Lines of justified type are usually a whole number of picas long or a whole number and one-half.

Line length or measure is referred to as being so many picas or as so many picas and points long. Thus "15.6" would mean a measure of 15 picas and 6 points or 15½ picas. Lines of justified type are usually a whole number of picas long or a whole number and one-half.

Line length or measure is referred to as being so many picas or as so many picas and points long. Thus "15.6" would mean a measure of 15 picas and 6 points or 15½ picas. Lines of justified type are usually a whole number of picas long or a whole number and one-half.

Line length or measure is referred to as being so many picas or as so many picas and points long. Thus "15.6" would mean a measure of 15 picas and 6 points or 15½ picas. Lines of justified type are usually a whole number of picas long or a whole number and one-half.

Line length or measure is referred to as being so many picas or as so many picas and points long. Thus "15.6" would mean a measure of 15 picas and 6 points or 15½ picas. Lines of justified type are usually a whole number of picas long or a whole number and one-half.

Line length or measure is referred to as being so many picas or as so many picas and points long. Thus "15.6" would mean a measure of 15 picas and 6 points or 15½ picas. Lines of justified type are usually a whole number of picas long or a whole number and one-half.

Line length or measure is referred to as being so many picas or as so many picas and points long. Thus "15.6" would mean a measure of 15 picas and 6 points or 15½ picas. Lines of justified type are usually a whole number of picas long or a whole number and one-half.

Type

3-25 Normal type spacing (*above*) and the same letters *kerned* in phototypesetting to bring them closer together.

Type

3-25 Normal type spacing (*above*) and the same letters *kerned* in phototypesetting to bring them closer together.

Such spacing is measured in units and half-units; loose and tight generally refer to $+\frac{1}{2}$ and $-\frac{1}{2}$; very loose and very tight refer to $+1$ and -1. These capabilities vary among machines, and the designer must be aware of such matters. Minus $\frac{1}{2}$ unit settings can allow about 5 percent more characters per line of type, and minus 1 can allow about 10 percent more characters per line.

Wordspacing can also be referred to as normal, loose $(+\frac{1}{2})$, very loose $(+1)$, tight $(-\frac{1}{2})$ and very tight (-1). In most cases, if other than normal letterspacing is used, it should be combined with matching wordspacing—that is, $-\frac{1}{2}$ unit letterspacing with $-\frac{1}{2}$ unit wordspacing. Figure 3-24 shows the effects of various combinations. The first setting is with normal spacing, whereas the remaining four are with loose, very loose, tight, and very tight settings.

Most type is set with normal or with $-\frac{1}{2}$ unit spacing. The selection of the proper spacing is not a simple matter. These guidelines may prove helpful:

1. Type set all caps should be letterspaced, unless the letterstyle is condensed. Note the words that follow:
   NO LETTERSPACING   WITH LETTERSPACING
2. Display type can be composed with tighter set than text type.
3. Condensed type can be set more tightly than wider type.
4. Faces with small center body (x-height) require little, if any, letterspacing.

Greater freedom can be exercised in the spacing of display type. A look through a number of magazines will prove very beneficial in terms of learning techniques used in linespacing as well as word- and letterspacing.

On many machines, limited letterspacing can be used in special cases. Look at Figure 3-25, the phototypeset placement of the *y* under the *T* is an example; this treatment is called *kerning*.

Some typographers decide on wordspacing that best suits the typeface and apply it throughout the composition. When this is done, the composition must be *ragged right*—that is, the lines are of different lengths. They have a common starting point on the left, however, and are thus *flush left*, as shown in Figure 3-26. When all lines are even, right and left (as they are in this book), copy is said to be *justified*.

On the pages that follow, the reorganization and its effect on various banks are more fully explained in sections which include the photographs of the senior officers who are responsible for individual areas.

3-26 Ragged right composition.

Composition with ragged right or the less common ragged left has a more even tonal appearance than justified composition because word-spacing is the same in all lines. Such composition is thus very effective for narrow measures.

Other Uses of the Point

The point is used for measuring interline spacing—that is, the extra space placed between lines of type. Such spacing is called *leading* (pronounced "ledding"). Type set without such extra spacing is said to be *set solid.* This terminology, though it was inherited from metal typesetting tradition, is in current use.

Because many phototypesetting machines are capable not only of adding space but also of reducing space between the lines, leading is also commonly called *linespacing,* the reduction of interline spacing being called *reverse leading, minus leading,* or *back leading.* In any event, leading and linespacing are measured in points (and $\frac{1}{2}$ points in phototypesetting).

If type is set 10-point with 1 point linespacing or leading, it is referred to as 10/11. If reverse leading of 1 point is done, the designation is 10/9. In Figure 3-27, the lines are set 10-point solid, leading 1 point, leading 2 points, and with -1 point leading.

Generally, text type is set with one or two points added; faces with small x-heights may require no leading. Display sizes can be linespaced with greater freedom. See Appendix B for the specifications for this book. Note that its text is 10/12; the captions are 9/10. The varying linespacings of the display—the heads—are expressed as "points B/B," meaning number of points base to base, that is, baseline to baseline of the x-heights of specific lines. Very free treatments of display sizes of type can be seen in advertising headlines in national magazines, where there are fewer restrictions than in books.

Reverse leading also makes it possible to set two or more columns of type on some phototypesetting machines. After one column is set, the paper or film can be backed up to allow another column to be set.

Other Uses of the Pica

In addition to line length (a horizontal measurement) the pica is used to measure:

1. width of column (horizontal)
2. depth of columns (a vertical measurement)
3. size of margins between columns and also between type areas and the outside of pages
4. size of illustrations

Several factors influence the selection of linespacing. The design of the type face is one. Faces with larger x-height require greater leading. The length of the measure is another. The longer the measure, in general, the greater the linespacing required. Finally, there is greater need to linespace the smaller text sizes, 5- to 8-point, to increase legibility.

Several factors influence the selection of linespacing. The design of the type face is one. Faces with larger x-height require greater leading. The length of the measure is another. The longer the measure, in general, the greater the linespacing required. Finally, there is greater need to linespace the smaller text sizes, 5- to 8-point, to increase legibility.

Several factors influence the selection of linespacing. The design of the type face is one. Faces with larger x-height require greater leading. The length of the measure is another. The longer the measure, in general, the greater the linespacing required. Finally, there is greater need to linespace the smaller text sizes, 5- to 8-point, to increase legibility.

Several factors influence the selection of linespacing. The design of the type face is one. Faces with larger x-height require greater leading. The length of the measure is another. The longer the measure, in general, the greater the linespacing required. Finally, there is greater need to linespace the smaller text sizes, 5- to 8-point, to increase legibility.

Several factors influence the selection of linespacing. The design of the type face is one. Faces with larger x-height require greater leading. The length of the measure is another. The longer the measure, in general, the greater the linespacing required. Finally, there is greater need to linespace the smaller text sizes, 5- to 8-point, to increase legibility.

Several factors influence the selection of linespacing. The design of the type face is one. Faces with larger x-height require greater leading. The length of the measure is another. The longer the measure, in general, the greater the linespacing required. Finally, there is greater need to linespace the smaller text sizes, 5- to 8-point, to increase legibility.

Several factors influence the selection of linespacing. The design of the type face is one. Faces with larger x-height require greater leading. The length of the measure is another. The longer the measure, in general, the greater the linespacing required. Finally, there is greater need to linespace the smaller text sizes, 5- to 8-point, to increase legibility.

Several factors influence the selection of linespacing. The design of the type face is one. Faces with larger x-height require greater leading. The length of the measure is another. The longer the measure, in general, the greater the linespacing required. Finally, there is greater need to linespace the smaller text sizes, 5- to 8-point, to increase legibility.

Other Uses of the Em

In addition to being a unit of spacing, the em is also used as a measurement of quantity of type. One would calculate the amount of composition in a space 15 picas wide and $7\frac{1}{2}$ inches deep, if type were 10 point, as follows

15 × 12 = 180 points wide
180 ÷ 10 = 18 (10-point ems or set ems per line)
$7\frac{1}{2}$ × 72 (points per inch) = 540 points deep
540 ÷ 10 = 54 lines of 10-point type
54 × 18 = 972 ems of composition

If the composition were 12-point type, there would be 15 set ems per line, 45 lines of type, and thus 675 set ems of composition.

The Agate Line

Sometimes referred to as *line,* the *agate line* is a measure of advertising space. The cost of advertising has often been quoted by the agate line, which can be defined as one column wide (horizontal) and $\frac{1}{14}$th of an inch deep (vertical). The agate line should not be confused with a line of type. Referring to an advertisement of 28 lines can mean either an advertisement that is two inches deep and one column wide—written 28 × 1—or one that is one inch deep and two columns wide—14 × 2, spoken of as "fourteen on two." However, this measurement is being replaced by modules called Standard Advertising Unit.

The Metric System

Points, picas, units and inches are terms common in the typographer's work-a-day jargon. Some day, it is believed, these terms will give way to metrication. Even today, many chemicals, paper, film and other printing supplies bear labels showing metric equivalents. In Europe there is a definite trend to the metric system for measuring type sizes and spacing.

3-27   *Opposite page. Left column:* This type is set in Garamond, 10-point on a 14-pica measure. The paragraph at top is set solid, or with no leading. In order below that paragraph, it is set with the following leading: 1 point, 2 points, − 1 point. *Right Column:* This type is set in Century, 10-point on a 14-pica measure. Note that it has a larger x-height than Garamond. The paragraph at top is set solid. In order below, it is set with the following leading: 1 point, 2 points, − 1 point.

The following table shows points and picas with equivalents in inches, centimeters and millimeters. The figures, which are to the nearest ten-thousandths, are based on (1) the accepted U.S. standard that one inch = 2.54 centimeters (a metric yard = 39.37 inches), (2) one pica = .1660 inches, and (3) one point = .013837 inches. The latter two measurements were accepted by the printing industry in the United States in the late 19th century.

Metrication Conversion

points	inches	cm	mm
½	.0069	.0175	.1753
1	.0138	.0351	.3505
2	.0277	.0704	.7036
3	.0415	.1054	1.0541
4	.0553	.1405	1.4046
5	.0692	.1758	1.7577
6	.0830	.2108	2.1082
7	.0969	.2461	2.4613
8	.1107	.2812	2.8118
9	.1245	.3162	3.1623
10	.1384	.3515	3.5154
11	.1522	.3866	3.8659
12	.1660	.4216	4.2164
picas			
2	.3320	.8433	8.4328
3	.4980	1.2649	12.6492
4	.6640	1.6866	16.8656
5	.8300	2.1082	21.0820
6	.9960	2.5298	25.2984
7	1.1620	2.9515	29.5148
8	1.3280	3.3731	33.7312
9	1.4940	3.7948	37.9476
10	1.6600	4.2164	42.1640

Type Composition

There are two methods of composing or setting type: *hot* and *cold.* Hot refers to the traditional method of composition with metal type, whether by hand or machine. For more than 400 years after Gutenberg's time (c. 1450 A.D.), all type was composed by hand, letter by letter, em space by em space, line by line. Mechanized composition is actually only 100 years old.

Our most modern typesetting methods—using photography or computers to produce what we call *cold type*—are now capable of assembling more than 10,000 type characters per second (cps). Using deep-set rules called composing sticks and picking characters from job cases, the hot type "hand peggers" were speedy if they could manage one cps.

Because cold type is the main method of composition today, let's discuss it first.

Cold-Type Composition

Type composed by any means other than hot metal is referred to as *cold type.* Such composition is achieved by direct imaging of characters onto film or paper. There are several methods: (1) phototypesetting, (2) photodisplay machines, (3) electronic composition, (4) direct impression or strike-on, and (5) transfer lettering.

Phototypesetting Machines

These machines operate on a common principle. They print typefaces and other symbols onto paper or film by flashing a light through film negatives of the desired symbols. One such system is shown in Figure 3-28.

High-quality negatives of the various symbols in a font are contained in the type disk in the example. The disk spins at a high rate of speed. The Xenon lamp flashes a brief fraction of a second, just long enough to "stop" the desired character. The beam of light strikes the prism in the escapement system and is reflected toward the paper or film. En route, the light beam passes through the rotatable lenses for enlarging or reducing the image. The escapement system moves horizontally, which makes possible the composition of lines of type. In many machines the paper or film is capable of vertical movement, making possible reverse leading. In some machines the negative image carrier is stationary and the light moves.

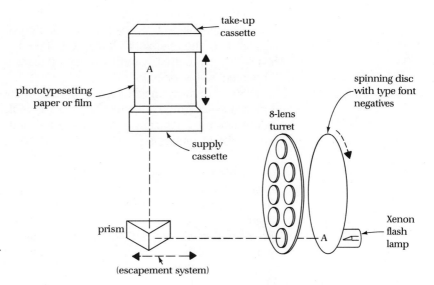

3-28 Optical system of a phototypesetter.

The symbol negatives are not carried on disks in all machines. In some they are in the form of filmstrips that are affixed to drums; other machines use flat grids, to which the negatives are attached. The film fonts are interchangeable. The various machines differ in many other ways, such as number of fonts on machine, type sizes available, speed of composition, paper or film widths, maximum line lengths and flexibility in terms of spacing, tabbing, mixing of letterforms, reverse leading and so on.

Two types of phototypesetters are in wide use today. The simpler type is called a *direct-entry* machine. In this application, the operator works at a keyboard that is part of the machine. The other type of phototypesetter is a *remote-entry* machine; access in this case is not direct but comes from different operators in locations remote from the machine.

Direct-Entry Machines. These are the most widely used photocomposition machines today and may be found in printing plants, business offices, advertising agencies and so on. Generally, they do not match the large, remote-entry machines in capacity of production.

Input comes from typewriterlike keyboards with additional keys to control word-, letter- and linespacing; *quadding* left (setting ragged right); quadding right; centering; tabbing; kerning; reverse leading and so on. On some machines the operator is signaled when nearing a line's full measure; the operator then decides on where to hyphenate the word, if necessary, or how to space out a line to justify it and thereby avoid hyphenation. Some machines offer the operator the option of using a computerlike processor for making the *h&j* (hyphenation and justification) decision. Such a processor is a part of the machine and contains basic logic rules for making these decisions. In some cases, small computers are used which store in memory an *exception dictionary* of words that cannot be accurately hyphenated by the logical rules.

Basically, type is set as it is keyboarded. Thus, speed of output is a function of the operator's typing skill. If the machine is not capable of h&j decisions, output is further limited because such decisions require 30 percent of the operator's time.

Some of these machines display only a few characters—less than a measure—at a time and then cast the accumulated line before another can be started. Characters and spaces are stored in a buffer memory and are displayed much as numbers are displayed on an electronic calculator.

More recent direct-entry machines make possible the display of at least 40 lines of characters on a *VDT* (*video display terminal*) before they are set in type. The operator, using special function keys on the keyboard, can edit the display copy before it is typeset. Some larger direct-entry machines can store beyond the 40 lines in a minicomputer memory until they are ready for composition. The VDT is further discussed in Chapters 7 and 8.

Some of the direct-entry machines are capable of storing copy for future use and also accepting input from keyboards that are off-line from the system.

Remote-Entry Machines. These phototypesetters are more adaptable to the requirements of larger printing plants and publishers of newspapers and magazines. They operate at higher output speeds because they can accept a number of different inputs coming from remote locations. In general, these machines are capable of functioning with more different faces and sizes as well as more *formats* (typographic requirements for composition) than the direct-input machines. They are usually integrated into large computer-controlled typesetting systems such as those discussed in Chapters 7 and 8.

Photodisplay Machines. These machines are used primarily for setting display size words. Phototypesetters (both direct-entry and remote-entry) are capable of enlarging smaller sizes to display, using special lenses, as shown in Figure 3-26. However, text and display sizes were traditionally separately designed. The smaller faces were slightly more extended and more space was allowed between characters. When enlarged appreciably, these characteristics were exaggerated.

Special machines are used for setting traditionally designed display sizes, as shown in the example of the portable unit in Figure 3-29. Spacing of headlines may be done visually, and the operator can place characters in positions other than "normal." Some equipment can apply special optical treatments, as shown in Figure 3-30.

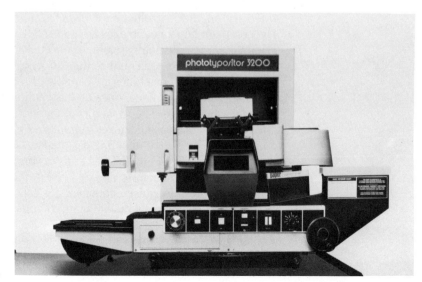

3-29 A portable typesetting unit. It is helpful for display typesetting for in-house production.

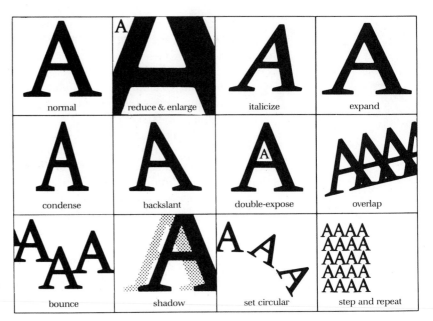

3-30 Optical treatments of photodisplay type. (Photo Typositor ® type reproduced by permission of Visual Graphics Corporation)

However, photodisplay machines are relatively slow, as their operation requires manual selection of characters and exposure one at a time on paper or film. Some are limited to setting lines on narrow strips; others can compose several lines on sheets of paper or film. They are cost-efficient, however, and permit in-house production of graphics that might have been "jobbed out" at a higher price.

Electronic Composition. Because these typesetters compose on a video screen, they are often termed CRT (Cathode Ray Tube) machines. The computer-generated images are focused by a lens onto paper or film, usually by a remote-entry system. The Video Display Terminals (VDTs) of most newspapers today utilize the CRT concept.

Some of these machines are capable of composing more than 3,000 newspaper lines per minute once all information is received from remote terminals. In one newspaper application, such a machine can turn out full-size pages of classified advertisements, complete with rules, in about one minute. More about this process, called pagination, in Chapter 17.

The flexibility of the CRTs extends beyond that of phototypesetters; in addition to the capacity to do larger areas, they are capable of broader computer control. Because characters are generated on a video screen, they can be electronically manipulated to appear as roman, italic, backslanted, condensed, expanded or bold—even in combinations of such treatments. They can generate line art along with type, and it is also possible to scan continuous-tone art, such as photographs and drawings, and convert tones to dot form in the digital computer, later to be output as halftones.

3-31 An electronically generated letter, enlarged. (Courtesy ANPA Research Institute)

Descriptive patterns for the generation of symbols are either stored in computer memory in digital form or matrix grids are scanned by CRT (not the printout tube), which translates character descriptions into digital coding. In either case, the descriptive coding is used to direct the action of the printout CRT beam. This electronic beam "paints" the shapes of the characters on the screen much as the beam puts a picture on a home television screen. The shapes of the characters are formed by parallel, vertical lines, as many as 1440 per inch. The greater the number of these lines the greater is the definition of the characters, but the slower is the composition rate. Some machines generate characters by means of closely grouped dots. The type sizes of these characters range from 4- to 80-point. Figure 3-31 shows an electronically generated letter.

Direct Impression

Also referred to as *strike-on*, the direct impression method of putting typefaces on paper involves the use of a special typewriter with interchangeable typefaces. Direct impression is limited to composition of text sizes only, but it serves well when low cost of composition is an overriding factor. Strike-on typefaces have low unit count values; thus finesse in letter- and wordspacing is limited.

On some machines copy must be typed twice. At the first typing the amount of wordspacing for justifying is determined by the machine; on the second typing the line is spaced to full measure. The most widely used system records the copy on magnetic tape at first typing, which is done on a nontypesetting typewriter. The typist is unconcerned with typeface, line length, linespacing and justifying. The tape is then fed to a processing unit that operates a typesetting typewriter. The latter justifies lines but cannot hyphenate. When hyphenation of a word is necessary, the operator must be on hand to make that decision. The operator must also stand by to change fonts, if the job calls for mixing of faces, as well as to set the composing typewriter for line length and leading.

Transfer Type

An increasingly popular method of preparing small amounts of distinctive display type is by *transfer*. Type fonts are carried on thin, waxy, acetate sheets that are laid over a design and then transferred by burnishing the sheet. This rubbing moves the letter from the sheet and affixes it to the layout (Figure 3-32).

These sheets are relatively low in cost and are available in an amazing variety of type styles, pi characters, borders and patterns. One manufacturer's catalogue boasts thousands of designs. Their only problem seems to be the potential for chipping of the transferred lettering—but a little acrylic spray should provide adequate protection.

These transfer sheet designs are becoming more popular in magazine and newspaper use, especially for special sections. They also are finding favor with advertising designers, who are using them to polish comprehensive layouts.

3-32 The application of transfer type.

Hot Type Composition

Hot type is the setting of characters, rules and borders cast in metal. Such type may be precast as individual symbols (*foundry type*) and assembled by hand. More commonly, composition is by machines that manufacture type as they are operated, either as a line of word symbols (raised faces) on a body of type called a *slug,* or as single letters. Three kinds of machines are used: linecasters, the Monotype, and the Ludlow.

Linecasting Machines

There are two *linecasters:* The Linotype and Intertype, both of which cast a line of characters on a slug. An operator at a keyboard assembles a line of brass molds, called *matrices* or *mats,* together with expandable spaces between words. When the assembled mats and spacebands approach full measure, the operator makes h&j decisions; occasionally the operator may drop extra word- and letterspacing materials between mats and bands by hand; when the line is adjusted, the machine is directed to cast the line.

Composition is relatively slow; a skilled operator can cast perhaps four or five newspaper lines per minute (lpm). Some linecasters, operated by computer devices that calculate h&j, can set perhaps 12 lpm.

The range of type fonts on a linecasting machine is limited; most linecasters carry only two, generally the roman and either the boldface or italic type style; a few machines may carry four or more fonts but each in only one size. Most linecasting machines are limited to setting 5- to 24-point and maximum line length of 30 picas. The faces available are not all aligned to a common baseline, as are phototypesetter faces, making the mixing of different families within one line more of a problem than in the case of photocomposition.

Extra spacing between lines can be accomplished by casting the leading area as part of the slug. But linecasters do not offer the minus leading or tight letterspacing flexibility of phototypesetting.

The Monotype

The Monotype machine casts lines of type from molds, but a letter at a time. Keyboard and caster are separate units. The operator at the keyboard perforates a paper tape, coded for letters and spacing. The operator makes all h&j decisions when the keyboard signals that composition is near the end of a line. Like the linecasters, the Monotype casts leading as part of the type. Linespacing flexibility is therefore limited. Sizes 4- to 14-point can be set on the Monotype machine, but font-carrying flexibility is limited. Because it does not cast slugs, the Monotype is better adapted than the linecasters for setting tabular matter and scientific materials.

The Ludlow

Like the linecasters, the Ludlow casts slugs. It is used primarily for casting display sizes. The operator of the Ludlow hand sets mats, which are then placed in a casting machine where the slugs are cast.

A Final Word

Understanding type—its origins, development and use—is crucial for an understanding of graphic arts and production processes. We hope this chapter has provided a substantial foundation for such understanding. In succeeding chapters we will concentrate on such matters as readability of typography, creative use of type and copyfitting. All of these areas will help round out your design and production skills.

4

Effective and Creative Uses of Type

Fashion and fancy commonly frolic from one extreme to the other, from the razor-edged fine lines and ceriphs of type, to the unnatural shape of turning all the ceriphs and fine strokes into fats, and fats into leans. From the broad Egyptian, to the tall condensed, by turns take the lead, until the ingenuity of the type founder produces something new, to please the fancy of the printer, who of course wants to be in fashion.

—from an 1838 Printer's Manual

Sometimes it seems there is nothing so constant as the desire for change. This observation certainly finds a lot of support in typography, where the rush for a "new" look and an obsession about innovation have always been characteristic. Perhaps because the written word is such an integral part of our society, we have always tried new ways to look at our alphabet. Melville's *Moby Dick* will never change, but the style, size and measure of its type always will be dynamic.

Making correct typographical decisions is a classic duel between form and function. Such a clash reveals an irony that puts design and content at cross-purposes: Both sides want to be read and understood,

66

but designers see a need for inviting, stimulating packaging, while the producer of the words fears that design may overwhelm the content.

Effective communication requires a stable, blissful marriage of form and function. Both parties must understand their roles and interdependence. This chapter will examine challenges facing the designer in working effectively and creatively with typography; it will review topics related to readability and appropriateness of typography in order to discuss the *form* of the printed word; and it will also provide examples of how typography can enhance or defeat communication.

Let's begin with two topics of great concern to all typographers: *readability and appropriateness.*

Readability

For the typographer, readability is an *imprimatur,* a license to practice. For the researcher, it is countless experiments and tests to determine acceptability and comprehension. For the reader, it's a simpler proposition: If the type is too small, too odd, too tight, too wide, or just plain overwhelming, it will make reading a chore.

Figure 4-1 shows how the *Chicago Tribune* capitalized on readability concerns when it purposely "squeezed" copy (thanks to the lens work on a phototypesetter) to show a problem that its new Standard Advertising Unit program would solve.

Readability is generally defined as *speed and accuracy of recognizing and comprehending printed material.* Comprehension, of course, is the key: Type design that is received and comprehended *faster* could be assumed to be more legible. A serious, exhaustive study of legibility was undertaken more than a half century ago by the British Medical Research Council. It made this attempt at a definition, which no doubt seems amusing today:

> Legibility has to do with reading. Normal reading refers to an act performed most commonly by an individual in an ordinary sitting position in full light, with words set in horizontal lines one below the other, printed, as to about 90 percent in lowercase, as to about 10 percent in uppercase, in black ink on white or cream paper. The letters, spaces and lines are of sizes and proportions which vary within certain limits. The matter is held at distances from the eye varying generally from between six and sixteen inches. A legible type means one can easily read under these conditions.[1]

It is not the intention of this chapter to review the volumes of work and major findings of such researchers as Burt, Patterson, Tinker, and Zachrisson, although it is interesting to note that not much significant research on readability has been reported in the last 20 years. However,

1. R. L. Pyke, *The Legibility of Type* (His Majesty's Stationery Office, 1929), p. 25.

4-1 A typographical "squeeze." Capitalizing on concerns over readability and typefitting, the *Chicago Tribune* successfully reached its advertisers with this message. (Copyright 1984, *The Chicago Tribune*)

we do want to present some general findings and trade practices related to readability, such as: typeface, size, leading, line length, justification and margins.

Typeface

The old typographical rule, "roman for body, gothic (sans serif) for display," is receiving a stiff challenge, if recent design practice is an indicator. Sans serif faces are becoming increasingly popular for use as text matter, especially for advertising copy and for magazine use. However, publications that run longer, more continuous amounts of text matter (such as newspapers and books) still favor roman faces.

With their serifs and contrasting strokes, the roman faces still provide ease of reading. The main objection to sans serif, it seems, is its monotony of stroke. But there are sans serifs—and then there are sans serifs. Consider this passage about the meeting of journalist H. M. Stanley and missionary-doctor David Livingstone in Africa in 1871. The passage is set in two sans serif faces, Helvetica and Optima Italic, and Stanley relates the meeting:

> As I advanced slowly toward him I noticed he was pale, looked wearied, had a grey beard, wore a bluish cap with a faded gold band around it, had on a red-sleeved waistcoat, and a pair of grey tweed trousers. I would have run to him, only I was a coward in the presence of such a mob—would have embraced him, only he being an Englishman, I did not know how he would receive me, so I did what cowardice and false pride suggested was the best thing.

> *I walked deliberately to him, took off my hat, and said: "Dr. Livingstone, I presume." "Yes," said he with a kind smile, lifting his cap slightly. I replaced my hat on my head, and he puts on his cap, and we both grasp hands, and I then say aloud: "I thank God, Doctor, I have been permitted to see you." He answered, "I feel thankful that I am here to welcome you."*

Which sans serif face seems more readable to you? Is either better than the roman face selected for this book? With such a limited sample, these are difficult questions to answer; for example, amount of copy and other factors we'll soon discuss will affect your response.

It seems obvious that a publication wanting to change its typeface(s) would pre-test its new choice(s) to ensure readability and acceptance. In research completed in 1974 under the auspices of the American Newspaper Publishers Association, J. K. Hvistendahl of Iowa State University reinforced the old typographical rule when his sample of 200 newspapers showed a marked preference for roman over sans serif for newspaper body type. He also found that readers were able to read the roman face *significantly faster* in three out of four comparisons of type set in both $10\frac{1}{2}$- and 14-pica widths.

A good laboratory for *your* typeface research is the 1700 daily newspapers and 10,000 magazines published in the United States. Scan as many of these publications as is practical and see what faces strike your fancy. Ask: Is the face *comfortable* to read? Is it too *monotonous*? Is it too *light*? Too *dark*? Does the design call too much attention to itself? Would it look better as a display face? An excellent source for typeface review is the quarterly publication of the International Typeface Corporation, *U&lc* (Upper and lower case). Its text matter is purposely set in a variety of type groups. It's a great opportunity to make comparisons not only of faces, but of leading and measure, too.

Type size

There is less debate about the legibility of various type sizes. Many researchers agree that type in the 10- to 11-pt. range is the most readable for continuous text matter. This is certainly true for many books, such as this one, which is set in 10 pt. Many newspapers, however, still run columns of copy in 9 pt.; and because it is a selection they want to read, there seems to be little complaint from classified ad readers that the type there is usually about six points high.

Even with substantial leading, long runs of textual matter below nine points are going to cause a strain on the reader. Some newspapers have even increased their body copy to 10-pt. and widened their columns to encourage more readership. But what of sizes larger than 11-pt., not commonly used for long runs of text? In 1982 Meg Ashman, a graduate student at the University of Oregon's School of Journalism, researched whether larger faces would be more readable for older readers. Her careful testing revealed that for normally sighted older readers, there were *no* significant differences in readability between 11-, 14-, and 18-pt. Times Roman.

As a related issue, if you compare paragraphs set in 11- and 14-pt. type with normal leading, you can see that the larger point size looks strange on a narrow measure, perhaps causing perception problems for the reader:

Every profession has its secret language, which is intended to keep nonpractitioners in the dark. Talk of *Bodoni, Kennerly, Optima,* and *Zapf* is surely as confusing to the uninitiated as is the utterance of *subdural hematoma* to an anxious parent in the emergency room of a hospital.

Every profession has its secret language, which is intended to keep nonpractitioners in the dark. Talk of *Bodoni, Kennerly, Optima,* and *Zapf* is surely as confusing to the uninitiated as is the utterance of *subdural hematoma* to an anxious parent in the emergency room of a hospital.

More on this when we discuss *line length.*

Sound business practice affects a designer's judgment about type size. Larger sizes will occupy more space, consume more paper and ink—and perhaps hike the postage bill because of increased weight. However, there are times when the discreet use of a display size, such as 14- or 18-pt., works well as text matter. It may give prominence to the lead paragraph in a magazine article, inviting the reader to spend time with the rest of the article, which will be set normally.

One instance in which you should consider larger text sizes involves the use of reversed type (white on black or a light color against a darker background). Size should be slightly increased to prevent the type from being overwhelmed.

Leading

There are several dependable rules on leading, and they all focus on *moderation.* Don't be stingy with leading, and don't overdo it. Here are three guidelines:

1. For ordinary text sizes, one or two points of leading are adequate.
2. For faces with a small body (small x-heights), 1-pt. leading is sufficient.
3. As the length of line increases, the need to insert leading increases. However, little is usually gained by 3- or 4-pt. leading, unless the line measure is extraordinarily wide.

Line Length

Again, moderation is the key. *Short measures* (usually defined as *less than a full alphabet* of the type in a designated size) will hurt flow, as the reader will jerk to and fro to absorb phrases and clauses. *Too long* a measure (usually defined as that *in excess of two full alphabets* of a designated type size) will also hurt rhythm, as many readers may lose track of the line they are scanning. So what is just right? Many designers think that $1\frac{1}{2}$ alphabets is a good standard.

Length of alphabet is a workable criterion because it takes into account the width and boldness of letters. When an "alphabet" is not available for measuring you can take the type size, say 10-pt., and multiply it by $1\frac{1}{2}$ to get an *optimum* line length—in this case, 15 picas (10 $\times$ $1\frac{1}{2}$). Remember, however, that an extended face looks more satisfactory on a longer line than does a condensed face of the same size on that same measure.

Generally speaking, it is better to err in favor of a longer measure. A wider measure permits better wordspacing and reduces the number of hyphenations.

Justification

Most body copy is justified, which means that it is set even (flush) on both sides. However, the use of ragged right (unjustified) is increasing, with no apparent adverse effect on readability. In fact, the use of ragged right can speed composition and eliminate the need to hyphenate words. On the other hand, there seems to be little justification (!) for running copy ragged left, unless is it used in small doses or if it is set around an illustration for effect. The eye is used to returning to a common point;

The highway has been rising imperceptibly from the lakeshore, he doesn't know how far, perhaps a thousand feet, so that after he leaves it the road lurches unpredictably into ravines, hills swell beneath him, he knows the land drops sharply to Georgian Bay just beyond a particular clearing by a stand of evergreens.

The highway has been rising imperceptibly from the lakeshore, he doesn't know how far, perhaps a thousand feet, so that after he leaves it the road lurches unpredictably into ravines, hills swell beneath him, he knows the land drops sharply to Georgian Bay just beyond a particular clearing by a stand of evergreens.

The highway has been rising imperceptibly from the lakeshore, he doesn't know how far, perhaps a thousand feet, so that after he leaves it the road lurches unpredictably into ravines, hills swell beneath him, he knows the land drops sharply to Georgian Bay just beyond a particular clearing by a stand of evergreens.

4-2 Fully justified, ragged right and ragged left composition.

long stretches of ragged left thwart this tendency and affect readability. (Note Figure 4-2, which shows fully justified composition as well as ragged right and ragged left.)

Margins

These are the blank areas around the printed area of a sheet. Traditionally, there have been little if any margins around newspaper copy, although the so-called "white space" that separates headlines, copy, and illustrations has become a more vital factor in newspaper design. (See Chapter 15.) In books, margins comprising 50 percent of the sheet are considered ample; however, some researchers feel that reader preferences regarding margins are mostly a matter of esthetics.

Progressive margins are used most frequently for books. The *narrowest* margin is the inner one (at the fold); the next larger is at the top of the page (head margin). Margin width increases at the outside, but the widest is at the bottom (foot margin). These margins move clockwise on odd-numbered pages and counterclockwise on even-numbered pages. Thus, odd- and even-numbered pages are held together by narrow margins at the center.

Figure 4-3 shows an example of progressive margins. Note, however, the "new" look of the left-weighted margins in Figure 4-4. This allows narrower measures for smaller typefaces as well as providing ample space for illustrations without breaking into body copy. Note also the various approaches to margins in Chapter 14, "Magazine Design."

Other Readability Factors

In no particular order, here is a list of "recommendations" drawn from research and actual practice:

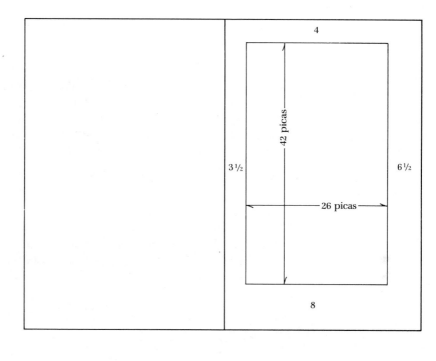

4-3 The traditional system of progressive margins on a book page.

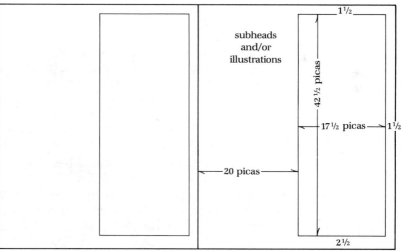

4-4 Book margin treatment with the new "left-weighted" system.

1. Regardless of typeface used, *caps and lower case* (clc) is preferred to material set in all caps. However, this does not negate the effective use of a small amount of all caps as display matter.
2. Type set *vertically* or *diagonally,* even in small amounts, is generally hard to read and should be avoided.

3. *Boldface* and *italics* are more effective when used for emphasis than for long runs of text.
4. An excessive amount of text matter that is set in display size risks a decline in readability.
5. Do not use too many faces in one body of work. Families may clash, with the resulting disharmony marring your design.
6. Avoid reversing (white on black) for long runs of body copy. This is especially true for material reproduced on newsprint, where ink tends to fill in letters. When reverses must be used, select larger, bolder faces.
7. Avoid text over illustrations or tinted areas, unless you are certain of sufficient contrast and a "clean field" for the words.
8. Long copy should be broken for easy reading. There are several techniques for doing this. Indent paragraphs at least one em, or if graphs are flush left, add extra space between them. Use subheads of a contrasting face or weight. Consider using boldface or italics at points of special emphasis in the text.

Appropriateness of Type

Appropriateness or compatibility of type is another concern of graphic arts professionals. They know that the overall effect of the printed message is greatly influenced by the look or feel of typography. Appropriateness in this context has three meanings, including: (1) selecting faces according to the psychological implications they carry; (2) using readability rules to fit the education and age levels of readers; and (3) using faces harmonious with other elements in the design.

Psychological Implications

The apparent psychological qualities of a font of type can create a feel or mood that a designer can use to heighten the intended effect of the message. As you look over typeface examples in Appendix A, several adjectives should come to mind: strong, bold, light, fanciful, raw, delicate, simple, sophisticated. If a face carries such a feeling, then designers should be careful that the "personality" of the type meshes with the mood and aim of the message.

For example, although the typeface Windsor *sounds* like an appropriate face to announce the christening of England's newest prince, it is much too heavy and bold for the quiet, tasteful decorum of such an event:

Her Majesty the Queen requests the honour of your presence at the christening of Henry Charles Albert David of the Royal House of Windsor.

Lubalin Light

Caslon Italic

P.T. Barnum

4-5 What "mood" or personality do you think of when you see these typefaces?

It is more appropriate to use a lighter, more dignified face, such as Tiffany Light Italic:

Her Majesty the Queen requests the honour of your presence at the christening of Henry Charles Albert David of the Royal House of Windsor.

Judging the personality of a typeface is, of course, a subjective evaluation. But even a quick look at several faces (see Figure 4-5) could bring agreement on the "mood" of those designs. Using *Gorilla* or *Circus* as a headline face for a story on a cloistered nunnery most certainly would cause a personality clash between typography and story. While this is an easy example to point out, you should be aware of the subtle inferences that other type can create.

Readability and Age

Although we mentioned earlier a research study that showed type sizes larger than 11-pt. were not necessarily more legible for normally sighted older readers, it is a safe assumption that slightly larger, bolder faces with more generous leading can help both the very young and very old move from line to line with more ease. But it also follows that where reader interest is naturally high, any problem with readability may not be an insurmountable barrier to comprehension and retention.

Harmony

In order to give unity to printed communication, type and other elements must be in harmony. This includes margins, indents, leading, wordspacing, paper choice, printing process and even ink. So much can go wrong from rough idea to finished product that the graphic arts professional must previsualize, test, work up comprehensive layouts—and most importantly, learn from experience.

Given all the rules and pitfalls of typography, how difficult is it to be creative with type? Can a design be both functional and expressive?

Of course—the best designs are. Let's examine how creativity enhances communication.

Creative Use of Type

Symmetry, ornamentation and firmly fixed rules of design marked the so-called "old typography." Its newer version, however, has these characteristics:

1. more asymmetrical design
2. wider acceptance of sans serif body type
3. greater use of ragged right composition
4. use of larger, more dominant display faces, including hand-drawn ones
5. greater use of white space and the relaxation of progressive margins
6. daring combinations of faces, especially for logos and titles

Let's look at some examples of these changes.

There is a quiet dignity and elegance about symmetrical arrangement of type. Each line is centered, with equal amounts of white space at either end of the line. It is simple and logical. Compare Figures 4-6 and 4-7. In 4-6, the formal balance is easy to read, but the same can be

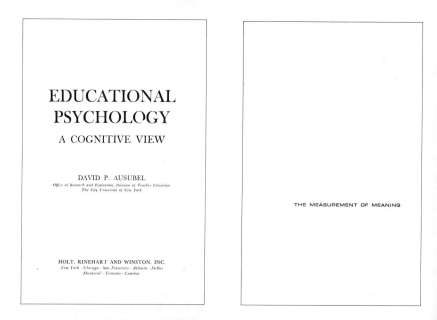

4-6   *Left:* Formally balanced, all-type layout. (Courtesy Holt, Rinehart and Winston)

4-7   *Right:* Asymmetrical, all-type layout. (Courtesy University of Illinois Press)

4-8 Asymmetrical layout with type below optical center.

DANGER
SIGNS
OF
CANCER

said of the simple but unbalanced 4-7. In fact, there is something compelling about such a small amount of type against such a strong field of white. We can see how effectively the principle of contrast works here. In many asymmetrical designs, the space becomes dominant, with type more understated.

Another example of asymmetrical layout is in Figure 4-8. Display type lines up so that its size is consistent with the height of the first column of type. But *all* type is below the optical center of the layout (a higher position that the eye prefers to the mathematical center). Yet there is a strong sense of balance and control in this layout.

Consider, too, the formally balanced example in Figure 4-9. Is its type design symmetrical? Yes. Even though the copy runs ragged right, there is logic and order in its presentation. In many ways the emphasis of its shapes is similar to the well-balanced title in Figure 4-6.

By running copy in ragged measure to fit the contour of a bunch of Chinese chard, a Stouffer's ad breaks symmetry (Figure 4-10) but still maintains an interesting balance; and the use of italic type and odd-angled borders provides excellent asymmetrical treatment of display and text in Figure 4-11.

Creating Special Display Faces

One of the greatest challenges facing designers and typographers is the creation of a type design that serves as an appropriate and inviting logo, title or trademark in a printed communication. Consider the various designs made by agency owner and designer Mary Fish as she created a

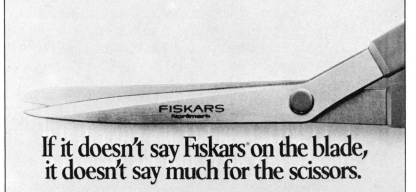

23 million people could be fooled this year.

This year, 23 million people may think they're buying a pair of Fiskars scissors and end up with an imitation.

The reason is simple. Fiskars designed the original lightweight scissors. They perfected it. They introduced it. And then, 44 other companies started copying it. Most even went so far as to use orange handles. But that wasn't quite far enough. It takes much more to make a fine pair of scissors. Like Swedish stainless steel blades that let you glide through yards of fabric without faltering. And comfort-molded handles that actually become an extension of you, offering a lifetime of effortless cutting.

So don't let the look-alikes fool you. If it doesn't say Fiskars on the blade, it's merely an imitation. And that doesn't say much for those other scissors.

FISKARS
Normark

If it doesn't say Fiskars® on the blade, it doesn't say much for the scissors.

Normark, Minneapolis, Minnesota 55423 In Canada, Normark Limited, Winnipeg, Manitoba R3T1T9. Manufactured by OY Fiskars AB Finland. Normark® Corporation is sole importer, marketer, and national distribution.

4-9 Symmetrical layout with body copy set ragged right. (Courtesy Normark Corporation)

new logo for a manufacturer of furniture and fixtures, New Wood. As you can see in Figure 4-12, she tried to create a common *W* that seemed to join the end of New and the beginning of Wood. Her first three efforts seemed strained, but as you can see in Figure 4-13, she made a design that allowed her to reverse a second *W* over the first. Using functional, bold sans serif faces, she gave the manufacturer a "new" look.

Consider the contrast in the logo of *American Educator* magazine (Figure 4-14). Although its design stresses an imbalance of sorts, it is clean and functional. Not so with the example in Figure 4-15; it just tries

4-10 Type "wrapped around" dominant illustration effectively breaks symmetry and grabs attention. (Courtesy The Stouffer Corp.; agency: HBM/ CREAMER; photography: George Cochran; designer: Elmer Yochum)

too hard, flanking the design with dominant letters around "American" and throwing in a reverse that multilates some serifs on letters. The design is overdone because the design rule of "less is more" has been violated. Understatement often works more effectively. Consider, for example, the design of the logo of the Lane Transit District (Figure 4-16).

Automating the $8 billion newspaper industry

Some 63 million newspapers printed in the U.S. every day. $600 million spent for more productive equipment in the last three years.

Video typewriters. Electronic editing systems. Computerized phototypesetters. Automated offset presses. Automated inserting equipment. More.

Harris. Printing. Electronics. Joined.

Write for an annual report.

HARRIS
Harris-Intertype Corporation.
55 Public Square. Cleveland, Ohio 44113.
Communications and information handling.

4-11 Display and text in an asymmetrical treatment. (Courtesy Harris Corp.)

Initial Letters

As mentioned in Chapter 2, large initial letters can create a point of focus for the reader, when display-sized type is integrated into body copy to signal a starting point. The initial should not attract too much attention, however. Consider the two examples in Figure 4-17. In the first a plain rising initial starts the paragraph. In the second, the initial flies over the

NE///OOD

NEWOOD

NEWOOD

4-12 Designer's first efforts for new logo seem strained because of difficulty in creating common "W" to link words.

NEWOOD
FIXTURES & FURNITURE

4-13 Many rough sketches and designs later, a new and successful logo is created. Note the distinctiveness of the common "W." (Courtesy Mary Fish Advertising and Marketing)

4-14   Varying type size, thickness and shading produces a distinctive logo. (Courtesy American Federation of Teachers)

4-15   An example of overdone typography and design.

4-16   Using space around letters to create an arrow helps provide a sense of movement. This is an example of clean design that produces a distinctive, memorable logo. (Courtesy Lane Transit District)

4-17   Several approaches to the use of the large initial letter to focus reader attention on the text.

4-18   This bold, decisive design serves as a "banner headline" for a series of features in *Texas Monthly* magazine. (Courtesy Ray-Mel Cornelius, Designer/TEXAS MONTHLY)

paragraph along with several other larger-set words of the sentence. There must be a happy medium between these extremes. Looking for the compromise that satisfies both form and function is a key to successful design.

A Final Word

As we mentioned at the beginning of this chapter, change will always pursue the design and use of type. But there is a logical basis to typography. It is not a free art; it is called to task; it must explain its function. Orderly and direct design of type is always better received than trickery and distortion. Yet there will always be room for freshness of style—as long as the design does not interfere with meaning.

5

Traditional Copy Processing

Copy preparation and processing are primary factors in implementing effective printed material. The techniques involved when computer-related technology is used will be explained in Chapter 6. Traditional methods for getting words ready for printing are still much used, however; they are discussed in this chapter.

For all printing, the words of an author are valuable raw material, but they must be thoroughly edited and processed before they can appear on the printed page. This editing is the last line of defense against error, against misunderstanding by the compositor and the readers, and against sloppy appearance. When the compositor receives copy, that copy must be accurate in every detail, or errors will certainly mar the final result. Furthermore, without specific and detailed instructions, its appearance in type may not even resemble what was desired. And, as every novice who has been sent in search of a "type squeezer" knows, copy must fit prescribed areas: Lead type slugs or lines of phototype cannot be compressed after they have been set.

On the other hand, it takes only one instance of less copy than that needed to fill a space to show that too little copy is as bad as too much.

83

<u>Correction Desired</u>   <u>Symbol</u>

Change from:

        3 to three. . . . . ③

        three to 3. . . . . (three)

        St. to Street. . . . . (St.)

        Street to St. . . . . (Street)

Change capital to small letter . . . . ∅

Change small letter to capital . . . . d̲̲

To put space between words. . . . . the⌋time

To remove the space. . . . . news⌒paper

To delete a letter and close up . . . . judg⌒ment

To delete several letters or words . . . . shall ~~always~~ be

To delete several letters and close up . . . . . . super⌒intendent

To delete one letter and substitute another. . . . . rece⌃ve

To insert words or several letters . . . . of ⌃the⌃time

To transpose letters or words, if adjacent . . . . . recⁱeᵛe

To insert punctuation, print correct mark
in proper place:

comma	⌐	parentheses	(
period	⨯	opening quote	ᵛ
question	⸮	closing quote	⸜
semicolon	⸲	dash	—
colon	⸴	apostrophe	ⱽ
exclamation	!	hyphen	⸗

To start a new paragraph. . . . . ¶ or |It has been

To center material. . . . .⌐Announcements⌐

To indent material. . . . . The first
                            day's work

Set in boldface type . . . . The art of̲

Set in italic type . . . . The art of̲

To delete substantial amounts of copy, draw
an X over the area and box it in.

To set several lines in boldface type, bracket   (The first
the lines and mark <u>bf</u> in the margin.   (day's work

5-1 Copy-editing symbols. Symbols are used at the points where changes are
to be made in the manuscript.

There are two solutions to this problem: extra leading (white space) between lines or writing additional material. Either solution will require more work for the compositor and will increase costs.

Therefore, three important aspects of copy preparation must be understood: copy correction, copy marking (with typesetting specifications), and copyfitting.

Copy Correction

Fortunately for the student, the basic techniques of traditional copy correction are the same for all media—whether copy is being prepared for newspapers, magazines, books, promotion pieces, or advertising. A universally accepted set of symbols makes this task relatively fast and efficient. These symbols are easy to learn because they are functional and are based on common sense.

Copy to be set should be typed double- or triple-spaced. All corrections can then be made at the spot of error, either on the line or above the line. Figure 5-1 shows both the symbols for correcting errors in typewritten copy and those used for typesetting instructions; the latter are discussed in more detail later. Figure 5-2 shows a story that has been edited, using these symbols.

5-2 A copy editor, using the standard symbols shown in Figure 5-1, has corrected this story before approving it for typesetting.

∧ Make correction indicated in margin.

Stet Retain crossed-out word or letter; let it stand.

. . . . Retain words under which dots appear; write "Stet" in margin.

X Appears battered; examine.

⚌ Straighten lines.

√√√ Unevenly spaced; correct spacing.

// Line up; i.e., make lines even with other matter.

run in Make no break in the reading; no ¶

no ¶ No paragraph; sometimes written "run in."

¶ Make a paragraph here.

tr Transpose words or letters as indicated.

ƨ Take out matter indicated; delete.

ƨ Take out character indicated and close up.

¢ Line drawn through a cap means lower case.

9 Upside down; reverse.

⊃ Close up; no space.

Insert a space here.

□ Indent line one em.

⊏ Move this to the left.

⊐ Move this to the right.

sp Spell out.

⌐ Raise to proper position.

⌐ Lower to proper position.

w.f. Wrong font; change to proper **font.**

Qu? Is this right?

l.c. Put in lower case (small letters).

s.c. Put in small capitals.

caps Put in capitals.

c.+s.c. Put in caps and small caps.

rom. Change to roman.

ital. Change to italic.

⚌ Under letter or word means caps.

⚌ Under letter or word, small caps.

— Under letter or word means italic.

∼ Under letter or word, boldface.

⌄ Insert comma.

⌄/ Insert semicolon.

:/ Insert colon.

⊙ Insert period.

/?/ Insert interrogation mark.

(!) Insert exclamation mark.

/=/ Insert hyphen.

ⱽ Insert apostrophe.

⟨⟨ ⟩⟩ Insert quotation marks.

ℰ Insert superior letter or figure.

∧ Insert inferior letter or figure.

[/] Insert brackets.

(/) Insert parentheses.

⊣ One-em dash.

$\frac{2}{M}$ Two-em parallel dash.

bf Boldface type.

s₍ Set *s* as subscript.

s⁽ Set *s* as exponent.

5-3 Proofreading marks and symbols. These marks are used to correct errors in typesetting and are placed in the margin. A caret or other mark is used within the column of type to show where the correction is to be made.

The correcting process does not end with typewritten copy, of course. When the copy has been set into type, galley proofs are read to detect and eliminate errors made by the typesetter. There is seldom enough space between the lines on a galley proof to enable a proofreader to use any of the symbols shown in Figure 5-1 at the point of error. Even with enough room to do so, the typesetter would have to read through complete proofs to find the symbols instead of being able to see each correction at a glance. Therefore, special *proofreading* symbols are used *in the margin* to correct material that has been set in type. A mark may also be made at the point of error. Many proofreaders for newspapers and magazines draw a line from the point of error to the correction in the margin; most readers for book publishing firms do not. When guidelines are drawn, care must be taken to avoid obliterating the remainder of the line to be corrected. The symbols for marginal marks (Figure 5-3) are basically the same for either system. A marked proof is shown in Figure 5-4.

Convict escapes

Kim E. Campbell, 27, didn't wait around to be congratulated for his rescue efforts in the crash of a united Airlines jetliner -- it would have meant a trip to the state prison.

Campbell, a prison escapee, was aboard the plane under escort by a corrections officer who was returning him to oregon.

Witnesses said Campbell who was not hand-cuffed, helped passengers out of the wreckage after the crash and worked tirelessly without fear for his own safety.

Corrections Officer Roger Seed said he and Campbell were both seated in the rear of the plane. Shortly before the crash, a stewardess asked the two to assist in the emergency exit.

"I was in charge of opening the rear energency a door and Campbell volunteered to assist people down the slide," Seed said.

Seed said Campbell remained inside and lifted people down to the ground eight feet below.

"In my estimation Campbell risked his life to help these people. He couldb the first one off the plane Seed said.

Campbell, serving concurrent prison sentences for two convictions of robbery escaped from a Tillamook forest camp last January and was recently arrested in Denver.

Seed said Campbell stayed on the plane until all passengers were helped off. Campbell then helped Seed back on the plane to check for other passengers.

Then, said Seed, "he disappeared into the crowd."

5-4 A specimen galley proof as corrected. The number of errors has been intentionally exaggerated here to show a wide variety of symbols. Actual proofs should have very few errors.

Many errors creep into printed material because someone fails to follow through after the galleys have been corrected. If errors are detected at the first reading, revised proofs with corrections should be checked, for a compositor can err when setting a correction in a line or when substituting corrected lines. Instead of pulling the line containing an error, the compositor may take out another one and replace it with the one corrected. The result is double-talk that can destroy all meaning for the reader.

There is usually another opportunity for corrections to be made even if revised galley proofs are not called for, but this final reading should not be used for detecting errors in typesetting. These last proofs are made in the form of pages or, in the case of advertising, of the completed ad. These proofs provide a chance to check if the material is positioned properly, if headlines are with the right story, if the captions are with the correct picture and so on. To delay typesetting corrections to this point is wasteful because it takes more time to unlock a form or alter a pasteup to exchange lines than it does to make the change when the type is still in galleys.

Compositors accept responsibility for their errors, marked as PEs (printer's errors), but charge for time spent correcting errors that were not detected in original copy or remaking lines for an editor or author who has merely changed his or her mind (AAs, or author's alterations). These revisions become more expensive as the material moves into the advanced production stages.

Publications with their own mechanical departments can hide the cost of author's alterations or other laxities because there is no bill that must be paid by the editorial department. But the cost remains nevertheless.

Some publications require duplicate sets of galley proofs, one for marking corrections and the other to be cut apart and pasted on layout sheets. The set to be corrected is usually on white paper; the other is often on colored stock. Proofs for pasteup bear markings across the type area to identify the storage location of the type or film negatives. For offset printing, this helps the compositor's makeup person find the proper type if the compositor is to do the camera-ready pasteup; or it helps the makeup person find the proper negatives for stripping into page positions. For letterpress printing, the proof markings help the compositor locate the actual type for making up pages.

Press proofs are also obtainable, and in some cases this additional safeguard may be warranted. But if the person who must check the proofs is not on hand when the material first goes on the press, expensive press time can be wasted, because the time the job is on the press must be paid for whether the press runs or not.

Regardless of precautions, errors occur. Absolute vigilance from the beginning of the typed copy to the final production steps keeps them to a minimum. Nothing can be taken for granted; it is amazing how easily errors seem to occur in such obvious places as headlines and titles in large display type.

Marking Typesetting Specifications

Before a compositor can set a single line of type, at least ten basic points of information—the specifications (or specs)—must be supplied:

1. type size (expressed in points)
2. type family (Century, Cheltenham, . . .)
3. family branch (bold, condensed, extended, . . .)
4. letter posture (italic or roman)
5. letter composition (caps, lowercase, . . .)
6. leading
7. line length (expressed in picas)
8. appointment of space (flush, centered, . . .)
9. wordspacing
10. letterspacing

Theoretically, then, the instructions for setting the type for this book would read: 10 point Cheltenham light roman caps and lowercase, leaded 2 points, set by 26 picas, flush left and right, normal wordspacing and letterspacing. However, much of this information does not have to be written on every piece of copy. Depending on the circumstances, it can be taken for granted that some of the instructions are understood by the compositor.

In body copy, for example, it is assumed that the appointment of space is to be flush left and right. Only exceptions must be marked. Letter composition is considered to be as shown in the copy; that is, typed capitals are to be set as capitals, lowercase letters are to be set as lowercase. Compositors also set copy with roman letter posture and with no leading and only normal word- and letterspacing unless there are indications to the contrary.

The marking of copy for titles and headlines is also simplified because of the following assumptions that are mutual to editor and compositor:

1. posture is roman unless marked;
2. machine leading is not needed unless marked;
3. line length is to be "line for line";
4. letter composition is to be as shown in the copy; and
5. word- and letterspacing are to be normal.

But whether by mutual understanding or by specific copy marking, a line of type cannot be set unless the compositor has the ten points of information. This is especially true of "transient" material, as distinguished from periodical copy. The procedure for periodicals differs because the regularity of issue permits considerable uniformity.

Newspaper Procedure

Marking copy for the mechanical department of a newspaper is simplified by several factors. The selection of type sizes, style and leading is a decision of management and is seldom subject to change. Column widths (line lengths) are standard, although there may be some variation on the editorial page for by-line columns or special features. Speed in processing copy is essential and time is at a premium. Because headlines have such a direct effect on the character of a newspaper, they are standardized as much as possible.

Copy is channeled through one central (universal) copy desk, a number of departmental desks, or both. These desks are directed by people who are expert in the English language and versed in the newspaper's style and its composing and pressroom procedures; they prepare copy quickly and efficiently for the mechanical department.

Because body type specifications do not change, much of the copy is sent to the composing room with no marked instructions other than those for exceptions (multicolumn leads, special treatment for editorials or columns, and so on). Standardization applies to headlines too. A comprehensive schedule that visualizes all possible headlines and gives all the information a headline writer may need is prepared by the editorial department for the composing room. Each headline is keyed by a number or letter; to give the composing room all necessary information about the final appearance of a headline, the writer simply labels the headline with any agreed-upon designation, such as "#1" or "AA," and this immediately refers the compositor to the type size, face, and so on, similarly marked on the comprehensive schedule.

To ensure that headlines are placed over the correct stories when pages are made up a "slugging" system is used. The body copy is slugged

5-5 Typesetting instructions for newspaper typesetters are kept to a minimum because specifications as to size, style and line length are usually constant. The slug, *Writer recalls*, is essential to insure that the story will be placed under its correct heading. Only the numerals 1-9 are necessary to let the typesetters know that the standard type in the usual column is required.

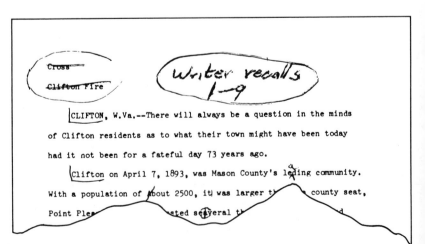

5-6 The beginning of the story edited in Figures 5-2 and 5-5 is shown here in proof form. Note that the slug is the first line of type. Once the story's position on the page is located and the story is ready to be placed, the slug line is discarded.

Writer recalls
   CLIFTON, W. Va.--There will always be a question in the minds of Clifton residents as to what their town might have been today had it not been for a fateful day 73 years ago.
   Clifton on April 7, 1893 was Mason County's leading community. With a population of about 2500 it was larger than the county seat, Point Pleasant, and it boasted several thriving industries and coal mines.

with a word or two to identify the story. Many newspapers use the first two words of the headline as a slug. For example, Figure 5-5 is the top of the "Clifton Fire" story used earlier to show copyreading symbols. Here it is shown as it would look after being marked for the typesetters in the composing room. Note that the slug has been changed to "Writer Recalls" because the headline as written by an editor reads "Writer Recalls County's Worst Fire." The only typesetting instruction is 1-9, a concise way of ordering the story to be set one column (14 picas) wide in 9-pt. Palatino leaded one point, the standard usage at this paper. Any exceptions to standard use would require more detailed type specifications.

Figure 5-6 shows the beginning of the story as set. Note that the first line is the slug. When the body of the story is placed under the headline that this slug represents, the slug is discarded.

It is also common for a one-word slug to be assigned to stories before headlines are written. The headlines then will be slugged with that same word. Once the proper headline is placed in position, the slug lines from the story and the head are discarded.

Other special problems for the newspaper are handled with equal efficiency. Continuing stories (which are set in type in intervals as they develop during the day), stories that must be changed slightly between editions and stories that must be set before a headline has been written require special markings. These vary from newspaper to newspaper, but are always conveyed by techniques that simplify the communication of instructions, from the editorial department to the composing room.

Body and headline copy are usually sent to the composing room on separate sheets. Traditionally, the display sizes are set on machines other than those used for straight matter (the usual body type), and if headlines and body copy are on the same sheet, the compositors cannot set both at the same time.

Newspaper Makeup Instructions

A newspaper must be put together in a hurry. Virtually every step of the makeup process is based on approximation, rather than on exact

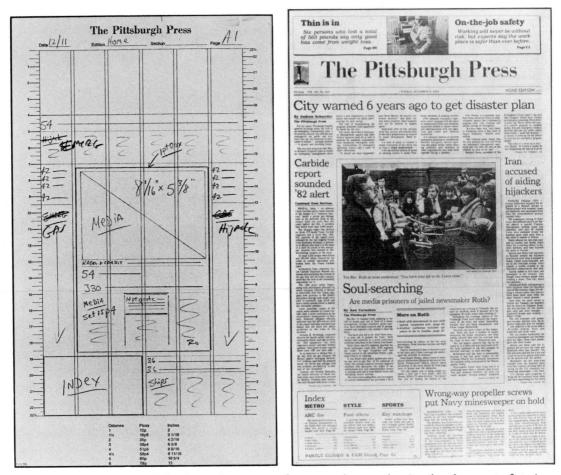

5-7 A typical newspaper front page dummy showing the placement of stories and the slugs identifying them for placement. The page resulting from it is on the right. (Courtesy *Pittsburgh Press*)

calculation. As stories are processed, their length is estimated and each is recorded with pertinent data on an inventory sheet usually called a *copy schedule.*

This information is used for page dummies. As the makeup person prepares the dummy, he or she writes the slug for each story in the position on the page that the story seems to merit. The makeup person indicates the probable length of the story with an arrow and shows the placement of illustrations by drawing an X through the space. The dummy then serves as a pattern as the stories and headlines are put in a form prior to stereotyping or printing. Figure 5-7 shows a typical newspaper page dummy marked up.

5-8 A typical markup: an ad layout marked with instructions for the printer. It shows placement of each visual element and gives specifications for display type. By setting display type from the markup, the printer can be certain to take care of any variations in spacing. The markup also is the blueprint for placement of all elements. (Though rough in appearance, the markup is precise in placement of elements.)

Advertising and Brochure Procedure

The marking of copy for advertisements is quite different. In most cases a full *markup* (Figure 5-8) is used for communicating instructions about typesetting and makeup to the printer. It is best described as a drawing of how the ad is to look when printed. All display lines are lettered in exact position, illustrations are sketched in, and body type areas are indicated by drawn lines. Instructions for type sizes and styles are written with colored pencil and circled next to each bit of display type or in the margin. The body type areas are identified by letter—A, B, C and so on.

Body copy is provided in typewritten form, is marked with typesetting instructions and is slugged with the corresponding letter from the markup. By following these instructions and checking with the markup, the mechanical department or printer can create an exact replica of the ad as designed by the advertiser or the agency. The same procedure is followed for flyers, handbills, direct-mailing pieces and other brochures.

COPY A, LEADER COATS
10/12 NEWS 2 x 14 PICAS

5-9 Advertising and brochure copy is slugged by the alphabet (Copy A, etc.) to identify its location, but the slug must also identify the specific ad in which the copy must be placed. Typesetting specifications must be specific. Justification of lines to be flush left and right is assumed.

Once again The Leader, Athens' leading department store is getting the jump on the fall season with its annual coat sale. Values have never been better. Every coat in our large stock is on sale this week. Every style, every material, a every weight can be found at extra special prices.

Where efile can you find all-wools for only $69? Only at The Leader and ony at our spring sale of afll coats. Buy now and save.

For your convenience, parking is free at the city garage on Washington St. Just bring your ticket for stamping at any sales station in our store.

Figure 5-9 shows the Copy A for the "Pre-Season Coat Sale" ad. Its slug *"Copy A, Leader Coats"* will ensure that it will be placed in the spot for Copy A in the ad so identified. Note that much fuller type specifications are needed than for newspaper copy. For all nonperiodical copy type specs must include every detail not subject to standard assumption.

In Figure 5-10 we can see copy with a variation from standard assumptions which must therefore be specified; this copy is set so lines are aligned on the left but irregular on the right in lines not exceeding 12 picas in length. The copy could also have been set in lines exactly as typed. If so, the specs could be: *10/12 News 2, line for line.* It must be remembered in this instance that beforehand knowledge of how long these lines will be when set is essential when calling for "line-for-line" setting. The discussion on copyfitting later in this chapter points out how this knowledge is obtained. Having type set to allow for initial letters or thumbnail pictures also calls for special instructions and some typefitting knowledge. Plus or minus letterspacing as illustrated in Chapter 3 can also be included in type specifications.

Copy A Leader Coats

Once again **The Leader,** Athens' leading department store is getting the jump on the Fall season with its annual coat sale. Values have never been better. Every style, every material, every weight can be found at extra special prices.

Where else can you find all-wools for only $69? Only at **The Leader** and only at our Spring sale of Fall coats. Buy now and save.

For your convenience, parking is free at the city garage on Washington Street. Just bring your ticket for stamping at any sales station in our store.

5-10   Here "Copy A, The Leader" has been set with ragged line endings, and the type specs on the typewritten copy would have had to specify "ragged right" to produce this result.

Magazine Procedure

The preparation of magazine material is usually a cross between techniques used for newspapers and those used for advertisements. Sometimes articles are prepared with full markups by an art department, or the editor may follow a fast course like his or her newspaper counterpart, but in most cases a middle ground is followed.

Often there is no headline schedule; titles follow no set typographical pattern. They are lettered in position on a dummy, with typesetting instructions entered as in advertising markups. The relative stability of column measure and the other aspects of body copy permits the use of minimum marking for such material. For example, the specs for Figure 5-11 would be: *Aramco, The China Trade, one-column.* As with the ad slug shown earlier, the printing job (Aramco) and the specific portion of that job (an article on trade with China) and all type specifications are thus detailed. Consequently, proofs of the type will be delivered to the proper source, the title will get on its proper article, and the type will be set in column measure, size, and face normally used by the source.

Because there is usually sufficient time between issues, a magazine dummy is made by pasting galley proofs of text material or specimen copy of body and caption type in position, with the titles lettered in by hand (Figure 5-11). Rough layout sketches in miniature or full size often precede the completion of this dummy. Also, if the magazine is to be printed by any of the photomechanical printing processes (offset and rotogravure), camera-ready pasteups may be required. Making these pasteups, called *mechanicals,* is discussed in Chapter 13.

5-11 A magazine dummy with galley proofs pasted in position and the display type lettered in position and marked for the compositor. *Below:* the printed pages show how accurate the dummy was. (Courtesy *Aramco World*)

Book Procedure

Perhaps the best example of care and precision in processing copy is in book publishing. Books must be more carefully edited and produced than any other printed product. More permanent in nature than newspapers and magazines, they are relied on by readers for authoritative and accurate material presented in legible fashion. Also, there usually is more time for meticulous attention to detail than in other media.

This attention to detail starts with the raw manuscript and proceeds to the final dummying stage. The photographs in Figure 5-12 show that, with design specifications already established, each set of facing pages is carefully crafted after all type is set. This pasteup dummy is the blueprint for mechanicals prepared later or for the stripping of film negatives of type and illustrations into exact page positions for making offset printing plates (or for preparing page forms for letterpress printing).

Copyfitting

The planner of any kind of graphic communication is vitally concerned with copyfitting. It is important to the editors of newspapers and magazines, the advertising designer, and the public relations person who puts together booklets and brochures. Without copyfitting, unnecessary costs are incurred or attractive layouts are destroyed, or both. If more type than needed is set, the payment for the *overset* is wasted cost. Titles that cannot fit a given space must be rewritten and reset with unnecessary loss of time and money. Areas of text type that fail to fill their allotted space can jeopardize the effect of a good design.

Depending upon the circumstance, copyfitting may be rough or extremely accurate. There are several methods for copyfitting, each suitable to its purpose. Newspapers, for example, have no time for complicated copyfitting methods. Stories are written so that they can be cut from the bottom up without destroying meaning. If the stories are too short, filler material is used. Consequently, estimation is based on the number of words in a column inch. Depending upon the point size, column width, and leading, this figure usually ranges from 30 to 40 words per column inch. When reporters use a uniform setting for line lengths on their typewriters, this figure can be converted into lines; that is, four typewritten lines equal 1 inch.

Estimating body type space needs on a "words per column inch" basis may be adequate for many newspapers when column widths and type size are standard, but it is not accurate enough for any other purpose. In figuring space requirements for display type, even newspapers require an extremely accurate system—one that takes into account the varying widths of letters as well as the inherent differences in various type styles. This system, called *unit counting,* is discussed in detail later in this chapter.

The most accurate and most commonly used method for estimating space needs for body copy is based on counting characters, a character being any letter, number, space or piece of punctuation. Although it does not make allowance for varying widths of letters, the character count method is sufficiently accurate for the precise work of preparing copy for advertisements, promotion pieces, and magazine pages. Type designs—even those considered standard and not condensed or ex-

5-12 Steps in dummying two pages of a book. (Photos by John King)

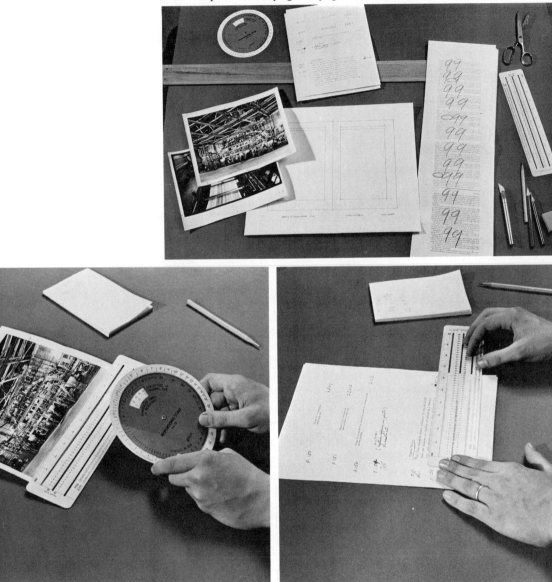

Left: First step: size the illustrations. Decide on placement of photographs and text. Assess each photo and decide whether to crop. Reduce (or enlarge) each photo with all these factors in mind, with the aid of the scaling wheel.

Right: Determine caption width and depth. As with the illustrations, decide on best dimensions and positions for caption copy. Measure the original copy and calculate the area from the number of characters.

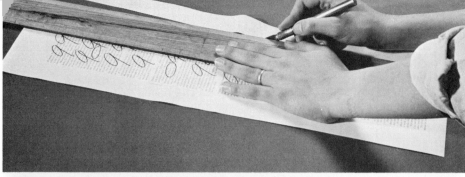

Wax the back of galleys in preparation for pasting. Numbers on the face of the galleys were put there by the typesetter and show the location of the type at the typesetter's shop. Then trim galley margins.

Place the waxed galley in position on the dummy page. Care must be taken to be sure all elements are properly aligned and follow basic page format.

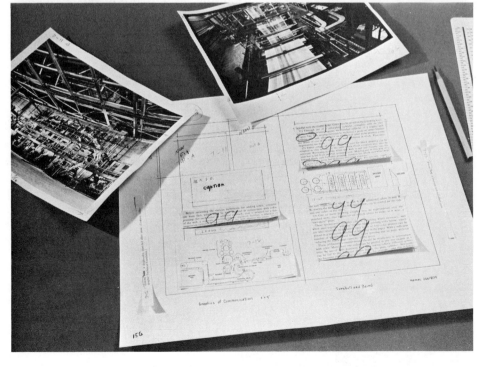

Finish dummy pages. Note outlines of sized photos at upper left (bleeds) and caption boxes. The line illustration at lower left and the type are ready to be pasted in position. The dummy will now go to the printer, who will follow it carefully in making up these pages.

panded—vary considerably in the number of characters that will fit into a line, and the character count method compensates for these variations.

Character Count Copyfitting

The first step in estimating space by way of the character count method is to obtain information about the specific type size and face from a printer or type manufacturer. Accurately compiled tables showing the number of characters that will fit in various line lengths or the number of characters in each pica of line length are readily available from these sources. The table on page 101 shows the characters per pica of 28 selected typefaces in various sizes. These tables are based on normal typesetting; if special tight or loose spacing is going to be used, information relating to that spacing has to be obtained.

Copyfitting problems are in only two forms: finding the depth of space needed for a manuscript on a layout that is being made, or finding the amount of copy to write to fill a space on a layout that is already completed.

In either case, copyfitting boils down to the two basic steps of determining how many lines of type will be involved; and how many characters fit into a line. Some changing of units of measure (points to picas and vice versa) is also often involved, but essentially there are only two major steps.

Finding the Amount of Space Needed on a Layout

The first step in finding out how much space is needed is to find out how long the copy is in terms of characters. The simplest way to find this out is to count an average line of the typewritten material and multiply it by the number of lines in the typing. When doing this, all lines should be counted as full lines, including those that end paragraphs. Next, the number of characters that will fit into a line of type (from our table) is divided into the total number of characters in the article to find the number of lines of type that will be involved.

With this accomplished, we have an answer of sorts, but usually we want to convert the number of lines of type into picas so that we can proceed with drawing the layout with a line gauge marked off in picas. We convert lines to picas by first multiplying the number of lines times the line thickness in points and get an answer in points. To convert points to picas, we divide by 12.

As an example, let us use the two-page manuscript in Figure 5-2 and compute the space we would need to have this set in lines that are 18 picas long if the type is to be 10-point Kennerly leaded one point (10-point type on an 11-point line).

Step 1 Find out how many characters there are in the manuscript. To complete this step, count an average line in the manuscript (we

Characters per Pica of Selected Typefaces

Characters per pica of a number of selected typefaces are presented here as a tool for practice in copyfitting. Copyfitting can be accurate only when the characteristics of the individual type design are taken into account, since typefaces of the same size use different amounts of space according to the design of their faces. In addition, the space required by many typefaces varies slightly according to the manufacturer (e.g., the Baskervilles of two type makers may differ) or according to the method of composition (e.g., Linotype Palatino differs from Linofilm Palatino). And if special tight or open spacing is specified, the space variations must be taken into account during copyfitting.

	Point Sizes							
Face	**8**	**9**	**10**	**11**	**12**	**14**	**18**	**24**
Baskerville	3.22	2.96	2.64	2.46	—	—	—	—
Bernhard Modern Roman	3.59		2.99		2.54	2.15	1.74	1.31
Bodoni with Italic	3.13		2.6		2.36	2.11	1.64	1.28
Bookman	3.11	2.88	2.6	2.37	2.21	1.84		
Caledonia	3.12	2.87	2.63	2.44	2.26	2.00		
Caslon 540	3.39		2.91	2.56	2.21	1.86	1.49	1.06
Cheltenham	3.56	3.2	2.99	2.72	2.53	2.15		1.42
Clarendon	2.6	2.4	2.3		2.0			
Cloister	3.56		3.11	2.97	2.75	2.45	1.93	1.46
Cooper Black	2.6		2.03		1.75	1.42	1.09	.83
Dominante	2.6	2.5	2.3		2.0			
Egmont Light	3.4		2.7		2.3	2.2		
Electra	3.2	2.88	2.68	2.5	2.4			
Franklin Gothic	2.66		2.1		1.89	1.63	1.26	.98
Futura Medium	3.6		2.87		2.42	2.11	1.61	
Garamond with Italic	3.37	3.18	2.95	2.7	2.59	2.3	1.77	1.38
Goudy Old Style with Italic	3.36		2.74		2.42	2.01		
Helvetica	3.03	2.68	2.45		2.10	1.97	1.53	1.17
Kaufmann Script			3.12		2.84	2.54	1.94	1.5
Kennerly			2.5					
Melior	3.08	2.75	2.48		2.14			
Optima	3.28	2.95	2.67		2.29	1.97	1.53	1.17
Palatino	3.08	2.75	2.48		2.14	1.87	1.44	1.11
Park Avenue					2.83	2.54	2.07	1.64
Scotch Roman	3.18		2.85	2.7	2.26	1.87	1.45	1.12
Stymie Bold	2.92		2.29		2.02	1.67	1.31	1.03
Weiss Roman	3.76		3.16	2.93	2.58	2.27	1.7	1.37
Weiss Italic	4.54		3.51	3.38	2.92	2.66	2.09	1.69

will use the second line) and find that there are 64 characters in that line. Then count the number of lines, short ones included, to find that there are 41 lines, 21 on the first page and 20 on the second. By multiplying 41 times 64 we find that the article contains 2624 characters.

Step 2 How many characters will be in each line of type? By looking at the table of characters per pica (CPP) we find that an average of

2.5 characters will fit into each pica of 10-point Kennerly. Therefore, 45 characters (2.5 × 18) will fit into each 18-pica line.

Step 3 By dividing the 45 characters in each line of type into the total number of characters to be set (2624), we find that the typesetter will have to produce 58 lines and then still have 14 characters left over, so 59 lines of type will have to be set. (When this answer produces a fraction, always round up to the next *higher* number of lines, because the typesetter will have to set another line, short though it may be.)

Step 4 Convert from the number of lines (59) to points by multiplying by line thickness (11 points); 59 times 11 equals 649 points. Note here that line thickness includes leading.

Step 5 Convert from points (649) to picas by dividing by 12 points in a pica; we find that we will have to allow $54\frac{1}{12}$ picas of depth on our layout.

Finding the Number of Characters to Write to Fill a Space

In many situations, the amount of space for copy is already definitely fixed on a layout, and only enough characters to fill that space must be written. The first step in these situations is to measure the width of the copy area to determine how many picas will be in each line of type. Then we use a scale to find the number of characters to write for each line of type. Then we measure the depth and convert it to points so that we can divide by the thickness of a line to find the number of lines that will fit into the area. When we know the number of lines and the number of characters in a line, we simply multiply the two to get the total number of characters.

As an example, let us assume that we have an advertisement in which a copy block is to be filled with 9-point Baskerville type with one extra point of white space for each line (9-point Baskerville on a 10-point line).

Step 1 We measure the width of the block and find that it is 15 picas.

Step 2 We look in the scale and find that the typesetter will set 2.96 characters in each of those 15 picas, so we multiply the two to find that there will be 44.4 characters in each line of type, which we will round off to the closest full character, 44. Use of the decimal would give us a slightly more accurate answer, but it is not worth the effort.

Step 3 We measure the depth and find that it is 18 picas, which is 216 points (18 picas times 12 points in a pica).

Step 4 We divide the line thickness (10 points) into the depth (216 points) and find that 21.6 lines will fit. Here we round off to the *lowest* whole line; 22 lines will not fit into the depth, and in terms of depth there is no such thing as a fraction of a line. If we can enlarge the block by 4 points, then we could fit 22 lines into the block. Assuming we have no authority to change the layout, we stay with 21 lines, and go ahead and write 21 lines each with 44 characters in it for a total of 924 characters. Extra white space between paragraphs would fill out the type to 216 points.

Making Copyfitting as Simple as Possible

Editors and graphic designers often don't like copyfitting; working with figures is not appealing to verbal and artistic individuals. But the job must be done. To simplify copyfitting we can use some shortcuts. For example, on a magazine or other publication with standard column measurements, copy paper can be printed with vertical lines to mark the beginning and ending for each line of typing. By spacing these lines so that the number of characters that can be typed between them is the same as the number of characters that the typesetter will produce in the columns, we can avoid a lot of counting. Each typewritten line is the equivalent of a line of type. Or at least, we can force manuscripts to be typed with standard line settings so that we know how many characters are in a line without counting an average line.

In any instance involving standardized typeface and line length, copyfitting can be made extremely simple; it is really not a serious problem for magazines. For ads and other variable work, little can be done except to follow the steps outlined previously. The results are worth the effort.

For general estimating—judging the number of pages involved in a booklet—a *word count* system can be used for copyfitting, but the results are not very accurate. In one of these systems, a table showing the number of words per square inch is used. Another system uses an estimation of 3 ems per word if type is 10 point or smaller, and 2.5 ems per word if type is 11, 12, or 13 point. Words vary so much in length that either of these systems can be effective only for preliminary work; they also do not take into account the different space requirements of different typefaces.

Fitting Display Type to Space

Even the character count method is inadequate for computing the space requirements of headlines, titles or other lines of display type. For ads, brochures and magazine pages, it is usually best to trace or hand letter display type to exact size for layouts, thus guaranteeing precise fitting. Tracing letters from type examples is helpful in getting size and spacing just right while lettering. Pastedown or transfer type can also provide for accurate fitting of display type.

The hand lettering of display type to exact size is not as difficult as it may seem to be. According to the point size of the type, two parallel horizontal lines are drawn, as in Figure 5-13, where the two lines are 36

5-13   For ads, brochures and magazines, tracing of display type, or lettering to size without benefit of tracing, is the best means for assuring that type will fit the space allotted. Drawing lines for the bottom and top of the body, plus the lines for bottom and top of the center body letters (x-height), are vital to be sure the size is correct.

points apart. Next, a base line must be drawn sufficiently above the bottom line to allow for descenders. A final guideline sets the top limit for center-body letters. By using reasonable care in setting letter widths and placing letters as in Figure 5-13, the lettering will so closely approximate the type that fitting to space is assured. Serifs may be added when appropriate to give the lettering a finished appearance, but that is not necessary to make fitting accurate.

For newspapers, fitting display type to space constitutes a very special problem. Although some newspapers now have adequate time and staffing to design and letter headlines individually, most of them have to rely on a counting system that sets line maximums for this job. Called a *unit-count* system, it gets reasonable accuracy by taking into account the variation in width among letters.

Unit Count for Headlines

In the unit-count system, characters are assumed to fall into four categories: thin, normal, wide, and extra-wide. Normal letters are assigned one unit, thins are assigned one-half, wides are one-and-one-half, and extra wides are two. Although characters vary considerably more than these four categories allow for, the slight inaccuracy is tolerated in the interest of simplicity of counting.

For newspapers with headlines containing only capitals, as well as headlines containing capitals and lowercase letters, the assignment of units is made as simple as possible in each case.

For capitals and lowercase headlines, the following allotments are made:

all lowercase letters and numbers 1 unit
except

m and w	$1\frac{1}{2}$ units
f, l, i, t, and 1	$\frac{1}{2}$ unit
all capital letters	$1\frac{1}{2}$ units

except

M and W	2 units
I	$\frac{1}{2}$ unit

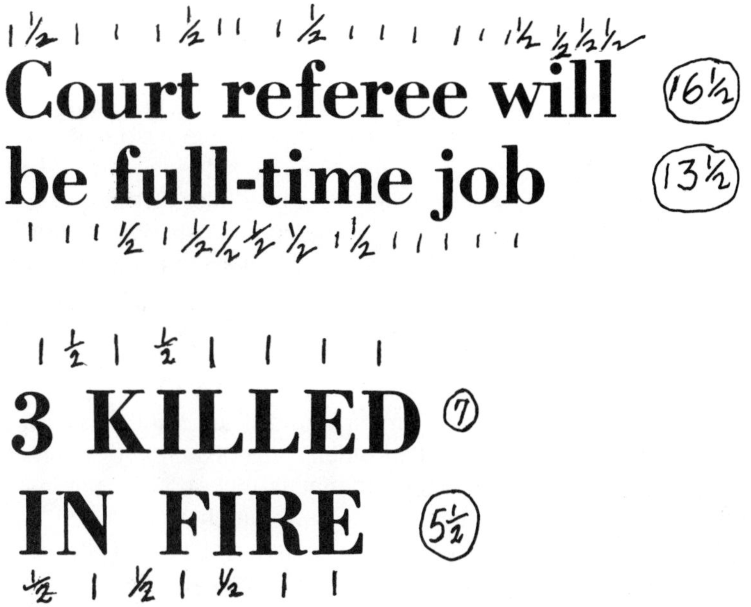

Court referee will (16½)
be full-time job (13½)

3 KILLED ⑦

IN FIRE (5½)

5-14   To be certain that newspaper headlines fit, a unit count based on variation in letter widths is used. The unit count is shown at the end of each line. Note the different assignment of values for caps and lowercase as compared with all capitals.

spaces	1 unit
punctuation	$\frac{1}{2}$ unit

Depending upon the design of the type, occasionally *j* and *r* are assigned only a half unit. Other variations can be made, but these assignments meet most situations.

The unit count for headlines of *all capitals* is different from that of both capitals and lowercase. For simplicity in counting, the basic capital letters are assigned one unit in all-cap heads. The unit allotments in all-capital display lines are:

all letters 1 unit
      except

M and W	$1\frac{1}{2}$ units
I	$\frac{1}{2}$ unit
spaces	$\frac{1}{2}$ unit
punctuation	$\frac{1}{2}$ unit

Note how the two headlines in Figure 5-14 are counted.

Virtually all the work connected with display types involves writing lines to fit a given space. It is therefore a matter of ascertaining the maximum number of units for the line, and then writing within that limitation. In newspaper offices these maximums are shown on a headline schedule. Originally, they are derived by setting lines composed of a normal assortment of letters and spaces and counting the units in these lines. Character counts shown for display type in printer's type specimen books may also be used as line maximums.

Whatever the source, the maximum count per line has to be observed. The temptation to squeeze an extra half unit may be strong if the wording of the title or headline seems especially good—and occasionally such fudging on the count pays. But when it fails, the waste of time for the writer to rewrite and for the compositor to reset the line is inexcusable. The gamble is not worth the effort and expenditure.

As already noted, the traditional copy-processing methods described in this chapter are steadily being replaced by electronic devices and procedures. Video display terminals and computers as described in Chapter 7 are splendid devices for many aspects of copy preparation, but in none of their functions are they appreciated more than for copyfitting. Video terminals that show a running total of characters in the story being typed save the chore of counting a line and multiplying the characters by the number of lines. Other terminals that are fully programmed for copyfitting can give the depth in picas exactly at any time and with virtually no effort on the part of the terminal operator.

Headlines can be typed onto a terminal screen and the units that do not fit into a line dropped to a second line, showing at a glance what the count problem is without the necessity of any human counting. Until there is no traditional copy processing, however, there is no way to avoid the tedium of character counting and unit counting for accurate typefitting.

CHECKLIST: **Some Points to Remember**

1. Getting words into print involves correcting at several stages, fitting copy to space, and marking copy with instructions for printing.
2. All copy corrections (those made in typewritten material) are made at the point of error, within the line.
3. All proofreading corrections are made in the margins bordering the type, although the errors are located with a mark in the column.
4. There are universally accepted symbols for making corrections in typewritten material (copyreading symbols) and for making corrections on printers' proofs (proofreading symbols).
5. Although there are ten specific points a printer must have to set type, many of those are assumed without marking. For body type, assumptions are that lines will be justified; the letter composition is as typed; the posture is to be roman; there will be no leading; and the weight, width, and spacing are to be medium.
6. Newspaper type specifications are minimal because the type and its usage are standardized and repeated from day to day.
7. A slug line of one or two words is used to identify news stories so they will end up beneath the correct heading.

8. Traditional newspaper layout requires use of a headline schedule, a copy schedule, and dummy sheets. The headline schedule lists and shows the headline patterns that are available; the copy schedule is an inventory listing each story as it is processed; and the dummy is a pattern for placing the stories on a page.

9. Marking copy for ads, brochures, booklets, and books—because they are not periodical and standardized—must be specific and detailed.

10. A slug line identifying the printing job and labeling the location within the job with an alphabetical identification is required on all transient copy.

11. Fitting body copy to space is essential for any printed communication to be as effective as possible. Although newspapers use a rough number-of-words-per-column-inch calculation, other media rely on an accurate character-count system.

12. The space-utilization characteristics of any body typeface are available from printers through CPP information, which gives the number of characters that will fit, on average, in a pica of line length.

13. Copyfitting with the character count method hinges on
    (1) the number of characters involved;
    (2) the number of characters that will fit into a line of type; and
    (3) the number of lines of type that are involved.

14. Newspapers fit headlines to space by using a unit-count system that allows for variations in letters: one-half for thin; one for medium; one-and-one-half for wide; and two for extra wide. A maximum number of units in any common line is predetermined and must be followed in writing headlines if the headlines are to fit into their allotted widths.

15. Designers of ads, brochures and magazines often will hand letter display type precisely to size as their method for ensuring that the titles will fit the spaces provided.

6

Computerized Copy Processing

Computerization has been introduced into virtually every facet of contemporary American society, and the area of graphics of communication is no exception. In fact, the communications media and the printing industry have been on the leading edge of developing applications for this technology.

Words, on their way into print, are now almost certain to filter through a computer in one fashion or another. The blending of computers and telecommunication transmission has produced electronic copy processing systems that are marvels to behold. These systems have invaded all the media, from the smallest newspaper to the largest metropolitan daily and from the smallest specialized magazine to the circulation giants.

Advertising and public relations organizations have also been affected by the modern methods of getting words into print. The printing industry as a whole has been revolutionized from top to bottom because of computer and other electronic technology.

For publishers, these systems are the fastest and most economical methods ever devised for getting words into print and from point to point.

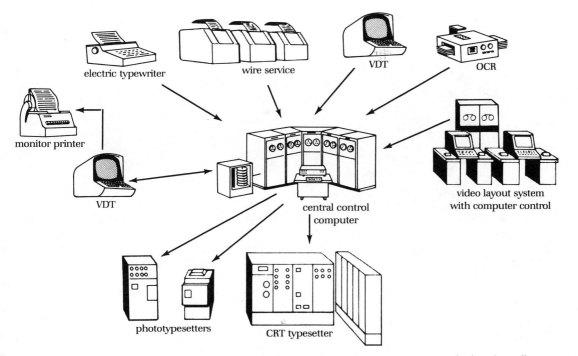

electric typewriter

wire service

VDT

OCR

monitor printer

VDT

central control
computer

video layout system
with computer control

phototypesetters

CRT typesetter

6-1   Computerized copy processing systems vary immensely, but they all start with various input devices and end with type, including some that also position the type. This diagram shows the common input devices: (1) typewriters, (2) wire services, (3) video display terminals, and (4) scanners (Optical Character Recognition devices). Output is by phototypesetters or cathode-ray tube typesetters, both of which provide photographic images to be carried to plates for printing. Although the diagram shows a central control computer, many of the other devices in systems contain their own capacity to store and control digital information.

For writers and editors who use them, they are essential tools of their trade. For students, the computer systems are an exciting part of their preparation for a professional career in mass communications.

Now, not only must students be proficient on a typewriter so that they can carry out their roles as writers, editors, graphic designers and the like; they must also be prepared to transfer their skills to other machines in computerized systems which are involved in getting words, art work and complete communications into print.

Unfortunately for everyone concerned, computerized systems are not all alike. Scores of manufacturers have designed and marketed systems, each with its own particular capabilities and features. There are sufficient similarities, however, to permit easy assimilation of the differences that do exist. In this regard, some understanding of the evolution of these systems can be helpful.

6-2 The writer (left) for the *Detroit News* and the editor (right) for the *U.S. News and World Report,* although working for different media doing different editorial chores and with slightly different-looking video display terminals, share the advantages and problems of computer copy processing. Virtually all media now rely on computers for some aspects of copy processing. (Courtesy *Detroit News* and *U.S. News and World Report*)

Early Uses

The need to make printing production more efficient was at the heart of early attempts to use computers and electronic transmission systems to prepare and produce print media. The labor-intensive nature of the industry was tending to restrict and reduce media and their activities, and every effort was expended to eliminate the need for human labor in all steps involved.

Typesetter Linecasting

Mechanizing the old-fashioned linecasting typesetters was probably the first effort directly related to this goal. Perforated tape that made use of the old teletype code eliminated the need for a keyboard operator for these machines. The binary digit principle, using a row of six possible holes as the basis for coding, was thus employed. Some newspapers still use a computer system based on the code shown in Figure 6-3, although most of them have moved to the more common eight-level coding.

As many of you probably already know, digital computers employ the *binary digit,* called a *bit,* in their operation. A bit is one piece of information, the equivalent of the answer to a *yes* or *no* or *true* or *false* question. This one piece of information can also be conveyed by a punched hole in a tape to mean "yes" and no hole to mean "no," or a positive electric charge to mean "yes" and a negative electric charge to mean "no," and so on. Computers operate on this basis. As they record and

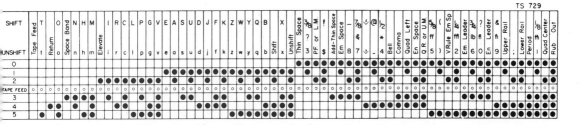

TS 729

6-3 An easy-to-visualize digital coding system. Perforated tape, still in use for some older processing systems, provides a good example of the conversion of alphanumeric characters to the dots, numbers or perforations. Using only six bits for a byte, there are adequate variations (64) for all letters, numbers, punctuation and basic typesetting symbols in this old code. The eight-level codes, common to most computer systems, provide 256 variations.

process information, circuits are either open or closed, switches either on or off, and transistors either conduct electricity or do not.

Codes based on rows of a sufficient number of bits to create enough variations to form a number for each letter of the alphabet, plus other symbols, form the basis for digitized communication symbols. Called a byte, each row of bits represents one letter of the alphabet (or some other necessary symbol) as is shown by the sixty-four variations available in the six-bit bytes in Figure 6-3. Bytes of eight bits permit the 256 variations ordinarily employed in computers.

Hyphenation and Justification

To have perforated tape replace keyboard operators, printers also had to use the storage capacity and processing capability of digital computers to do the hyphenation and justification involved in producing columns of type. To do this "h&j" (as it was called) bulky minicomputers were moved into type composition departments in newspapers and printing plants throughout the country. The ridiculous task of manually correcting perforated tape then became a necessary skill in these plants.

Cold-Type Composing Systems

Spurred on by the development of cold-type composing systems, particularly the composition of columns of type on photo paper, publishers encouraged computer system vendors to produce systems that could eliminate all manual aspects of typesetting, including devices and methods to:

1. enter words into storage

2. remove words from storage for editing
3. transfer the words to a typesetter
4. produce columns of type on photopaper

Entry-Only Systems

Some of the earliest systems, used mostly by newspapers, provided only for entry and storage. Typewriters with ball-type elements containing a bar code or a particular type style were used to produce copy that would be scanned by an *optical character reader* that would digitize the copy. The reader, called a scanner or OCR machine, produced a perforated tape that could operate a typesetter. Although such systems are still in use, the difficulty in making corrections and coding typesetting instructions made them inefficient. To make corrections one had to retype the faulty portion of the copy and rescan it.

As a refinement of this basic approach, some typewriters were wired directly to a typesetting machine. The problems of editing and coding typesetting instructions still prevailed, however.

VDT Systems

The ultimate goal for typesetting systems was to eliminate a re-keyboarding of material going into print. Minimizing keystrokes was the maxim for system engineers to follow. The use of *video display terminals* to enter and recall material from computers was the answer. Newsrooms and magazine offices in the 1970s resounded with talk of VDTs or CRTs as the new terminals were installed. Calling a terminal a CRT (standing for *cathode-ray tube*) was common early on, but is now better used to describe typesetting machines that use video tubes for almost instantaneous typesetting of large quantities.

The third goal, transferring words to a typesetter, was first accomplished by the use of perforated tape, but *on-line* systems with terminals and other devices hooked together (*interfaced*) by cable were quick to follow. Writers at VDTs composed copy and used keyboard commands to store their copy; editors withdrew the story with keyboard commands and, after making necessary alterations, sent the copy directly from their terminals to the typesetting machines.

These typesetting machines originally were photocomposing machines; an exposure of light through film letters created the image in column (galley) form on photopaper. Headlines were composed separately on direct-entry keyboard machines capable of producing several sizes and styles of type on a strip of paper that could then be cut apart to form the lines of headlines. These machines, though still widely used, have been replaced to a great extent by phototypesetters that can do area composition (produce type in columns under a headline covering the columns) and the CRT typesetters that produce computer-generated type

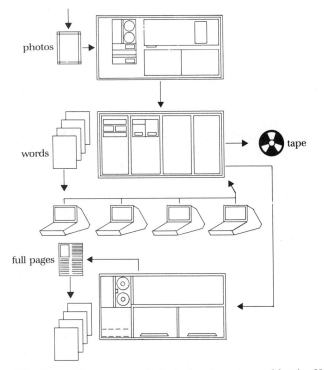

photos

words

tape

full pages

6-4 One of the most sophisticated systems is used by the *U.S. News & World Report.* Photos go directly into a scanner to be digitized and stored for later use. Copy is keyboarded at VDTs, entered into storage and recalled for editing. Page layout is done at a VDT, and the output is a complete page, including illustrations. (Courtesy *U.S. News & World Report*)

and illustrations in full-page form using only the time it takes to get the light from its TV tube to expose photopaper.

Pagination and Transmission

All facets of pre-press activity are now computer-compatible. These include the four steps mentioned earlier in type-composing systems on through the arrangement of material into full pages (*pagination*) and their direct imaging onto printing plates or the printing surface itself. The digitizing of photographs was one of the last hurdles to be overcome, because of the large memory capacity needed. The current and future marvels thus occurring are described in detail in this book's final chapter. Here it should suffice to remind students that digital material can also be transmitted from point to point by any telecommunication system. Thus reporters composing copy at their computer terminals can send it to distant editors, and editors can send stored pages from their offices

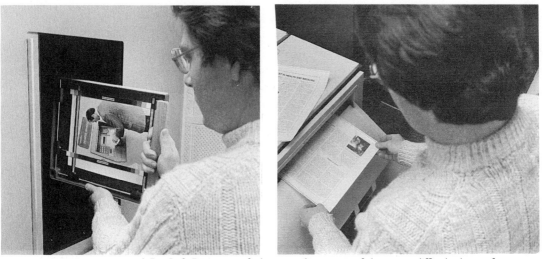

6-5   *Left:* Digitizing of photographs is one of the most difficult chores for a computerized system because of the great storage capacity involved when a photo is scanned in thin lines, picking up 256 shades of gray. It can be done, however, and shown here is a photo being inserted into a scanner at *U.S. News & World Report.* Output is a halftone reproduction in place on the appropriate page in the magazine. (Courtesy *U.S. News & World Report*)

6-6   *Right:* The output of the system used by *U.S. News & World Report* is full pages with body type, display and all illustrations in place. (Courtesy *U.S. News & World Report*)

to distant printers via their computer terminals. Color photographs were successfully transmitted and prepared for reproduction through computer action in the 1984 Olympic games.

The PC and Graphic Systems

The personal computer pushed its way into millions of American homes in the mid- and late 1980s, providing a source of amusement (game-playing) and the potential for enlightenment, as well as the capacity to help with many chores. At that same time, PCs burst into the editorial offices and art and production departments of media everywhere. Advertising and public relations agencies were also inundated.

The earlier specialized portable VDTs that had become tools for sports writers, wireservice writers and newspaper remote bureau personnel were an indicator of what was to come, but publishers and other media executives were not fully prepared for the speed with which PCs moved into common use.

Suddenly writers had no need to report regularly to the office; using inexpensive, small PCs that were complete with *modems* (devices to

6-7 Personal computers of every variety have worked themselves into the lives of journalists. The specialized systems designed for newspapers and other media are being forced to accommodate the PCs being used by staff members. (Photo by Ralph Kliesch)

connect one computer with another via telephone lines), they could file their written material in the office computer or typesetter from any remote location. Funeral directors, with their PCs, could file obituaries directly with the newspaper without requiring a reporter to call for the information. Preparation of graphs, charts and other images could be done on many PCs and then moved through the production system. Data for long, complicated stories could be carried by writers or editors on small discs to which they could readily get access with their PCs. And so it went, with one task after another falling into the range of the personal computer. Again, it should be said here that the potential of miniaturization of computer activity because of microprocessor technology is discussed in our final chapter. But the day-to-day role of the writers, editors, artists and designers in getting words and images into print cannot be understood without relating their functions to computer technology.

For anyone planning a career in any activity connected with the process of getting material into print, a basic knowledge of working with computer terminals and systems is essential. Unfortunately for everyone concerned, computerized systems and PCs are not all alike. Scores of manufacturers design and market systems and computers, each of which has its own peculiar capabilities and features. Without getting involved with the many brands such as Apple, IBM, Atex, and Itek, let's look at some basic elements common to most systems. Variations are too numerous to know or remember, but it is at least beneficial for newcomers to know that such variations do exist and to know what questions to ask about them.

The approach here will be to try to delineate what should be common knowledge for anyone about to use electronic copy processing systems as they now exist in newspaper, magazine, advertising, and public relations offices.

Working with Electronic Systems: Some Basics

One of the most important things for newcomers to understand while sitting down at a keyboard entry device, whether it be a VDT in the office or a personal computer in some other setting, is that they are involved in the operation of a system, and the end goal of that system is to prepare printed material.

Proliferation of personal computers among staff members of many publications became one of the major problems discussed at publishers' meetings in the mid-1980s. With specialized systems already in place, publishers found many advantages and uses for PCs, but also faced what sometimes seemed to be unending problems of interrelating them with the system. It should be remembered that anything done at a keyboard or, for that matter, anything *not* done at the keyboard that interferes with the flow of words and images through the system and into print is defeating the purpose of the system.

It must also be remembered that systems sometimes do *crash,* and precautions against these system breakdowns are essential. Checking and double-checking the system can avoid many disasters. If you think you have recorded your story in the system, check to be sure that it has been received there before clearing your terminal. Along this same line, you should know that anything written on a VDT screen must eventually come off the screen, but no one wants it to vanish unintentionally. Sometimes one accidental touch of a key results in the loss of a story, so beware of keys labeled "clear," "kill," or something similar. Although many processing systems provide safeguards against accidental clearing of screens and losing the results of hours of work, others, unfortunately, do not.

It is also important to remember that work at a VDT keyboard has two facets:

1. typing characters onto a screen, much like typing them on paper
2. using the keyboard to communicate with other elements in the system

The first of these presents very few difficulties; some slight variations in keyboards can be a nuisance, but these can be learned very quickly. It is the second of these facets that is new and different and consequently can be troublesome. It is helpful in this regard to remember that each key that is struck represents a digital piece of information. In talking to a computer or other element in a system, a small letter instead of a capital or one extra space in a command can totally change the meaning of that command. The figure *1* and the small letter *l* are totally different in digital code; the same is true of capital *O* and *zero*.

Accuracy in typing intrasystem commands is thus essential, but so is the mere typing of a story on the screen. In computerized electronic systems, the writers and editors at the keyboard are the final authorities regarding what gets into print; there no longer are printers to blame for errors in typesetting. Full control rests with the writers and editors, and the pressure upon them to maintain a high level of accuracy is greater than ever before.

All of these cautions seem to make working with an electronic copy processing system a fearful prospect, but actually it is not. Writers and editors like the fact that they have total control over their product, and, once they become accustomed to the new machines that are involved, they are almost unanimous in their enthusiasm for them.

Learning the VDT Keyboard

The first thing to confront anyone sitting down to write into a computerized system is the keyboard—or perhaps we ought to say *keyboards*, because they usually are divided into segments. Although there is wide variation in detail among keyboards of various systems, there are some common traits. All of them have, for example, the *basic keyboard* containing the normal characters and numbers found on any typewriter. All of them also have, in one form or another, a set of *editing* keys with which to make changes on the screen and a set of *function* keys that are used to communicate with other parts of the system. Many keyboards

6-8 Keyboards of video display terminals in common use by mass media are not much different from those of personal computers or electric typewriters. Supplemental keypads for specialized functions represent the largest difference.

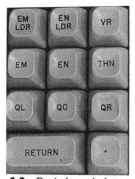

6-9 Basic knowledge of typesetting terminology can be of great help in adapting to VDTs in publication offices. As this key pad shows, some terminals use standard printing terms such as em, en, quad left and em leader to identify the keys that specify, respectively, a space the width of the type size; a space one-half the width of the type size; space out the line so it will be flush to the left; and place ellipses one em apart.

also have a group of typesetting keys. The labels and locations of these keys vary, but for a system to operate, they must be there in some form.

The basic keyboards are "old hat" to anyone who has ever used a PC or an electric typewriter. The letter keys are there, and in the same place, and there are also shift and shift lock keys, but here is where the first variation from a typewriter will probably occur. As the shift lock key is depressed, the shift key does not depress, and the lock key pops right back. So there is no way to know that the shift is on unless, as some terminals provide, the key has a light bulb that comes on when the shift is locked.

You should also know of some other probable differences in basic keyboards. For example, keyboards may provide a different method for typing quotation marks. Typesetters set beginning quotation marks that are different from the ending marks, and, because VDT keyboards produce type, they must provide for differentiating between beginning and ending marks. Terminals usually will have one key that will seem to be an apostrophe and/or comma that can be struck with the shift key down to get one half of the other quote mark. Striking the key twice in each instance provides for the double mark in type.

As pointed out earlier, an electronic copy processing system is based on digital information, and one byte on tape or in wire signals equals a character. By depressing the single open quote key, we provide one byte of information that will cause a typesetter to form one little black mark; a second depression of that key will produce the other byte and the other mark. Usually, striking one key (such as for a small letter) produces one byte and that byte will equal the desired character. That byte shows on the screen as a letter, and later will go through the computer as impulses, tape holes or magnetic dots. For capital letters, two bytes are needed, one to specify a capital and the other to specify the letter; therefore, to form a capital letter we must hit two keys, the shift key and the character key.

There probably will be a *return* key somewhere on the board, but it will not return a typewriter carriage because there isn't one. The return key will, however, serve a similar purpose of moving the action on the screen from the end of the line to the beginning of a new line. In some systems, it is also used for the last key stroke in all commands that are given to a computer.

Ending lines at the keyboard is not a problem for VDTs. Most systems permit endless typing, each line filling the maximum number of characters that the screen can accommodate with no hyphenation required. A *word wrap* feature is usually available; either automatically or at the command of a keystroke, the system will end each line at the end of the last possible word. In some systems the keyboard operator may be able to dictate hyphenation at his or her keyboard, but hyphenation is usually the function of the computer. At any rate, it pays to be wary of putting hyphens at the ends of lines; striking the hyphen key creates

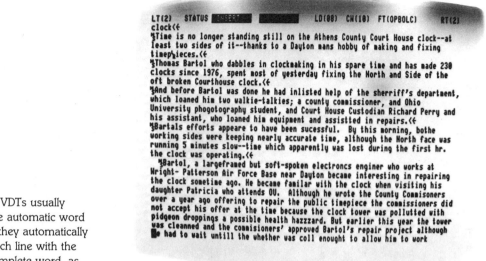

6-10 VDTs usually provide automatic word wrap; they automatically end each line with the last complete word, as shown on this screen.

a byte of information, too, and hyphens can then appear where they do not belong in typesetting. The hyphen key may also have some special functions.

There is thus nothing in the basic keyboard to be really concerned about; the few peculiarities that may appear are quickly and easily mastered.

The Cursor and Editing Keys

Any text change or correction that is usually made with pencil and paper can be carried out on a video screen with keys on the keyboard and something called a *cursor*. The cursor is a small block of light, usually about the size of a character, that can be moved to any position on the screen. Cursors usually blink so that they can be spotted quickly, and they can be in the form of a rectangular block or an underline. Regardless of their physical appearance, cursors all serve the same purpose; to locate, on the screen, the action that results from keys. The use of the cursor is the most important single difference between typewriters and terminals, a fact that causes one common error: the use of the space bar instead of cursor control keys.

When the space bar is touched, it creates a blank space on the screen; when that blank space travels through the system in a digital code, it is a byte of information. Striking the space bar will not move the cursor; it will simply place more blank spaces at the cursor location or eliminate letters at that location. The only way to move the cursor, and

6-11 Most terminals will have cursor direction keys conveniently located. Speed of cursor manipulation is extremely helpful in building efficiency of editing with keyboard instructions.

thus change the location of the characters called for by key strokes, is with the cursor control keys.

The speed of editing at a terminal is directly related to the speed of manipulation of the cursor, and it is wise to quickly learn all shortcuts that are available; precious time can be wasted while moving the cursor space by space when it can be positioned instantly.

After the cursor is in position, any necessary changes can be made with the other editing keys, which make it possible to *insert, overstrike, delete* and *move* any character, word, paragraph, or block of material.

One keystroke will usually place a terminal into either the insert or overstrike mode. Striking the insert key, for example, will set up the terminal to permit the insertion of as little as one letter to as much as several paragraphs just ahead of the cursor position. In what seems to be a magical manner, all the material, from the cursor on, just moves out of the way and allows room for each character as the key is struck. If, however, the terminal is in the overstrike mode, as each key is struck, the new character appears in place of the old character, which just vanishes from the screen. Thus terminals permit totally neat overstriking, not like typewriters that place one character over another with the usual result that no one knows which character is intended to be there.

Once proficiency moving the cursor has been obtained, editing with cursor and keyboard can be done as rapidly as with pencil-and-paper methods, and often more rapidly.

System Function Keys

Most of the variations among systems occur in the use and labeling of keys involved in intrasystem communication: for video terminals to talk to computers and computers to talk to typesetters, and so on. Custom engineering of systems has caused these variations to be so great that they can be discussed here only in the most general terms.

Let us look at system keys from the standpoint of the function they perform for the user, beginning with the writer and concluding with the editor.

From the standpoint of a newspaper reporter or magazine writer, video terminals are tools for composing their thoughts into words that are then turned over to editors for further processing. The writers' involvement in the system is minimal; they want to put their stories where editors can find them and where, should the need arise, they too can find them again and get them back for further work. In pencil-and-paper terms writers put their stories on a spindle or in an "in-basket" where they and their editors can find them.

In electronic system terms, the writers must put their stories in storage. In order for such storage to be useful, it must involve a foolproof filing system so that stories can be located and recalled when needed. For this purpose, computers are better than humans, and in the filing process computers can prepare a list of every filed item almost instantly. If the humans using the system are careful, there is almost no chance of error.

Most systems are highly restrictive in the number of characters that are available for assigning file names, and this restriction must be known by all writers. If the limit is six digits, there is no way to "fudge" on that limit; in that sense computers are rigid and unyielding. Also, some computers take file names absolutely literally: If a reporter enters "Fire" as a file name for a story and erroneously types "fiRe," the computer will accept it and record it in that fashion. Any listing (called *directory* or *queue*) of what is in storage will record it as "fiRe," and for recalling that story, the name must be exactly the same. Anything else (Fire, fire, FIre, FIRE) will not work.

6-12 Computerized systems provide file names for stories and will show, on command, a listing of all files, such as this directory. Subfiles, such as those of a page editor, are often called queues and can be called to the screen by keyboard command.

In filing stories at large installations, such as the *New York Times* and *Washington Post,* is may be necessary for writers to tell the computer in which queue or directory to put their work because departments may have their own listings as part of a larger directory. At smaller newspapers, there may be just one centralized storage area.

The use of system commands for filing and the like may seem to be complicated and difficult to understand, but actually they become routine very rapidly. Even with multiple files, for example, a reporter usually writes into only one (e.g., sports) and is not concerned with the others. And in almost every instance, "crib sheets" are located at every terminal listing the keystrokes involved in all common commands. Such crutches help the newcomer but are soon forgotten because they are no longer needed.

The first step in using any system command is to make sure that the receiving hardware can "hear" the command and thus receive it. In many systems this requires a keystroke, which can be compared to picking up a telephone receiver and dialing a number. The result of this operation is to hook the terminal into the system, to put it "on-line" with the other devices. For some systems it is important also to be sure that the terminal is "off-line" when it is functioning as a typewriter; for others, the "on" switch that gives the terminal power immediately puts it on-line with the computer.

Calling Stories out of Storage

Recalling stories from storage is usually carried out in one of two ways. The first of these is to call the directory to the screen and place the cursor next to the file name of the desired story. One keystroke will then bring that story to the screen. The other way is to use the keyboard to execute a command such as "Get" followed by the file name of the story. In this way you are telling the computer to "get" the story and bring it to the screen.

In either case, the entire story often does not appear in view; sometimes the system provides only the first few paragraphs, or there may not be room on the screen for the complete story. To take care of this problem, VDTs have *scrolling* capacity. The portion of the story on the screen can be rolled up or down to permit viewing of other portions.

Putting Stories into Type

Besides correcting the work of writers, editors usually write the headlines or titles and mark the story and the headline for typesetting. Systems engineers have designed terminals so that these same functions can be carried out with keystrokes.

Most VDTs provide for quick, routine selection of boldface or italic type options because sometimes even the reporter would like to specify these options. Placement and terminology may vary, but one can usually find these keys easily. If not labeled *italic* or *bold*, they may be called

UR (for upper rail) and *LR* (for lower rail) because of old linecasting machine terminology. Upper rail traditionally has meant the optional choice (either bold or italic), and lower rail was the normal choice. When using such keys at a terminal, you must remember to mark the beginning and ending of the option. If one word is to be in italic, the italic key (perhaps *upper rail*) must be struck before the word is typed, and another key (perhaps *lower rail*) must be struck to have the typesetter return to normal setting. Otherwise, large unwanted blocks of italic or bold can show up in proofs.

Other typesetting keys often found on VDT keyboards include *flush left*, *flush right* and *centered*. Where traditional terminology is used (i.e., upper rail and lower rail) these keys are usually labeled *quad left, quad right*, and *quad center*. The result is the same self-explanatory positioning of type on lines. Type is normally justified, which means that each line is automatically made to be flush to both edges of a column.

Beginnings and endings of paragraphs are also important elements of information to convey to a computerized typesetter. Most systems have keys plainly labeled, and many have one *paragraph* key that serves to start and end a paragraph. Other systems have traditional typesetting terminology: *em* for starting paragraphs and *quad left and return* to end paragraphs. TTS tapes for linecasting machines used those terms to tell the automated machine to indent one em to start a paragraph, and to put in quads at the right to make the last line be flush to the left.

Super Shifts and Pi Characters

Typesetters set many characters that do not appear on an ordinary typewriter keyboard, including such typographical miscellany as stars, bullets, check marks and so on. These miscellaneous strange characters are called *pi* characters, a term that also comes from printing tradition: Type pieces that were not in a proper bin (all mixed up and in disorder) used to be called *pi*.

In order to sort these characters out on a VDT, the keyboard provides for what is called a *super shift* or *double shift* function. When the regular shift key is pressed, the capital is called for instead of the lower case letter. When the super shift key is struck, followed by a normal character key, a specific pi character is called for. The pi characters available vary from system to system and are listed in system manuals where they may be consulted as needed.

Formatting

VDTs usually have some provision for *formatting*, a simplified method for communicating complicated typesetting instructions. Format keys permit one key to communicate a list of typesetting instructions that are used frequently. Example: One key can tell a typesetter what kind of type to

6-13 In most editorial offices, a list of basic commands for the system is posted on each terminal. After using terminals only a few days, most staff members find they no longer need to refer to the list. (Courtesy *Hudson Register-Star*; photo by Robert L. Ragaini)

use for a by-line, how to position the words in the line, what column measure is to be set, and the leading that is required. The computer will have been programmed to follow these instructions when the appropriate key is struck. Formatting is especially helpful when headlines and body type are written together at a terminal and composed as area composition by the same typesetter. Small systems may only provide for a few special formats; the first portions of the system installed in the *New York Times* in 1976 contained 180 formats that could be designated with a *uf* (use format) key plus the number of the desired format.

Although some keyboards contain tabular keys like a typewriter, it is more common to use format keys for tabulated materials such as football scores, stockmarket reports and the like.

Wire Service Copy

The processing of wire copy (the stories that come to a newspaper from organizations such as the Associated Press and United Press International) can be much easier in an electronic system than with traditional pencil-and-paper methods.

With transmission being only from computer to computer (AP's computer to the newspaper's computer) stories can travel much more rapidly—a full day's news in a matter of minutes. Traditional teletype transmission is at a medium typewriting speed. Sending long stories in the slower speed always has presented a problem for the wire services and their clients, whose deadlines vary greatly. In order to make sure that a client with an early deadline can get at least a part of all the news, stories are sent in "takes," which must be put together at deadline time to form as complete a story as possible. New developments during a day's news cycle are handled with periodic new beginnings (new leads) that must be incorporated with earlier takes. The new high-speed transmission from computer to computer cuts such piecing of stories to a minimum.

Whether a newspaper receives high-speed or traditional transmission, processing of wire copy is carried out in the same fashion as locally written copy. Wire news is recorded in storage as it arrives, each with a file name and each listed in a directory. Directories and files can be called forth to video terminals where the stories can be headlined and corrected before going into type.

Sometimes wire copy is received into storage in Teletypesetter form with all the hyphenation and justification codes already in it. To permit quick elimination of these commands, terminals are usually equipped with a *wire strip* key. Striking that key strips the copy of all the h&j commands, and displays the story on the screen in standard form.

Split-Screen Merging

Large metropolitan newspapers often get different variations of news coverage from more than one wire service and prefer to blend these versions into one more comprehensive story. This is one area in which pencil-and-paper editing has been simpler, but systems have been developed to make electronic merging of copy equally efficient.

To make story merging easier, systems provide for splitting the VDT screen so that two stories can be displayed side by side. With the ability to move words, paragraphs, and blocks from one column to the other, the editor can blend the stories without too much difficulty. As the editor works, he or she can also type in his or her own paraphrasing whenever desired. Without the split-screen feature, editors must work with one version on the screen and the other in typed form, and much more keyboarding is required.

Getting Hard-Copy Printouts

Especially in the handling of wire copy, editors may wish to look at *hard copies* of story segments with which they are working. Hard copies are paper copies as contrasted with *soft copies* which exist in electronic form in computer storage or on a video screen. Reporters and writers also often want hard copies, and systems usually provide printout devices to deliver these copies. These printout devices can be nothing more than teletype devices operating at typewriter speed, but they often are high-speed computer printout devices that will give story copies in seconds.

The procedure for getting a printout is often very much like the procedure involved in sending copy to a typesetter because it is simply a matter of sending the copy to a different machine—in one case it is the typesetter and in the other case it is the printout machine (often also called the *line printer*).

Fitting Copy and Headlines to Space

One of the chores now readily done by computerized systems is fitting type to space, including headlines. Done manually, this copyfitting is boring and difficult for some, but nonetheless absolutely vital. Carried out in a computer system, it is virtually effortless.

To fit body copy, a computer must know the same information that is involved in manual copyfitting: the font of type, length of line and leading between lines. When the proper keyboard command is given, it will divide the number of characters in the copy by the number that will fit into a line of type to find the number of lines of type. The lines of type will then be converted into a unit of measure, usually either picas or inches. These computations are carried out internally, of course, and for the user the only actions required are to keyboard the three items of required information and ask for the answer.

6-14 Some systems provide copyfitting calculations from keyboard commands. Here (A) shows the story will be 8.5 column inches long when the 10-point type is set leaded to 12 points (B) in a column width of 15 picas (C) if the typeface is Optima Bold (D).

Display type as used in headlines is fitted for each line. When the computer is told the size and style of type, it will respond with the length of line or, if a line limitation is given to it, it will show the cutoff point for the desired line length.

CHECKLIST: Computerized Copy Processing: Some Helpful Hints

1. Sharpen your keyboarding skills through steady use of a personal computer or a typewriter. Although it is easy to correct copy on computer terminals, a high level of accuracy eliminates many frustrations that can come from errors in typing commands into a system.

2. Understand the basics of computer copy processing systems. This understanding helps you to know which questions to ask concerning any new situation. Remember, as a writer you must know how to put your material into storage; as an editor you must know how to get it out, correct it and then send it into type. In any system there will be short, precise commands for accomplishing these tasks, and the right question can bring a quick solution to any problems. If crib sheets are not available, make your own handy aid for keyboarding these commands.

3. Before using any system, quickly read any procedure manual that accompanies it. Although it is not possible to absorb everything a manual contains, a quick reading will usually eliminate most points of uncertainty and permit quick adjustment to the system.

4. Practice, practice, practice with any video system terminal or personal computer you can get access to. In spite of wide differences among them, "hands on" experience goes a long way in removing fears and developing necessary skills for working with a system.

5. Learn basic typesetting terminology; most systems will employ terms whose roots are in traditional typesetting.

6. Be aware that errors seem to be more difficult to see on a video screen than on paper; at least, many newspapers have discovered that more errors go unnoticed when VDTs replace typewriters. Special care is necessary to pick up typographical errors out of what appears to be a perfectly clean, error-free screen.

7. Remember that systems do crash occasionally. Keep backup copies until there is no possibility of loss because of system breakdowns. A hard copy printout or your own disk provides good insurance against system disasters.

8. Above all, remember that computerized systems put full responsibility for accuracy and quality of final typesetting into the hands of the editorialist. In these systems, the type compositor is you, not some handy scapegoat called the printer.

Images in Graphic Communication

Although the hackneyed adage "One picture is worth a thousand words" defies proof and begs argument, the basic value of images in graphic communication is beyond dispute.

The pervasiveness of images in our communication systems is without question; we start to learn our verbal language from picture books and move on to maturity in a world of television, motion pictures, and illustrated magazines, books and newspapers.

Indeed, television seems to have launched us into an age of images, made us a nation of viewers rather than readers. All print media have responded to television's impact with more, bigger, and better illustrations. Orators without "visual aids" to supplement their verbal presentations are swimming against the stream of images that seems to be flooding communication today. Even highway signs have been evolving from verbal to visual images to achieve instantaneous communication with motorists.

This increased emphasis on images for communication is not surprising. As we look back to the early attempts of human beings to communicate graphically, we can see that pictures were the first message form. The caveman's pictograph demonstrated an appreciation of the communicative potential of illustrations at the earliest stages of graphic communication. What we now see seems simply to be the completion of a cycle that again places pictorial images in a position of primary importance.

Completion of the cycle has been the result of technological innovations that have made the use of illustrations easier and more effective. These inventions—photography, photoengraving, motion pictures, television and then the omnipresent computer—have each taken us a step further in our reliance on illustrations for communication.

Information Graphics

The most spectacular development in image presentation by the mass media has been in what we might call *information graphics* or *information images.* These are the charts, graphs, diagrams, and pictographs used to relay statistical and other types of information through visual image.

In simple form, these drawings have been a part of print media for years, but the success of *USA Today* and other contemporary newspapers whose pages burst with colorful charts and diagrams of every kind has brought these image forms to new levels. Microcomputers with remarkable graphic versatility and sophistication also have brought graphics to desk and table tops in offices and homes almost everywhere. Computerized videographics, with the added dimensions of sound and motion, have increased the general awareness of and sensitivity to information images through video games and special effects in TV programs and motion pictures set in outer space. Even sports fans have come to expect their TV football commentators to show a "graphic" periodically to bring them up-to-date with past records, totals, comparisons or other data.

As one of the leaders in presentation of information graphics, *USA Today* presents us with a good example of their use in a print medium. *USA Today* maintains a staff of 13 graphic artists working staggered shifts around the clock. Working at top speed with the traditional tools of graphic artists, they complete their work an hour before deadline to allow ample time for page designers to do their work. During slow periods, especially during the night shift, advance drawings are made for anticipated fast-breaking news events, such as airline crashes and other disasters.

An average of 39 pieces of informational art is prepared daily at *USA Today*. Its weather page with its large map has been a popular feature, as has its use of colored boxes of information that have been called *factoids*. High circulation figures, more than a score of awards from the Society of Newspaper Design, and the compliment of imitation by others have attested to the value of this emphasis on color and graphics.

Graphics by Computer

Television, with its need for color, speed, animation, and unusual effects, has been the leading medium in using the computer for generating graphics, but the future possibilities for other media seem endless.

A look at the use of computer graphics by CBS News can give us a glimpse of that potential. The news department's graphic artists produce an average of 35 graphics a day, plus the usual advance work such as that done by *USA Today* artists mentioned earlier. Some of the work is done with the traditional drawing board and art supplies, but much of it is now computerized.

Four computers provide the capability for generating the great variety of symbols, maps, charts, diagrams, flags and other graphics required for news telecasts. One computer with a viewing screen lets artists draw with a stylus, call from a menu a wide variety of textures and elements, then arrange the elements and "paint" large color areas with an almost limitless range of hues. A variety of typefaces is also available.

Another computer, this one with a keyboard, provides animation capability. Still another lets artists feed in pre-designed components such as photos, transfer letters and two-dimensional renderings of three-dimensional objects. These can then be called back for incorporation in later creations. With another computer, basic designs can be given special effects such as fades, dissolves and soft wipes.

Computerization makes it possible for CBS News to have a compact library of disks, permitting quick recall and reuse of more than 70,000 graphic designs on file there.

At this writing, graphics by computer were much more common in nonprint media than for newspapers, magazines and other print media. Principal cause for the lag in use by print media has been a technical one that should be solved shortly, as indicated in Chapter 17. Unlike television and film, print media have not yet had direct reproduction capability of computer graphics. A hard-copy printout from an ink-jet printer or an impact printer that serves as original copy for printing has been all that was available. Efforts to develop direct computer-to-paper, fully paginated printing systems are underway, however.

In the meantime, print media graphic artists have been using the computer to simplify their task and improve their products. At the *New York Times*, a computer system is used to input data and then display, on terminal screens, charts of different kinds to help determine which seem to do the best job of presenting the data (Figure 7-1). A hard-copy printout becomes a tracing plot for finished artwork, and more than one may be combined with type and other art to form the finished graphic

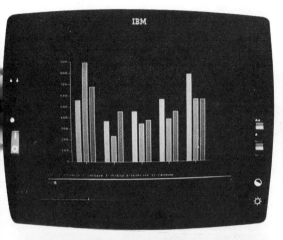

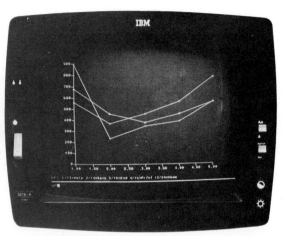

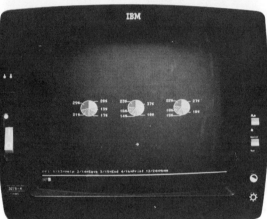

7-1 At the *New York Times*, the difficult and time-consuming job of plotting charts and diagrams accurately is done by a computer. With just three key strokes, the visual display of the information can be changed to any of the three forms shown here. The circular pie charts automatically change the data groups to percentages, and the bar charts are scaled by the highest number automatically. (Courtesy the *New York Times* Map and Chart Department)

(Figure 7-2). This then becomes the original artwork that must be entered into production in the same manner as other artwork.

Freelance graphic artists can now turn their personal computers into complete graphic-design workstations for studio use. Drawings are made with a stylus on an electronic tablet and displayed in full color on their monitor. From menus displayed on the screen various *pixels* (picture elements) can be selected for incorporation into the drawing, and, with a keyboard, type fonts can be selected for titles and other verbal display. Excellent informational graphics can thus be created in minutes instead of hours.

Computer assistance in preparing informational graphics for print media offers tremendous potential for improved communication of complex material, but there are also dangers. The primary danger is that the illustration, designed to simplify the message, may itself become so complicated that readers cannot understand it.

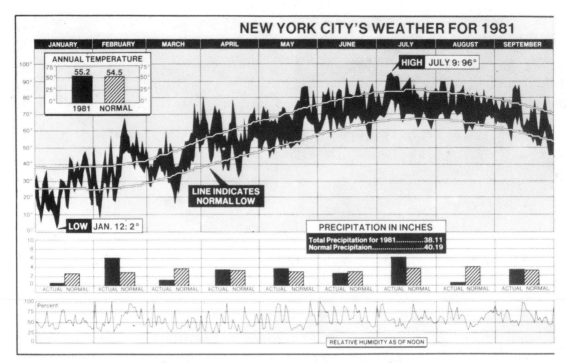

7-2   A portion of the finished art for a computer-assisted graphic in the *New York Times*. (Courtesy the *New York Times* Map and Chart Department)

Some Basics About Information Graphics

The ability to make more complicated charts and diagrams faster because of computer assistance places greater responsibility on designers and editors to make certain that such artwork is held to the function or functions intended for it.

A look at the basic components of such illustrations along with their capabilities can be helpful in that regard. In Figures 7-2 through 7-6, we see these basic components individually and in combination, with or without the benefit of shading or color that can make them more helpful or complex. The *pie chart,* a circle split into segments to show parts of a whole, the *line chart* to show trends over time, the *bar graph* to show comparative amounts, the *pictograph* to add visualization of items compared to the bar graph's comparative amounts, the *diagram* to show how a task is done or devices and systems work, and the *map* to show locations—all are foundations on which to build.

In two-dimensional form, with one explanatory function, each of the basic drawings is effective. Duplicating them in one drawing, such as two line charts to show comparative trends, or combining them, such as using pie charts on a map, can also be effective. Each complicating

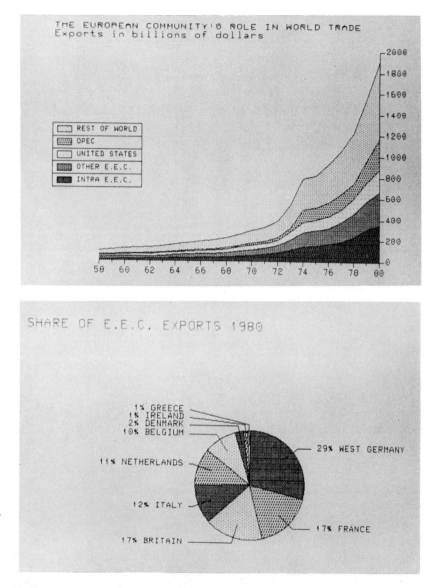

7-3 These are the computer versions of the line graph and the pie chart incorporated by the artist into the finished art shown in Figure 7-2. (Courtesy the *New York Times* Map and Chart Department)

factor, however, must be evaluated to avoid ambiguity and, in some cases, outright inaccuracy.[1]

Artist, editor, and computer must work in harmony to meet what seems to be a need for splashier, more colorful, more complicated information graphics—brought on by reader exposure to video and film graphics—without thereby creating obstacles rather than aids to communication.

[1]An excellent book full of such examples is *The Visual Display of Quantitative Information* by Edward R. Tufte (Graphics Press, 1983).

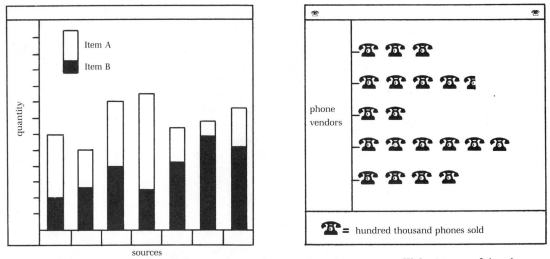

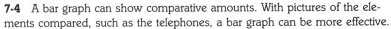

7-4   A bar graph can show comparative amounts. With pictures of the elements compared, such as the telephones, a bar graph can be more effective.

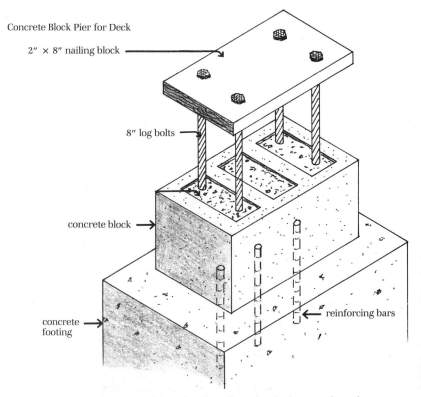

7-5   To show how to lay a footer for the pillar of a deck or to show how complicated systems work, a diagram can be most helpful.

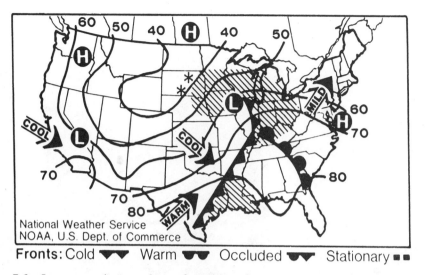

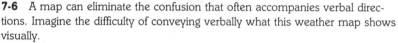

Fronts: Cold ▼▼ Warm ▼▼ Occluded ▼▼ Stationary ▪▪

7-6 A map can eliminate the confusion that often accompanies verbal directions. Imagine the difficulty of conveying verbally what this weather map shows visually.

Entertainment Graphics

As comic strips attest, illustrations can also be used to *entertain* readers. Political cartoons, such as those drawn by Thomas Nast for *Harper's Weekly* more than a century ago as well as Doonesbury and others of today, have shown that entertainment can also carry an editorial punch. Immediate changes in circulation figures for newspapers result when changes are made in comics and cartoons, proof that they are important parts of printed communications.

Photographs

As explained in more detail in later chapters, one of the basic functions of illustrations is *to attract and get attention.* Magazine editors, advertising designers and other media practitioners have long realized that a striking illustration is perhaps the best means for attracting a reader's eyes to a page or design. Although all forms of illustrations can accomplish this function, the photograph has been the primary choice. Photographs, because they are true-to-life duplicates of images that the human eyes see in the world about them, can compel attention quickly and forcefully. The emotions or reactions that are aroused as we view life about us can be stimulated and catered to by photographs better than by any other means.

Photographs are also primary tools for the communicator who wants to *inform* his readers precisely of what took place at an event or hap-

7-7 For many purposes, photographs are unmatched in the ability to show things as they happened or as they are, as shown in this photo of tornado destruction. (Courtesy Richard Dibon-Smith/Photo Researchers)

pening. Auto accidents, sports action, parades and other such news events can be shown to readers through photographs more effectively than with other kinds of illustrations. The devastation of an earthquake, as shown in Figure 7-7, defies verbal description. Because of the importance of photographs in graphic communication, a full chapter devoted to picture editing follows this one.

The Production Aspects of Illustrations

So far in this chapter we have looked at illustrations from the standpoint of the original form of the illustration as created by an artist or photographer. Before illustrations can be viewed by masses of readers, however, they must be produced in quantity by a printing process. As we consider illustrations from the production standpoint, different terminology, different categories, and different concepts emerge.

As explained later, in Chapter 13, many printing processes are available for the mass reproduction of words and illustrations. Some of the technicalities of the production of illustrations vary among these different processes. But for the three primary printing processes most production terminology and procedures are the same; these similar procedures are discussed here and the technical differences are explained in later chapters.

Basic Types of Reproductions of Illustrations

From the standpoint of mechanical reproduction, there are two basic types of illustration each of which contains some subtypes. These two kinds of reproductions, *line* and *halftone*, are best explained by briefly tracing their production steps.

Line Reproductions

Some drawings, such as pen-and-ink renditions, are composed of only solid tones, black lines on a white background, called *line drawings*. When printed, they are called *line reproductions*. Figure 7-8 shows a basic line reproduction. In order to reproduce Figure 7-8, the printer followed a relatively simple photographic procedure. The original artwork, done with pen and black ink on a white background, is first photographed in order to get a production negative. During this photographing, the image may be enlarged or reduced, with reduction being more common. Line illustrations are usually drawn larger than the reproduction in order to minimize flaws that might be present in the original drawing. The negative that is created is then used to transfer the image to a metal surface for use on a printing press. This image transfer is possible because of the sensitivity to light of the films and metals that are used.

For example, when the line illustration is mounted in front of the lens of a large camera (called a *process camera* or an *engraver's camera*), light is beamed toward the illustration. That light reflects from the white background and strikes the film in the camera, making it black in the background. The dark lines of the illustration reflect no light, thus letting the film remain clear in the image areas. The developed negative, therefore, is dark (opaque) in the nonprinting area and clear in the printing area. The image it contains is a reverse image of the original drawing. This image is transferred to a light-sensitive metal sheet by beaming light through the negative to the metal. Light thus exposes the metal sheet where it is to carry ink but leaves the nonprinting area unexposed. The

7-8 A drawing that contains only lights and darks and no middle tones is called, when printed, a *line reproduction.*

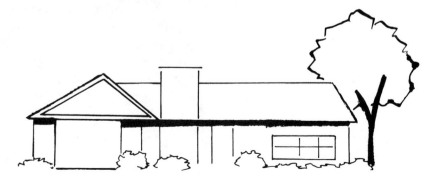

metal sheet can then be chemically developed or etched with acid for printing, depending on the printing process to be used. In either case, the light-exposed portion of the plate carries ink and the nonexposed area does not.

Halftone Reproductions

The reproduction of illustrations that contain tones between the extremes of white and black is more complicated and puzzling. These reproductions, called *halftones*, are necessary for all photographs, wash drawings, oil paintings, watercolors or any other original illustration containing *continuous tones.* The continuous tones that lie between white and black in a photograph cannot really be carried to paper from a printing plate—either black ink is deposited on the paper or it is not. The illusion of middle tones is created by breaking the printing image into tiny dots, each of which will carry ink from plate to paper; if the dots are small and widely spaced the area will appear to be light, and if they are large and closely spaced they will create a darker image. Figure 7-9 was made with a coarse screen to make the dots readily visible.

The dot pattern for halftones is created through the use of a screen in front of the film in the engraver's camera. The screen, either on glass or film, is composed of parallel lines that intersect at right angles. Although these lines are usually too fine to be seen by the naked eye, under

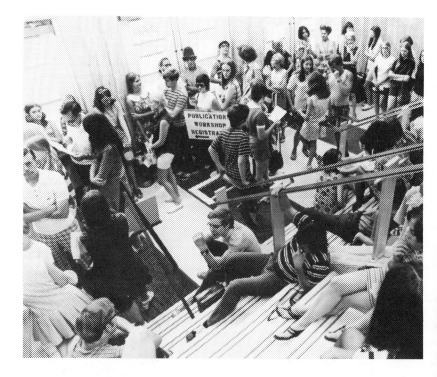

7-9 This halftone, made with a coarser screen than the paper permits, contains a dot structure visible to the naked eye.

7-10 The dot pattern is submerged in this fine-screen halftone. This is an example of a basic reproduction of a photograph, oil painting or other continuous-tone illustration that is called a *square-finish* halftone.

a magnifying glass the screen pattern they create looks much like the screen used for a household door or window. The coarseness of the screen is dictated by the number of lines per linear inch, and the designation of the screen desired for halftone reproduction is of considerable importance. Figure 7-10 shows how a fine screen submerges the dot pattern in a halftone.

Screen coarseness varies usually from 55 lines to 175 lines per linear inch. Traditionally, the coarser screens have been used by newspapers and other media being printed on rough paper. Newspapers still using the traditional printing method are restricted to about 55 to 85 line screens. Media using other printing processes or finer paper (i.e., magazines) can employ the finer screens. Generally speaking, the finer the screen, the better the reproduction. Consequently, in specifying the desired screen, one must consider the printing process to be used, the paper and the quality level desired.

How Halftone Reproductions Are Made. With the specified screen in the camera, the photoengraver places the copy on a copy board in front of the lens, puts the film behind the screen in the camera, and proceeds to make one or more exposures.

Halftone negatives may be made with only one exposure, like line negatives, but photoengravers usually take a series of short exposures in order to get greater tone control and to retain detail in the extreme light and dark areas of the copy.

As the light is beamed to the copy, it reflects back through the lens opening and the screen to the film. Because the light that goes through the lens is reflected from the copy, it varies in intensity directly according to the lightness or darkness of the various areas of the copy. A photograph of a man with a white shirt and dark suit, for example, will reflect light strongly from the shirt and weakly from the suit. Note in Figure 7-10 the variation between the light dome and the dark trees.

When the light pierces the thousands of tiny holes in the screen, it is broken into thousands of small beams. The intense light spreads, as it goes through these apertures, breaking the screen lines into clear dots on the negative. The dots vary in size and shape and are connected or separated, depending upon the amount of light reflecting from the copy. Because of this variation in the dot structure the tones in a photograph or similar illustration can be captured on film, transferred to a plate and finally produced in the printing process.

The developed halftone negative looks to the naked eye like a standard photographic negative. With a magnifying glass, however, the thousands of dots created by the lines of the screen can be clearly seen. The image is composed completely of dots, both clear and opaque. One can readily realize how tiny the dots are by understanding that the number per square inch is always the square of the screen size; a 50-line screen produces 2500, a 100-line screen produces 10,000 and so on.

Halftone negatives are transferred to a plate surface by the exposure of light through the negative to the light-sensitized metal. On the finished plate, each of the dots that was clear on the negative becomes a tiny printing surface; the metal surrounding these areas has either been treated to repel ink or has been etched away so that it cannot receive ink. Areas that were dark in the original copy will have many relatively large and closely grouped dots to carry ink to the paper. Consequently, as the plate is printed, most of the paper will be covered with ink in these areas, and these areas will be dark to the eye. Light areas of the copy will contain relatively small dots widely spaced and will be light when printed.

The Magic of the Dots. One point about halftone reproductions should be emphasized. The dot pattern of a standard halftone, though it varies considerably, is present over all portions of the negative and consequently will be present over all portions of the finished plate. Therefore, there are no pure black or pure white areas in a standard halftone. In areas that seem to be pure white in the original, some dots will stand to carry ink to paper. Areas that were pure black are marred by the presence of tiny clear dots. Figure 7-11 shows a picture of a cogwheel seemingly containing blacks, whites and grays. However, the enlargement on the right reveals the presence of dots throughout.

In spite of the fact that halftones rely on dots to create the illusion of tones, when the proper screen has been selected the reproduction can be excellent. To the viewer, unaided by a magnifying glass, the dots on a halftone reproduction blend with the background to form a faithful reproduction of the original, as Figure 7-10 shows.

The principle of blending dots with the background can easily be illustrated by any student. By holding a newspaper at normal reading

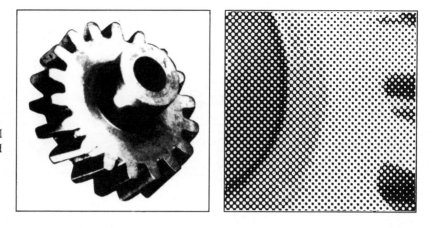

7-11 *Right:* A small portion of the silhouette halftone of the cogwheel at left has been enlarged to show how the dot structure produces shades of tone. (Courtesy S. D. Warren Company)

distance, all the letters and characters can be seen clearly. These represent the dots of a halftone. If the newspaper is pinned to a wall and you step back several paces, the letters and characters appear as masses of gray; the difference in tone created by columns of standard type matter as compared with areas of boldface type is the best illustration of how the dots make tones vary in halftones.

Tint (Tone) Blocks. It is possible, because of the dot magic of the halftone process, to reproduce areas of any given size in a uniform tint, or tone, of the color being used in a printing job. These tints can be produced in any percentage of the full density of the color.

For example, when black is being used, a 50 percent gray (just half the density of solid black) can be printed from a plate made to that specification. Other desired percentages, such as 20, 30, or 80, can also be obtained (Figure 7-12).

7-12 Screen tints provide panels of color or tone, sometimes as background for type. Shown here are 10, 20, 30, 40, 50, 60, 70, 80, 90, and 100 percent tone values.

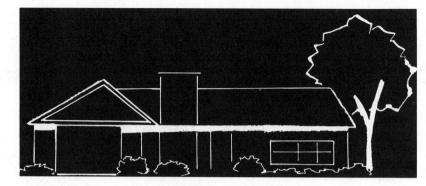

7-13 Tone values of a line drawing are reversed when the drawing is reproduced as a *reverse line* illustration.

These "tint blocks," as they are called, are prepared through the halftone process. Instead of photographing an illustration, a white board is put in front of the camera and the desired tone is achieved by controlling the amount of light going through the screen to the film. Any screen, 55-line, 133-line, and so on, can be used.

Solid tints (100 percent of the tone) are made by exposing the plate area through a clear, unscreened film.

The impression that an additional color was used in printing is often created by screened tint blocks. When red ink is used, for example, a tint appears as pink; when brown is used, tan results. Tint blocks behind type areas of another color are effective in drawing attention to areas that would otherwise be weak in display.

Creating Special Effects for Line Reproductions

Reversing Tones. When it is desired, the values in a line drawing can be reversed for reproduction; that is, the black areas in the drawing can be made to print as white and the white areas as black. Figure 7-13 shows the effect created by a *reverse line* reproduction. Figure 7-8 showed the same illustration reproduced in standard fashion.

To obtain a reverse line reproduction, a normal line negative must first be made. Then, by placing the line negative over another sheet of film and exposing it to light, a negative can be produced on which the values are the same as the original copy. The lines that were black on the original drawing are black on the negative; the other areas are clear.

When the second negative is transferred to the printing plate, the areas that were white on the original will be exposed on the plate surface and thus be made to carry ink to paper.

7-14 Type can be treated as a line drawing and reproduced with reversed tones.

Reverse Type

7-15 When middle tones are created by hatch marks or other lines, a pen-and-ink drawing can be reproduced as a line illustration.

Common uses for reverse line illustrations are for signatures of advertisers or in other cases when an especially bold, black area is desired. Words in type can be line illustrations and treated as such for production, as shown by the reverse line reproduction in Figure 7-14.

Creating Middle Tones. Line reproductions can be used only for illustrations that contain no middle tones—only the extremes. However, artists can produce illustrations that appear to have middle tones but in fact do not and are reproducible as line illustrations. Drawings done with a pen, as shown in Figure 7-15, can be produced as line illustrations when the shading is composed of hatch marks or other lines. Brush-and-ink drawings are also acceptable for line reproductions. They have a somewhat different flavor from those made with pen and ink, especially when the *dry-brush* technique is used. To create such drawings, the artist uses a brush that is virtually dry. To get ink coverage, the artist rubs the ink on the paper instead of flowing it on. By using rough illustration board for the surface, the artist introduces grays into the drawing because the ink does not seep between the high spots of the illustration board.

Coquille board, for example, has a surface composed of scores of small raised dots. By drawing on it with crayon or ink, the artist coats only the peaks of these dots. The dots then provide an illustration that looks like a halftone although no screen is used in its reproduction. Pencils used on a special velvety paper and charcoal on a rough paper expressly made for that purpose also create interesting effects without being reproduced as halftones. But pencil, crayon, and charcoal drawings on smooth paper usually must be reproduced as halftones, or the grays and softness of tone that characterize these drawings will be lost in the reproduction.

Applying Shading Mechanically. The most common method for adding shading to line illustrations is a mechanical one called *Benday.* The method gets its name from the inventor of the original system used by engravers as they artificially added shading to the relief line plates needed in traditional printing. The term Benday now more commonly refers to the shading sheets used by artists for adding tones to line illustrations. These shading sheets are available at most art supply stores in a wide variety of patterns; common trade names are Craftint and Zip-a-tone. They usually are adhesive-backed clear acetate sheets on which the patterns of dots, hatch marks, and the like have been printed. The artist applies the piece of patterned acetate over the desired area and then trims and peels away the excess, leaving the pattern precisely where desired. Benday shading has been added to our line illustration in Figure 7-16.

Another system employs drawing board (i.e., Craftone or Doubletone) that has been preprinted with shading patterns that are invisible to a camera until developed. The artist draws a line illustration on the

7-16 When shading is added by the Benday process, a line drawing can still be reproduced as a line illustration.

board, then paints the areas to be shaded with a developer that brings out the preprinted pattern. With one kind of board (Doubletone) a second developer can be used to bring out a second, deeper shade of tone, thus providing the drawing with four tones: black, white and the two added shades.

Line Conversions. An interesting technique that came into vogue in the early 1970s is the use of a line reproduction for a photograph or other continuous tone illustration. To achieve this special effect, the original illustration is photographed as a line illustration would be—without a screen in the camera. All the middle tones are then lost and a highly contrasty representation (Figure 7-17) results. When the subject of the illustration is clearly recognizable without the middle tones, this treatment creates the impression of an artist's line drawing of the subject.

Types of Halftone Finishes

In addition to the wide variety of line reproductions available, the designer of modern pieces of graphic communication also has at hand an equally varied assortment of halftone treatments.

A basic halftone reproduction is called a *square-finish* halftone because it is a common rectangle (as in Figure 7-10). Any variation from a square finish requires special effort and time during production. This extra time and effort results in some added cost, the amount of which depends on the printing process that is involved as well as the amount of time and effort. In spite of extra cost, however, the use of a multitude of special finishes is common among all print media.

Special Geometric Shapes. The simplest variations from the norm of a square-finish halftone are special geometric shapes ranging from *circles, ovals* and *triangles* to the most elaborate geometric designs.

The oval shape is used to create on "old time" impression for a photo, because photos often were framed as ovals in the early days of

7-17 A *line conversion* reproduction of the photograph in Figure 7-10. When the subject is clearly recognizable, a line conversion gives the interesting artistic effect shown.

7-18 The *oval* is only one of many geometric shapes available for the reproduction of illustrations. This shape gives a "historical" feeling to a photograph.

7-19 Softening the edges of a halftone creates a *vignette* reproduction.

photography. Other irregular shapes can provide a directional emphasis in a design; some are given rather bizarre dimensions to add to their attention-getting value.

Vignette. This finish provides a soft edge for a photo; instead of sharply delineated dimensions, the reproduction has an edge that fades into the background. The general shape of the vignette edge may be quite irregular or it may be more standardized as it is with the oval impression created in Figure 7-19. A feeling of age or beauty is often being sought when the vignette finish is ordered. The removal of the dot pattern gradually from the edges creates the vignette; this work is accomplished partially by an artist but requires careful, detailed attention in production also.

Silhouette. Also called *outline,* this finish is as the name implies; the background of the photo is completely eliminated so that the central subject stands in sharp outline or silhouette against a blank background. The dot pattern that ordinarily is present in the background is completely removed from the halftone negative before it is exposed on metal for printing. This treatment serves to avoid distraction from the background and to give emphasis to the central subject by the sharp contrast between the subject and surrounding area.

Mortise. A *mortise* halftone is one containing a cutout (Figure 7-21). If the cutout is from the outside it may be called a *notch* halftone (Figure 7-22). Notches or mortises are usually rectangular cutouts; the most common is a rectangle cut from one corner of a square-finish

7-20 Outlining or silhouetting the central subject can help emphasize it because competing background details are eliminated.

7-21 A *mortise* halftone contains an interior cutout.

halftone. In traditional printing, irregular mortises were difficult to saw from the metal engravings that were used; modern printing systems have afforded the opportunity for greater versatility in this regard. For some printing systems any irregular shape can now be masked out of a halftone negative with little difficulty.

7-22 A *notch* halftone contains a cutout from the outside.

Mortises are usually made to provide for the insertion, within the halftone area, of type messages or other illustrations.

Highlight (Dropout) Halftone. Special care and handling of a halftone negative can give a reproduction that is devoid of dots in some areas. A model's teeth in a toothpaste ad, for example, can be made pure white by painting out the few dots that ordinarily would carry ink to paper. Special attention given to exposure and development during the making of a halftone negative can virtually eliminate the dots in a highlight (light gray) area, but hand painting with an opaque fluid is usually required.

Photoprints. The use of a screened, continuous-tone photoprint provides an efficient, versatile method for highlighting halftones and producing other special effects. The making of a screened print is identical to the making of a halftone printing plate except that it is made on photographic paper; this screened print, therefore, contains the usual dot pattern needed to reproduce the various tones. If a highlight effect is desired, the dots can be painted out with white paint on the photoprint. A screened print can be photographed as a line illustration because each dot is copied just as if it were part of a Benday pattern.

Advertisers use screened prints a great deal because they often want to highlight portions of an illustration in order to focus attention on particular features of their products; the screened print also makes it possible to paste all elements of an advertisement together to form a single line illustration ready for an engraver's camera. Any possibility of error in the arrangement of material in the advertisement is thus eliminated.

Special Screens for Special Halftone Effects. Special halftone screens that will produce tonal variations while adding mood effects to reproductions have become a common tool for the designer of graphic communications.

Screens are made up of concentric circles, parallel lines, parallel wavy lines, thin irregular lines resembling old steel engravings, mezzotints, wood grains and patterns of various materials such as twill and burlap. Each special screen pattern produces continuous-tone reproductions with a special flavor (see Figure 7-23). Especially good for giving variety to subjects that must be shown repeatedly, these mood screens, along with line conversions (Figure 7-17) and posterization, became especially popular with designers in the 1970s. Because these special screens often are used to make screened photoprints which are then photographed as line illustrations, the special-effect illustrations are also called line conversions even though they reproduce continuous tones and screens are used in making them.

Also in vogue in recent years has been the enlargement of the dot pattern in a halftone reproduction to such a magnitude that the reproduction resembles a line illustration made with dots (Figure 7-24, a small part of Figure 7-22).

Posterization. Posterization, another mood device, is especially effective when two colors can be used but it can also be effective without an added color (Figure 7-23). To achieve posterization, the wide range of tones between black and white is reduced to a single middle tone. This middle tone often is reproduced with one of the special screens and/or in a second color.

All the special screen effects for halftones tend to have one thing in common: They seem to convert standard photographs into artistic renderings. Effectively used, they add a desired dimension to a piece of graphic communication.

Combining Line and Halftone in One Illustration

It is possible for an artist to use a pen to create a line drawing on the face of a photograph thus combining a line illustration and a continuous-tone illusion. This procedure, however, would result in a reproduction containing a screened line illustration because the drawing would be broken into a dot pattern by the screen used in the engraver's camera. (Remember: There are no pure whites or pure blacks in a halftone.) Letters (such as type in a headline) can be handled in the same way but with the same shoddy results.

7-23   Artistic effects for photographs with special screens. (Photo by David Vine, line conversions by Joel A. Levirne, Graphic Images, Ltd.)

Concentric circle (bull's eye) screen

Straight-line screen

Etching screen

Mezzotint screen

Linen-texture screen

Three-tone posterization

7-24 Deliberately enlarging the dot pattern of a halftone is sometimes useful to produce a special effect.

To get sharp, clear line illustrations on the face of halftones, separate negatives are made for the line and halftone portions of illustrations; these negatives are then exposed together on the printing plate to form what is called a *combination* illustration.

There are two kinds of combinations, one in which the line illustration appears in dark lines and the other in which the illustration appears in white lines (Figure 7-25). The first of these is a *surprint combination,* also known as an *overprint, overburn,* or *double burn.* To produce it, the halftone negative and the line negative are separately made as they ordinarily would be. The line negative is then exposed on the metal sheet, followed by the exposure of the halftone negative in the same position. Its many names come from the fact that these two photo printings or "burnings" are necessary. The plate produced in this fashion will reproduce the line illustration in pure blacks while the halftone takes care of the continuous tones. The other combination is called a *reverse combination* because it produces a reverse line illustration on the face of the halftone. To prepare a reverse combination, the halftone negative, the line negative, plus a reverse line negative (film positive) must be made. The two of these negatives that are needed (halftone and reverse line) can be placed together in position on a printing plate for a single exposure. The single exposure is possible because the background of a reverse line negative is completely clear and does not hold back any light.

A common use for surprints and reverse combinations is to get words across the face of a halftone. Figure 7-25 shows both types of

7-25 *Left:* A surprint combination. *Right:* A reverse combination that also has an outline finish at top and a vignette finish at bottom.

combinations, plus some other treatments. Any and all of the special finishes can be used in concert in order to achieve a special communication goal.

Bleeding Photographs and Other Illustrations

Good design usually dictates that white space surround type and illustrations, thus framing the content and holding it within bounds. The use of margins for magazine, newspapers, books and other printed matter stems from this concept. Unity of presentation and contrast for the content against the white surroundings are undeniable benefits.

There are instances, however, when, for one reason or another, there is a need to let illustrations expand and seem to be endless, unbound by a frame. Action pictures, panoramic scenes and other subjects often will gain an added visual dimension if they *bleed* (run off the edges). One need only look at photographic covers of magazines to realize that bleeds seem to be even larger than they are.

Within magazines and books, bleeding of photos can also open up additional room for copy because it is making use of marginal space. And after many marginal pages, a bleed page can give a definite visual relief.

To achieve a bleed, a pica or $\frac{1}{8}$ inch must be added to any dimension that will include a trim edge. This bleed allowance, as it is called, takes care of variations in folding and trimming that otherwise might leave a ribbon of white at the edge. It insures that the photo will run off the edge even if the trim is short or at a slight angle. An $8\frac{1}{2}$-inch by 11-inch magazine page, therefore, requires an extra pica of width and two picas of depth to take care of top, outside and bottom trim edges.

Adding Color to Illustrations

Simply stated, color is added to printing by running a printing press with the desired color of ink in the press; for each color desired the paper must receive an impression by being run through the press again or by passing through another unit of a multi-color press. The same can be said of illustrations, with the addition that a separate illustration must be reproduced on a printing plate for each color. Therefore, line illustrations can be printed in as many colors as one might desire. Sunday comics are good examples of line illustrations in full color (the three primary colors plus black). Line illustrations in only two or three colors are also common. The preparation of artwork for multicolor reproductions is described in Chapter 11.

Halftones can also be reproduced in color, and it is even possible to reproduce a black-and-white photo in more than one color. Take, for example, the situation in which an editor has a black-and-white snow scene to be used on a page that will also be printed in blue ink. The editor can order the work necessary for a *duotone* reproduction that will appear in blue and black, a combination that would add a special chilly feeling to the reproduction. The editor will require two halftone negatives specially made to avoid the clashing of halftone screens that occurs unless the screen angle is changed as the two negatives are made. This clashing produces an undesirable *moiré* effect (Figure 7-26). Because of this moiré one cannot use clippings from printed material to serve as the original for halftone reproductions.

When two halftone negatives of the same subject have been properly made (one is usually toned down also) they can be used with excellent two-color results. Brown with black for desert scenes and green with black for forests and meadows are especially effective.

Sometimes a color is added to a halftone area by printing a tint block with the halftone, thus adding a flat color uniformly across the surface. This method is easier and cheaper but produces less spectacular results.

Originals in color, such as color photographs, slides, oil paintings and the like can also be faithfully reproduced, but in a different manner. In those cases, the different colors must be separated from the original to permit different impressions for each color. All colors can be recreated in print by separating the three primary colors and black from the original, then printing from plates made to carry each of the primaries and black to paper. Other colors are formed by the blending of the four inks.

7-26 The "screen door" look of this halftone is caused by the clashing of two halftone screens. It is because of this moiré effect that a picture clipped from a publication usually cannot be original copy for a second reproduction.

Called *process* color, printing from color separations is discussed further in Chapter 11.

Production Treatment Is Secondary

This chapter's fairly extensive discussion of production treatments for photographs and other images must be kept in proper perspective. Silhouette, vignette, reverse and other such treatments can be helpful in making printed communications sucessful and must, therefore, be part of our storehouse of options. On the other hand, nothing is gained from the use of a production technique that does not add to the effectiveness of an illustration. Even color should not be used for the sake of color alone. As we have already said, form is secondary to content. In the next chapter, the qualitative selection and editing of pictures and other illustrations for maximum effectiveness of communication will be discussed; the techniques of this chapter are only means to that end, not the end itself.

CHECKLIST: Some Points to Remember

1. For production, illustrations are divided into two types, line and halftone. Line illustrations contain only fulltones or none; halftones contain continuous tones blending from the lightest to the darkest.

2. Special treatments for line illustrations include reversing (making black in original white in reproduction) and Bendaying (adding a dot or other textured pattern to give the effect of middle tone).

3. Line charts show trends over time, bar graphs show comparison of quantity, and pie charts show relative sizes of the parts of a whole. Pictographs use pictures of items, rather than just bars or sections, to show quantities.

4. Schematic diagrams are vital in presenting technical information about how a process or mechanical device works.

5. Continuous-tone originals, such as photographs, are ordinarily reproduced with square finish, that is, with right-angle corners. Other shapes are possible, however.

6. Continuous-tone originals can be reproduced without background (silhouette) or with the background seeming to fade away (vignette).

7. Reproductions of continuous-tone originals are made by being screened to form dots to carry ink to paper, creating the various tones. Special screens using parallel lines, concentric circles or textured patterns can be used for special effects in the reproductions.

8. A continuous-tone original can be reproduced in the full-or-no-tone style of a line drawing with the production technique called a line conversion. Addition of a middle tone in the same or an additional color creates what is called a posterization.

9. Line copy and continuous-tone originals can be combined in a single reproduction; a line illustration (including type) superimposed on a halftone creates a surprint combination. When the line copy is reproduced in reverse, the reproduction is a reverse combination.

10. In using illustrations as background for type, sufficient contrast must be maintained for good legibility; only the lightest areas should be surprinted and only the darkest should be reversed.

11. Vignette treatment can help create a soft impression, one of beauty or age; silhouettes can help add force to the presentation of products in ads because of the elimination of background and increase in contrast.

8

Illustration Editing

Chapter 7 discussed the functions and forms of illustrations in graphic communications. This chapter takes a more qualitative look at illustrations, with a special emphasis on photography. In fact, almost every statement made here about photography could also be applied to line art or any other illustration. In this chapter, we are concerned with effective editing of illustrations for maximum visual impact.

There is a sad but predictable irony in visual communications today. Everyone seems to have a camera, and many have distastefully labeled themselves "shooters" as they toy with their automatic light metering systems, sonar-like focusing and motorized film advance. Perhaps this state of the "art" received its most appropriate commentary several years ago when a gorilla photographed herself in a mirror with an automatic camera; that image appeared on the cover of *National Geographic*, and that gorilla was paid handsome cover rate.

Even though we seem to have a world of photographic paparazzi busy at work, many of our publications continue to be innundated by irrelevant, dull and trite illustrations. The irony is that ever since the first

8-1 Picture editors face many challenges, not the least of which is finding a balance between form and function. Each image they review must be evaluated for its ability to work with content and design. They would by delighted with Patrick Sullivan's exciting sports photograph, which has strong design and excellent content. (*Courtesy Patrick Sullivan/Kansas City Star*)

use of the halftone engraving more than a century ago, people have been saying that ours is a visual age. One would think that with the growth of technology and sophistication, we would see strong visual communication in today's mass media. Not so. It is improving, but slowly.

One reason for this problem is a lack of "visual literacy." There are many pictures and illustrations available, but people aren't always sure how to use them for maximum graphic impact. In most work situations, there is an uncertain road between exposed film and final publication. A sentry of sorts waits on that road, deciding which traffic will pass—and in which form it will reach its destination. That person is an editor, whose task seems deceptively straightforward: to produce visual communication that is concise yet strong in content, that reflects both simplicity and innovation in design, and that works meaningfully in concert with the written word. The picture editor faces an important and sometimes overwhelming task (Figure 8-1).

Many misconceptions hamper picture editors. Perhaps they think they have too little technical experience to make good photographic judgment. Some editors think that a photograph or illustration is only a space-filling adjunct to the communications package. Others believe that skill in picture selection, layout and design require a strong fine arts background. These are unfortunate views because they undermine and damage the visual product.

Illustration editing is both a natural and necessary function in print production. Given the myriad of images that are being produced in mass communications today, there is much need for selectivity, interpretation and presentation.

This chapter concentrates on three areas, especially as they relate to photographic editing: picture selection, basic elements of layout and design with pictures, and the legal aspects of picture use.

Factors in Picture Selection

It may seem odd to you that a competent photo editor *does not* have to be a gifted, sensitive photographer. Indeed, many photographers would make terrible editors. Many photo editors today may be capable of critiquing and using a photographer's work but would be out of place trying to do the photographer's job. Nonetheless, it does help the editor to have *some* technical experience in photography, both in the darkroom and in the field.

But the requirements of visual literacy remain paramount. As an editor, you must be able to review many images in a relatively short time. You will have to ask of the image: What does the picture "say"? Is it spontaneous? Is it accurate? Will the audience understand what you and the photographer are trying to communicate?

The aim of any picture editor or photographer is a solid critical standard. It has three components: technical, contextual and philosophical.

Technical Considerations

There are several technical factors that editors must consider in the selection and use of photographs. Before these are listed, however, it must be emphasized that these considerations are downplayed in favor of powerful content. A good example is Figure 8-2, Stanley Forman's 1977 Pulitzer Prize–winning picture of a black man in Boston being attacked by an anti-busing demonstrator who was "armed" with an American flag. This is a strong testament to the editor's creed that *form should follow function.*

But generally, there are several accepted standards of technical quality.

The Image Should Be Properly Exposed and Developed
An underexposed picture (Figure 8-3) lacks shadow detail, and its clarity suffers even more in reproduction. Its negative (Figure 8-4) is obviously thin, and the print completes the tale of woe. An overdeveloped negative (Figure 8-5) will give a print of high contrast, blocked whites and excessive grain (Figure 8-6). Even with the most modern printing methods, these pictures will suffer from an exaggerated form of what normal prints do in reproduction: They will have a contrast gain and a loss of shadow detail.

8-2 Although this picture is somewhat blurred and low in contrast, the hurried, dramatic nature of this anti-busing demonstration brought the photographer his second Pulitzer Prize in two years. (*The Soiling of Old Glory,* © Stanley Forman)

There is no substitute for a normally exposed and developed negative (Figure 8-7) and the resulting print with a normal tonal range and detail (Figure 8-8). Even with a less than desirable reproduction process, this print will be published with good clarity and definition. It is important to set a consistent standard for photographic quality; one economic benefit of this shows up in the halftoning process, when prints are screened for reproduction. If the prints are consistent in tone and detail they can be more effectively "gang photographed" (rephotographed in a grouping of one exposure on a larger negative sheet). Not only does this save money,

8-3 An underexposed photograph. Note its lack of shadow detail.

8-4 The negative of the print in Figure 8-3.

8-5 An overdeveloped negative. Note its high contrast.

8-6 Print of the negative in Figure 8-5. Its contrast and excessive grain make it unsuitable for high-quality reproduction.

but such consistency in tone and detail gives an element of harmony to one's layout and design.

Exposure Requirements for Color. As you will see in Chapter 11, correction to color imbalances that are due to poor exposure, improper development or use of film improperly matched to lighting conditions can be very expensive. The public is becoming more attuned to color. It can recognize poor-quality color, and that will affect the readability and acceptance of your printed product. In addition, because color transparencies (slides) and prints have to be separated into four printing plates for reproduction—yellow, magenta, cyan and black—any error in color exposure or development probably will be magnified in this preparation.

In normal color exposure, colors are properly saturated; that is, they have normal values, and their detail is not obscured by high contrast.

The Image Must Have Acceptable Focus

Some people equate grain pattern on a print with poor focus. However, films that have a tight, sharp grain pattern may be "soft" because the light rays that intersect in the camera to form an image have not been properly aligned. That softness is related to improper focusing of the image—an operator problem—and this weakness can detract from the effectiveness of the image. When a negative or print is "sharp," the image is clear and crisp around its focal point, and the eye is aware of edge sharpness around the area of intended focus.

Editors must understand the difficulties that cause focus problems. Low-light situations that require use of large apertures (f-stops) can hamper depth of focus and accurate focusing. Having to hand-hold long lenses in low light can also affect focusing. If the problem seems chronic, however, discuss it with the photographer. In most cases, an editor should

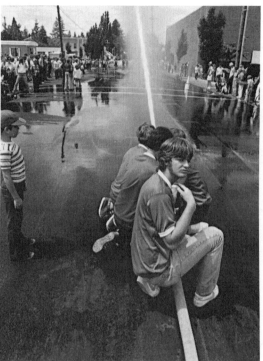

8-7 A normally exposed and developed negative.

8-8 Print of negative in Figure 8-7. Note its good tone and detail.

demand to work with crisp, clean images—no matter how grainy the film is because of the emulsion speed required. These images are clearer and have more impact. They put no constraints on picture size. So— establish a standard for sharpness and stay with it.

An editor cannot always discern sharpness and detail from a contact (proof) sheet alone (Figure 8-9). That print may be too dark or on a textured paper. It is *always* a good idea to look at the negatives on a light table to make a final judgement.

Print Quality Should Be Consistent and Professional

A good print (Figure 8-10) should contain a normal range of tones from deep black to textureless white; it should be light enough to reproduce well; and it should have good detail, especially in shadow areas and skin tones. It is a poor statement about editing and selection if an editor accepts prints that are excessively contrasty or that are overly manipulated, such as in Figure 8-11, where excessive "burning in" of an area creates abnormally dark tones.

Two other technical matters have a bearing on print quality and selection.

8-9 A proof or "contact" sheet. These small images give an editor an idea of relative exposure and detail, but they are not infallible about image sharpness. Always refer to the negative for your final judgment.

8-10 A high-quality print with no manipulations and with good range of tones.

8-11 An overly manipulated print that draws unnecessary attention to its unnatural form. The darkness on the edges is caused by a process called "burning in."

The Textured Print. A print surface that is not smooth can cause problems in photographic reproduction. A surface that has a pebble or linenlike texture could dull detail and cause troublesome light flare when halftone negatives are made. Plain-surface prints, whether glossy or matte, are best.

8-12 An example of "direct flash" exposure. The raw light of an electronic flash unit bleaches skin tones and throws off distracting shadows.

8-13 When the light from the flash unit is "bounced" or diffused, the shadows are removed, and the skin tones look more natural.

Using Direct Electronic Flash. This raw, undiffused light casts unacceptable shadows on the subject and often washes out skin tones (Figure 8-12). In most lighting situations, this type of flash is unnecessary and unprofessional. Insist on a more diffused, natural lighting situation, such as electronic flash "bounced off" a reflective surface before it strikes the subject (Figure 8-13).

Content Considerations

In evaluating content of photographs for publication, an editor needs to be a bit of a reporter. What *information* do the pictures contain? It is vital that an editor uses a picture that communicates with accuracy and impact, rather than just picking one that is "graphically pleasing." Indeed, content evaluation is the most difficult aspect of picture selection.

Three factors are important in content consideration: relevance, simplicity and impact. If a photograph or illustration meets these criteria, it is a strong and usable image.

Relevance

How well does the picture complement the assignment or story? You won't like your response to that question if: (1) you assign a picture session without giving "detailed" information about the story to the photographer; (2) you make picture selections *before* you see the completed story; and (3) you try to lay out the pictures *before* you have seen the complete photographic take. In other words, your picture editing won't work unless you have the conviction (and practice) of having your pictures work in partnership with the copy in your communications package.

A photograph is relevant—and usable—if it helps to communicate the theme of the story or presentation, if it illustrates a major point in the story, or if it can stand as an informational device with very little copy.

A photograph flirts with irrelevance if it is only *incidental* to the story theme or if it gives an image contrary to the story's emphasis. In this context, the photograph does little more than fill space.

Copy and art must be coordinated and complementary. The impression must be singular. Consider the following example.

If you were editing a story with art about an elderly, asthmatic woman who was being forced, by economic circumstance and bureaucratic bumbling, to face another winter in her ramshackle house without proper heat and fuel, which one of the following images would you use to illustrate this story? Figure 8-14: The woman stands cheerfully outside her small cabin with her favorite dog. It is well-composed, but the mood is wrong for the story because we lack a close view of her environment. Figure 8-15: We see more of her isolation and infirmity here, and we are aware of her dependence on wood as fuel. But the mood is not quite right yet. Figure 8-16: This interior view of her two-room cabin shows her "family," her possessions and the wood stove on which she cooks frozen TV dinners, and next to which she sleeps on winter nights. The sign on the wall is her statement of philosophy; we somehow learn more about her in this picture.

Of the three images, Figure 8-16 is clearly the most relevant to a story about this woman's plight. The others only suggest that information.

An editor might ask, "Why not use a wide exterior view of her cabin with her in the foreground?" A response, with the factor of relevance in mind, would be that

1. she lives *inside* the cabin and
2. the outside image is too posed and static.

It takes time to make good photographs. For the photographer, it means being sensitive and establishing relationships with subjects. For the editor, it means patience with a photographer trying to get the "right" image and the high standards to accept nothing less.

Remember—a picture doesn't just help story content. It is an *integral* part of it. Understand the purpose of the assignment and the theme of the story, and picture selection will come more easily.

8-14 through 8-16   This series provides different views of the elderly woman's living situation. Figure 8-16, however, has the most impact for the proposed story.

8-17 A picture that could have been improved with reduction in background clutter.

Simplicity

This is an important factor in both photographic composition and page design. In terms of content, it is important that a picture has a dominant theme and is not hampered by extraneous detail. A simple, direct photograph aids both recognition and understanding.

Study some of the work of the world's great photographers, and while you may note different styles, you also will see the clarity and simplicity of their images. They are direct, even to the point of being overwhelming. Look, for example, at work by W. Eugene Smith, Walker Evans, Dorothea Lange and of such contemporaries as Brian Lanker, Mary Ellen Mark and Joel Meyerowitz. For the most part, their images contain only a few elements. Usually, there is one strong element supported by several key but lesser details. These pictures are composed for clarity, not clutter.

A look at several photographs will help you understand the criteria for simplicity and directness.

In Figure 8-17, the bucket brigade member is dominant, but the clutter of crowd detail is evident because of good depth of focus. A change of angle to the right and a depth reduction with a larger lens aperture would have made this picture much easier to view.

8-18 and 8-19   Note the difference in clarity between these pictures. Figure
8-19 obviously is a much clearer and direct image.

8-20   This is an example of how a clear,
dominant foreground
creates a distinctive im-
age. Note how back-
ground is thrown out of
focus.

In Figure 8-18, the face of the chimney sweep is slightly obscured, and a tree interrupts his outline. But in Figure 8-19, both his face and outline are clearer. This difference in "lines" is really not subtle; it is what makes one picture so obviously better than the other.

In Figure 8-20, the wheel chair marathoner is dominant—he is the picture's key element. Although the photographer used a wide angle lens that normally creates greater depth of focus, he used a large f-stop (aperture) to suppress that depth. In so doing, he blurs the crowd in the background. The picture is more simple and clear because it stands in relief.

An image must have *subject focus*, just as a news story should establish its theme in the lead paragraph. You must expect this of your photographers, and your editing must reflect this understanding.

Impact

A picture might be relevant and have a clear, thematic focus, but it must also be able to stir reaction. When a picture has impact, the viewer is overcome by the mood and meaning of the image. The viewer is drawn closer to the story. The attraction may be pathos or humor, but it is magnetic. Rosanne Olson's picture of a young leukemia victim undergoing a painful bone marrow test (Figure 8-21) is a good example of an image with impact. With only the young boy in sharp focus and all the arms of the unseen people around him out of the camera's depth of field, the picture draws in the viewer with its emotion and simplicity.

In addition to having impact, a strong picture has solid, *relevant* content and strong, *simple* focus. There are no frills, no excesses. When your picture has met the test of these factors, you can be confident of your picture selection.

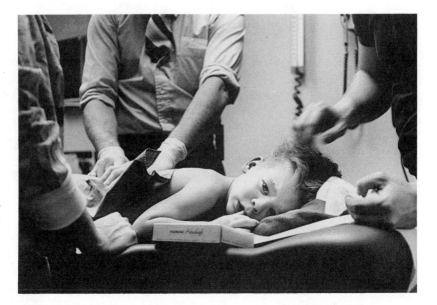

8-21 Visual impact. Strong focus and uncluttered content in this picture of a young leukemia victim give a dramatic, unmistakable message.
(© Rosanne Olson)

When the Photography Is Below Par

What happens when your photographic take doesn't meet your expectations? What if all those photos are weak and there is no time to repeat the assignment? Unfortunately, this is not a rare occurrence. When this happens, you usually have three options.

Use no photographs at all. This should be done only if the image truly detracts from the presentation. Poor focus, technical problems and irrelevant content may force you into this decision. Don't be too concerned about eliminating a picture if you have others on the page. Don't weaken your publication by using poor photography.

Downplay picture sizing and placement. This is a reminder not to make a weak picture too dominant on a page. One of the biggest mistakes editors make when they have a "visual rebirth" is to anchor all pages with a large photograph. Images deserve a large size only if their content warrants it. If the photograph is poor but necessary to the story, be discreet in your sizing.

Be creative in cropping and use of graphic devices. There are many ways to dress up a page or layout when images are weak. This "silk purse from a sow's ear" approach can be helpful, but it is superficial at best. It is no substitute for solid content. Don't overdress.

Philosophical Considerations

It is appropriate to discuss technical and content aspects of picture selection, but where does philosophy fit in? How do you quantify personal tastes and attitudes and present them in textbook fashion?

Obviously you don't. The purpose of this brief section is to make people aware of their philosophies and of the attitudes of their audiences. Here is a sampler of questions. Perhaps you can add a few, too.

1. When does a picture seem "posed" to you? Under what circumstances would you use it?
2. When would you discard normal content considerations in favor of a striking image that has stronger graphics than relevance? (Example, you have a technically weak and routine "moment" picture of the winner of the state high school pole vault competition, but you also have a well-exposed image of the tenth-place finisher who throws down his pole in disgust after failing at a mediocre height.)
3. What is your definition of "embarrassing" content? Under what circumstance would you use it?
4. Assuming that you have the choice in your publication, do you prefer black-and-white or color pictures? Can some images only convey their impact in black and white?
5. Which picture do you prefer—the abstract image that suggests different things to different people or the concrete, direct image that leaves little room for interpretation?

Some of these questions may seem futile because you may think that technical and no-nonsense content factors will force your tastes and attitudes out of the decision-making arena. But many of your preferences do stay with you. You should try to understand them. A simple checklist of your photographic likes, dislikes and bad experiences can start your review. Consider, for example, the editor who adamantly states that he dislikes grainy film, any shadows on faces outdoors (he demands that photographers use fill flash in those situations), and any picture selection that will face the "wrong" way on the page. Yet others might retort that a well-focused but grainy image can be stark, dramatic and graphically pleasing; that "studio" conditions outdoors not only are unrealistic but badly contrived; and that a picture with strong content can't be automatically dismissed because of a problem with page position.

Like this rigid editor, many of us need to air our photographic attitudes before letting them control too many of our picture selection decisions.

The Role of Illustration in Layout and Design

Publication designer and author Allen Hurlburt stresses that picture selection and picture layout are part of the same process. Trying to create an effective layout without knowing the choice and personality of the typography, or without feeling the meter and impact of the copy is to engage in a blissful—but ignorant—exercise in drawing shapes around oceans of white space.

Although this book does not focus on all aspects of layout and design, several of its chapters give an overview of general principles. This section focuses on several tenets that editors and designers should follow.

Art Should Complement the Copy

Photographs and copy should not go trailing off in different directions. The purpose of a layout is to create a visual package of information. If the copy focuses on one topic and the art brings up totally new or unrelated information, you have the main elements of layout at cross-purposes. The reader will be confused. On the other hand, the copy should not be a giant-sized caption for the art. Together, *both* elements should bring harmony to the page.

Have a Strong Illustration Anchor the Page

Just as the lead paragraph of a story should bind the reader to the copy, so too should the lead picture draw the reader. Using too many small illustrations creates visual confusion. Select an image that will showcase

8-22 and 8-23   Excellent page design with strong use of photographs. Note the dominant photograph and the smaller one that anchors the page. Examine the basketball photograph (8-23) and observe how it meets all the tests of a strong image. (Courtesy the *Springfield (OR) News* and *Betty Udesen*)

the page and illustrate the key story. In Figure 8-22, this newspaper's front sports page contains just two pictures, but one is obviously dominant. This gives the page a clean, strong design, a characteristic also seen in the main photograph (Figure 8-23). Look also at the various page design examples in Chapters 14 and 15. Which page looks strong to you?

Many Photographs Benefit from Cropping and Sizing

Some photographers and editors may claim that the real strength of composition lies in the "full frame" of the image, but this school of thought doesn't consider the reality of photography, especially photojournalism. Weak angles, insufficient time to get close, clutter, and most important, "buried" content are reasons why we may change the shape of an illustration, emphasize certain portions, or play size up or down. Consider

8-24 and 8-25   Note the difference in impact and content focus between these two pictures. Searching for the proper content in a full-frame picture and cropping it appropriately can have great reward. (Courtesy *Oregon Daily Emerald*)

the photograph in Figure 8-24. It is a well-focused picture of volleyball action, but its full frame (shown with the distinctive black borders of the negative frame) reveals too much clutter and weak emphasis of theme. Compare it with its cropped and re-sized version in Figure 8-25. Just as you will seek a dominant picture for your page, so too should you try to make the "raw material" of the image as refined and dominant as possible.

Don't Leave Content Trailing in Form's Wake

This is another way of saying that seductive packaging of material will not always save weak illustrations. True, there is usually benefit in strong design, but choosing an illustration for its design strength rather than for its content diminishes the information function of your publication. Be sure that you communicate information in addition to design.

Legal Aspects of Illustration Use

In addition to properly selecting illustrations and using them effectively in layout and design, an editor must be skilled enough to detect potential legal problems in picture use.

The main legal concerns of the picture editor are defamation, commercial appropriation and ownership.

Defamation

Illustrations can be as damaging to a person's reputation as mistake-laden or malicious copy. Pictures are said to be defamatory when they cast a "false light" on an individual or group. Ironically, it is usually the accompanying text that throws a picture out of its context and causes the entire presentation to be damaging. Consider the woes of a metropolitan newspaper when it discovered that its picture story about prostitution downtown used an illustration that identified an innocent passerby as a procurer. That person actually was in another frame of the proof sheet. An important rule here is to make sure that the context of the story and the presentation fit in with the true content of the picture. Editors: Talk with your photographers before, during and *after* the assignment. They were there!

Commercial Appropriation

Suppose that your publication printed a touching but humorous picture of a tearful child watching helplessly as a dog eats his spilled ice cream cone. Suppose also that 10 days after that publication, an advertising agency contacted you and wanted to use that picture to illustrate its care for children in the products it makes. In those two actions you would have a perfect case study of how a news or human interest photograph, used legally in its original context, becomes distorted and manipulative if permission is not secured. Such a mistake is costly; hefty damages can be assessed in such lawsuits. The correct procedure here would be to secure a "model release"—permission from the subject to use the photograph in the context stated by the agreement. This use is, of course, paid for, but that cost won't match the financial loss suffered if the publication is sued for unlawful appropriation.

Ownership of Work

Since passage of a revised Copyright Act in 1976, authors and artists have enjoyed more ownership rights. Today, if a photographer sells you several prints for use in your publication, it is assumed that he or she *owns the copyright* of that work and is only selling you a limited, one-time right to use it. Under the law, the only time it is assumed that the publication owns all right to the work is

1. if the work's creator is a staff employee, not a freelancer
2. if the creator signs a document acknowledging that he or she is turning over all rights to that work to the publication.

Editors should also know that just because a freelancer is assigned to do work that has been conceptually developed by the publication, that work still is the property of the freelancer unless an agreement to the contrary is negotiated. Remember that if a freelancer is going to agree to that, he or she will ask for a much higher fee because of the revenue loss from not being able to resell that work at a later date in another market. This also may be the case when you purchase stock or file photographs from a picture agency or syndicate. Find out what you are buying and its terms. Always commit these arrangements to writing to avoid legal headaches later.

An Editor's CHECKLIST

When working with illustrations and the people who make them, remember these main points:

1. The content value of an illustration far outweighs its importance in design or form. Clean, functional design does not have to depend on the content of the illustration for success in form. However, presentation of information fails when weak content is glossed over by flashy design.
2. You must demand strong technical work, especially in photography. Content still rules, but a constant lack of technical expertise will hurt your product.
3. When searching for content, examine the illustration according to its context. Then see if that matches the intent of the copy. When they match, your presentation will be more cohesive.
4. An illustration does not always have to be used. Content, as always, is your criterion. When you have weak illustrations, strong design and creative typography can make a more effective presentation.

5. Most photographs can be cropped. Look inside each photographic frame and see where the simplest, most direct information lies. The same is true for sizing; strong pictures deserve large sizing.

6. Remember that defamatory pictures, those used to promote a product or concept without the subject's consent, and those whose ownership has not been agreed to contractually can be costly headaches for a publication. Be aware of your legal standing, and let professionalism and strong ethics be your guide.

9

Preparing Illustrations for Production

Photographs and other illustrations are "copy" for the printer, as are the text and titles included in printed messages. As component parts of a piece of printing, they undergo the same basic processing steps as those involved in word editing: correction of errors, marking of printing instructions and fitting to space.

As pointed out in the previous chapter, photographs, like news stories or magazine articles, are sometimes verbose, poorly constructed, too large, too small or mechanically flawed. They must be edited to tell what they are supposed to convey, reconstructed to give emphasis where it is needed, and reduced or enlarged to fit space.

Much of the editing suggested in Chapter 8 is accomplished through a process called *cropping*, the figurative cutting away of parts of the photo to leave only pertinent portions for reproduction in print. Cropping is figurative because rarely will portions of a photo be literally cut away with scissors or blade. Instead, small marks called *crop marks* are used to denote the portion of width and depth desired to be included in a reproduction.

177

Crop marks, therefore, are tools for improving the impact of illustrations. On the other hand, they are vital tools for insuring that illustrations will appear in print as planned. In this sense, crop marks are used to communicate with printers and to force illustrations to fit their space.

Cropping for Production

Cropping for production and cropping for content must obviously go hand-in-hand. However, to provide emphasis here on crop marks as production tools, we will set aside (insofar as it is possible) cropping to improve the content of illustrations. This emphasis should not be taken to mean that the content of an illustration is ever totally forgotten.

Placing Crop Marks for Production

Every illustration that enters production should contain four crop marks. These marks set the dimensions of a drawing or photograph; without them, the illustration has no established width or depth. Although printers sometimes will assume that the lack of crop marks means that the

9-1 No photo or other illustration is ready for production without four crop marks: two to set the width and two to set the depth. The two setting the width can be either at the top or bottom, and those setting the depth can be on the right or on the left. They cannot, however, jump from one side to the other. (© Duncan McDonald)

9-2 This line illustration also requires crop marks to set its dimensions. The marks should include within them all portions of the drawing that are to be included in the reproduction; the distances between them provide the dimensions for computing enlargements and reductions.

entire width and depth of the original is to appear in print, that assumption cannot be counted upon.

Four crop marks are required because two are needed to show the width and two are needed to show the depth, or length. One might think that eight would be better, but unless a tilt of the image is desired, four will do the job without creating the danger of an *undesired* tilt or out-of-square reproduction. In Figure 9-1, notice that two crop marks at the bottom clearly mark off the portion of the photo to be included in the width, and two on the right clearly show the depth. It should be obvious that two additional marks across the top to show width would have to be *absolutely* synchronized with the ones shown at the bottom or confusion about the exact dimension would result. Such accuracy of placement is almost impossible to insure. Consequently, we usually use four crop marks *only*, with absolute certainty of accuracy in production.

Crop marks must not appear in the printed reproduction, so they should be placed outside the image area, if possible. Certainly, we would not draw lines on the surface of the photo because (1) some portion of that line would be almost certain to drift into the image area, and (2) unless a grease pencil is used, the lines would ruin the photo for future use or for recropping to accommodate a change of mind.

Line drawings and other artwork need crop marks as much as photos do. If necessary, overlay sheets can be used to carry marks and other instructions, but no illustration is ready for production without the four crop marks. As we can see in Figure 9-2, crop marks are placed on drawings so all parts of the drawings fall inside them.

Marking for Production

With crop marks in place, instructions as to kind and size of reproduction can be added to complete the job of marking for production. As indicated in Chapter 7, there is a variety of reproductions available for illustrations—including line, reverse line, Benday line, square-finish halftone, geometrical shape halftone, special screen halftone, mortise, notch, vignette, silhouette, surprint combination, reverse combination, duotone and process color. These descriptive names must be indicated in instructions for the printer, usually on the backs of photos and somewhere in the margins of the artboard used for drawings. Overlay sheets are used to show the location of notches, mortises, silhouettes and line portions of combinations.

The desired size for a reproduction is usually noted in combination with any other instructions and can be specified in inches or picas or as a percentage of the original size. Because a line gauge in picas is usually used in doing layouts, it is more common to carry pica measurements over to illustrations from their use in columns, margins and other spatial dimensions. And the fact that printers must know the percentage of enlargement or reduction as they set their process cameras to get reproduction negatives causes many editors and graphic designers to stipulate the percentage of original size they want for the reproduction.

Illustrations can, of course, be reproduced the same size as the original. The stipulation *same size* or *ss* results in a reproduction with the same width and depth as the original. Although enlargements and reductions are easy to order, the two-dimensional character of illustrations often creates a sense of confusion among novices.

The discussion that follows concerning figuring enlargements and reductions requires an understanding of these two points: (1) percentage of enlargement or reduction of illustrations affects both dimensions, and (2) reproductions are always the same shape as the cropped original. Therefore, if an 8″ X 10″ photo (width is always the first dimension) is ordered as a 50 percent reduction, the width would reduce 50 percent to 4″ as the depth reduces 50 percent to 5″. Also, because the 8 X 10 is a vertical rectangle (deeper than it is wide), the reproduction (4 X 5) will have the identical shape. Keep these two principles in mind.

Figuring Percentage of Enlargement or Reduction

To figure the enlargement or reduction of an illustration as it enters production, we need only to divide one original dimension (let's say the width) into the corresponding reproduction dimension (width) and the answer is the percentage. Please note that the unit of measure (inch) must be constant. For example, if we have an original 8″ wide and it must reduce to fit a space only 4″ wide, we divide the 8 into 4 and find that the reduction is 50 percent. In graphics, reduction percentage always relates to the *percentage of the original*; that is, an 80 percent reduction is the reduction *to* 80 percent.

We must understand here also that we figure percentage of reductions or enlargements for two reasons: to know what percentage to specify *and* to be able to know both dimensions of the reproduction so we can complete layout plans. We can, of course, divide one dimension into the other to find what it will be. Generally, however, it is easier to set up two ratios, such as: $8/4 = 10/X$. For two ratios to equal one another, the products of their means and extremes must be equal, so $8X = 40$. Di-

Figuring Percentage of Reduction for Illustrations: Step by Step

1. Divide one original dimension into its corresponding reproduction dimension, being sure to use the same unit of measure for both. The answer is the percentage of the original in which the illustration will be reproduced.

9-3 The distances between crop marks establish an original width and an original depth. These dimensions establish a shape, either a vertical rectangle, a square, or a horizontal rectangle.

viding on both sides of the equals sign by 8, we find that $X = 5$. This method is the foundation for using mechanical devices that complete this figuring without any mathematical calculation.

Figuring Proportions of Enlargements or Reductions

As noted earlier, not only will enlargements or reductions affect both dimensions equally, but the shape of the reproduction is always the shape of the original. There is no way to take an original that has finally been cropped to be a vertical rectangle and reproduce it as anything but a vertical rectangle. The same is true of squares and horizontals (see Figures 9-4, 9-5, and 9-6).

Let's illustrate this point with some obvious figures. We have a photo cropped to 30 picas wide and 60 picas deep, a rather extreme vertical with the width only half the depth. All reproductions from this rectangle will have that same shape, with the width only half the depth, such as 15 picas by 30, 10 by 20, and so on. Look at the stages in Figures 9-4, 9-5, and 9-6. Starting at the left are vertical rectangles that have gone through a series of reductions. Their shape is constant. Squares when enlarged or reduced are still squares, and horizontal rectangles remain horizontal.

We can use two sets of ratios here also, with these ratios expressing the shapes of the rectangles. If an original is 30 by 60 and is reduced to 15 picas wide, the ratios would be: $30/60 = 15/X$, so $30X = 900$, and $X = 30$. We can find any missing dimension from the other three, just as we could with the ratios used in connection with percentage of enlargement or reduction. Here, however, we can use different units of measure for the original than for the reduction; the 5-inch by 10-inch original when reduced to 15 picas wide will also be 30 picas deep. Just remember which dimension will be involved in the answer if you mix them in the ratios.

9-4 *Left:* This photo, reduced to 50 percent and then to 25 percent of its original size, maintains its extreme vertical shape while changing its size. Remember that the original dimensions, hence the shape, are established by the crop marks. (© Duncan McDonald)

9-5 *Above:* Cropped to be square in its original size, this photo must remain a square as it is enlarged or reduced for publication. (© Duncan McDonald)

9-6 This horizontal photo remains in the same horizontal shape as it is enlarged or reduced. (© Duncan McDonald)

Some Everyday Picture-Production Problems

Everyone involved with printed communication is involved with scaling and proportioning illustrations. Rarely can we reproduce an illustration the same size as the original. Photos, for example, are usually provided as 11 X 14 inches, 14 X 11, 8 X 10, 10 X 8, 5 X 7, or 7 X 5, the six shapes in three standard sizes of enlargements generally made by photographers. These originals will then be reproduced in sizes ranging from a half-column width in a newspaper to full pages in a magazine or newspaper. Working with enlargements or reductions stems from one of two directions:

1. to find out how much space to allow on a layout plan, or
2. to find out how to change the shape of the original through cropping to make it fit a reproduction shape.

Let's look at some of these common examples from various media, doing our computations by hand. Once we understand the principles involved, the use of calculators and mechanical aids will do all the figuring for us.

Scaling Before Layouts Are Finished

Finding Depth When Width Is Known

The most common problem for newspaper editors is to receive a photo that is about 8″ wide and 10″ deep, showing the face of a person (a "mug shot"), that is to be used, essentially as is, in one column. In such situations, editors first use the required four crop marks to establish the original dimensions of the photo. As they do so, they make it as easy as possible for themselves by avoiding fractions; newspaper layout practices, by necessity, are not precise. Assuming that crop marks were set at 48 picas for width and 60 for depth ($8″ \times 10″$), editors probably would divide the 48 into the 14 picas of column width to determine that the percentage of reduction is approximately 29. To find the depth that the reproduction will occupy on the layout, they probably would then multiply the 60 picas in the original depth by 29 percent to know that it would be about 17.5 picas.

If they use ratios, they probably would simplify as much as possible and use inches: $8/2.3 = 10/X$, and solve to find that the depth would be almost 2.9 inches.

Finding Width When Depth Is Known

Magazine editors, also working with established column widths, probably would go through the same procedure with most of their photo processing. Sometimes, however, the depth is critical but the width can vary, so the figures for depth are used to figure percentage of reduction. At any rate, because one layout dimension is usually flexible, the problems are elementary and routine because there is an established pattern to them.

A typical problem to find reproduction width would start with a photo cropped to 8 inches wide and 7 inches deep. The reproduction width is flexible but depth is fixed at 18 picas. Translating the 18 picas into 3 inches, the percentage of reduction would be approximately 42 (7 divided by 3). The width needed would then be 42 percent of 8, or about 3.4 inches. We can find the same answer by using the reduction ratios, $8/X = 7/3$, $7X = 24$, and X, again, equals about 3.4 inches.

Figuring How to Crop to Fit Space

For designers of advertisements, brochures, posters and other transient materials, the problems of figuring enlargements and reductions can vary considerably. The greater freedom of layout and design now being felt by newspaper and magazine designers has tended to increase the number and complexity of problems with which they must deal. Whenever layouts are made first and copyfitting and photoscaling are done second, these special problems quickly show themselves.

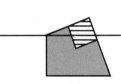

Scaling to Find Reproduction Dimensions to Complete Layouts: Step by Step

A. Thinking in terms of percentage of change (keep units of measure constant):

1. To find depth of the reproduction when width is known, use distances between crop marks as original dimensions and use the ratios:

$$\frac{\text{Original Width}}{\text{Reproduction Width}} = \frac{\text{Original Depth}}{X}$$

2. To find reproductive width when depth is known, use the same ratio in this manner:

$$\frac{\text{Original Width}}{X} = \frac{\text{Original Depth}}{\text{Reproduction Depth}}$$

B. Thinking in terms of constant shapes:

1. To find depth of reproduction when width is known, use distances between crop marks as original dimensions and use the ratio:

$$\frac{\text{Original Width}}{\text{Original Depth}} = \frac{\text{Reproduction Width}}{X}$$

2. To find reproduction width when depth is known, use the same ratio in this manner:

$$\frac{\text{Original Width}}{\text{Original Depth}} = \frac{X}{\text{Reproduction Depth}}$$

Scaling to Fit Completed Layouts

The key to understanding photoscaling problems that stem from the need to crop originals to fit a layout is to think in terms of shapes, working from the layout back to the original illustration. If the layout calls for a square, the cropped illustration must be square; if the layout calls for an extreme vertical, the original must be an extreme vertical, and so on. Figuring is done before final crop marks are placed.

Use of two ratios relating to shape (proportion) and not percentage of reduction provides the efficient way to handle these cases. For example, let's suppose a magazine editor finds a picture that he desperately wants to use as a full-page bleed on this month's cover. The shot is a panoramic view of a mountain range and is 10 inches wide and 8 inches deep. A full-page bleed in a standard magazine measures 52 picas wide and 68 picas deep ($8\frac{1}{2}'' \times 11''$ plus an extra pica for each trimmed edge). Obviously, the reproduction must be a vertical shape and in this case it will be an enlargement. The editor would set up the reproduction ratio (52/68) and then see if the 10×8 can be converted into a vertical of the same proportion. All of the 8-inch depth will be used because to do otherwise makes the shape-changing still more difficult. He is then working with:

$$\frac{52}{68} = \frac{X}{8} \quad \text{So } 68X = 416, \text{ and } X = 6.1 \text{ inches.}$$

Assuming that the mountain scene can be cropped in width by 3.9 inches to 6.1 inches, it would be so marked and enlarged to fit. When this kind of cropping means deleting necessary detail from an illustration, it must be abandoned in favor of a change in layout or a new illustration that will conform to the desired shape.

We should repeat here that content in any printed communication is of primary importance, with form secondary. This principle applies to photos as it does to all other copy. Then, one might ask, should a layout *ever* dictate shape and size of illustrations? Shouldn't these dimensions be entirely a factor of what is in the original illustration? The answer to these questions is modified by reality; there are many instances in which size, shape and content must mutually be respected, and even some cases when content gives way slightly for form.

The preceding example of the full-page bleed for a magazine is a good example; some portions of the photo that might otherwise be included could be edited out to gain the advantage of a bleed shape and size. But *serious* injury to the communication capability of the original would not be tolerated.

Brochures, ads, posters, magazine ads and book pages are much more likely to be tied to form than are newspapers or newsletters, for example. Many of these media are carefully designed with the thought that all components will be made to fit the desired packaging. But even in such cases, though the designers scale photos as we suggest here (to fit the layout), prior planning results in photos basically composed to fit the layout shapes. The figuring, then, is just to guarantee a perfect rather than approximate fit.

For example, it is rare that an ad would be laid out to show a horizontal illustration, but the artist or photographer would present a vertical original. Basic shape would have been a stipulation of the original assignment. But even so, if an 18-pica by 20-pica vertical rectangle has been drawn in place for an ad, the original provided might very well be 5″ × 7″. To check its fit we start with: $\frac{18}{20} = \frac{5}{7}$. But does it? Five times 20 equals 100, and seven times 18 is 126, so the original needs some cropping to fit the space. In this case the seven must be cropped so that 18 times the new depth will exactly equal 100:

$$\frac{18}{20} = \frac{5}{X},\text{ so } 18X = 100, \text{ and } X = \text{approximately 5.5 inches.}$$

If about 1.5 inches can be cropped from the depth without spoiling the effectiveness of the photo, crop marks to make the original 5″ × 5½″ will be marked on the photo. The percentage of reduction would then be 60, the 5-inch width reducing to 18 picas (3 inches).

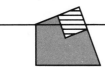

Scaling to Fit Layouts: Step by Step

1. To crop a vertical to fit a horizontal space:
   A. Make the original depth the unknown and solve with these ratios:

   $$\frac{\text{Original Width}}{X} = \frac{\text{Reproduction Width}}{\text{Reproduction Depth}}$$

2. To crop a horizontal to fit a vertical space:
   A. Make the original width the unknown and solve with these ratios:

   $$\frac{X}{\text{Original Depth}} = \frac{\text{Reproduction Width}}{\text{Reproduction Depth}}$$

3. To find which dimension must be cropped to alter a shape:
   A. Fill in both these ratios with figures:

   $$\frac{\text{Original Width}}{\text{Original Depth}} = \frac{\text{Reproduction Width}}{\text{Reproduction Depth}}$$

and cross multiply the means and the extremes. If they are equal, no change in original dimensions would be necessary. If they are not equal, the larger number is the product of the reproduction dimension times the *original dimension that must be cropped.* (If OW times RD is larger, width must be cropped; if OD times RW is larger, the depth must be cropped.)

Use of Proportion Wheels

Human effort and human error are reduced to a minimum by the use of mechanical devices called *proportion wheels* or *circular scalers* when preparing photos for reproduction. Personal calculators are also useful, but proportion wheels are designed especially to carry out all the calculations ordinarily involved in picture editing.

They are available at most bookstores and art supply houses for a small charge, but are also often available free from printers or other graphic art specialists, such as photoengravers. Usually made of cardboard *or* plastic, proportion wheels consist of two circles rimmed with numbers. The inner circle of numbers can be rotated.

The secret of the operation of the proportion wheels lies in the fact that any two numbers lined up across from each other on these wheels form a ratio (for example, 2 over 2) that is equal to all the other ratios around the wheel (for example, 1 over 1, 5 over 5, and so on). When the inner wheel in this case would be moved so the outer 2 is over 4, all ratios would be proportionate, 1 over 2, 4 over 8, 5.5 over 11, and so on up to 50 over 100.

Note the proportion wheel in Figure 9-7. It shows how to use the device for figuring percentage of reduction and missing dimensions based on percentage of reduction. In this case, the original dimensions are on the inner circle, and the reproduction figures on the outer. The wheel has been set to show that an 8 × 10 illustration is to be reduced to 4 by *X*. The wheel tells us that the new depth will be 5″ because that number is above the 10-inch dimension of the original.

By using the wheel in this fashion, we can look into the window marked "Percentage of Original Size" and find that the percentage of reduction is 50. When the 8″ width reduces to 50 percent of its original size the 10-inch dimension will reduce to 50 percent of its original size. Remember, here the same unit of measure must be used for all dimensions.

The wheel in Figure 9-8 is being used differently. Here we line up original dimensions across from each other, let's say 48 picas over 60 picas, and then look to the left for the reduction of the width to 20 picas and find the reproduction depth (25 picas) across from it. In this instance, we could mix our units of measure if it helps. Assuming that we had measured the photo in inches (8″ over 10″), we could still look across from 20 picas and find that the new depth would be 25 picas. In this case the wheel is reflecting proportion (shape), not percentage of reduction. The figure in the window would *not* be the percentage of reduction. That percentage could be found by moving the wheel to have the 48 picas of original width under the 20 picas of reproduction width and the figure in the window would reveal the correct 33.3 percent reduction.

We can use the wheel in Figure 9-9 to show how to find a missing

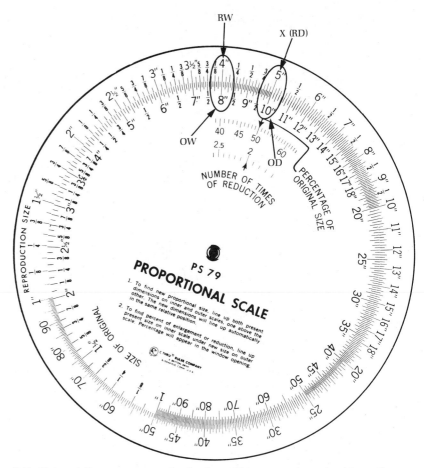

9-7 Determining percentage of reduction with a proportion wheel is easily accomplished by placing one reproduction dimension over its original counterpart. In this case we have the 4 over the 8. The percentage of reduction is shown in the window, and, in this case, it is 50 percent. Because all ratios formed around the wheel are equal, we can also locate the 10-inch original dimension on the inner wheel and find the reproduction depth (5 inches) just above it. As the 8 inches reduce 50 percent to 4 inches, the 10 inches will reduce 50 percent to 5 inches.

original dimension, i.e., an original dimension that must be cropped if the shape of the original is to be the same as the reproduction. This is the kind of problem that emerges when one is scaling illustrations to fit a layout.

In this case the layout dictates that the finished dimensions must be 20 picas by 25 picas and our uncropped original might be 10″ by 8″. Without figuring, these numbers should reveal that the reproduction will be a vertical and the 10″ by 8″ original is horizontal, so obviously the 10″ must be cropped to something less than 8″. Looking at the wheel in

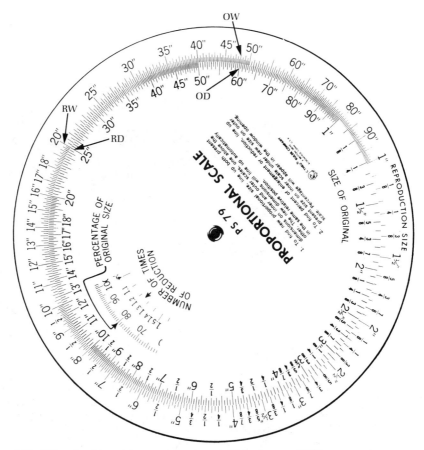

9-8 This wheel is set to use ratios to establish shapes. In this case, we can use inches for the original and picas for the reproduction. With the original figures lined up one over the other, we can look to the reproduction width (20 picas) on the top row and find the reproduction (25 picas) directly beneath it. The figure in the window is *not* the percentage of reduction.

Figure 9-9, we would set 20 over the 25 and look to the left and find the 8 on the inner wheel. The cropped width ($6\frac{3}{8}''$) is across from it. Should these shapes not be obvious, we could multiply 10×25 and find 250, and then 8×20 and find 160. This would indicate that the $10''$ width would have to be cropped.

Proportion wheels are marvelous devices; no one who scales many illustrations should be without one. But for novices, it is essential that they understand what is being done with the figures, or the wheel is really no help at all. In fact, some strange reproduction shapes can result when someone is trying to use a wheel without an appreciation of scaling (percentage of reduction) and proportioning (shapes being constant).

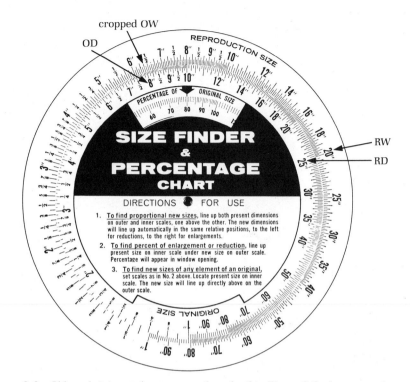

9-9 Although it is set the same as the wheel in Figure 9-8, the proportion wheel shown here can be used to illustrate the solution of a different scaling problem. Assuming that our layout is completed and the reproduction *must* be 20 picas by 25 picas, we can find that ratio on the wheel first. If our photo is 10 inches wide and 8 inches deep, we can see that the original width will have to be cropped to the amount shown just above the 8 (6⅜ inches).

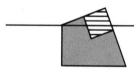

Using Proportion Wheels, Step by Step

1. To find percentage of reduction and missing reproduction dimension, place original dimension under its reproduction dimension and percentage of reduction will be shown in window. The missing reproduction dimension will be above the equivalent original dimension. Units of measure must be constant.
2. To find any missing reproduction dimension by lining up proportions, place the original width (outer wheel) over the original depth (inner wheel) and any *unknown* reproduction dimension will be across from the other *known* reproduction dimension.
3. To find any missing original dimension (missing because it must be cropped to be of the right shape for reduction), place the reproduction dimensions across from each other and the missing original dimension will be across from the known original. A sense of shape should reveal which original dimension should not be cropped.

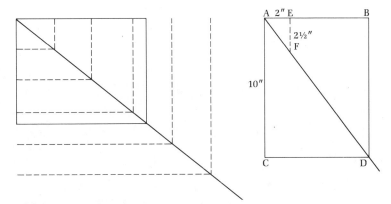

9-10 *Left:* Diagonal system of photograph scaling works because any rectangle formed by right angle lines from adjacent sides to a diagonal is the same shape as the original rectangle. Missing dimensions can simply be measured without any figuring involved.

9-11 *Right:* Finding depth when width is known: Measure reproduction width (2 inches) across width A-B. Then measure from point E to find the reproduction depth, E-F.

Use of a Diagonal

Another method for scaling illustrations uses a diagonal line or a mechanical scaler employing the diagonal line principle to do the same things we just did with a proportion wheel. Any missing dimension arising in scaling photos for reproduction can be determined in this fashion. No mathematics are involved; the work is done entirely by measuring dimensions.

Figure 9-10 illustrates this principle. With a diagonal line set off to bisect a rectangle from one corner through the other, any rectangle then formed by right angle lines from adjacent sides to the diagonal forms a rectangle that has the same proportions as the original. In Figure 9-10, the dotted lines represent what could be new dimensions for an original photograph being reduced or enlarged.

Figure 9-11 shows how the diagonal is used to solve a typical problem. The larger rectangle represents a photo cropped to be 8 inches wide and 10 inches deep. The reproduction width must be 2 inches and is measured across the top. A perpendicular from that point to the diagonal (line E–F) is the depth the reproduction will be, $2\frac{1}{2}$ inches.

All inaccuracies in drawing lines affect the accuracy of the answer when using the diagonal method. If the perpendicular is not exactly at 90 degrees, or if the diagonal slightly misses a corner, the answer will be slightly inaccurate.

Figure 9-12 shows the use of the diagonal to find the width when the depth is known. The procedure is identical to that used in Figure

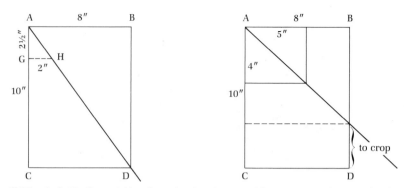

9-12 *Left:* Finding width when depth is known: Measure reproduction depth (A-G) 2½ inches along depth A-C. Measure perpendicular G-H to the diagonal to find the unknown width of the reproduction.

9-13 *Right:* Finding amount to crop: Lightly draw a rectangle with the reproduction dimensions. Draw a diagonal for that rectangle. Measure the distance from the diagonal's intersection to the bottom right corner. This is the amount to crop. The distance from B to the diagonal represents the cropped original depth.

9-11, except that the perpendicular is drawn from the side (because the depth is known) to the diagonal.

Figure 9-13 shows the use of the diagonal method to solve a problem when both dimensions of a reproduction are known and information about how much to crop the original is needed. In this example, the diagonal bisects the rectangle formed by the reproduction dimensions and not the original picture. The amount to be cropped is found by measuring the distance between the intersection of the diagonal with the line B–D and the corner D.

Diagonal lines used to solve problems as shown here can be drawn lightly and carefully on overlay sheets and the necessary dimensions for solving the problems may also be drawn on the sheet. Ruled mechanical scalers, shaped as an L and containing an adjustable, pivoting rulerlike device, save time and effort. By adjusting one L to the other so the pivoting rule serves as the diagonal, one can quickly discern any needed dimension.

Choosing a Scaling Method

The scaling or proportioning method used is relatively immaterial; whatever is easiest for the user will ordinarily suffice. Most editors and graphic artists prefer to use mechanical devices, such as proportion wheels. For beginners, however, an understanding of the simple mathematics involved is essential if they are going to be able to successfully use a mechanical aid. Beginners must also understand the purposes behind the figuring; that they are either trying to find a missing dimension so that they can complete a layout, or trying to find what cropping must be done so that an original will have the correct proportions to fit a layout that has already been executed.

Other Necessary Production Specifications

All original illustrations require some additional marking of instructions, besides crop marks, if they are to be reproduced as desired. This marking includes size of reproduction, a specification of the screen if needed, and any special finishing to be used in the reproduction.

Specifying Size

Either a percentage of enlargement or reduction or the reproduction width and depth must be clearly specified for all illustrations; if dimensions are provided, the best location for this information for photographs is on the back. Ordinarily the width is given first, in either picas or in inches. Glued order blanks, fastened to the back, are best for stating dimensions; otherwise instructions should be lightly written or with grease pencil so that the pressure does not harm the emulsion of the photograph. For drawings, there is usually ample marginal space on the front for all instructions.

Specifying Screen and/or Metal

For continuous-tone reproductions, the screen to be used must be specified. As pointed out in Chapter 7 the fineness of the screen determines the quality of reproduction—the finer the screen the better the reproduction. In letterpress printing, however, this statement is true only insofar as the fineness of the screen and the smoothness of the paper are properly matched. Fine screens require smooth papers in letterpress; in offset lithography good reproduction of fine screens can be obtained on rough papers.

Other chapters on illustrations and paper provide information on the proper matching of screen and paper, but generally speaking, screens with under 100 lines per inch are used with rough papers in letterpress, and finer screens require the smoother calendered or coated papers. The common screen for high-quality work is 133-line.

For letterpress engravings, the metal to be used must also be specified as either zinc (rougher screens) or copper (finer screens and longer runs).

9-14   An airbrush can be used to eliminate disturbing background in a photograph. (Courtesy of Anthony Scaravilli; © 1986 Anthony Scaravilli)

Specifying Special Finishes

The standard reproduction of any illustration is as a rectangle, called a square-finish. Any other reproduction may require some special treatment and special instructions.

Even with photos ordered to be produced as square-finishes, some altering other than cropping might be in order. For example, an artist can *airbrush* photographs to remove disturbing background or to emphasize certain portions of the subject (Figure 9-14).

The platemaker can do the airbrushing, however, and also manipulate camera settings to make some gray areas white (*highlight*) in the reproduction. Highlighting of some areas of commercial products is routine in advertising reproductions.

Through the use of special plate finishes as described in Chapter 8 (silhouette, partial silhouette, vignette, geometrical shapes), the appearance and shape of photographs can be changed when they appear in print.

Although airbrushing and retouching require special skills, journalists can get special plate finishes without an artist's assistance. Through the use of overlay sheets journalists can adequately communicate their desires to the platemaker who creates the special effect as the platemaker makes the plates. To order silhouettes, for example, an overlay sheet is fastened snugly to the photo and then the subject to be silhouetted is lightly outlined with a soft pencil. To avoid misunderstanding, "outline" or "silhouette" should be written in the area surrounding the line.

Vignettes can be indicated in similar fashion. The beginning and ending of the fade-out area can be drawn on an overlay. Mortises, notches, and geometric shapes (circles, ovals, irregulars) can also be shown on an overlay. The change in size brought on by enlargement or reduction in platemaking *must always be considered* when working with overlays.

An overlay sheet is also used to show desired highlight areas for highlight halftones and to locate line work on combination plates, both reverse and surprint. For letterpress printing, combination plates are expensive, but on many occasions they are especially effective. If type matter or line illustrations must appear over a halftone (in white or in the color of the halftone) a combination plate is required. Along with the halftone copy, reproduction proofs of type matter or sharp black-on-white line drawings must be provided to engravers so they can make good combination plates. These techniques are also used in offset lithography, but they do not involve special *plates*. The special treatment needed in each case centers around the *negative* preparation in lithography.

Photomontages (composite pictures made by combining several photos into one) are usually made by pasting the photos together on mounting board. They can also be made by the photographer, in which case the negatives are used to print several subjects on one sheet of photographic paper. The edges of the component photos can be sharp or blended into each other by an airbrush or by retouching. The component photos require no special instructions for reproduction.

As explained earlier, overlays are usually used to show the location of special treatments, but verbal instructions are also needed.

A typical marked photo might, therefore, have a tissue overlay showing the portion to be outlined, four crop marks to show the dimensions to be used, and these verbal instructions on the back:

$3'' \times 5''$, 133 line silhouette halftone

Such complete instructions eliminate most misunderstandings; the original illustration should be kept free of all other markings. Such things as the original dimensions of the photo or other numbers on the original can only cause confusion and error.

Processing Line Drawings

Although they are the simplest and cheapest of illustrations, pen-and-ink drawings are highly versatile and effective. In letterpress printing, the required line etching is simple to make and is the least expensive kind of photoengraving. In offset, there usually is no special treatment and no extra charge is required for line drawings. If the drawings are created in the same size as desired for reproduction, they can be pasted in position with type matter and processed with no special treatment or added cost. If they must be reduced or enlarged separately, a slight charge is usually involved.

For best reproduction, these drawings are done on white bristol board with black ink; the primary production demand is for sharp, clear, black lines on a contrasting background. Although a pen is most commonly used, brushes can produce good line illustrations also, as described in Chapter 7. The quality of reproduction is often enhanced when original drawings are reduced for reproduction; any drawing that can be reduced to 50 percent of its original size will lose many minor flaws that might have been present in the original art.

Line drawings and other artwork must be crop marked just as photographs are as they are being processed for publication. Although crop marking is usually not needed to change the shape or content of a line illustration because the illustration usually is drawn to specifications, crop marks are needed to set the dimensions to be followed. As with photos, four marks are needed: two to set the horizontal dimension and two for the vertical.

Any drawing that contains only pure darks and pure whites is reproducible as a line drawing or reverse line drawing. This includes those that will appear to have middle tones because of Benday shading or drawn dots or lines; it is important to recognize the wide variety of artwork included in the line-drawing category. Cartoons, bar graphs, charts, diagrams and maps are usually prepared for line reproduction.

Color in Illustrations

The preparation of copy for color reproduction is explained in Chapter 11. As mentioned there, both line and halftone copy can be reproduced in color. Full-color photographs or film transparencies, oil paintings, watercolors, and other original full-color continuous-tone materials are reproduced by the halftone process through color separation. It is wise to determine the preferences of individual engravers or lithographers before submitting copy for separation negatives and plates. For color in line illustrations, separate drawings keyed for exact positioning must be provided for each color. Enlargements and reductions are possible for color reproductions just as they are for black and white.

CHECKLIST: **Reading Proofs of Illustrations**

Although the errors in illustrations differ from the misspellings, wrong fonts, transposed lines, and the like, that creep into type matter, they nevertheless demand careful attention. Engravers and lithographers provide proofs of their work with illustrations, just as printers do with type, and these proofs should be checked in time for necessary corrections to be made before deadlines.

It is difficult to discern some illustration errors; others are easy to spot. With a little care and practice, anyone can detect the common failings. Some of these errors result from poor work by the engraver or lithographer, but many are the result of improper preparation. Wherever the fault lies, it is essential to detect and correct all flaws before the final printing.

Here are some common failings:

1. Wrong dimensions. This error often can be traced to the person who marked the original copy, but occasionally a production person will err in figuring the percentage of reduction, or a camera operator may shoot the copy incorrectly. But whether an editor placed a crop mark incorrectly or an operator set the camera improperly, the negatives or plates must be remade to fit their space. The only debate is about who pays the extra cost.
2. Imperfections on the edges. Photo reproductions with jagged edges need not be tolerated. Engravers can smooth plate edges, and lithographers can recut mask openings to eliminate such blemishes.
3. Content not as desired because plate dimensions do not follow the crop marks. Sometimes an illustration will be reproduced in the

desired size, but material that was to be cropped out may be included in the reproduction. If the original was correctly marked, the illustration is redone at no charge.

4. Scratches. Engravers and lithographers try to handle negatives and plates with care, but unsightly scratches sometimes do appear. Circle them on the proof so that the cause of the flaw can be located and corrected.

5. Spots. These should also be circled on the proof. Although spots often are only the result of a bad proof, it is possible that they are actually in the reproduction. If they are merely proof flaws, a new proof will prove the fact; otherwise the error must be corrected in the negative or plate.

6. Proof too gray or too contrasty. A good halftone requires accuracy in the determining and making of several camera exposures. Bad camera work or etching can cause a halftone to be a poor reproduction of the original. Mark the proof "too gray" or "too contrasty," and the engraver will deliver a better plate if the evaluation was reasonable.

7. Some faint handwriting on surface. Poor editing can be the cause of this problem. Any handwriting done on the back of a photo may show in a reproduction. If this shows up on a proof, the reproduction must be redone at the cost of publisher or supplier, whichever caused the flaw.

8. Paper clip marks on edge. This is also usually the fault of the editorial staff, not of the engraver or printer. Paper clips should not be used on photos; they often scratch or dent the emulsion. Such scratches or dents will appear in any reproduction.

9. Hairline cracks. These usually result from improper handling of the photo. Photos should not be rolled or folded, otherwise emulsion cracks will result.

10. Dark line on part of an edge. Improper cropping can cause this failing. Lines should not be drawn to indicate a dimension of a photo; only marginal crop marks are needed. Any line drawn to show cropping will appear in a reproduction if it is slightly off angle.

Some imperfections in illustration reproductions can be seen only with a magnifying glass; others may only show up when the plate is put on a press. But most shortcomings that can cause serious difficulties can be detected by careful inspection of proofs. Time so spent is certainly worthwhile.

10

Elements of Printing Production

Printed communications begin with a plan that is followed by or jointly prepared with the words and illustrations needed to accomplish the goals of the communications. These steps are considered *editorial* activities, with the work being done by professionals such as reporters, writers, editors, photographers, artists and graphic designers. They are, of course, the steps with which this book is most directly concerned. But, as pointed out in the first chapter, these steps cannot be separated from the actual *production* of the printed material. Although much of the production work is carried out by tradesmen, the professionals involved in the preparation of graphic communications must, like architects, be knowledgeable in production. This knowledge is not intended to permit the professionals to do the tradesmen's work, but, instead, to insure that the work as carried out follows the plans and specifications essential to the final product.

The invasion of printing production by the computer in the last two decades has somewhat blurred the distinction, however, and made the knowledge of production even more essential for those preparing printed media.

199

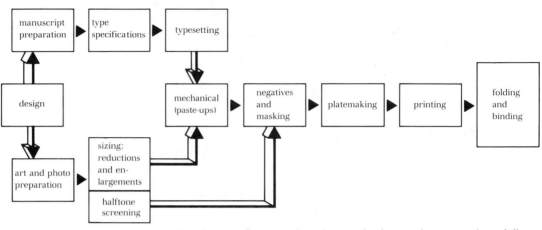

10-1   This diagram illustrates the steps involved in producing words and illustrations into print, using the common printing processes.

Basic Production Steps

As shown in the flow chart in Figure 10-1, printing production begins with the composition of type and preparation of illustrations. Type, once composed in an attractive and legible face of adequate size and reasonable line length on photo paper and proofed, is placed in position on a white background to become part of what is called a *mechanical* or *pasteup.* To be a mechanical, a pasteup should be accurate and clean enough to be photographed for the printing process. A mechanical may also have the illustrations in position, although they may be handled separately. To be on the mechanical illustrations must be of the proper size, and if they are photographs they must be *screened* in advance. These screened photoprints are made up of tiny dots created by a halftone screen and can be photographed in their various shapes and sizes along with the type and line drawings that would also be on the mechanical. As explained in Chapter 6, computer pagination eliminates the need to paste up a mechanical.

The negatives that are created when photographing the mechanical must then be placed in position in an opaque sheet in combination with any other pages or special negatives that are to be on the same printing plate. This process of putting negatives into position with adhesive tape is called *stripping.* The sheet containing the negatives is called a *flat* or *mask*. The openings cut to make room for the negatives are called *windows,* and the negatives are stripped into the windows of the mask with cellophane tape.

Plates are made from flats by exposing light through the negatives to the plate beneath. Plates are then made ready to accept ink in a

10-2 These photos taken at the *Athens* (Ohio) *Messenger* show the steps involved in getting a newspaper off the presses and on its way to readers. (Photos by Ralph Kliesch)

10-2a Editorial and advertising staffs use video display terminals to keyboard copy and file it in the computer.

10-2b Video display terminals are used to retrieve copy from a computer, correct it, write a headline for it, and add formatting specifications for the typesetter.

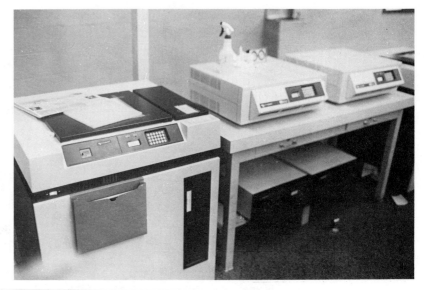

10-2c These type-setters are on-line to the computer and its terminals. Copy in digital form moves into them from terminals or computers and is converted into phototype at tremendous speeds.

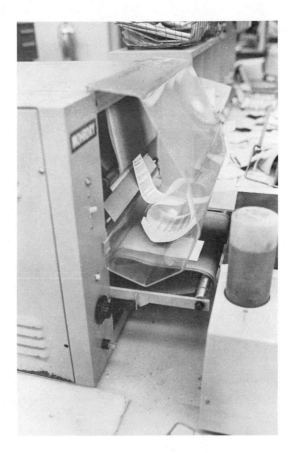

10-2d Copy emerges from a processor and dryer in column form with or without a head-line, ready to be positioned on a mechanical.

10-2e *Left:* Before going onto the mechanical, type columns are trimmed.

10-2f *Right:* Photos from local photographers or these laser photos from Associated Press are evaluated, scaled, and cropped, to be photographed again.

number of different ways varying according to the printing process that is involved. Plates are placed on a *press,* then inked on the image area, and the ink is carried to paper, again in different ways, according to the printing process that is used. Paper may be fed into the press in sheets (*sheetfed*) or from a roll (*webfed*), and may be printed on one side or perhaps it may be *perfected* (printed on both sides with one run through the press). The kinds of presses vary according to the size and number of printed pieces needed as well as the printing process involved.

Proofs for correction are usually provided when type is in column form (*galley proofs*) or pages (*page proofs*) or on the press plate (*press proofs*).

10-2g With a dummy to show the location of all items, the type, line drawings, and screened photoprints are fastened to mounting board with wax or rubber cement.

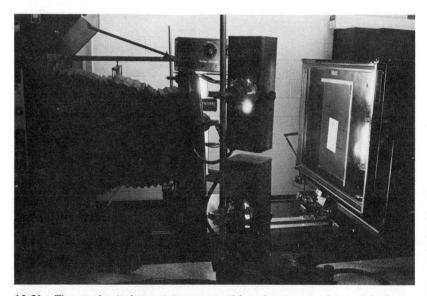

10-2h The mechanical containing type and line drawings is photographed to produce a negative. Photos are re-photographed through a screen and enlarged or reduced to fit a dummy.

10-2i The page negative is checked, and dust spots or other imperfections are opaqued with pencil or brush.

10-2j The negative image is transferred to a flat aluminum plate by exposing light through the negative to the plate.

10-2k The plate is wrapped around a cylinder on the rotary press.

10-2l The web is started through the units, each carrying a plate sized to contain two pages.

10-2m Complete papers emerge from the folder at the end of the press, ready to be bundled and loaded onto distribution trucks.

Computers may be involved in virtually every production step varying according to the stage of technology to which the printer has moved or, as with several other steps, according to the printing process being used.

Basic Printing Processes

Although there are many printing processes, we can accept one as the basic process because it is so widely used and two others as secondary processes because of their versatility and use. Several others are worthy of mention because they have specialized uses. The basic process is called *photo offset lithography* or *offset,* and the two secondary ones are *letterpress* and *rotogravure.* All three use metal images to carry ink to paper, but offset prints from a flat surface, letterpress from a raised image, and rotogravure from depressed areas. Some of the specialized processes described later in this chapter are plateless processes.

Fundamentals of Offset

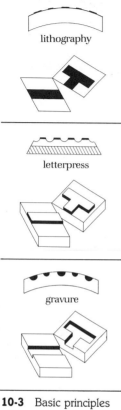

lithography

letterpress

gravure

10-3   Basic principles of the three common printing processes, offset printing from a flat plate, letterpress from raised images, and gravure from depressed images.

Offset is a chemical process of printing that gets images on paper by utilizing the principle that grease and water do not mix. A flat plate, usually made of aluminum, is photographically exposed and treated so the image area will receive a greasy ink and the non-image area will receive water and repel the ink. On the press, the plate never touches the paper; the process gets its name because the ink from the plate is first offset onto a rubber surface that squeezes the ink into the paper.

Offset presses are *rotary,* that is, the type image is rotated as printing occurs. As can be seen in Figure 10-4, the plate is wrapped around one cylinder that contacts another cylinder covered with a rubberized *blanket* that, in turn, pushes the image into paper as the paper passes over an *impression* cylinder. As each impression is made, more water is applied to the non-image area and more ink, repelled by the water on the non-image area, is applied to the image area only.

Both sheetfed and webfed presses are in common use for offset.

Prepress Production Steps

The basic production steps listed above apply to offset lithography. Because platemaking and other preliminary steps are photographic, any method of type composition can be used for offset printing. Computerized photocomposition methods are common, but hand lettering, paste-down letters, transfer letters, strike-on (typewritten) letters, proofs from metal type or any other original source that can be photographed may be used.

Type, line illustrations, and screened prints of photographs all represent what the printer calls *line* copy and are photographed on the mechanical. For better quality, photographs and other continuous-tone artwork such as oil and watercolor paintings are produced separately as screened negatives and stripped into separate flats. In these cases, the flat containing the line copy and the flat with the halftone copy must be separately exposed in proper position on the one plate. This making of two exposures on one plate is called *double burning.* Superimposing type over halftones also requires double burning.

Any colors in addition to black require separate flats and separate plates. The mechanical from which black printing is to occur usually is the *key* mechanical and those for colors are on clear acetate and taped in position over the key mechanical. Correct positioning of each *overlay* or *flap* mechanical is assured through the use of matching *registration marks* on each mechanical (they look like gunsights).

Advantages and Uses

Offset is now the basic system of printing in the United States because it has some distinct advantages over its traditional competitors. These advantages include:

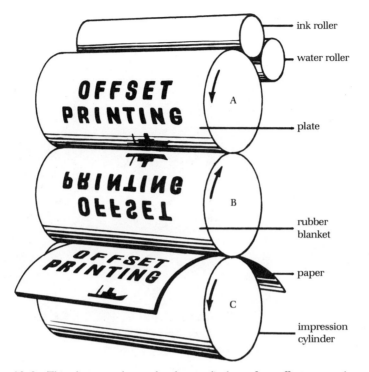

10-4 This diagram shows the three cylinders of an offset press: the one on top containing the aluminum plate, the one in the middle containing the rubber blanket that receives the image from the plate, and the one on the bottom that serves as the platform to hold the paper as the blanket cylinder squeezes the image onto the paper. (Reprinted from *Printer I & C,* Navy Training Courses, U.S. Government Printing Office)

1. The ability to use all kinds of cold-type methods for type composition, thus keeping cost to a minimum.
2. The ability to reproduce type clearly and distinctly. One of the ways to identify offset is to look at type under a glass; other systems produce a less precise letter image.
3. The ability to produce quality reproduction on a wider variety of paper surfaces. The squeezing action of the rubber blanket gets ink into the crevices of rough paper stock better than other processes can.
4. Cost-free reproduction of line illustrations and less costly reproduction of photographs and other continuous-tone illustrations. Because it prints from a flat surface, offset does not require acid etching of engravings for illustrations.
5. Efficient press operation; rotary presses are faster than other types, and the flat, thin offset plates are ideal for rotaries. Some processes require special preparation or adaptations of type and plates in order

10-5   Any letters that can be photographed can serve as type for offset, including the paste-down letters this graphic artist is using.

to use rotary presses. Also, except for adjusting the ink-water balance, time-consuming makeready is avoided.

6. Easy storage of plates, flats and mechanicals. Prepress materials for other processes are often too bulky to make storage feasible.

7. Adaptability to computerization. Cold-type composition and photographic steps in production have permitted offset printers to incorporate computer assistance faster and in more production steps than some other systems.

These advantages of offset have made it the most common method of producing newspapers, magazines, illustrated books and miscellaneous brochures of all types. For students preparing for a career involving any printed medium of communication, offset is the process they should know best. As writers, editors or graphics specialists for a newspaper or magazine, they are very likely to find that their publishers have chosen offset as the best production method for their publications. Or if their career is in advertising, public relations or publishing organizations and their work involves the selection of printing methods, they will find that offset must be seriously considered for most of their work.

Instances in which the selection of offset would be almost certain include:

1. Short-run (under 1000) pieces that involve type and illustrations.
2. Any number of copies that require reproduction of many photos on rough or cheap paper and good quality of reproduction is desired.
3. Any piece of printing composed mainly of drawings such as charts, diagrams and cartoons.
4. Any moderate to medium-long run printing requiring good photo reproduction plus the size and speed of webfed rotary presses. As runs exceed 100,000 copies, rotogravure becomes competitive; at a million copies or more, rotogravure tends to replace offset totally.

Many special factors can influence the choice of a printing process, and we can present only generalized conclusions here. In many instances printers whose expensive equipment for other processes is idle will price their work in that process below normal in order to keep their equipment from remaining idle. In some areas, a printer using what normally would be the better process may not be available. In any case, the versatility of offset requires that it be given careful consideration when any printing is being planned.

Fundamentals of Letterpress

Because it is the traditional system of printing, letterpress perhaps requires less explanation than other methods. A number of characteristics and ramifications of the system, however, should be noted.

It takes only a moment's thought to realize that letterpress can be defined as a direct, mechanical system of printing from raised surfaces. But the words "mechanical" and "raised" point to characteristics that are of considerable significance to anyone who is either preparing material for reproduction by letterpress or considering the system's quality and cost levels.

Prepress Operations

For printing to be done directly from a raised surface, words and illustrations must, in some way, be "carved" or molded in relief in a substance sufficiently hard to withstand wear from constant applications or pressure. It should also be apparent that equality of pressure for all elements against the sheet being printed becomes a matter of necessity for a high level of quality in this process.

These two requirements point directly to five matters of importance to users of the letterpress process:

1. Traditionally, words and letters have had to be cast in metal to be reproduced.

10-6 Preparation of a book by offset lithoghraphy. (Courtesy Vail-Ballou Press)

Type and line illustrations are pasted in page mechanicals. The mechanicals are photographed with a process camera to get negatives of each page. Page negatives are stripped into a mask of opaque paper to form a flat, in this case containing 64 book pages. The images on the negatives in the flat are transferred to an aluminum plate by beaming light through them (burning). If photos are to be used, they would be stripped into a separate flat and "double burned" onto the plate containing the line images from the other flat. On the press the plate transfers images to the blanket, which then lays ink on paper. The large sheets then are folded and bound into appropriate covers.

10-7(a)   Engravings and metal type must be locked in place in pages for their raised images to carry ink to paper in traditional letterpress printing. Newspapers such as the *Pittsburgh Press* have modernized letterpress methods so plastic plates with a raised image **(b)** can be made by exposing light through page negatives **(c)** and be thin enough **(d)** to wrap around cylinders of high speed presses. (*Pittsburgh Press* photos by Greg Blackman)

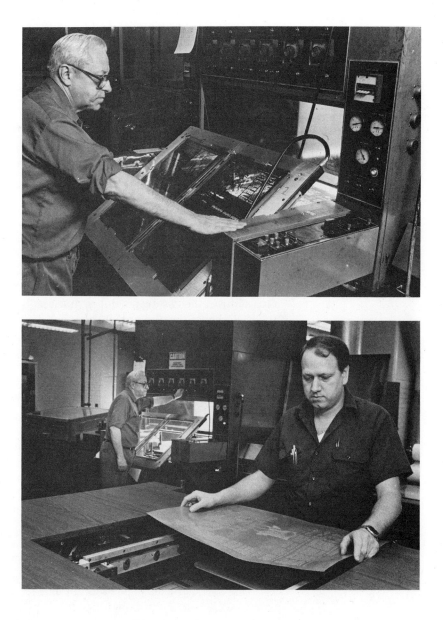

2. Illustrations must be separately manufactured in plate form to be re-produced.
3. For fine quality of reproduction for photographs, a smooth, coated paper is required.
4. Time and skill are required in "making ready" a press form so that the pressure of each element against the paper is equal, thus giving an even application of ink.
5. Traditionally, letterpress has required the casting of curved metal plates

as a duplicate of an original page of type and engravings in order to use presses with higher speeds.

Let us look at each of these items to see how they are of importance to the journalist who works with the letterpress process.

Type Composition

In traditional letterpress shops, the mechanical preparation of copy starts with a skilled technician, the *compositor,* who may operate a machine, such as the Linotype, Intertype, Monotype, or Ludlow typecaster, or may even set by hand the pieces of type stored in *cases* (drawers). Type cast from molten metal is called *hot type* and its use has been fundamental to letterpress printing for centuries. Compositors of hot type have served extensive apprenticeships, are strongly unionized, and are relatively well paid. Thus, hot-type composition has been a costly part of letterpress printing for many years.

Automation of hot-type composition has been effected in many plants through the use of tape-driven machines; tape that is punched by a typist drives the casting machines much in the fashion of the old player piano. Perhaps most important, however, has been the introduction of photochemical prepress methods for rotary letterpress, thus permitting cold-type composition (see the section on wrap-around plates).

Plates for Illustrations

The need to have a raised surface for printing all kinds of illustrations by letterpress has also been an important factor in any comparison with other processes.

The traditional letterpress method for reproducing illustrations is to create acid-etched metal plates on which the nonprinting area is cut away in acid baths, leaving the image area in relief. Even the simplest pen-and-ink drawings require the manufacture of separate metal plates called *line* engravings; photographs or other illustrations containing continuous tonal variations require a complicated procedure of breaking the image into dots on the plate surface, plus the subsequent complicated acid etching that makes the dots stand in relief and thus be able to carry ink to the paper. These plates are called *halftone* engravings.

The special plates needed for all illustrations are one of the costly aspects of letterpress printing; they also tend to restrict somewhat the use of illustrations. Because each line drawing or photograph is a separate added cost, and because the cost for each illustration increases with the size of the illustration, there has been a tendency to use fewer and smaller illustrations than otherwise.

Procedurally, photoengravings in letterpress require working with still another production specialist, the engraver. The time allowance for the engraver's work has to be coordinated with the printer's deadlines. In some operations, notably those of newspapers, the printer also operates an engraving department, thus reducing scheduling problems.

Some electronic machines are now in use that make plastic or metal plates for letterpress illustrations without acid etching. Most of these machines employ the principle of an electric eye scanning the illustration and sending electronic impulses to a hot needle that etches dots or lines on the plate surface. Some of the restrictions in size and number of illustrations tend to be reduced in situations where these machines are installed; the cost of their operation tends to be fixed, thus making the unit cost less with added use.

Paper Requirements

The relief characteristic of letterpress printing necessitates the use of extremely smooth paper in order to get good reproduction of photographs. For high fidelity in reproduction, the dots in a halftone engraving must be extremely small; these tiny raised dots are lost or smudged in the hills and valleys of the coarse surface of cheaper papers. Consequently, the hard, smooth finish of more expensive papers must be provided for fine photographic reproduction. When coarse papers must be used because of cost, the engravings are made so that their dot structure is much larger, with a resultant loss of quality. Many magazines offer excellent examples of the beautiful reproduction of photos that can be achieved in letterpress printing on smooth papers; newspapers, because they are printed on the cheapest kind of paper, offer examples of poorer picture quality.

Importance of Makeready in Letterpress Printing

Theoretically, type set for letterpress printing is *exactly* 0.918 inches high, and all plates are mounted at *exactly* the same height. Perfect impressions depend on this exactness. But perfection, of course, is seldom attainable. Compensating for the imperfections in type and plate height, as well as other factors affecting pressure, is accomplished through a procedure called *makeready*. Makeready is vital to letterpress printing because it establishes the level of reproduction quality. Fine presswork can be obtained only by carefully adding tissue paper under low areas and by cutting away packing where impressions are too heavy. This work on the press cylinder is time-consuming and costly, but it makes possible the finest kind of printing. Other printing systems that do not rely on a raised surface for putting ink on paper do not require a makeready operation.

Special Requirements of Rotary Letterpress

Letterpress presses can be either *platen, cylinder* or *rotary.* The fastest of printing presses is the rotary press, which is so designated because the type and/or plates rotate on a cylinder as they carry ink to the paper.

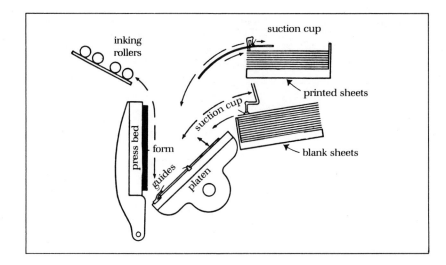

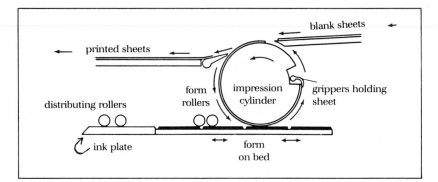

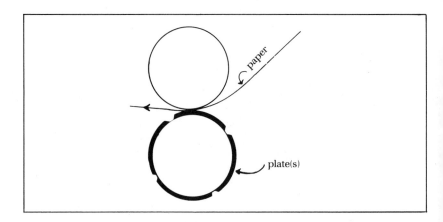

10-8 Letterpress printing presses are of three types: platen, flatbed cylinder, or rotary. Rotary presses are faster than the others but require cylindrical plates that can carry the images to paper.

Stereotyping

Until recently the only way to use the rotary principle in letterpress was first to put the type and plates together in a flat form, and then duplicate that form on the surface of a curved plate that would fit around a plate cylinder. This was usually done through *stereotyping,* a method of duplicating that uses a papier-mâché or fiberboard mat to serve as a mold for a casting in molten lead. In stereotyping, the mat is placed over the page form and subjected to great pressure, forcing the relief areas of the form to be depressed in the mat. When molten lead was put on the mat in a cylinder-casting box, the lead would contain, in cylindrical form, the relief printing image of the original form. Stereotyping made modern newspaper production possible; the speed with which modern metropolitan newspapers are printed would not be possible if printing had to be done from a flat form.

Wraparound Plates

The necessity of stereotyping, although it has been a boon to newspaper printing for decades, has been somewhat of a hindrance to letterpress printing in competition with other processes. Some loss of quality that occurs during the duplicating process, plus the need to maintain a stereotyping department, have served as disadvantages. However, new techniques to permit rotary printing by letterpress without stereotyping have become available in recent years. The most significant of these techniques are those that permit the use of cold type as well as eliminate the need for stereotyping. In these systems, page pasteups are photographed and the negatives thus created are used to expose the printing image on a single thin, flat sheet of magnesium or other metal, or plastic. The metal or plastic sheet is then shallow etched to create a relief image. This lightweight, pliable plate can then be wrapped around a "saddle" and used on the printing cylinder of a rotary press. Most newspapers now use these plates instead of stereotypes.

One of the more spectacular systems for making these plates involves the use of laser beams. The Gannett Company, the publisher of a large chain of newspapers has successfully tested such a system. According to Gannett, its system successfully passed field tests under normal operating conditions. A series of multiple laser beams, directly from photocomposed pasteups, produced lightweight, combination metal and plastic plates at the rate of one every two minutes and performed satisfactorily in runs of up to 200,000 impressions.

Platemaking systems such as these seem to be an indicator that many newspapers will continue to be produced on letterpress presses much longer than has been forecast by many experts. Not only do they enable the use of the latest photocomposing systems, but they permit the owner of expensive rotary presses to forgo purchasing offset presses.

Advantages and Uses

One of the primary advantages of letterpress printing is that it is the traditional method of printing in this country. Since its invention by Gutenberg in the 15th century, letterpress has served as a primary system for mass production of words and pictures. Consequently, presses and prepress equipment for letterpress can be found in most print shops and many publication production departments. The heavy investment in this equipment has slowed the move to discard it, and in some places no other printing method is available.

Throughout its history, letterpress has demonstrated its ability to produce excellent quality work in black and white or color on flatbed cylinder presses that can be adjusted and made ready to suit the quality demands of the most fastidious user of printing. Letterpress also retains an advantage in the production of type-only periodicals with moderate press runs. Once hot type is produced on linecasting machines, the type can be put in a page form and then on a press without further reproduction steps. Offset and other processes require that their cold type be photographed, stripped into a mask, and then exposed on a plate before printing.

The necessity for making acid-etched engravings for all illustrations used with hot type remains a disadvantage in comparison with offset, but in publications work, particularly, the disadvantages associated with hot-type composition are steadily being eliminated. Many newspapers, for example, though they have converted entirely to cold type and related prepress preparation, have been able to retain their expensive rotary letterpresses by making raised-image plates for them by photochemical methods.

Although many observers and prognosticators in the printing industry have concluded that letterpress is suffering from a terminal illness and that its demise will occur shortly, such predictions are still premature. The elimination of hot-type composition is well on its way (linecasting machines are no longer being manufactured in the United States), but that should not be confused with an elimination of the printing process. Printing from a raised image remains a viable system of printing that must be understood by those planning careers involving the preparation of printed material.

Fundamentals of Gravure

The terms *gravure* and *intaglio* are used to describe the printing process in which images are transferred to paper from ink-filled depressions in a surface rather than from inked lines in relief or material on a flat surface.

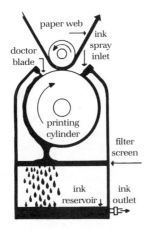

10-9   A diagram of a rotogravure press.

A typical application of the process in its simplest form is the engraving of calling cards or formal invitations. The lines to be printed are cut into the surface of a plate. The plate is coated with ink and then wiped clean, leaving ink only in the depressed areas. When paper is pressed against the plate, it picks the ink out of the depressed areas, thus coating the image in relief on the paper.

However, the simple engraved invitation can be considered only a distant relative of the fine reproductions of photographs and works of art that can be achieved by gravure printing. These are the result of adding photography and rotary webfed press operation to the process, thus creating *rotogravure.*

High-speed rotogravure presses work on the same principle as the one with simple engravings. Basically, it is a matter of filling wells with ink, scraping the excess ink from the surface, and applying paper to plate with pressure (Figure 10-9).

The rotary press prints directly from an acid-etched copper cylinder using a watery, fast-drying ink. As the cylinder revolves, it goes through an ink bath and is then scraped clean by a steel knife called a *doctor blade,* thus leaving ink only in the wells of the image area. The ink is sucked onto the paper surface when the paper is brought into contact with the plate.

Prepress Operations

All prepress operations that relate to copy preparation are the same for gravure as for offset. Cold-type composition is pasted up to form mechanicals that are photographed. Separate continuous-tone originals are also photographed, but without a screen and with low-contrast film as compared with the high-contrast film used for the mechanical.

Gravure's unique capability in the reproduction of photographs stems from the different use of a screen for getting tonal gradations in these reproductions. The screen itself is different; instead of being made up of intersecting opaque lines on film, it is formed of intersecting clear lines. The use of this screen is also different.

First, the screen is placed over a sensitized gelatin transfer sheet, called a *carbon tissue,* that is big enough to cover a full printing cylinder, and light is exposed through it. The gelatin on the sheet is thus hardened in the screen pattern, because the lines forming the screen are clear. Next, a film positive of the image area is placed over the cylinder and light is exposed through it. Areas that are to carry full ink (type, for example) thus get no light through the film positive, leaving the gelatin coating soft except for the lines created by the screen. Non-image areas get total exposure to light and total hardening of the gelatin; middletone areas would get medium exposure and medium hardening, and so on. Finally, the gelatin coating will determine the amount of ink the cylinder will apply. When acid is applied to the cylinder surface, it creates depressed areas of varying depths: In non-image areas no depression is formed, type areas are depressed to full depth, middle tones are depressed to middle depth and so on. When ink is applied, it is carried to the paper in varying amounts according to the depth of the etching.

Advantages and Uses

The picture sections of Sunday newspapers, mail-order catalogs, magazines, reproductions of paintings and a great variety of product containers and wrappings are among the items printed by the gravure process. The chief asset of the process, reproducing highly faithful copies of photographs and paintings (both monotone and color), is possible because the thin ink in the wells of the plate spreads enough during printing to virtually eliminate any screen or dot pattern. In addition, variations in tone result from the thickness of the ink deposit instead of from a dot pattern, and photographs are reproduced with a special quality that cannot be achieved otherwise.

Type reproduction by photogravure is another matter. Type matter and illustrations are transferred together through a prescreened carbon tissue to the plate. Type matter is therefore screened. Because of this and the watery consistency of gravure inks, the text material of a gravure job is less sharp than it would be if prepared by other systems. One of the means of discovering whether or not a piece has been printed by gravure is to check the fuzziness of the type matter.

The use of gravure in commercial printing has expanded with the call for more printing on materials such as cellophane, new plastic films and foil. New composition methods, a boon for offset, have also aided gravure. Expected improvements in platemaking also promise much for the future of gravure. One of these improvements is electronic engraving, which skips the chemical etching step in platemaking. The process, developed in Germany, is coming into increasing use in Europe and the United States. This system involves scanning of color separation prints and electronic activation of a diamond stylus that mechanically engraves the copper plate.

The increased use of rotogravure has been especially noticeable among large-circulation magazines. In recent years several magazine circulation giants announced either total or partial conversions to gravure, including *Reader's Digest, National Geographic, McCall's, Redbook, Ladies' Home Journal* and the reborn *Life.* Although most of the changeovers to gravure were at the expense of letterpress, some of the work had previously been done by web offset. In all cases, the press runs were in the millions.

In summary, rotogravure is best suited for high-quality reproduction of photographs, in large press runs (minimum of 100,000), with the advantages becoming most pronounced when press runs reach a million copies. The high cost of plating and etching cylinders makes short runs uneconomical, and the fuzziness of type reproduction caused by the prescreening of cylinders reduces its effectiveness for type-only uses.

Computerized Imaging Systems: Jet and Electrostatic Printing

Most current efforts to improve printing systems are being directed toward the development of totally computerized systems, systems that would start with the digital information in a computer and end with a printed image, skipping all traditional typesetting and page composition steps.

As pointed out elsewhere in this text, the digitizing and storing of all information used in printing is possible, including the graphic elements such as photos and drawings. It is also possible to position those elements on pages through the computer. In other words, all prepress functions are within the capability of the computer; the "front-end" operations in printing have all been perfected.

Presses, however, are still huge, cumbersome, noisy, inefficient, and expensive. It is no wonder that the American Newspaper Publishers Association and other interested parties are devoting much of their resources and time to the development of new imaging systems. Most encouraging of these experimental systems are *jet* and *electrostatic* printing.

Fundamentals of Jet Printing

Fundamentally, in jet printing the digitized information in a computer is used to direct ink through minute nozzles to form alphanumeric or dot patterns as they spray an image on paper. Neither large rotating cylinders nor pressure is needed to form the printed impressions, just a web of paper rolling under a jet or jets.

One of the jet printing systems that has received considerable attention has been the A. B. Dick Videojet system. It uses only a single nozzle guided by a computer so it oscillates over the paper to deposit ink, much as the electron gun produces an image on a cathode ray or television screen. Another system, the Dijit Printer, uses a full bank of nozzles to form tiny jets of ink into necessary images by way of computer programming.

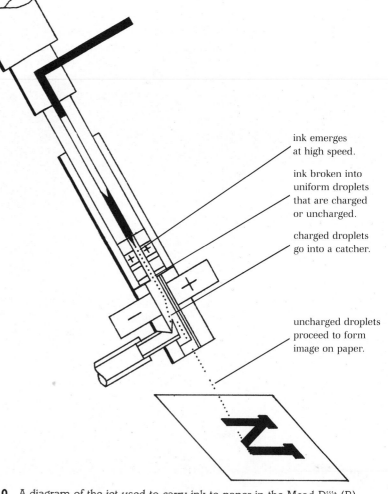

ink emerges
at high speed.

ink broken into
uniform droplets
that are charged
or uncharged.

charged droplets
go into a catcher.

uncharged droplets
proceed to form
image on paper.

10-10 A diagram of the jet used to carry ink to paper in the Mead Dijit (R) plateless, pressureless, and computerized printing system.

Advantages and Uses

The advantages of pressureless printing are immense and obvious. Printing on delicate breakable surfaces that cannot be printed on by traditional systems becomes feasible, the wear of plates pounding against paper and impression cylinders is eliminated, and prepress operations are totally automated.

In its current experimental stage, jet printing has been used for printing on containers and packaging materials and for addressing the millions of federal income tax forms as they emerge from a web press running at 700 feet per minute. Some typewriters using the jet principle have been introduced. The forecasts for a wide variety of uses of jet printing including the printing of newspapers and other publications are optimistic.

A linkage of jet printing with facsimile transmission may make this current optimism seem pale when compared with future reality. In newspaper and magazine publishing, for example, this might be the ultimate solution to pressroom and distribution problems. With all text and graphics gathered and arranged in page form in metropolitan editorial offices, pages could be sent by facsimile to one or several computerized jet printing facilities where the required number of copies could be printed as close as possible to their ultimate destination. Or for book publishing, consider this solution to the problems of determining print orders, storing copies and periodic updating. Authors could compose their work on any computer input device (a typewriter that writes on magnetic tape or perforates paper tape, for example). The work, after being fed into a computer, could be drawn out and edited to the publisher's satisfaction and returned to the computer in page form. Orders for the books could be directed, not to the publisher, but to any satellite jet printing plant located near a bookstore or near the customer. The printer could then call the computer and, in return, receive facsimile page transmission in sequence; these pages would automatically emerge ready for binding and distribution locally. Only those books sold would be printed; warehouse storage and remainders (unsold books) would no longer exist.

Fundamentals of Electrostatic Printing

Electrostatic printing relies on the attraction of positive and negative electrical charges to each other to achieve printing: A powder with one type of charge is attracted to an image area with the opposite charge.

One such system developed by Electroprint Corporation resembles jet printing to a great extent. With holes in a bar that are controlled by a computer, charges are transferred according to a program through holes into a cloud of ink, causing ink droplets to be deposited on the paper.

Another system developed by the Stanford Research Institute involves the use of a screen stencil through which powder is applied to the printing surface via electrostatic attraction. An electrostatic charge is used to suck the powdered ink (toner) to the printing surface.

In yet another system, a laser beam directed by a computer produces a charged pattern on a plate or drum that will then pick up toner and transfer it to paper. The images on the plate or drum can be quickly erased and replaced by others. This system, like jet printing, has the capability for being the basis of a totally computerized image system, but it is still in the experimental stage.

Advantages and Uses

These electrostatic systems have the same advantages as other computer-controlled, impressionless systems. They have been used in computer printout machines to get super-high speeds as compared with strike-on machines, to print on such exotic surfaces as pills, eggs and fruits and to serve as the basis for office copiers.

Some Specialized Printing Systems

Many printing systems that have specialized advantages or combine aspects of the three basic systems are available when circumstances warrant their use. Here are some of those systems and their potential uses:

Screen Process

Known to many students as the method for putting lettering and designs on T-shirts, screen printing also is used for posters, billboards and glass bottles because it provides for heavy, bright inks that can be squeegeed onto surfaces without heavy pressure on the surface to be printed.

Collotype (Photogelatin)

This is the only system that will reproduce photos and other continuous-tone originals without breaking the image into a screened dot pattern. Thus large numbers of public relations or advertising photographs can be created by the collotype method and disseminated for use as original copy for other printing methods.

Flexography

A letterpress system using flexible rubber plates, flexography can lay down heavy solid ink areas as does screen printing. Milk containers, cardboard boxes, gift wraps and brown grocery bags are often printed by this process. Foil, plastic films and tissue paper also serve as surfaces for flexography.

Quick Printing

So-called quick print establishments under this or similar names are common everywhere. A combination of electrostatic and offset printing, this system is totally automated. Paper masters made electrostatically are fed through offset duplicators to produce small bulletins, newsletters and other similar pieces of communication rapidly and at low cost.

Letterset

Also known as *dry offset,* letterset is best described as offset letterpress because it is a combination of those two basic processes. Shallow letterpress plates deposit their image on a blanket cylinder and printing occurs from the blanket. It is offset printing without water and letterpress printing that incorporates the indirect printing principle of offset.

Thermography

Also a combination of methods, thermography starts with copies printed by offset or letterpress, but with special nondrying inks, and adds a powder to the image area. When the powder is fused to the ink by heating it, the image on the paper is in relief, just as it is with traditional engraved (gravure) printing. It is a less-expensive substitute for simple applications otherwise calling for gravure.

Getting the Job Done:
In the Office or at the Printer

Selection of the process to be used is one of the first steps in getting a printing job done. As indicated in other chapters, other early steps are planning, scheduling and selecting a printer. Planning involves a format (size, shape and style) for the *medium* (newspaper, bulletin, magazine, booklet, advertisement and the like), determining strategy, and executing that strategy through words and illustrations. Scheduling involves deadlines for all steps involved (writing, editing, typesetting, photographs, layouts and the like). All of these steps are important and present complicated choices. None is more important, however, than the selection of a production partner, the printer.

Sometimes the choice of a printer is not difficult—the printer and the user may be one and the same. Computerized typesetting, electronic data transmission and automated duplicating systems have revolutionized printing so that, in many cases, all of it can be done "in house," meaning within the editorial operation. This is especially true when the output of automated duplicating systems is adequate for the needs of the publisher. In most cases, however, there is a division of labor with the editorial staff responsible for all steps up to the preparation of mechanicals and the printer responsible for *photomechanics* (making negatives and plates from the mechanicals) and presswork, folding, binding, and any other finishing step that might be required.

Regardless of circumstances surrounding any particular situation, it is essential that the responsibilities for all parties concerned be firmly established. This understanding is usually best accomplished through the use of *specifications* and a *contract* based on the specifications, or an agreement based on common understanding.

In dealing with outside printers, for example, it is impossible to compare prices without extremely definite and complete specifications that form a basis for a binding contract. With inside printers, a mutual understanding of responsibilities without the formalities of a contract can be accomplished.

Printer's Specifications

Specifications (called *specs*) must include every aspect of production, and their compilation actually serves as a review of the steps involved in the reproduction of words and pictures. These steps are

1. Format
   a. What will be the size and shape of the final product?
   b. What is the "type page size" (the dimensions of the page within margins)?
   c. What column arrangement is planned?
2. Type composition
   a. Who will set the type?
   b. What type sizes and designs will be used?
3. Number of copies
   a. How many copies are needed? Allowance should be made for the printing trade practice allowing a printer to deliver plus or minus 10 percent of copies ordered.
4. Number of pages, if appropriate. Is there a separate cover?
5. Frequency of issue, if applicable
6. Papers
   a. What color, finish, and weight are desired?
7. Number of photographs or approximate percentage of surface expected to be occupied by photographs
8. Page layout
   a. Who will prepare the mechanicals?
   b. Will mechanicals include screened photoprints (Veloxes) or must photographs be stripped into flats separately?

9. How many colors are to be used?
   a. Will full color (four-color process) separations be required? If so, how many and what size?
   b. How many pages will be in color?
10. Finishing operations
    a. How is the final product to be folded?
    b. What kind of binding is required?
11. Delivery or distribution
    a. Is printer to handle mailing or other distribution? If not, what delivery arrangements are required?
12. Proofs
    a. Proofs of all type should be provided for correction and approval when it is first set.
    b. Proofs of all pages should be provided so that placement of items can be corrected and approved before plates are put on the press.
    c. Are press proofs required?

Quality and Service

Detailed specifications can ensure mutual understanding between printer and publisher, but they cannot ensure satisfactory quality and service. Careful investigation of a printer's record for quality and experience in producing the kind of material desired is essential. Selection of the best process and printer, if matched by effective content and graphic design, will result in effective communication in print.

CHECKLIST: Some Points to Remember

1. Offset lithography is the most used system of printing; letterpress and rotogravure are secondary.
2. Offset printing uses flat aluminum plates, letterpress prints from raised images, and gravure prints from depressed areas.
3. The basic prepress steps in printing production are typesetting, reducing or enlarging illustrations and screening those with continuous tones in the original, pasting up a mechanical, stripping negatives into a flat and burning the plate.
4. Computer pagination makes it unnecessary to paste up a mechanical. Although most computer systems cannot yet accept unscreened photographs, pagination of line copy only is fairly common.
5. Rotogravure printing does an especially good job with photos, but does poorly with type, and is most often used for large runs of publications using many photos. Minimum run is about 100,000.
6. Letterpress printing from raised metal letters and etched photoengravings is largely being replaced by offset because of the expense of metal typesetting, engraving of photos, the better quality of paper needed, and the makeready of type and plates before printing.

7. Although the printing systems are different, the preparatory steps for rotogravure are the same as for offset; the same is also becoming increasingly true for letterpress printing.

8. Posters and billboards, because they require heavy applications of ink in large areas, are often printed by screen process.

9. Except for developing them in a darkroom, the only way to get screenless reproductions of photos suitable to be screened for other printing processes is with the use of the photogelatin process.

10. Computer-generated imaging, making plates and other preliminary parts of traditional printing systems unnecessary, is employed in jet and electrostatic systems of printing.

11

Communicating with Color

One way to understand and appreciate color is to imagine a world without it. Consider, for example, a land of glossy white posterboard occasionally punctuated by mountains that look like white enameled tents. A brilliant, white sun hovers in a white, textureless sky. One day, onto this seemingly stark stage is placed a giant, triangular section of glass— a prism. As the sunlight strikes the glass, an orchestra of color plays across a field of white. Performing in careful measure, ribbons of red, yellow, green, blue and violet dramatically change the landscape.

Although this experience seems surreal, it nonetheless teaches several important and practical lessons about color:

1. White light is a combination of all color in the visible spectrum of light.
2. Colors separate according to their wavelength along this electromagnetic spectrum.

3. This principle of separation is similar to the one that guides the use of color in graphic arts.

It is not the purpose of this chapter to delve into the physics of light and the scientific characteristics of color. However, you should understand the use of color in graphic arts. There are several areas of necessary focus: the vocabulary of color; the function of color in graphics; types of color printing and the separation process of color reproduction; cost and quality control in color printing; and guidelines for the effective use of color.

Vocabulary of Color

Look at Figure 11-1, the electromagnetic spectrum of energy and radiation. Notice how small a space that visible light—from the short wavelength violet to the longer length red—occupies. All visible color is contained in this band. When the entire band is present, it is perceived as white; when only a portion of that band exists, it is because an object has absorbed most of the other colors and has reflected only its *hue* (a synonym for color). When apparently white light struck the prism in our chapter opening, that light was being bent and separated according to its wavelengths, which is why we could see color. The same principle occurs in the formation of a rainbow. Light strikes drops of rain, which act as a prism; what appeared to be white sunlight is separated into colors.

In the graphic arts, however, we consider white to be the absence of color. White, then, becomes our palette of communication: We can communicate in color only with the application of selected pigments.

To understand how color is applied, it is important to understand these terms: primaries, complements, value and chroma.

Primaries

Primary colors are the dominant ones in any spectrum. They are more *solid* colors; ones in between these primaries are known as intermediaries because they require mixing of primaries, e.g., blue-green (turquoise), to get their hue.

There are, however, several sets of primaries. The *reflected light* primaries are commonly labeled *red, blue* and *green.* These relate to the dominant areas of the right, left and middle of the visible spectrum. In reflected light, yellow exists in a narrow band between the more dominant red and green. However, as most of us learned when we started mixing finger paint in grade school, combining yellow and blue actually creates green.

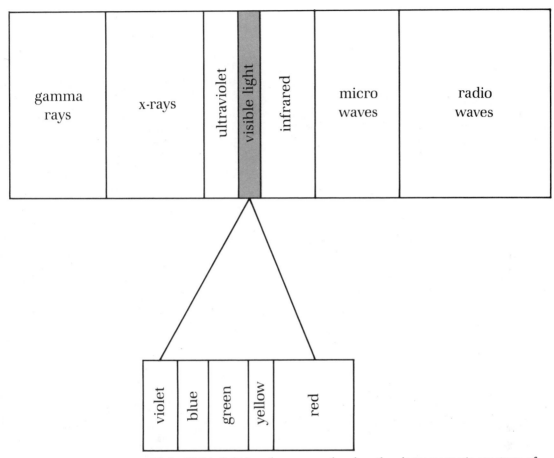

11-1 Visible light is only a narrow band on the electromagnetic spectrum of energy.

This illustrates another use of primaries, the *pigments*, used in painting and printing. In painting, the primaries are *yellow, red* and *blue*. In printing and in photography, they are *yellow, magenta* (reddish blue) and *cyan* (bluish green). In printing, these would be called *process colors*.

Understanding primaries is a critical factor in learning how to mix and correct colors. For example, mixing levels of cyan and magenta can create various shades of blue. In painting, mixing tints of red and yellow produces orange. In graphic arts, your understanding of color can help you order corrections to color reproductions. For example, skin tones and sky hue may need adjustment because of improper filtering or pigment mixing.

It is interesting to note that with only a few primaries as base hues, more than 250 color designations are listed by the U.S. Bureau of Standards.

Complements

A complementary color is the opposite of its primary. A good illustration of this can be seen in color photography. In making a color print from a negative, all colors are reversed. If the negative is of an American flag, the red portion of the flag on the negative material will look somewhat cyan; when that negative is printed, cyan's opposite, red, will show up on the positive print.

Look at the representation of a color wheel in Figure 11-2 (page C-1), and you will see how complements work. If a complement is the opposite of a primary, the opposite is also the contrasting color. Note where magenta lies on the color wheel. As the opposite of the primary green, magenta exists as a blend of blue and red; the opposite of red is cyan, or a blend of blue and green. Because cyan exists in the absence of red (where only blue and green remain), it is called a *subtractive primary*. More on this when we discuss the color separation process.

Value

Value refers to the lightness or darkness (tone) of a hue. A color can be lightened by being mixed with a lighter hue of the same color or by the addition of white. Pink, for example, is a high value color; brown is low. Printers can lighten a color by *tinting* it; they can do so with the use of a screen or by blending that color with white. They can also darken or *shade* the color by blending it with black or overprinting it with a screened black.

Chroma

In the 19th century, the American painter Albert Munsell created a color system utilizing *chroma* to define the intensity or saturation of a particular hue. A color such as red can be high on the saturation (chroma) scale but lower on the value scale when compared, for example, with yellow. In other words, yellow is lighter (of higher value) than red, but the quality of the red can be more intense or saturated if it doesn't contain much grey. Test this theory out the next time you're looking at new cars. Ask to see two convertibles on a sunny day. One should be maroon, the other, peach-blossom pink. The maroon car will look darker, but its color will seem deeper, more intense. It is of low value, high chroma. The pink (whew!) car will be very bright, of high value, but it will look so light that it seems somewhat washed out. Its chroma is obviously low.

When you evaluate color, then, you are examining *hue, value* and *chroma*. Is the actual color what you wanted, or has it shifted too much? Does the lime look too much like a lima bean? Is the color too light? Has too much white been added? Is the green too dull? Has too much grey been added? You must be prepared to discuss these issues with printers and designers.

Functions of Color

The wise use of color creates the same effect as good design: It

1. attracts attention
2. develops associations
3. aids retention and
4. creates a pleasing atmosphere

Attracting Attention

This is the major use of color. Contrast is the basis of attention. Thus, when you add a bright color to a piece printed in black, you should be guaranteed more attention-getting value. (Remember—black is considered a color in the printing field. So, if you printed a piece with black for the type and blue for the line art, you would have a two-color job.)

Color should be applied to the design elements of the greatest significance. But it should be placed with discretion. Cluttered or loud use of color will detract from your message. Complements, value and chroma can aid you in your color selection. For example, blue and green are not complementary colors (as far as the color wheel is concerned), but their juxtaposition can create a pleasing contrast, especially if their values and chroma contrast. So, a lighter value blue and a lower value green with a greater chroma could provide a pleasing and attention-getting combination.

Four helpful hints for planning color contrast are:

1. A tint of a particular hue is stronger against a field of middle grey than against the full strength of that hue.
2. Warm colors (red, yellow) are higher in visibility than cool ones (blues).
3. Contrast in values—light versus dark—is greater than contrast in hues—blue versus yellow.
4. The darker a background, the lighter a color appears against it.

Developing Associations

It is natural for people to associate different colors with different products. Red is happily associated with cherries, but the thought of green for fresh meat is not a pleasant one. Color suggestions of coolness and warmth suggest formality and informality. Red implies life and moods such as action and passion. Blue connotes distinction, reserve and serenity. Green is nature; purple is splendor and pomp. A black-and-white image could be criticized or admired for its apparent starkness or saturation of tone.

However, many associations are not so obvious; personal judgment may pale in the face of research findings. Testing reactions to comprehensive color layout or a set of separation keys can help prevent disaster.

Aiding Retention

In describing something, we are likely to refer to its color. This is because color has high memory value, a feature that the communicator can capitalize on. A color should predominate because it helps readers remember what they saw. Think of the use of yellow and red in MasterCard and McDonald's advertisements. Advertisers are particularly interested in reader recall and repeat certain colors in their campaigns in order to establish product identification.

Creating a Pleasing Atmosphere

The misuse of color in a message is worse than using no color at all. Poor choice and application of color can repel readers after their attention has been aroused. Consider a brochure with a bright blue headline printed against a field of yellow. That's relatively attractive. But you open the brochure—and the rods and cones of your eyes start "breakdancing" as they try to discern a message of reverse (white) type against that yellow field. The choice of yellow here has caused a terrible strain, and the message will not be read.

Colors, as well as black, grey and white, should be arranged in accordance with the same principles in layout: balance, contrast, rhythm and harmony.

Balance comes from proper placement of elements by weight or visual emphasis. Colors add further weight, according to their hue and value. When used with black for a two-color job, the color should be given relatively light weight so that it will not draw undue attention from the black. If a heavier color is desired, perhaps a lighter screen or tint of the black can be used unless there is too large a quantity of typesetting.

Contrast is necessary for image recognition. Contrast in values is more significant than contrast in hues. For this reason, when color serves as a background, care should be taken not to let it detract from other elements. For example, a dark-colored background will make a lighter hue seem even brighter. If the background and applied color are of the same relative value, however, the contrast between those two elements will flatten out and seem more bland.

Rhythmic use of color is achieved through repetition at various points in the printed piece. Spots of second color can be used effectively to guide the reader's eye through the message.

As we mentioned in Chapter 2, harmony helps create order and unity in your message. Harmony with one color and black may change to disorder when another color is added. Selected hues that work together harmoniously are an important part of the design function.

Types of Color Printing

Color printing is divided into two categories: *spot* and *process.*

Spot color uses solid or tinted colors that normally do not overlap with each other to create new hues. An example of spot color is a black and white grocery ad that features the store name and some prices in red. This color has been applied in additon to the black, requiring two inks and two plates for the job. Here each color comes from a *separate original;* each has its own mechanical.

Process color refers to specifically screened printing that requires the separation of hues from original color art (a term encompassing both drawings and photographs) in order to reproduce them. This is a more complicated and costly procedure, as you will see.

Today, most process color work is called *four-color,* which applies inks from four successive runs on the same page to reproduce the original art. These colors are applied in this order: *yellow, magenta, cyan* and *black.*

A good way to tell the difference between spot and process color (even if spot color blends) is to pick up your Sunday newspaper and look at both the comics section and any color photograph.

The comics and the photograph are printed with essentially the same colors, but their application is different. In the comics, a character might have a solid (nonscreened) swatch of yellow for her hair and a slightly screened (lightened) version of red for her face. There is no dot pattern for the solid colors and very simple, even-patterned dots for any lightened or mixed color (Figure 11-3, page C-1).

For the photograph, however, *all* colors are screened and carefully applied, one over the other at varying angles, to create careful gradations in tone and shadow. Instead of simple dots in the face of the subject, the photo will contain almost triangularlike patterns containing magenta, cyan, yellow and black, as the black-and-white representation in Figure 11-4 (page C-1) shows. Obviously, the process color is going to be truer, better detailed—and more expensive.

Two terms important to the understanding of color printing are *separation* and *register.* Let's deal with separation first.

Separating Colors for Reproduction

In the separation process, originals in color are rephotographed or scanned through special filters and screens to create individual printing plates for *each* of the inks required to make the reproduction. In the four-color process, that means four plates, or *runs,* are needed to reproduce the image. In a four-color run, the yellow is applied first. The yellow image then receives the magenta, cyan and black inks in that order.

To create these plates, the color original has its four color components separated through filtration. Although this can be done on a process camera, most of this work today is done on highly sophisticated electronic scanners (see Figure 11-5, page C-2). With the scanner, color correction is more automatic, as transparencies (slides) or reflection copy (prints) are affixed to a rotating drum and are scanned by light beams. The digital information from this scanning is used to create exposures for the three printing primaries and black. In many cases, this scanning will be done by laser beam.

Even if the process is accomplished by the older separation cameras, the filtration principle is the same. To create the *yellow* component, a *blue* filter is used. That filter transmits only blue light; because this is a photographic process, its complement (opposite) will be the color printed—in this case, yellow.

A *green* filter is used on the *second* exposure. It rejects red and blue, leaving only green's complement, *magenta.*

The *third* exposure, made through a *red* filter, rejects green and blue, leaving only red's complement, *cyan.*

The *last* exposure creates a simple *black* proof. This is critical because it helps create better shadow and line definition. Figure 11-6 (page C-3) attempts to show how these four plates are created.

It is important to realize that while both separation and press proofs come to you in color, the plates themselves are relatively colorless prior to inking, showing only sections of the reproduction. Figure 11-7 (page C-4) shows what portion of the print is contained on a cyan plate. Obviously, application of the other three inks is necessary to complete this image.

Registration

As explained in other chapters, *registration* refers to the positioning of the image impression on the printed sheet. The proper alignment of one color with another is called *correct register.* We have all seen improper register; the comic pages again serve as a good example. When the colors in a *Peanuts* strip aren't properly aligned, the blue of the sky may droop into Snoopy's white face; Charlie Brown's blue shorts may bleed their color onto his pink knees. Poor registration looks somewhat like

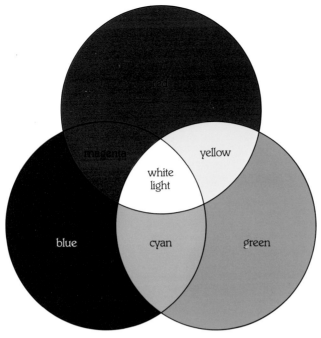

red

magenta   yellow

white
light

blue   cyan   green

11-2 A diagram of a color wheel showing primaries and complements.

11-3 A closeup image of the comics shows how *spot color* is applied. Note the even dots.

11-4 The complicated dot pattern of process color. The dots merge because one color is applied over the other. (Courtesy Woodfin Camp / Annie Griffiths)

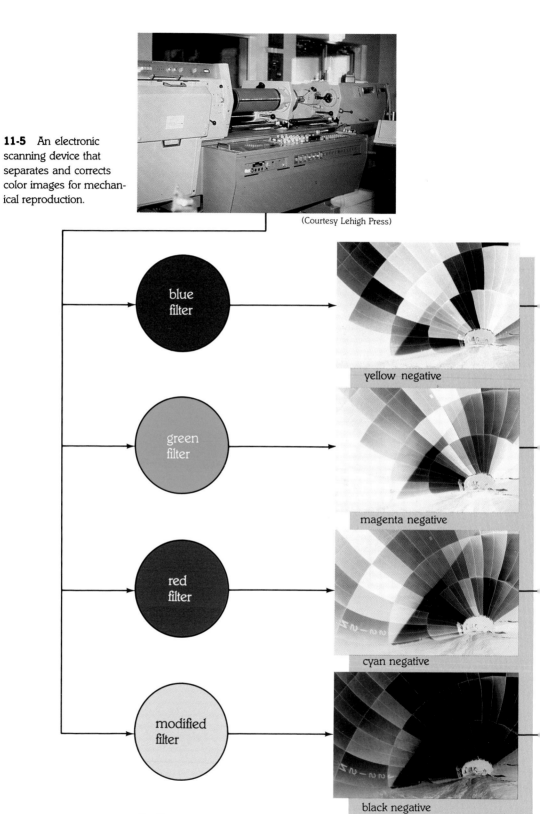

11-5 An electronic scanning device that separates and corrects color images for mechanical reproduction.

(Courtesy Lehigh Press)

blue filter

green filter

red filter

modified filter

yellow negative

magenta negative

cyan negative

black negative

11-6 Color separation steps: the blue filter prints yellow; the green filter prints magenta; the red filter prints cyan; a final special filter prints black. In this process, "print" means to create a plate sensitive to that color.

4 – color reproduction.

(Courtesy Woodfin Camp / Annie Griffiths)

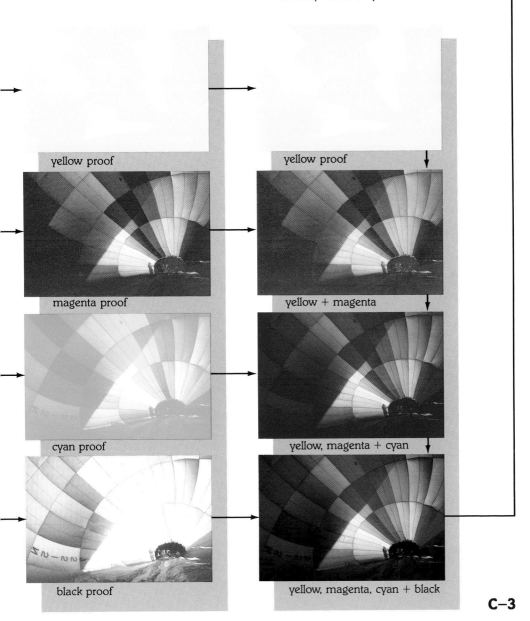

yellow proof

yellow proof

magenta proof

yellow + magenta

cyan proof

yellow, magenta + cyan

black proof

yellow, magenta, cyan + black

C–3

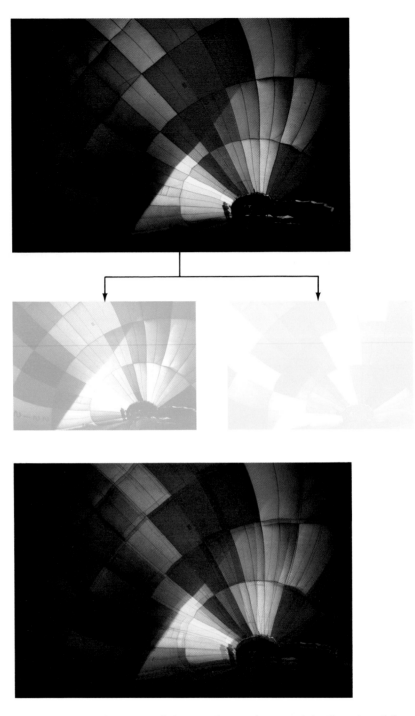

11-7 The cyan plate or proof shows only partial tone and detail, yet it and the black plate show the most. The yellow proof is the most difficult to discern. Unless *all* colors fall into precisely correct position, reproduction of any color will be poor, as the out-of-register image (bottom illustration) shows.

(Courtesy Woodfin Camp / Annie Griffiths)

C–4

viewing a 3-D movie without the proper glasses: Nothing is aligned; if you watch the movie that way for too long, you'll probably get seasick.

Process color requires more critical separation because of the tight overlapping of colors. In spot color runs, some colors may not touch and have *loose* register. When *tight* register is needed, most good printing presses will oblige, as they can maintain the position of an impression to within 1/1000 of an inch.

But in order to have the press do its work, the printer must receive accurate registration information for the plates. This is discussed in Chapter 12, "Preparation of Mechanicals." In the four-color process, all page negatives (screen colors) are carefully keyed with registration marks (Figure 11-8). These marks show the proper positioning of the image on the printing plates. If a page negative moves slightly in the making (burning in) of a printing plate, register will be affected. Likewise, poor tension on a paper roll or looseness in an offset blanket will hurt registration. Failure to maintain quality control in this area will cost time, money, and very likely, clients.

Cost and Quality Control in Color Printing

Because of the high cost of color work, even with today's faster, computerized presses, it is important to keep a careful watch on both expenses and the quality received.

To give you an idea of cost differential between black-and-white printing and the addition of color, consider a print job of 8 pages on 8 by 10 stock, with 10 photographs occupying one-third of the printed space, at a run of 5000. If that job had one color (spot) added to all pages, the cost would go up by at least *25%*. If the job was to be in the four-color process with all photographs separated and screened for color reproduction, the cost would be at least *200%* over the black-and-white expense.

The higher premium for four-color can be attributed to:

1. The need to have color originals filtered, separated and keyed for preproduction approval
2. The closer production work required to ensure that all colors will be in perfect register
3. The cost of the additional plates, ink and press, area needed.

Obviously, the product received must be worth the high expense. Separated color, made available for inspection through a color key proof (often called a *cromalin*) or through a press proof, must be inspected carefully. If the color, reassembled after scanning, has resulted in unacceptable color *shifts* (e.g., a skin tone that has too much magenta), corrections should be ordered. If the engraver or scanner is unaware of the type of inks that the printer will use in reproduction, a shift may occur in printing that cannot be seen in the cromalin. If the quality of paper is poor (e.g., it lacks sufficient enameling for high reflectance), the reproduction of certain colors may be too dull.

Beyond Four-Color

As if the cost and precision of four-color work weren't enough, there are also five- and six-color processes to consider.

A typical *five-color* project would involve the three printer primaries, the black plate, and another color that could not be mixed from the printer's ink fountains of four colors. *Silver* is a good example. It is becoming a popular background color against which to print process color because it provides more contrast and a sophisticated look. Not surprisingly, it is a more expensive project, especially considering that the silver may require another run through the press for a coating of special varnish to prevent smearing.

A *six-color* process might include all of the following plus another color not mixable from the printer primaries or able to be screened from them. It would generally be an application of *spot* color for a border or headline. You could tell this by looking at it under a lupe (a magnifying glass of at least 8-power); it would be unscreened, like the black text (often referred to as *line copy.*). Typical in this process might be the reproduction of a four-color photograph against a background of applied silver, with a specifically mixed color for the headline to contrast with black type. Although this process is indeed more expensive, it is not rare to see it; in exceptional earning years, you may see it in some companies' annual reports.

Four-Color Alternatives

Some daily newspapers, as well as other publications, have tried *three-color* reproduction of their photographs. In this less-expensive process, the black plate is eliminated in the photo reproduction (but used still for all line copy). While it is a cost saver, the results are less attractive than the traditional four-color approach. The most noticeable effects in three-color are the loss of contrast and edge definition (sharpness) in the image.

There are other color options available. As pointed out in Chapter 7, two of the most frequently used are the *tint block* and *duotone*. If a black-and-white photograph is regularly screened as a *halftone* and is overprinted with a tint block in color, it usually looks unrealistic, but the price is right. The tint block is usually better reserved for applications of spot color used in combination with black.

11-8 Registration marks. These are important keys for the worker who aligns page negatives on the platemaking machine. Improper marking leads to color that is printed "out of register."

A duotone, slightly more expensive, usually provides more pleasing results. In this process, *two* halftone screens are made of the original black-and-white image. The second screen concentrates on the middle tones of the picture. The whites and shadows of the picture remain fairly crisp because the color (the second plate) only takes on the middle (grey) tones of the picture. In an example of higher quality printing today, some photography books are featuring the *two-black* duotone process, creating black-and-white images with deep shadows, crisp highlights and a deep range of greyish, middle tones.

CHECKLIST: Points to Remember About Color

By no means an exhaustive list, the following points cover many frequently overlooked considerations that are applicable to both monochromatic and multicolor printing:

1. When using more than one color, reserve the darkest for the basic message and use the additional colors for mood or emphasis.
2. Color used behind type should be light to ensure legibility—the smaller the type, the lighter the background color should be.
3. Be *very* careful when running type in color. Some colors are too light to be used on white stock. Yellow is a good example. Use hues with lower value and higher chroma.
4. If both four-color process *and* black-and-white *halftones* appear on the same page or signature, consult both the engraver and the printer. If the black-and-white pictures are large and dark, they may require such heavy inking that the black process plates will have to carry an excess that may muddy the color reproductions.
5. When running type in color (other than black) on a page where process printing appears, be aware that two runs—in perfect register—may be required to get the proper color. For example, if a deep *orange* is required, two plates (*magenta* and *yellow*) will be required. A satisfactory result is possible if the type is large.
6. Likewise, when *reverse* (white) type is to appear on a color formed by overprinting two or more plates—for example, on a dark green made by printing a screened black on a light green—the reverse printing must be on both plates. Unless they are printed in very close register, the type will not appear as a clean white.

7. Type printed in reverse should be within a fairly dark area to ensure image recognition. As a general rule, avoid reverses against a tone of less than 40 percent of the full hue.

8. Restraint should be exercised in the use of additional color. Because of cost, clients often feel that color should be applied lavishly to get their money's worth. But an overuse of color can defeat the extra expense. Often a single spot of color is sufficient, or two can work together to enhance contrast. Use the principles of good design to guide you.

12

Preparation of Pasteups (Mechanicals)

After type has been set on photocomposing machines and illustrations have been scaled for reproduction, the next step in the preparation of copy for modern printing methods is the creation of what is called a *pasteup* or *mechanical.*

As its name indicates, a pasteup is a pasted version of a printing job ready to be photographed and made into a plate. The use of the term *mechanical* stems from the fact that the pasteup is to be "camera ready"—ready to enter the photomechanical steps of printing as a precise entity.

If there is more than one color, a separate pasteup is usually required for each color; in these cases, one of these pasteups is the *key* (or *base*), and all others must be matched precisely to it. (In special cases, such as overprinting a headline across a picture, two separate pasteups may be required for only one color.) The additional pasteups are made on transparent or translucent film; they are called *overlays.* Marks resembling gunsights, called *register marks,* are used to match up the pasteups. More is said later about this *register* or *registration* (precise positioning) of elements so that they match other colors or other elements.

243

To understand the whys and hows of pasteup preparation, the basic differences between line illustrations and halftones discussed in Chapter 7 must be recalled here. Line illustrations contain only pure tones and white, and none of the tones in between. Phototype fits this category, as well as any pen-and-ink drawing, and thus is included in what we call *line work*. Original illustrations containing various shades of tones, such as photographs, are *continuous-tone* illustrations and must be separately photographed through a screen before platemaking. For this reason, they often are not included on pasteups. In addition, each pasteup must be separately photographed, and the resultant negative is stripped into a mask for platemaking as described in Chapter 10. Hence a pasteup is also a piece of communication to the stripper who will guide it through the platemaking steps.

Who Does Pasteups and Why

Pasteups may be done by either the printer or the customer, but there is a definite trend toward having the customer prepare them. Most in-house printing operations now involve pasteups. It has always been common practice for advertising agency art departments to prepare mechanicals, and the development of cold-type composing systems has now made it a frequent chore for magazine and public relations personnel as well. In newspaper shops, pasteups are usually the responsibility of union personnel, but in some nonunion situations editorial personnel are also involved in preparing pasteups.

What Makes a Good Pasteup?

When properly done, a one-color pasteup contains all line work, so that only one camera exposure is needed to reproduce it. The primary role of the pasteup is to avoid tedious working with film during platemaking; it is much easier to paste each piece of display type and body type into position than it is to cut holes in a mask and strip pieces of film into position.

A good pasteup will also have all elements positioned *exactly*, with all elements of an even tone so that they will photograph well. A good pasteup will also be without blemishes and will have all instructions needed by a stripper clearly shown. Incorrect positioning, uneven type proofs, dirt and fingerprints, vague or missing instructions, and missing elements result in poor pasteups.

Some pasteup flaws can be corrected after the negatives are made by *opaquing* the negatives (painting them), but this should be avoided as much as possible. It makes no sense to do pasteups to lower costs and then add to costs by forcing someone else to paint out thumbprints or other blemishes that show as clear spots on a film negative. A good pasteup keeps opaquing to a minimum.

The photographs in Figure 12-1 show some of the tools and procedures involved in making mechanicals.

12-1 Some procedures in preparing a mechanical. (Photos by Neil Sapienza)

12-1a Good tools are needed for good mechanicals. Some of them are shown here: drawing board, T-square, triangles, pens, X-Acto knife, calipers, rulers, scaling wheel, light box, white paint, brush.

12-1b For precision alignment of proofs, use a T-square and triangle.

12-1c   This mechanical is nearing completion. Most of the waxed type proofs are in position. Use tweezers to handle small pieces, as here. Note the completed overlay for a second color, flipped back onto the table while final work is done on the key pasteup.

12-1d   For precision trimming of proofs, use a T-square.

12-1e   Preparation of a second overlay begins.

12-1f   Register marks are placed on the new overlay to insure precise alignment with the first overlay and the key.

Tools Needed for Preparing Camera-Ready Mechanicals

A Complete Preliminary Layout Is Essential

In order to prepare mechanicals well and efficiently, pasteup artists must start with an accurate and detailed plan for the job—a *layout*, or *dummy*, as it may be called. Without the complete plan at their disposal, pasteup artists have to expect many false starts and errors resulting from changes that must be made. Accurate copyfitting and photoscaling are essential parts of any such layout. No one can put a jigsaw puzzle together if the parts do not match or if pieces are missing.

A Suitable Surface Is Needed

The surface on which type proofs and other elements are to be pasted is extremely important for a number of reasons. First, the surface must accept the adhesive well and it must permit drawing with ruling pens without causing lines to spread and become fuzzy. The surface also must be dimensionally stable if any precision work is required; shrinking or other distortion cannot be tolerated for close-register printing.

In advertising agencies where mechanicals are prepared, not only to be photographed for platemaking but also to show clients in an impressive, neat and exact fashion what the finished product will look like, heavy and expensive illustration board is usually used for the key. In printers' art departments the preferred surface for the key, if *tight* register (also called *hairline* or *close* register) is required, is usually a polyester (plastic) material. The printer's preference is based on the need to have the surfaces for all parts of a mechanical of the same material—so that they all react the same way to moisture, heat and other conditions. A set of color pasteups with the key (black) pasteup on board and overlays for colors on film cannot be expected to stay in exact register; yet overlays must be transparent or translucent, so they obviously cannot be on boards. For newspaper and other periodical work where precision is not required, key pasteups are usually done on paper sheets that are preprinted, gridded, and tailored to the publication's format.

Grids, Jigs, Underlays

Preprinted forms for mechanicals can be extremely helpful, especially in periodical work. With a *grid* that has been precision-printed (do not try to make your own) with lines that are very close together, pasteups can be done quickly and with reasonable accuracy. Grids can be set off in picas, half-picas, fractions of an inch, or millimeters depending on their intended use. The grids may have heavier lines at regular intervals (perhaps at every sixth pica) if these lines can be useful. A center line from each dimension and crossing at the exact center can also be helpful.

A *jig* is a customized grid sheet (also called a *pasteup dummy sheet* or *dummy sheet*) that clearly shows placement dimensions for all standard elements: column lines, margins, trim edges, page numbers, running heads and so on. Any repetitive work, such as that involved in magazine, book and newspaper pages, can be made simpler with jigs. All printing on grids or jigs is in light blue, a color the camera and graphic arts film do not "see."

In order to avoid or reduce the cost of preprinted jigs or grids, an *underlay* printed in black can be prepared and used on a light table. Sometimes paper underlays will work, but they often are made as film positives because the lines are blacker and the background is clear.

Light Tables, Drawing Boards, T-Squares, Triangles

Grids and jigs are invaluable aids for any pasteup artist, but "eyeballing" with the aid of grid lines is not accurate enough for close work. A number of devices are used to increase precision.

A light source under the work surface is extremely helpful if the pasteup sheets are translucent. Tables with built-in fluorescent tubes under a glass top or what could be called lighted drawing boards are widely used.

Wooden drawing boards with metal edges, metal T-squares and clear plastic triangles are also useful aids. These devices should be constantly checked for accuracy by first drawing a line with the T-square guided at the left and then drawing another with the T-square on the other side; these lines must be absolutely parallel or something is out of square. Flipping the triangle for a second line can serve as a check on its accuracy.

If a large amount of precision pasteup is to be done, mechanical substitutes for T-squares are often used. These *drafting machines*, as they are called, have a geared head containing horizontal and vertical straight edges; the head moves about on an arm that can be pivoted into any position. The edge guides are always at right angles and prevent the misalignment that often comes when T-squares are not quite tight against a board edge.

The great advantage of using pasteup composition of pages is lost when the elements are not squarely positioned; off-angle work is the curse of printing processes requiring photomechanical prepress steps and must be avoided. Extreme care is essential at all times during the pasteup process.

Adhesives

Type proofs and other elements are fixed in position on a mechanical with a variety of materials or methods. Among these are wax, rubber cement, both single- and double-faced Scotch brand or similar adhesive tapes, and spray adhesives.

The most efficient and most common adhesive is hot-melt adhesive wax. Wax requires special applying devices, either hand-held or table-top models, to permit the wax to be melted and applied evenly. These devices usually apply the wax in parallel strips; sometimes double coating by running a proof through twice and in opposite directions is required.

The outstanding feature of adhesive wax is that it allows elements to be moved from one position to another; an element can easily be lifted and repositioned without losing its adhesive properties. It is important to use the right wax for the machine and for the paper it must adhere to, as well as the right temperature for melting. If these are correct, waxing is the cleanest, fastest and most convenient method of fixing proofs to the pasteup surface.

Rubber cement is the old standard. It can be used wet, in which case only the back of the element is coated and the element can be moved about somewhat as it is being pressed on a board or paper surface. Or it can be applied to both the element and the board, and then permitted to dry before being positioned. The latter provides better bonding but requires extreme care in placement because the bonding is instantaneous and no sliding is possible. The main disadvantages of rubber cement are general messiness, the fact that it will form a yellow stain, and its tendency to draw dirt around edges. It also tends to slow down pasteup work. Nevertheless, it is still in common use.

When pasteups are to go before a camera quickly and there is no need to retain them for any length of time, adhesive tapes are adequate. Double-faced tape at strategic places can hold elements in position if the camera operator is careful not to let edges get turned over when the mechanical is placed under the glass cover of the copyboard. Single-faced tape can be used if it can be kept clear of any image area; it can show in reproduction, especially of continuous tone.

Spray adhesives can be used, but they have the obvious disadvantage of settling on unwanted pieces even when great care is taken.

Getting the Job Done: Commercial Register Work

The purpose for which a mechanical is being prepared dictates the best procedure to follow in its preparation. Because pasteups for some periodicals are simpler and require less care than for some others, let us first assume that we are to complete a pasteup of that kind, with tight register of colors not being required. This kind of noncritical register is called *commercial* register.

All type proofs should first be gathered. It is poor practice to start without all proofs, but obviously this may sometimes have to be done in newspapers and other periodicals if deadlines dictate it. At any rate, the

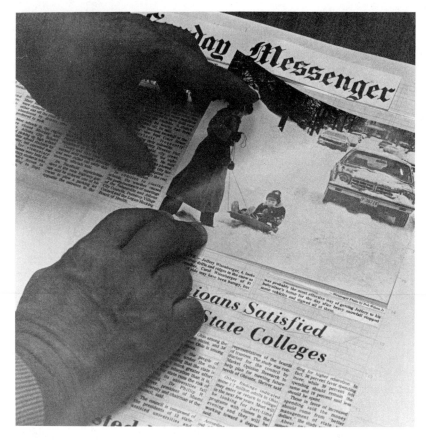

12-2 For most newspaper work, screened prints are fixed to the mechanical along with type and line illustrations. The mechanical is then photographed as if it contained only line copy.

type proofs must be carefully checked for imperfections. White specks in type can quickly be corrected with a pen; uneven development usually requires resetting, but it cannot be tolerated. Along with off-angle work, another curse of printing systems using photographic prepress steps is a variation in tone for type. To have the body type of one story darker than for all the others is not acceptable; even worse are the correction lines that are of a different tone. Good pasteup personnel carefully check all type proofs before sticking them down; it is much more difficult to make substitutions at a later stage.

Next, illustrations should be checked. Usually any line illustrations are drawn directly on the pasteup surface or prepared separately in exact size ready to be pasted in position.

Periodicals vary in their handling of continuous-tone illustrations. Often these illustrations are scaled to size and screened in a process camera to produce a screened photoprint. These screened prints can be pasted in position and then treated as line work (see Figure 12-2). They are, in effect, the same as Benday line illustrations—they are composed of screen-created dots that can be captured by a camera along with type or line drawings.

For finest quality, photoprints are not used, because there is a limitation to the fineness of the screen that can be used; therefore the dots created are large enough to be visible in reproduction. Also, in printing, every step involved in camera reproduction tends to decrease quality slightly, and the rephotographing of photoprints is an added step.

Use of Photomechanical Transfer (PMT)

Screened photoprints are often prepared on a *photomechanical transfer machine* (PMT) that automatically develops the screened print after it has been exposed through a screen in a process camera. Newspapers, particularly, make much use of this process. Use of the process camera and PMT for enlargement and reduction of both type and line illustrations is also common. (The treatment of continuous-tone reproductions for maximum quality is discussed in the next section.)

After type and artwork are gathered, they should be separated for color. For our example, we will assume that everything is black and white except a headline which is to be printed in red. We will therefore set aside the headline and work only with the remainder.

For maximum efficiency, all proofs should be coated with adhesive first, before cutting out each piece. The waxed proofs can then be placed face up on waxed paper for cutting and trimming; even small pieces will stay in place and stay free of dirt until they are positioned.

This is the time—before proofs are positioned—to draw or position borders and lines that are to print. Borders and *rules*, as they are called, are available as pressure-sensitive tape and in various thicknesses and styles. If these are used, they can be pressed into place. If rules are to be drawn, good ruling pens and undercut line guides (T-squares, triangles and rulers) must be used. Pens of mechanical drawing quality should be used and tested to make sure that the ink does not spread and fuzz out on the particular surface. The T-squares, triangles and rulers used as guidelines should be undercut so that lines will not smear when they are drawn; without the undercutting, ink runs under the edge. Although special ruling guides can be bought, they can also be "rigged up." The only requirement is that the edge be slightly raised off the paper when it is positioned for drawing; a strip of masking tape can do the trick.

What Lines Mean

So there is no doubt about which lines are to print and which are not, it is wise to coordinate their color with their purpose. Blue lines, because they have the same effect on film as if they were white, are for guidelines and instructions. They must be light blue, as mentioned; blues are dark only because they contain some black, and they can contain enough to be reproduced. (A nonreproducing blue pencil is essential in preparing mechanicals.) Black lines should be reversed for material that is to be reproduced. Red lines reproduce as well as black; their use should be restricted to placement lines that must show in a negative but will be removed before a plate is made.

Working with Type Proofs

With rules in place, trim all proofs, including illustrations. Type proofs should be cut, if possible, with an edge of at least $\frac{1}{8}$ inch around them; the raised plane of the proof can cast a shadow. If the edge is far enough from the image, it will be covered by the mask when the negative made later is stripped into position, and shadows will be no problem.

Corrections in type are always a problem when they must be made at this point. Pasting them over the proof adds still another layer to the pasteup that creates shadow problems in photographing. It is best to cut out the errors, if possible, and replace them with the corrected material. Patching in lines, and especially words, is often done, but it can lead to imperfections and lost corrections when the pieces fall off.

One tip for getting type proofs lined up: Make two short vertical cuts in the proof in line with the left vertical edge of the type, one just above the type, the other just below. Then by lifting the two corners you can align the type itself with a grid line or straight edge under the proof. In other words, the border on the proof is thus prevented from being an obstacle to lining up the type (see Figure 12-3). A light blue line along

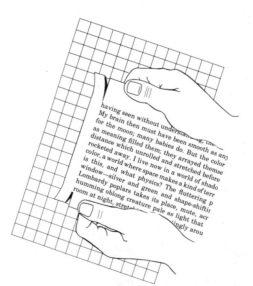

12-3 Aligning a type proof.

the edge of the type from top to bottom edge of the proof can serve the same purpose as the cuts.

To get screened prints sized and positioned accurately, they should be roughly trimmed only before they are pasted in position. The final cutting, following crop marks or a guideline, can be much more precise if it is done with the proof pasted in position rather than before it is placed.

Preparing Color Overlays

With type proofs, rules, and illustrations in position, we are ready to turn to the preparation of a mechanical for the red plate. Although the example we are using does not require close register, we should still use register marks to ensure proper positioning of the color image. Marks are available on adhesive-backed, pressure-sensitive clear tape or sheets, or they can be drawn, if necessary. Register marks (crossed lines about $\frac{3}{4}$ inch long) should be put in two places outside (but relatively close to) the image area on the key mechanical. The lines should be horizontal and vertical, not at some other orientation.

The second pasteup, for the red, must be on a transparent base because it will be laid over the key mechanical and integrated with it by sight. The first step here is to fasten the overlay securely to the base mechanical; the second is to place matching register marks exactly over those that can be seen on the key. Then, following the location shown on the layout pattern, paste the headline in position on the overlay (see Figure 12-4).

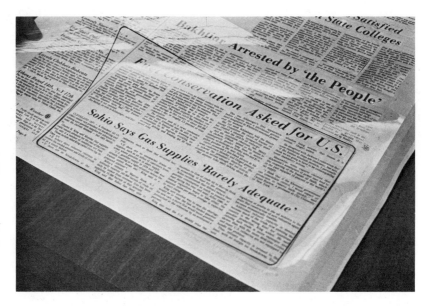

12-4 A transparent second-color overlay. The copy to be printed in red—in this case a box border—is laid over the key mechanical; and positioned with register marks. Note these marks near upper right and lower left corners of the box. (Register marks are opaqued from the negative before plate-making.)

The mechanicals are then ready for the steps involved in plate-making. Each one will be separately photographed, and their negatives will be stripped into two separate masks. They will be positioned in the masks by using the register marks, which will then be covered up before the light is beamed through the masks separately to form the two plates.

Preparation of Mechanicals: Tight Register Work

Some changes in technique are involved in preparing mechanicals that involve tight register and maximum quality for the best possible reproduction of photographs, maps, and other exacting artwork.

As already noted, most printers find that maximum accuracy is possible only if the key and the overlays are made of the same material; thus a transparent or translucent stable material such as polyester is used for all. Many printers, however, use illustration board for the key.

Most printers also say that really accurate register is only possible with a pin and punch system similar to the one they use to register the negatives into flats. This system requires that holes be punched in each mechanical so that, when these holes are used to fasten the mechanicals to properly positioned pins, the mechanicals will not move. However, many use only the register marks, relying on pasteup personnel to make sure that the crosslines stay lined up as they work. In any case, the register marks are essential.

Many printers also prefer to "break for color" when they are working with negatives, rather than work with two or more mechanicals. They can ensure absolute hairline register if, working from one mechanical, they make duplicate negatives and then block out those elements that do not belong in the color run that is involved. Many problems, including different degrees of stability in the pasteup surfaces and inaccuracies in register marks, can be eliminated because the negatives are identical. Many customers, however, still prefer to avoid a printer's charges for this work by preparing a separate mechanical for each color.

In some cases where positioning is tight (for example, a cutline that must be extremely close to a photo) or when line work is to be combined with continuous tone, separate pasteups may be required. The pasteups are then masked separately and exposed in sequence on a plate. This process is called *double burning*: The halftone is burned (exposed) onto the plate through one mask, and the line work is burned through the other mask. Separate pasteups to get tight positioning are necessary because the stripper cannot place two negatives (one a halftone and the other line) very close together; a fairly sizable strip of the mask is needed between the two or it will tear, bend, and slide out of position. Screened photoprints eliminate some of these double burns, but they are not used when top-quality reproduction is required.

Placement of Illustrations

To process continuous-tone elements separately, mechanicals must make provision for their accurate placement through the use of what are called "windows" because they end up as areas of clear film when the negatives are made. These areas on the pasteup must be totally devoid of light-reflecting capability. Red tone sheets that are pressure sensitive (will stick when pressed) are usually used. The tone sheet is put down just as if it were a screened print and is trimmed to the exact dimensions to be occupied by the photo. Black ink can also be used to color in these areas, but there is always a possibility of some reflection if small areas are missed or the ink is not black enough.

An advantage of using red sheets is that they can be seen through, but still not reflect light. This permits the use of photostats under them to identify the illustrations and show how they are to be positioned. It also makes trimming easier, because guidelines can show through.

The placement of illustrations can also be shown on a mechanical with a red outline. The identification of the illustration comes from a blue line drawing in sufficient detail to avoid any possible confusion about the identity of the illustration. A device called a *camera lucida* can be used to project artwork at the desired scale so this drawing can be quickly and easily done. The blue lines must be light enough so they will photograph as white. Or, the red keyline area might be labeled with a letter or number that will correspond with a letter or number on the original artwork. This last method is easiest for the pasteup person, but it has the greatest potential for error and is an inconvenience for a printer. For the printer, this means that the stripper must have the original copy of illustrations at hand in order to identify each negative.

Use of Photostats

Although it is perhaps the most expensive method of handling line work, the use of photostatic enlargements or reductions on the pasteup is foolproof and has many advantages. Photostats (often called *stats*) are reproducible and become an integral part of the mechanical. Many type display problems are solved with photostatic enlargements and reductions; reverses (white lines on a black background) are efficiently handled with photostats.

A photostat machine is useful because it makes enlargements and reductions directly on paper. A lens in the machine keeps the original image right-reading on the negative, but the image is reversed: Blacks are whites, and whites are blacks. In order to get a positive image, the negative print must be re-exposed in the machine. Therefore, reverses for logotypes and other uses are cheaper than positives.

Photostat paper has a minimum size, $8\frac{1}{2} \times 11$; thus "ganging" of illustrations can keep photostat charges to a minimum. This necessitates grouping illustrations that have the same percentage of enlargement or reduction, but the effort is worthwhile.

Care must be taken in ordering photostats so that there is no misunderstanding about whether the reversed negative print or the positive print is desired. Since the negative means one exposure and the positive two, the best way to make an order clear to the photostat operator is to express it in those terms: first print or second print.

Newer types of photostat machines (two trade names are Duostat and Statmaster) make stats in a process that requires only one exposure. In this case the lens produces a wrong-reading image on the negative. This image is directly transferred to the positive sheet during development, to form the right-reading positive stat. A reverse stat is made in the same way, but with specially treated negative paper. Thus the order to the operator of one of these machines need only specify a positive stat (often called a direct positive) or a reverse stat.

When ordering a photostat, size must be carefully specified, just as it would be for a printer's camera, and the type of paper (glossy or matte finish) must be designated. The less expensive matte finish is adequate for prints not to be used for reproduction, but only glossy prints give enough blackness for reproduction.

In publication offices with access to a production plant, a PMT machine is often used instead of a photostat machine. The PMT provides enlarging-reducing capability by means of a process camera; it produces photoprints mechanically. As mentioned earlier, the PMT can also produce screened prints of photographs and other continuous-tone illustrations that can then be treated as line work.

Screen Tints and Special Treatments for Illustrations

The screen tints discussed in the chapter on illustrations can be applied directly to a mechanical or they can merely be located on the mechanical and specified for insertion in the mask at the stripping stage. Any line illustration that is on a mechanical may also have some of its components screened in order to create some middle tones.

If screens are on a mechanical, they should be checked for flaws and replaced if necessary. It has been assumed in our discussion of mechanicals that they will all be reproduced without enlargement or reduction. They can be reduced, of course, and if they are, the effect of the reduction on any screen used on the mechanical must be considered.

Although it involves a stripping charge, it is sometimes advantageous to let the printer strip in a film screen rather than put one on the mechanical. Accuracy of reproduction is thus assured. It is possible, for example, to get distortion in a screen if it is applied to the mechanical over an irregular area of a pasteup caused by the edge of a type proof. The surface under a screen must be clean and smooth. If a printer is to apply a screen panel, the area should be precisely bordered by a red line on the pasteup.

Line work can be reproduced on a screen background by applying a positive photostat within a blue border on a pasteup; a negative photostat with a red border will result in a reversed line image on the screen. For the printer, the surprinting of the black line requires a double burn; the reverse image does not. Both require additional negatives and stripping. If the line image is to surprint (be in black) the tint must be light (a low percentage), and vice versa for a reverse.

Line work, including type, can also be reproduced over halftone reproductions to form surprint and reverse combinations as described in the chapter on illustrations. The procedure is the same as with tint screens.

Outlines and irregular shapes can be expedited by using red tone sheets cut to form the outline and placed in register on an overlay. The red "knocks out" the image wherever it is used.

Multipage Mechanicals

If more than one page is to be on a press plate, the work of the printer can be minimized by putting all the pages on a single mechanical. In order to do this, the way in which the pages must fall on the press plate must be known before the mechanical is prepared. The different ways in which pages can be arranged (imposition) depend on folding and binding and are fairly complicated. These subjects are discussed in Chapter 13. It should suffice here to point out that the imposition is critical, and no multipage mechanical should be attempted without full knowledge of it.

Guidelines and Dimension Marks

Guidelines, dimension marks and instructions are an important part of mechanical preparation. They are more complicated for multipage mechanicals, but some such marking is essential to any mechanical, both as an aid during its preparation and for the printer during later processing.

Actual finished size for any mechanical must be clearly marked, usually with blue lines forming the outline, and black corner marks emphasizing the corners. These marks show the *trim size*, the finished size of the printed paper after it has been trimmed. Corner marks are in black because they may be retained by the printer as trim guides; printers may also prefer to opaque them from the negative and use their own marks.

A *bleed* dimension is also marked if any portion of the image area is to go off a trim edge. The bleed edges should be shown with a red line.

Fold lines are shown with a short, dotted black line that is outside the trim line; it is a helpful guide during the preparation of the mechanical and may also be used as a guide by the printer.

Any guidelines used merely to determine accurate placement of elements, whether part of the preprinted grid form or drawn in place, must be light blue to assure that they will not be photographed by the camera and thus appear on the negative.

Call-outs (instructions written at the end of a line drawn from the point of reference) should be beyond bleed lines in marginal space or on a special tissue overlay.

CHECKLIST: Mechanicals: Some Helpful Hints

1. Remember that anything black, red or gray on a mechanical may end up in print; do not rely on a printer to remove all errors by opaquing.
2. Read all proofs carefully before starting; correction of type errors after a mechanical has been begun is inconvenient, to say the least.
3. Use full-page electronic "pagination" if it is available. The extra planning and markup is worth it; pasteups are only a poor substitute for full-page photoproofs from a computerized typesetter.
4. If full-page typesetting is not possible, at least use area composition to its fullest capability. The fewer the pieces involved in preparation of a mechanical, the fewer are the chances for error.
5. Keep cutting tools sharp, pens and brushes clean, and work area tidy and well lighted.
6. Keep checking T-square and the alignment of elements to catch any flaws as quickly as possible.
7. Use red film sheets instead of painting in black areas. Results are more certain and it takes less time.
8. Watch edges of individual pieces of proofs or illustrations. Dirty edges will appear as lines on negatives and require opaquing. For reverse solid areas, paint the edges black so that they will not reflect light and appear on the negative.
9. Use pastedown and transfer letters when unusual, "this time only" typefaces are required, but be especially careful with alignment and spacing.
10 When ruling lines, to get a good beginning and ending, place a piece of tape at each end before starting with the ruling pen. Then start the line over the beginning tape and run it beyond the ending tape. Line ends are then exact and free of flaws.
11. Keep a nonreproducing blue pencil on hand for writing instructions on mechanicals.

13

Imposition, Binding and Paper Selection

As they produce booklets, brochures, magazines, books or other such publications, printers ordinarily print several pages on a single sheet of paper. All of the pages that are to be printed on one side of a sheet must be positioned so that when both sides of the sheet have been printed the sheet can be folded and bound with the pages in proper sequence.

This arranging or arrangement of pages is called *imposition*. It is of great concern to printers because they are responsible for it, and any reprinting necessary because of an imposition error is a major financial loss for them. Although every effort is put forth by printers to impose sheets that result in correct pagination, it is not too uncommon to see pages upside down or not in proper sequence in publications produced under deadline pressure.

Imposition is also vitally important to editors and designers of printed material because of its effect on planning for deadines and for controlling costs.

Imposition Planning

To see how imposition affects planning for printing, let's first look at it in its simplest form. The smallest piece of printing, by necessity, contains at least two pages, one on the front of the sheet and the second on the back. If only one page is to be printed and the other is to remain blank, it would be possible to use a printing press only large enough to accommodate the small single-page-size sheet. If 1000 copies are needed, 1000 sheets are run through the press to be inked on one side.

On the other hand, if both sides of the sheet are to be printed, the option to use a press capable of printing two pages is available and might be much more efficient. Running the same small press 1000 times to ink one side, then turning the sheet over and running it through 1000 times again, would get the job done. But in this case it is likely that the job would be done "two pages up"; pages one and two would be printed on one side of a larger sheet, then the sheet would be turned over and "backed up" with page one behind page two and page two behind page one, as diagrammed in Figure 13-1. With the larger press, only 500 sheets are run through to be inked on one side and then turned over to be backed up, a total of 1000 impressions for the press, only half of what the smaller press required. A press capable of printing two pages up would also handle four pages efficiently, as shown in Figure 13-2. In general, use of the largest possible press results in economy of production.

13-1 Two pages can be printed on one side of a sheet and repeated on the reverse side so the sheet can be cut in half to form duplicate sheets of two pages. Only half as many press impressions are needed in comparison with printing one of the pages on the front of the smaller sheet, then printing the second page on the back. This is the simplest example of what would be called *work-and-turn* imposition.

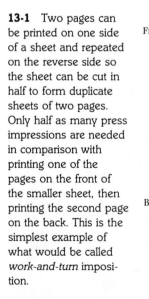
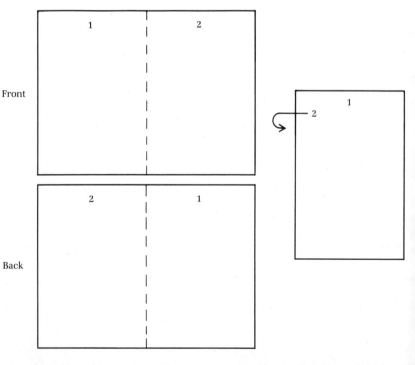

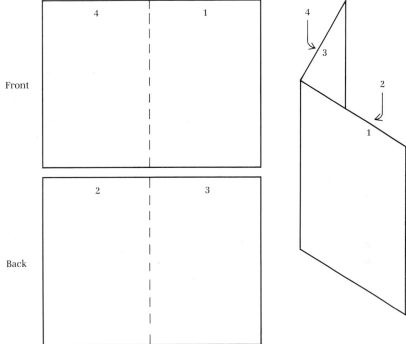

13-2 The same size press used in Figure 13-1 can be used more efficiently for four pages, two on one side of the sheet and the other two on the back, folded once. This is the simplest example of what would be called *sheet-wise* imposition.

Imposition and Signatures

Each sheet that is printed is folded to become one or more sections of a publication. Called *signatures,* they vary widely in number of pages. The example we have just used would indicate that the smallest signature is two pages (one leaf with two sides), but for all practical purposes, the minimum is four pages. One sheet folded only once produces four pages, so even the smallest folder, newsletter, or booklet will have at least one four-page signature. Printing-press capacities and sheet sizes are geared to multiples of four, printing two pages up for four-page signatures, four pages up for an eight-page, and so on through 16, 32, and 64.

There are numerous kinds of impositions, especially for the great variety of intricately folded pamphlets and folders that are produced and are discussed in Chapter 16. In any case, the imposition a printer uses is dictated by the press capacity, the number of pages involved, and the folding and binding that are to follow.

For editors and graphic designers, knowledge of at least the most basic characteristics of the printer's imposition is essential since much of the planning for using color and setting deadlines will depend on the kind of imposition that will be used.

For example, let us look at the problems of the editor of a small 16-page publication. If, as is typical, the printer plans to print half the pages on one side of a sheet and half on the other, the editor must know which pages go on which side of the sheet. The editor can then set separate deadlines for each unit of eight pages that must go on the press at the same time. Only when all eight pages are complete right down to the last photo and the last line of type is the form ready for the press.

If there is to be a color in addition to black on only eight pages, or fewer, the editor, knowing the imposition, can assign color only to those pages that fall on one side of the sheet. By so doing, the color is printed with only one additional press run; if one or more pages of color were to be assigned to each side of the sheet, two additional press runs would be required.

Imposition, therefore, is of great importance because press delays, missed publication dates and unnecessary color costs can be avoided by a planner who knows what method the printer will use.

Kinds of Imposition

For most purposes there are two basic kinds of imposition. One of these is shown in Figure 13-3: Half the pages in a signature are printed on one side of the sheet and the other half are printed on the back of the sheet. This method is called *sheetwise* and is preferred by most printers for most jobs.

In the other kind, as in Figure 13-4, all pages of a signature are printed on one side of a sheet for half the press run, and the sheet is then turned over for the same pages to be printed on the opposite side during the final half run. The sheet is then cut apart to form two signatures. Depending upon how the sheet is turned before it is backed up, this imposition has three variations—*work-and-turn,* which is most common, *work-and-tumble,* and *work-and-twist.*

outside form				inside form			
5	12	6	8	3	14	15	2
4	13	16	1	6	11	10	7

13-3 Sheetwise imposition of a 16-page signature would put eight pages on one side and a different eight pages on the other side, as shown here with pages 1 through 16.

13-4 When circumstances warrant, the imposition used for the same size sheet and press as shown in Figure 13-3 would be work-and-turn, thus producing duplicate 8-page signatures instead of one 16-page. Pages are arranged so the eight pages on the front of the sheet are duplicated on the back; then the sheets are cut in half to form twin 8-page signatures.

3	9	5	4
2	7	8	1

In work-and-turn, the sheet is turned so that the left edge becomes the right edge, but the front (gripper) edge remains the same. In work-and-tumble, the sheet is tumbled so that the back edge becomes the gripper edge when the sheet is being printed on the second side. In work-and-twist all edges are reversed. Because work-and-turn employs the same gripper edge for printing both sides, it is used much more than the other two techniques.

The sheetwise imposition shown in Figure 13-3 would produce a 16-page signature for a magazine. Suppose, however, that your magazine consists of 24 pages. Can this press efficiently handle eight pages? It can if a different imposition is employed, such as work-and-turn, with each impression producing two twin eight-page signatures. Note in Figure 13-4 that the same size sheet is used, and we are still printing eight pages up, the maximum for this press. In this case all numbers, one through eight, will be printed on half as many sheets. The sheet then will be turned over and the same eight pages will be printed on the other side. The sheets then are cut as shown by the dotted line to form duplicate eight-page signatures. Our earlier examples of two- and four-page signatures might help make this point clear. Folding sheets and numbering pages can also reveal how forms are being imposed.

In Figure 13-5, a 16-page work-and-turn imposition is shown. It should be noted that the sheet and press plate used for this signature would have to be twice as big as the one shown in Figures 13-3 and 13-4. It prints "16 up," in printing parlance, and the other was limited to "8 up."

In summary, sheet-size capacity of printing presses determines signature sizes and imposition used. If a printer has a press large enough

13-5 Work-and-turn imposition for a 16-page signature would require a press with a capacity to handle sheets twice as large as those used in Figures 13-3 and 13-4.

to print all the pages required for a work-and-turn imposition, work-and-turn will be used. But if the press capacity is only half of a desired signature, sheetwise imposition would be required.

Figure 13-5 also shows a rather specialized printing technique that is of importance to imposition. This is *split-fountain* or *split-roller*, a

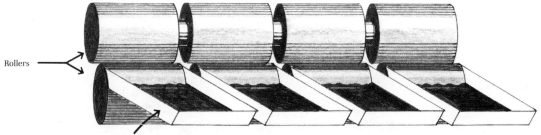

Rollers

Fountain

13-6 In split-fountain printing, the tray of ink (fountain) on a printing press is divided into compartments corresponding to split rollers. Different colors can be used in each compartment, thus permitting application of several colors with one run of the press. Each section of the roller carries a different ink to the plate.

technique that applies several colors to various positions on a sheet during one press run as shown in Figure 13-6. Once a sheet has been printed in black, several colors can be added with one impression if they are planned to fall in "channels."

Although the procedure varies, the ink fountain is usually split into several compartments (four, in Figure 13-6), which carry different colors. From these, the inking rollers, correspondingly split, carry the colors to their particular pages. As many colors can be printed simultaneously as there are sections of the roller. To plan color according to the channels covered by each roller section the designer must know the location of each page in a form.

This technique is used extensively by magazines to satisfy the color requirements of advertisers at a minimum cost. Roller splitting for a one-time-only job may be too costly, but for magazines that can use cut rollers repeatedly it can offer substantial cost advantages.

Imposition and Webfed Offset

There has been a marked trend in recent years for many publications to change over from sheetfed letterpress or offset to web offset. Imposition and its effects on the use of color and planning vary considerably when multiunit web perfecting offset presses are used. As noted earlier, web presses are those fed from a roll rather than sheets, and a perfecting press is one that prints both sides of the paper at the same time.

In general, the typical four-unit and six-unit web offset presses used for magazine and book work offer much greater use of color at lower cost; the expense involved in running a second unit, for example, usually is considerably less than putting a sheet through a press a second time.

The availability of several units and the possibility of using more than one web gives great color versatility when using web offset. This wide variation makes it impossible to give a complete analysis of web offset impositions here; printers will provide imposition sheets showing page positions for each variation.

Wraps and Tip-Ins

Although good planning dictates a consideration of imposition and signatures, it is not always possible to produce a publication that will adhere to large signatures.

An advertiser, for example, will frequently insist that a magazine ad be on a special paper or other material. The ad must then be specially handled and inserted into the publication. In book work it is not unusual for the publisher to want a special glossy paper for reproducing the few illustrations to be used and to order the rest of the book printed on a cheaper stock.

In these and other cases where standard signatures cannot be used, the printer will most likely take care of the problem with a *wrap* or a *tip-in.* The former is a four-page insert placed around a signature before it is bound. Because they can be stitched into the binding with their signatures, wraps are as durably bound as the rest of the magazine or book. Wraps are a problem to the editor, however, because he or she must plan their location carefully in order to get the desired continuity of subject matter.

It is possible, but more time-consuming, to place four pages within a signature rather than around it. In that case the pages are simply called an *insert,* if they are in the center of the signature, or an *inside wrap* if they are between the center and the outside.

A tip-in is a pasted-in two- or four-page section. Most tip-ins are of two pages—a single sheet. They are given a coating of paste in a narrow strip along the inner edge that is used to "tip" the sheet into position. Tip-ins are not so durable as wraps or inserts because they are not stitched during binding, but they are frequently used.

Although these inserting methods are commonly used, their use is restricted to situations demanding such treatment. Only when substantial costs are avoided or imperative special effects are obtained should the use of units other than standard signatures be considered.

Folding, Binding, Trimming

When the printed sheets come off the press, the work of the printer, as such, is completed. The printer may or may not process the work further; basically, the remaining work belongs to the bindery, or finishing specialists.

In most cases, bindery operations begin with folding, an often underrated step in publication production. Sheets sometimes must be cut before folding, but this step is avoided whenever possible. Even with the best cutting, the knife "draws" the paper as it goes through a stack, and a variation in page size results. Unbound circulars using bleeds, however, must be cut before folding.

Kinds of Folds

The most commonly used fold, because of its use for books, booklets and magazines, is the *right-angle* fold. Thus, a single sheet folded once becomes a four-page signature; folded again at a right angle it becomes an eight-page signature, and so on. An eight-page signature folded in this manner must be trimmed before the pages are free to be turned so that pages 2, 3, 6 and 7 can be read.

A *French fold* is an eight-page unit made with right-angle folds and not trimmed. French-fold leaflets are often used in advertising and promotion work.

Parallel folds may be either *accordion*, where each succeeding fold is parallel but turned in the opposite direction, or *over-and-over*, where each fold is in the same direction. Like the French fold, both of these folds require no trimming. See Figure 13-7 for common folds.

13-7 Some common folds for printed matter: (a) 4-page folder, single fold. (b) 6-page standard folder. (c) 6-page 4 accordion. (d) 8-page booklet or folder, two right-angle folds, also called French fold if printed one side and not trimmed. (e) 8-page right-angle folder, first fold short. (f) 8-page folder, two parallel folds. (g) 8-page accordion. (h) 8-page parallel folder, three-fold over and over. (i) 8-page parallel map. (j) 10-page accordion. (l) 12-page broadside, first fold short. (m) 16-page parallel booklet. (n) 16-page broadside.

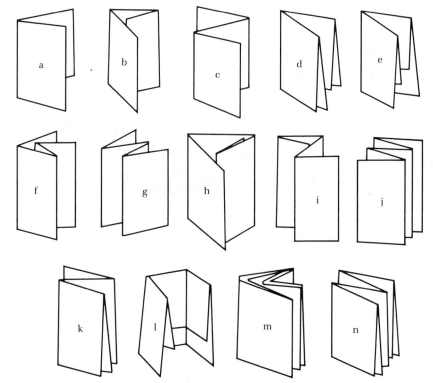

Methods of Binding

Binding may be either a minor or a major contributor to the cost of any printing job. With simple leaflets binding can be skipped entirely; for an elaborate sales presentation book it may be the major cost element. This influence on cost makes binding an important part of production planning. Binding also has a direct bearing on planning in signature units. This point can be more clearly seen with a comparison of two commonly used binding methods.

Saddle-Wire Binding

The most commonly used kind of binding, because it is inexpensive and adequate for many magazines and booklets, is *saddle-wire binding*. Signatures to be bound by this method are inserted one into the other, and wire staples are driven into the fold through to the center of the publication. As they are bound, the signatures resemble a saddle, hence the name.

Saddle-wire binding has some special advantages. Because there is no backbone, only a fold, pages will lie flat. Inside margins can be small, because the binding does not infringe upon the page. Separate covers can be used but are not necessary. Saddle-wire binding is limited, however, in the number of pages it can accommodate. Generally speaking, it is usable only for publications up to about $\frac{1}{4}$ inch in thickness.

Side-Wire Binding

Thicker magazines or booklets (up to about $\frac{1}{2}$ inch in thickness) may be *side-wire bound*. In this sort of binding, signatures are stacked on top of each other and staples are driven through from top to bottom. Because these staples are inserted about $\frac{1}{8}$ inch from the backbone, they prevent side-wire publications from lying flat when open. A separate cover is usually wrapped around and glued to the backbone of side-wire publications. Figure 13-8 illustrates these two binding systems.

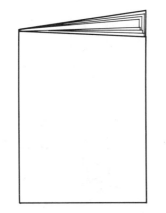
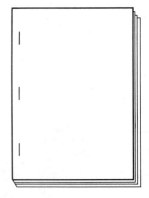

13-8 Saddle-wire binding and side-wire binding.

Once again, the effect of the mechanical operation on editorial planning should be emphasized. In this case, the pages that fall into each signature can vary according to the kind of binding. Except for the center signature, half the pages in each signature of a saddle-wire booklet come from the front of the booklet and the other half come from the back. Thus, in a 32-page booklet of two signatures, the outside or wrap signature contains pages 1 through 8 and 25 through 32. The center signature contains pages 9 through 24. On the other hand, all signatures in side-wire booklets have pages with consecutive numbering. Editors, therefore, must know which binding system is to be used as they complete the signatures to meet press deadlines.

The planner of a side-wire bound booklet or magazine must also allow a larger inside margin to compensate for the $\frac{1}{8}$ inch or more taken up by the binding.

Perfect Binding

The development of durable and pliable plastic adhesives has increased the use of the so-called *perfect binding*. This is a much cheaper method than traditional book binding, yet it can be used for volumes as large as municipal telephone books.

No sewing or stitching is needed in perfect binding. Instead, the backbone area is roughened by grinding, the pliable adhesive is applied to it, and lining cloth is then glued to the backbone. Perfect binding is used for both paperback books (Figure 13-9) and hardcover books.

Traditional Book Binding

The traditional method of book binding, sometimes called *edition binding*, has been in use for centuries. Books bound by this method are

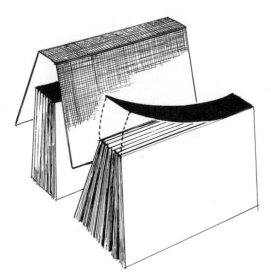

13-9 In perfect binding, lining cloth is glued to backbone, then a stiff paper cover is glued on.

13-10 In Smyth sewing, stitches hold the signatures together at the backbone.

sewn and *casebound;* as "case" implies, they are hardcover books. (Some sewn books are given paper covers, but this combination is not edition binding.)

After the signatures have been gathered, end papers are tipped (pasted) to the first and last signatures. Signatures are then sewn together (Smyth sewing), and the book is "smashed," or compressed before the three sides are trimmed. In Smyth sewing, signatures are saddle-sewn and sewn to each other at the same time. (Figure 13-10).

Books are often *rounded* and *backed* after trimming. They are said to be backed when the backbone has been widened enough to compensate for the thickness of the covers to be added. When rounded, the backbone is made to form a slight arc. It is then reinforced with mesh and paper, which are glued to it, and the *case* (cover) is attached by gluing the end sheets to it.

Loose-Leaf and Mechanical Bindings

Scores of loose-leaf and mechanical binding systems are being used today, ranging all the way from student notebooks to elaborate catalogs and price books.

The chief advantages of these bindings are that pages open flat, may be of different paper stock and even different sizes, and there is no need to be concerned about signatures.

All the mechanical binding systems use more or less the same principle. Sheets are punched with holes along the binding edge and are then bound together by plastic or metal rings or coils that are slipped through the holes.

13-11   Steps from imposition to sewing of signatures. (Courtesy New York Lithographing Corporation and Montauk Book Manufacturing Company, Inc.)

a.   Stripper lines up page negatives on a goldenrod flat according to folding and binding imposition. Light table enables him to follow ruled-up master form below.

b.   Exposed plate ready for developing and fixing.

c.   Banding skid of printed sheets for delivery to bindery.

d. Cutting printed sheets according to specifications.

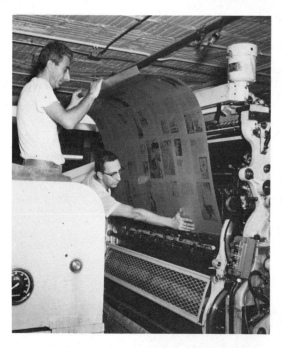

e. Putting finished plate on press.

f. Taking printed sheet out of delivery end of press.

g. Skids of printed sheets ready to be placed on folding machines in the background. Skid in left foreground holds stacks of sheets cut in half, each half containing a 64-page signature (32 pages on each side of sheet).

h. Smyth sewing signatures before binding. Spools of thread are at upper left. Stack of signatures is in front of each operator.

Paper Selection

Sheets and webs of paper are sized to fit common printing press capacities, and skillful imposition is essential for efficient use of paper. Printers will take care of correlating paper dimensions, imposition, and press capacity, however. For the user, other factors are extremely important and must be considered when selecting paper because of paper's effect on appearance and durability.

Paper shares full responsibility with type and illustrations in giving personality to any printed piece. Paper also contributes to the "voice" of the printed material. It can say quality or cheapness and speak loudly or softly. From the user's standpoint, this may be the most vital role of paper. But, although the color, weight, and smoothness must be judged according to their esthetic contributions, these and other characteristics of paper must be analyzed in other ways, too.

Practical properties, such as the ability to withstand age, are very important. Printed matter that is supposed to last for years may disintegrate long before its intended life span has expired if proper paper was not chosen. Or, faulty paper selection can cause printed pieces to fall apart at the folds before the material has completed its usefulness.

The cost of paper is always a determinant. Paper is priced by the pound, with the rate according to the kind and amount of processing needed to give it the desired qualities. Thus weight or thickness becomes significant, increasingly so if the finished product is to be mailed. A small difference in weight per piece can multiply postage costs by thousands of dollars if great numbers of pieces are to be mailed.

The user of printing is thus likely to be most concerned about these characteristics of paper: (1) the esthetic or psychological effect of its appearance and "feel," (2) its permanence, (3) its durability, and (4) its cost and weight.

Printers must share their customers' concern. But, because they are charged with the mechanics of production, they see these characteristics from a slightly different angle, regarding many other technical properties that have special meaning for them.

Printers must be aware of the opacity of paper, for example, knowing that appearance can be ruined if the inked impression on one side shows through to the other. They try to ensure that a printed piece is planned to fit a standard-size sheet of paper that matches press capacity. By so doing, they can minimize the unnecessary costs that increase through wastage from trimming.

A letterpress printer knows that only with a smooth-finish paper can fine-screen engravings be reproduced to a customer's satisfaction. The offset lithographer or gravure printer requires other special papers for good reproduction.

The chemical and physical properties of paper, such as acidity, porosity and surface-bonding strength, must be checked. Papers with high acid content are fine for some work, but are not permanent enough for many uses. Ink spreads after contact with paper according to the porosity of the paper; surface-bonding strength determines a paper's resistance to "picking," the undesirable release of small bits of paper surface during a press run. If picking is excessive, press time can be lengthened because of the need for frequent cleanups.

Printers must always be conscious of the grain of paper. As paper is manufactured, the watery pulp is carried over fine wire cloth and the pulp fibers tend to lie in the same direction. In this way, the fibers give paper a grain, much like that in wood. Grain direction is important because it affects

1. the ease with which paper will run through a press
2. the folding and binding

In a magazine or booklet, for example, the grain should run parallel to the binding so that the sheets will lie flat when open. The bindery must always be consulted to be sure the grain is in the right direction for folding and binding.

The printer, then, in addition to the end-use properties of paper that may be apparent to the customer, must also consider

1. opacity
2. sheet size
3. special properties for particular printing processes
4. capability of reproducing illustrations
5. chemical and physical properties that affect presswork, folding and binding
6. grain direction

It is therefore essential that the user of printing work closely with the printer in selecting paper for any job. A basic knowledge of kinds, weights, sizes, and finishes is important to permit the user to adapt his or her requirements to those of the printer.

Basic Kinds of Paper

Paper can be classified in many ways—for example, *wood* papers and *rag* papers. Most paper is made of wood pulp, but some is made of rags or a combination of both.

The cheapest paper is made by grinding bark-free logs into a pulp that is formed into sheets without benefit of any chemical action to remove impurities. This *groundwood* paper is commonly used for newspapers and disintegrates quickly because of its imperfections.

Wood-pulp papers of more permanence are treated to be rid of substances that cause fast deterioration. Called *sulphate, soda* and *sulphite* papers, they are used for all kinds of printing.

A 100 percent rag content paper is virtually imperishable, but is so expensive that its use is limited.

To order paper, one must know its four basic classifications, named by appearance and proposed use—*bond, book, cover* and *cardboard.*

Aside from its use for bonds and stock certificates, bond paper is standard for office use. Because its primary application is for letterheads and typewriter paper, it has a semihard finish that is ideal for typing or handwriting.

As the name implies, book paper is used for books, but it also is the vehicle for virtually every mass-printed medium of communication. It comes in textures ranging from rough to a smooth gloss.

Heavy and durable, cover paper has been formulated to withstand the extra wear on booklet and magazine covers and is available in many colors and finishes. Publications are often "self cover"—the cover is printed on the same stock and at the same time as the inside pages, but when special bulk or durability is desired, cover stock is specified.

Posters, stand-up advertising displays and direct-mail promotion pieces are frequently printed on a stiff, heavy paper composed of several plies, or layers. Cardboard stock may be referred to as *bristol board* or by a number of suppliers as *postcard.*

In addition to the basic classes, there are special papers for special uses. *Offset* papers have properties designed to compensate for the moisture and other problems unique in offset printing. *Gravure* or *roto* paper is especially made to absorb the large amount of ink applied in rotogravure printing. There are other kinds of paper, but most are variations of those already described. Much of the variety comes from giving standard papers different finishes or surfaces.

Paper Surfaces

Paper sheets are formed during manufacture when pulp is passed between rollers. This is called *calendering,* and the amount of calendering depends upon the desired degree of surface smoothness.

Paper with a minimum of calendering is called *antique* or *eggshell* and is widely used for books and brochures. It has substantial bulk and is rough in texture. Although it is not suitable for reproducing letterpress halftone illustrations, the nonglare surface of antique paper makes it desirable for lengthy reading matter. The bulk of antique papers is often reduced by additional calendering that is gentle enough not to eliminate the rough texture.

Fairly extensive calendering produces a smoother surface for paper called *machine finish.* Many magazines use this paper because of its good printing surface; *English finish* is very similar (slightly more calendering) and provides only slightly better letterpress halftone reproduction.

Supercalendered paper has been processed until its surface is slick enough to take all but the finest-screened letterpress halftone engravings. It also is popular for magazines.

Paper manufacturers, when confronted with the problem of finding a suitable surface for fine-screened halftones, developed *coated* papers. Originally these were brush-coated with a clay substance, and some still are, but most coating is now applied by machine as the paper is being made. Coated papers are expensive but essential for the finest quality of photographic reproduction.

Paper Weight and Sheet Sizes

Paper is priced by the pound but is sold in lots of a given number of sheets as well as pounds. Standard lots are a *ream* (500 sheets), a *case* (about 500 pounds), and a *skid* (about 3000 pounds). A *quire* is one twentieth of a ream and a *carton* is one quarter of a case.

It would be impossible to identify paper's weight by that of a single sheet. Instead, this vital element of paper, usually called *substance,* is expressed as the number of pounds in a ream of sheets of a basic size. Hence, paper would be labeled "100-pound" if 500 sheets of the basic size weighed 100 pounds.

Unfortunately, the basic size is not the same for all kinds of paper. Generally, the basic size is the one most suitable and efficient for the common uses of any particular paper. These sizes are shown in a table in Chaper 16. For example, that table shows the basic size for bond paper is 17 by 22 inches; it will fit most presses and will cut into four $8\frac{1}{2}$ by 11 inch sheets. The point to remember here is that 20-pound bond and 20-pound book paper would be totally different. In fact, we would have to order 50-pound book to get the same weight and thickness characteristics of 20-pound bond.

Although printers can use practically any size sheet of paper and cut it to fit, the waste is intolerable.

Some Special Finishing Operations

Some of the finishing operations may be carried out by the printer, but many of them are the responsibility of a binder or a firm specializing in the particular technique. In many cases, finishing techniques are used to increase the utility of the printed piece, but they are also often employed simply to enhance visual appeal.

The following list is by no means all-inclusive, but it does present the more commonly used techniques.

Die Cutting

Some printed pieces are much more effective if they are cut to special shapes. Any special shape—a company's product, a question mark, the outline of a state—can be made by die cutting. Several sheets of paper or cardboard can be cut at one time when *high dies,* very similar to rugged cookie cutters, are used. Some *steel-rule* cutting is done, however, on standard printing presses with only one or two sheets being cut at a time. For steel-rule cutting, the desired shape is cut into $\frac{3}{4}$-inch plywood with a jigsaw, and steel rules are cut and bent to fit the shape. The rules, when put into the cutout, are sharp enough and high enough to make the desired cut with each press impression.

Easeling

Finishers have stock sizes of easels that are applied to display cards and other printed pieces so that they can stand on counters, desks and tabletops. Either single- or double-wing easels are used, depending upon the weight of the board or the width of the base.

Embossing

Initials, seals, medallions and other designs can be raised in relief on paper or other material by running the material in a press between a relief die (below) and an engraved die (above). Embossing may be either blind (no color applied) or printed. Inks or paints are applied before embossing. The major expense is in the making of the dies, but careful makeready is also required.

Gumming

Labels and other stickers may be gummed by hand or by machine either before or after printing. Machines can apply gum in strips of any number and in any direction. Many printing problems are avoided if gumming follows presswork.

Indexing

Indexing is a die-cutting process for providing the tabs needed on such items as index cards, address books, telephone pads and so on.

Numbering

Most letterpress printers can easily and cheaply provide numbering because numbering machines can be locked in a chase with or without other plates and type matter. These machines can number consecutively or repeat.

Other printing processes require the use of special press attachments.

Pebbling

Any texture can be added to paper following printing by running the paper through rollers embossed with the desired design. Paper manufacturers offer a *pebble* stock, a paper with a textured surface, as well as other uneven finishes, but as a finishing term *pebbling* means the addition of *any* texture after printing. Linen and other clothlike surfaces are included.

Applying texture to paper as a finishing process instead of during paper manufacture eliminates the problems connected with running rough stock on letterpress machines.

Perforating

Either the printer or the finisher can do perforating. If it is done by the printer, ink is carried to the paper at the perforating line because the sharp rule used is slightly more than type high. A perforating wheel is attached to the cylinder if the technique is to be done on a cylinder press.

The kind of perforating found on postage stamps is the work of a finisher who uses a rotary machine that punches rows of tiny holes. The purpose of perforating is simply to make tearing easy.

Punching

Standard male and female dies are used to punch holes for the various styles of loose-leaf or mechanical binding.

Scoring

Scoring, like perforating, is done to make tearing easier or to aid in folding. A sharp steel rule is used to cut the outer fibers of the paper slightly; if heavy stock or cardboard is being used, the rule may have to cut partially through the board.

Scoring should not be confused with *creasing*, a similar operation in which a dull, rather than sharp, rule is used. Creasing is also an aid to folding, but its other purpose is to make tearing more difficult, not easier. The blunt rule merely compresses the fibers, making the stock more durable at the fold.

To avoid confusion, it is wise to tell the finisher *why* the technique is being requested.

14

Magazine Design

From the standpoint of both design and content, magazines are a hybrid form of periodical. They have some of the characteristics of newspapers, and in some cases actually are purveyors of news. But on the other hand they have a quality and a lasting value that would make them more closely akin to books. In fact, the common term for magazines among the professionals who design and produce them is *book*. Then, too, magazines resemble advertising in that great attention is given to their visual appeal, and they can, as in the case of house organs (public-relations magazines), go so far as to have basic goals resembling those of advertising.

This multicharacter aspect of magazines is illustrated in Figures 14-1 to 14-3: The newsmagazine employs standardized headlines in newspaper fashion; the scholarly magazine is in traditional book format; the public relations and consumer magazines have a flair that comes

14-1 As a weekly newsmagazine for journalists, *Editor & Publisher* standardizes its headlines in much the same fashion as newspapers do. In a recent redesigning, *Editor & Publisher* changed from predominantly one-column headlines to the horizontal ones shown on these pages. (Courtesy *Editor & Publisher*)

14-2 *Left:* Each issue of *Journalism Quarterly* and other scholarly magazines have the size and the appearance of books.

14-3 *Below:* Some of the best magazine design is done for public relations magazines. (Courtesy *Texaco Star*)

only from the application of special attention and artistic design principles that are characteristic of advertising. These differences point to the first principle for magazine design: The magazine's appearance should be functionally suitable to its basic editorial goals. The magazine that deals in spot news should look different from the one that is concerned only with abstract concepts, and the one that is headed for a scholar's bookshelf can be radically different from a magazine headed for a homemaker's coffee table.

But even within each of the many categories of magazines there are and should be substantial differences. Each individual magazine develops a character of its own, and physical appearance is a primary factor of that character. Magazines tend to take on human characteristics in the minds of their preparers and their readers. Editors become very sentimental about their books; one would think to hear them talk that their subject is their own child rather than a magazine. And many readers look forward to their favorite magazine as if it were a friend stopping in for a weekly or monthly visit for coffee and conversation. The layout of a magazine must, therefore, take into account the specific personality and character that its readers perceive it to have. The principle that magazine design must relate to a magazine's basic editorial role and to its own individual character serves as a foundation pillar for our discussion of magazine layout.

One other point relating to the impact of graphics on magazines must be made here. Visual appearance has been extremely important to magazines throughout most of their history. In the years since the advent of television, however, design has become increasingly valuable. Experimentation, some of it wild and bizarre, characterized some of the general consumer magazines as they entered their death throes in the 1960s and early 1970s. In these cases, it seemed that publishers were calling on graphics to be the life preserver for their drowning magazines. Although the rescue attempts didn't work, the effort did put still more emphasis on magazine design.

The importance of layout for magazines is reflected in their staffing. Immediately following the editor, the first person listed in the masthead is usually the art director whose responsibility is the design and layout of a magazine. For many magazines, the art director and editor work as virtually coequal partners. The art director creates the physical external personality of the magazine, whereas the editor molds the "spiritual," internal character of the magazine. Obviously, both must work with full mutual knowledge and cooperation.

Volumes have been written about magazine layout and design, and this one chapter cannot present an in-depth discussion of that subject. In the space we have here we can, however, give some basic principles and relate the essentials of communication theory and basic design to magazine layout so that journalism students, whether future newspaper reporters or magazine designers, can understand the "why" behind the skilled output of professionals.

The First Step:
Break-of-the-Book

The layout of a magazine actually begins with an editorial job called *breaking the book.* This task involves the allocation of the total amount of space among the ads, articles, departments and other editorial material that is planned for the issue.

Because advertising determines the existence of a magazine, it is usually placed first, with consideration allowed for editorial-department needs. Although advertisers may request, pay for, and get special position, they are vitally concerned with the success of the editorial portions. As a matter of fact, their requests are often in connection with placement at or near certain portions of a magazine. Cooperation between business and editorial offices negates difficulties arising from advertising placement. It is common practice for the ads to be located front and back with the center reserved for the main editorial section.

One of the minor layout problems associated with this practice is to alert the reader to the beginning of the content. The reproduction of the name plate is often used on the first editorial page to signal the reader.

Several studies have shown that a large percentage of readers peruse a magazine backwards. (This can be checked in a classroom survey.) Some magazines have, therefore, found it expedient to place some strong features as complete single-page units at the end of the editorial section. These serve as a starting point for the "backward" readers.

As the main editorial section develops, the pace should change frequently. Long articles should not be lumped together but should be relieved by single or fractional page articles.

Although the ads are placed first, the breaking of the book is primarily the responsibility of an editor; he or she is the one to make space decisions for editorial content.

But as the editor decides which articles get only one page and which get more, or which pages will get special color treatment and which will not, he or she must be aware of some basic production requirements.

These requirements stem from the fact that magazines are printed on large sheets of paper, usually big enough for 8 or 16 pages, and these sheets are folded into sections of the magazine. Each of these sections is called a *signature.* In order to let the printer work efficiently, the editor must complete pages in units corresponding to those that will be on the press at any one time. And, if the editor is to use color economically, he or she must plan color to fit in those same units of pages. This planning to meet production requirements was explained in detail in Chapter 13.

Magazine layout, therefore, is often the result of a team effort involving the advertising manager who places the ads, the editor who allocates space, the production manager who keeps printing costs in check and the art director who designs the pages.

The Dimensions of the Stage: Format

As pointed out in the chapter on design principles, all graphic communications are restricted by certain visual limits just as an actor is confined to the limits of the stage. Every page designed must fit the proportions that have been set for it.

The graphics equivalent of the actor's stage is the *format*, the shape, size and style of the publication.

The *format* of a magazine is a basic factor in its layout and is not subject to artistic whims. Magazines vary considerably in shape and size, ranging from small enough to tuck into a pocket to dimensions that equal the tabloid newspaper (Figure 14-4). Format is the result of one or more of three practical considerations: (1) ease of handling, (2) adaptability of content to format, and (3) mechanical limitations of printing-press sizes.

Ease of handling is the chief advantage of the pocket size of the *Reader's Digest, TV Guide* and many other small magazines. Easy to hold and to store, the small-size magazine is particularly suited to its contents, which consist mainly of text, with the illustrations secondary. The large sizes are best for emphasis on pictures, because the larger the photographs, the greater their impact. However, postage and paper costs have almost eliminated the larger "picture magazine" size.

Most magazines present text and illustrations on a relatively equal basis and use a format adequate for both—about $8\frac{1}{2}$ by 11 inches. Since this is the same size as standard typing paper, filing these pages is simple; also, the dimensions are familiar and comfortable for the reader.

Most magazines are vertical rectangles, a traditional shape substantiated by the difficulty of handling horizontal formats.

14-4 This photo of just a portion of the magazine rack in a college book store shows the great variety of formats now in use by magazines. (Photo by Ralph Kliesch)

Some Theoretical Bases for Magazine Design

The design principles discussed in Chapter 2 and based on communication theory apply just as strongly to magazine pages as they do to advertisements. The end goal of magazine pages is to get information into the mind of the reader—to have the reader get meaning from the pages. Because magazines are usually more concerned with concepts than with straight transferral of specific facts, the role of graphics is especially important; more so than for the newspaper, for example.

The transferral of concepts requires the utmost in sophistication of visual presentation. Visual syntax must be clear and correct; the order and simplicity that are characteristic of any good design are especially important if magazine pages are to accomplish their communication goals.

Achieving Meaning Through Orderly Presentation

The orderly design of magazine pages starts with the margins that are used to frame the content of the page. Margins are important for two reasons. First, they are either the ending or the beginning marker (or both) for verbal copy. Try cutting the margin from both sides of a magazine page and note the reading difficulty incurred without the frame of white to set off the line endings. Second, they help make pages and spreads attractive and unified by wrapping the elements on a page into one package with a border of white margins. In this respect margins act like the frame around a picture.

Margins are usually considered mandatory for type matter because of their contribution to legibility. But exactly what size they must be varies widely.

Many magazines follow traditional book margins because they are being designed in traditional fashion; most early magazines differed in appearance from the books of their day only because they had no hard covers. The scholarly magazine shown in Figure 14-2 is typical of book-like magazines.

Traditional book margins are progressive, with the bottom margin being the largest and the inside margin the smallest. The area inside the margins is called the *type page* because all type is required to be within that area. Type pages ride slightly high on a page because they are centered on the optical center which is slightly higher than the geometric center.

It is generally most important that the inside (*gutter*) margin be the smallest—ordinarily no more than half the size of the bottom margin. Gutter margins that are too wide destroy the order and unity of two facing magazine pages, and in most instances it is desirable to design facing pages as one unit. If each page is to stand separately, then extra white space at the gutter may be desirable.

14-5 The panel of white extending from the title on the left to the other side of this two-page spread helps unify the spread while contributing to the contrast of the elements, such as the title. (Courtesy General Mills *Family*)

As several of the illustrations in this chapter show, modern designers take great liberty with margins on magazine pages. Certainly no effort is made to have type fill out the full dimensions of the type page. But when there is extra white space available, most designers move it to the outside of the design, thus maintaining a white frame, however irregular it may be. Another common technique is the use of large panels of white to create movement in a design (Figure 14-5).

If a magazine's policy is to give special emphasis to pictures, *bleeds* can be especially effective. A photo is said to bleed if it runs off the edge of the page. Bleeds are a good device for any magazine because:

1. They provide a change of pace in comparison with the pages with unbroken margins.
2. They give more room on a page by adding the marginal space to the content area.
3. Most importantly, they offer extra magnitude for pictures; without frames, photos seem to go on and on.

Balance and Simplicity Help Create Order

Probably the most important contributor to order in magazine design is *balance*, the feeling of equipoise that results from a relatively equal distribution of weights with respect to the optical center of a design area.

Symmetrical design is readily recognized, easy to obtain, and widely used for single pages or two-page spreads in magazines. Most commonly, symmetry is created by so placing a dominant illustration that it encom-

14-6 Centering title, picture and text on a single page guarantees symmetry and the feeling of order. (Courtesy *Measure*, Hewlett-Packard Co.)

passes and rests on the optical center; the title and text that complete the page are also centered, thus assuring perfect balance (Figure 14-6).

Placing duplicate weights on each side of the vertical axis will also achieve symmetry (Figure 14-7); in magazines, however, there is usually a strong element that is centered on the axis.

For informal balance, weights are distributed at various distances from the vertical axis, with the lighter elements being put farther from

14-7 Placing a duplicate element on each side of the axis helps create a feeling of equilibrium, along with a dominant element placed on the axis. (Courtesy *Aramco World*)

14-8 The large illustration on the right near the axis and the lighter elements at the extreme left provide a feeling of equilibrium and stability without formal symmetry. (Courtesy *NCR World*)

the fulcrum in order to balance the heavier weights that are closer (Figure 14-8). Remember that weight comes from shape and tone as well as size.

For magazines, a page-to-page balance for spreads is also important. Readers, as they view a magazine, are almost always seeing two pages together. Except when they look at the front or back cover, the magazine is opened so that the eye can scan the two pages spread before them. These two pages thus form a design unit. Weights should be so distributed that balance exists between the two pages but not necessarily on each of them (Figure 14-9). Also, the white space in the spread should be so assigned that the two pages hold together; the combined space of the two gutter margins must be overcome with any device that is available. Techniques for binding two facing pages into one design are discussed later.

The handmaiden for balance in achieving the order in design that is so vital to communication is simplicity. We have long known from readability studies that simplicity in verbal language is essential for efficient communication; the same is true for visual presentation. Simple, straightforward visual syntax is important for magazines because of the conceptual nature of most magazine content.

Of first importance in visual syntax is a starting point that dominates all other components of the page or spread. In Figure 14-10, a drawing has been used for this purpose; the reader can be expected to start there and then move to the title and the text. Pages with two or more equally prominent elements can create confusion because the reader may be misled into starting at a point in the design that would be equivalent to the middle of a sentence.

14-9 A feeling of balance is created for these pages by the photo on the left being offset with the larger photo on the right that has been placed closer to the center. Placement of the title near the center also helps unify the pages.
(Courtesy *NCR World*)

14-10 Of first importance is a strong visual starting point such as the drawing in the upper left of this spread.
(Courtesy *Postal Life*)

Special care should be taken to be certain that a reader knows where the text of an article begins on a magazine page. One common typographical device for accomplishing this goal is the large initial letter, as shown in Figure 14-11. In the earliest days of printing, long before modern communication research, the value of special initial letters was realized, and they have not lost their value. Many magazine designers also have learned the value of what we might call an "end-of-design" graphic period. They place check marks, logotypes, star dashes or some

Nine Days in the Wilderness

14-11 A large initial letter can serve as a clue for readers to find the starting point of the text of an article. (Courtesy *Long Lines*, AT&T Long Lines Department)

other typographical dingbat at the end of the text of an article. These dingbats emphasize the end of a magazine article just as the period signifies the end of a sentence. Otherwise readers may be inclined to turn a page or move to a facing page, falsely expecting the continuation of an article.

Grouping, Gridding, Alignment

Simplicity becomes increasingly difficult to accomplish as the number of elements to be placed on a page is increased. This problem is solved primarily through the grouping of related elements. Note in Figure 14-12 how design elements, especially photos, are grouped to achieve simplicity. Note, too, how captions are handled to be close to the photos they accompany. Captions, if placed too far from their photos, become design elements in and of themselves and can contribute to clutter and disorder. The same thing can be said about subtitles; they ought to be close to and part of their main title.

Another way to bring order to magazine pages in spite of the large number of elements to be displayed is by the *grid* method, in which the page is first divided into basic segments, such as halves, thirds or quarters. Each segment is further divided into rectangles (Figure 14-13). Titles, photos and copy are then forced to conform to these rectangles. The rigidity of the grid system forces order and at least a relative simplicity onto what otherwise might be chaotic pages. The grid system requires careful preliminary planning and extreme accuracy in copyfitting and photocropping because if elements slop over any of the grid divisions

14-12 When a large number of display elements, especially photographs, are to be used, grouping is essential to avoid chaos. (Courtesy *Go,* Goodyear Tire & Rubber Company)

14-13 A geometric grid forces order into design when many display elements would otherwise tend to create disorder. (Courtesy *Exxon USA,* published by Exxon Company, USA; Editor: Downs Matthews; Art Director: Richard Payne)

the orderliness is lost. Figure 14-14 shows magazine pages in another grid pattern.

Alignment, which is a characteristic of gridding, is also helpful in creating order on magazine pages. Elements should be aligned as they are grouped so that the number of directions, as well as the number of elements involved on a page, is kept to a minimum. Analyze the accompanying illustrations to note how the photos are aligned with each other

New Discoveries In Sumatra

Exploring for new reserves takes oilmen deep into the sweltering jungles of Sumatra. In the relatively cool shelter of a tent, a CPI seismic crew adjusts its sensitive instruments (*facing page*) while other members of the team slog through the jungle to find the site of the next test shot. Top to bottom, left: workers and their families live in modern housing and enjoy a swim in the club pool at the Duri field; an oilman digs into a plentiful meal at a remote jungle location; trees are felled to use as foot bridges to cross swampy areas. The aerial view (*above*) shows a typical Sumatran riverside village. The red section of the map (*top, right*) indicates the area where P. T. Caltex Pacific Indonesia (CPI) has production; a helicopter (*above, right*) moves a portable housing unit for a drilling crew to a new jungle location.
Continued on Page 4

14-14 Grouping and plenty of white space provide unity and produce a semblance of Mondrian design. (Courtesy *Texaco Star*)

and with titles; how lines of titles are aligned with each other; how captions are aligned with the edges of photos or the edges of a column of type. Even alignment of an element within a photograph is considered by skillful designers (Figure 14-15).

Before a beginner places any element on a magazine page he or she should ask, "What should this line up with?" because the odds are that it should be in alignment with at least one other element. Brief study will usually show which one.

Controlling Direction

Once a reader has been directed to a starting point, he or she must be guided through the remainder of a magazine article until he or she has received the entire message. This guidance involves the use and placement of elements that create visual motion in desired directions. As pointed out in Chapter 2, this eye movement comes from reader habits but it can be directed by lines, both implicit and explicit.

With horizontal flow generally preferred to vertical, magazines have an advantage because of their two-page spreads. The proportion of the

A drilling rig provides a striking background as two oil field workers use some of their off hours to catch up on their fishing at the Pass-a-Loutre State Game Preserve. Other photos appear on Pages 12 and 13.

11

14-15 Note the alignment of the caption with the vertical direction of the oil rig in the page on the right. Alignment of photo with column, caption with photo, title with columns, and a caption with margins create order for the pages below. (Courtesy *Texaco Star* and *NCR World*, respectively)

Advertising Education

by Sharon Brock

Photographed by Doug Martin
Models courtesy of NONE Models
Photographed at Columbus Technical Institute

When the Columbus Ad Fed began a scholarship program last spring, members wondered where even a well-intentioned committee could find ad-striving students in central Ohio. "There is no advertising program around here," moaned one Friday luncheon participant. "Ohio University (Athens) is as close as we can come. What's wrong with you guys?"

Advertising education does exist in central Ohio, but it is true that none of the local universities or colleges have a formally structured advertising major.

If advertising education means learning about accounts, consumer behavior, marketing, radio and television production, promotional strategy, audience analysis, writing, layout and design, the courses exist. However, in most of the local college catalogues, these courses as they relate to advertising careers are better camouflaged than new taxes in an election year.

Capital University, home of Randal Merriman, Ad Fed's first advertising scholarship winner, has several options open to students interested in advertising, according to Dr. Armin Langholz, professor of speech communication.

Students would take four or five courses in the business area, some professional writing courses in journalism and English, and radio and television courses which include advertising, in the speech department. If a student wishes to specialize in the creative aspect of advertising, he/she would take courses in fine arts, design, graphics and photography.

Dr. Langholz said that his faculty tries to set up internships in advertising departments of agencies wherever they can find them.

Columbus Technical Institute (CTI) has a two-year business management associate degree which includes one course, Advertising 3808. This is a basic advertising course and is part of the marketing mix in that program.

Many of Columbus's creative ad people know about, or have attended, the Columbus College of Art and Design. It has a Division of Advertising Design with enough elective courses to develop the talent of any student gifted

enough to make it through CCAD's admission process. There are also some general courses in finance, literature, and writing to expand the background of CCAD's artists.

Franklin University has one overview advertising course, BSAD 219, as part of its marketing program.

Ohio Dominican college will list two courses in its new catalog, Promotional Strategy and Theory of Promotional Strategy, according to marketing professor Kipps Schaffer. She said these courses will be part of a business administration major. The focus will be on sales, with advertising an important part of each course.

Ohio Dominican's art department offers typography and graphic design which some students combine with business courses in anticipation of advertising careers.

Prof. Schaffer said the students work on course projects which give them a good idea of what an ad campaign is, and her faculty is in a continual search for internships which she said "are impossible to find in Columbus."

The Admissions Office personnel at Otterbein College said a student could combine writing and editing courses from the journalism concentration in the English department with courses from the business major to learn about the general field of advertising. Journalism at Otterbein is an interdisciplinary program so students could choose courses from many departments depending on whether their advertising interest is copy writing, creative, promotion or management.

At Ohio State, that all-encompassing institution in the center of the city which reputedly has a major in everything to accommodate its 52,000 Columbus campus students, advertising hides in several departments.

Business Administration/Marketing has promotional strategy, (including ad campaigns), consumer behavior and marketing research, retail and wholesale management. Communications has persuasive communication, radio and television production (including producing commercials), and broadcast audience analysis. The psychology department offers social psychology, human motivation, and other courses which use advertising as examples of how

continued on next page

ALASKA
Land of Conflict and Opportunity

by George Barlow

14-16 Lines that lead the eye across the gutter and help unify spreads are evident in both these examples, although display type and illustrations are also used. (Courtesy *Ad-vocate* of Advertising Federation of Columbus and *Aramco World*, respectively)

Alaskans seek a path to growth, but one that doesn't trample their life style or their state's beauty. Business writer George Barlow reports on how Alaskans are meeting the challenge.

Take a small American city—say Knoxville, Tennessee—and scatter its 400,000-plus population through an area one fifth the size of the Lower 48 states.

Put in the nation's largest oil field, add rich reserves of varied minerals, some of the most prolific fishing grounds in the west seas, and incalculable amounts of coal.

This is Alaska—the lively, diversified reality so different from the "frozen

Northland" image many "Lower 48ers" acquired reading Jack London and Robert W. Service in their youths.

That gap between mythical and actual is what makes many Alaskans believe that people in the Lower 48 don't understand Alaska's hopes and problems.

A list of those problems would include issues concerning the state's role to its lands and how land can legally be used.

Then there are conflicts over whether Alaska's oil, minerals, timber, and other resources should be developed to meet the state and nation's needs for energy and raw materials, or whether Alaska, along with its resource treasures, should be preserved as "The Last Great Wilderness."

Add to this the adversary positions in tax and regulatory matters that have often developed between the state and the private companies that have the

financial capability and experience to connect potential resource areas with population centers. Alaska actually has fewer miles of road than Connecticut. Many of Alaska's harbors are sealed by ice in winter.

Anchorage Times publisher Robert Atwood likens Alaska to a "warehouse full of goodies—but without aisles."

In it all adds up to a hard economic fact: many resource company' that does business in Alaska must be sure it has a profitable, high-grade resource to develop and must be capable of making enormous capital investments to bring its product to market.

In Alaska, the logistics of getting people, machinery, and supplies to resources and getting resources and products to market are complicated by staggering distances, rugged terrain, and extremes of climate.

Rail, truck, and shipping facilities are

limited. State highway networks don't connect potential resource areas with population centers. Alaska actually has fewer miles of road than Connecticut. Many of Alaska's harbors are sealed by ice in winter.

These problems are complex and intertwined. How they are sorted out and resolved will in large part determine Alaska's future. Alaska has the opportunity to become the model for other states wrestling with similar issues.

Superimposed over the questions and issues Alaska must settle are some hard physical facts about this remarkable state's raw materials and energy.

That, of course, raises the question of how Alaskans want to develop their vast resources—where, when, and to what degree.

Alaska's Republican governor, Jay Hammond, points to his Growth Policy

Council's recent report.

The paper supports continued oil exploration and balanced development of renewable resources such as timber, fish, and grain, as well as local agricultural and rural crafts and industry development to provide jobs.

State Commissioner of Commerce and Development Charles Webber is enthusiastic about development possibilities, but voices the caution expressed in many quarters.

Alaska has to do it better than it's ever been done before, he says. We intend to be a showcase not a boondoggle example.

While the nation needs Alaska's resources, and Alaska's people want jobs and revenues from those resources—in a framework that preserves life style and environment—development could be a long-range process.

Alaska won't be able to put together a development showcase overnight, no matter what decisions are made. And many observers agree that the state is on dead center because of Federal actions and Congressional delays in settling land issues.

Those observers point to the Alaska lands bill passed by Congress in November after four years of bitter debate and signed by President Carter in December.

The measure will confirm the state's title to virtually all the 104 million acres of land promised under the Statehood Act of 1958, and an additional 44 million acres Alaska's native groups were to have received under the 1971 Native Land Claims Settlement Act.

It also designates an additional 104 million acres as Federal lands—national parks, wildlife refuges, and conservation areas. Those lands, scattered throughout

12   13

17-by-11-inch area formed by two facing pages of the standard magazine format is ideal for the display of visual material. In order to get linkage between the two pages, however, the vertical gutter formed by the two interior margins must be overcome. An obvious line, created by a series of dots or an uninterrupted line, either full-tone or shaded, can produce horizontal movement between pages very easily (Figure 14-16).

Photographs that have been put together to form a horizontal line can also give horizontal direction (Figure 14-17). A regularity in the place-

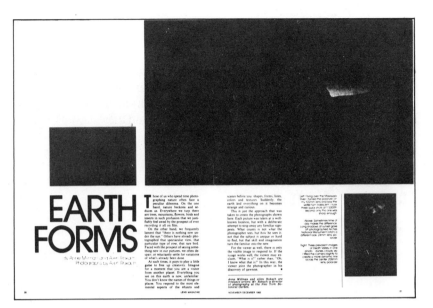

14-17 Two photographs joined to form a horizontal line aid the other elements on these pages in creating directional movement across the pages. (Reprinted with permission from *Lens*. Photographs by © Allen Rokach)

ment of illustrations can produce a sense of rhythm as well as directional movement (Figure 14-18).

Pages or spreads must always be designed with the realization that North Americans have been doing their reading in a left-to-right fashion since the first day their first-grade teacher unveiled the magic of reading to them. The visual syntax must take this custom into account, and the starting point should ordinarily be in the upper left. Other elements should

14-18 Placement of a series of illustrations in a horizontal line can produce a sense of rhythm as well as directional movement. (Courtesy *The Sohioan*)

follow movement to the right and/or down. In most of the illustrations in this chapter, it can be noted that the starting point is in the upper left and normal reader eye movement is followed from that point.

Deviations from that pattern should be looked upon in much the same fashion as a writer looks upon incomplete sentences and other grammatical variations from the norm: They should be used only for desired special effects, and they should make the overall communication more efficient.

Controlling Contrast to Achieve Harmony and Unity

To give the reader a starting point on a magazine page, one element is made to stand out from all others and is placed in a reasonable location, usually the upper left. To get the reader to move along at the end of the message, we provide other "stand out" elements at intervals. In these and other instances we are employing *contrast* to get our communication job done.

Contrast, as explained in Chapter 2, comes from differences: differences in size, shape, tone, textures or direction. Contrast is essential in magazine layout as it is in all layout because contrast makes each element discernible as an individual entity. Contrast can, however, be overdone. Too many elements shrieking for attention prevent or delay the reader's getting meaning from a message. All shrieks and no whispers can obviously mean that nothing will be heard. And, in the final analysis, it is hoped that each magazine article will be related in a single voice, not a multitude of shouts.

14-19 The balanced design and conservative typography go hand in hand while creating an interesting layout about a religious group. (Courtesy *The Review* of Imperial Oil Limited)

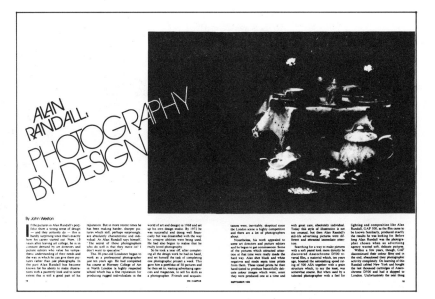

14-20 High style and contemporary design are suggested by the typography and design of these pages. (Courtesy *Lens On Campus*, photos by Alan Randall)

Therefore, contrast must be controlled. On each spread or page contrast must be controlled so that the overall message will be communicated in harmony and with unity.

Harmony results from controlled contrast, and from using types and other elements that are different enough to be seen but similar enough to blend well with each other. Harmony also comes from the selection of visual elements that are in keeping with the subject or readers of the message that is being communicated.

With regard to magazines, harmony between the subject and its presentation is of primary importance. Considerable effort is invested in trying to have title type and design reflect an article's subject. Figures 14-19, 14-20, and 14-21 show how type selection and basic page design can reflect an article's content.

14-21 Type, illustrations and white space are used in combination to get an effective design that reflects the article's content. (Courtesy *Long Lines*, AT&T Long Lines Department)

For Love of Barns

When its old barn burned, Philipsburg Manor suffered a great loss. But now it has a new two-hundred-year-old barn, moved there in pieces and reassembled by a man who reveres old barns for the glimpse they give of "where we came from"

by Peter V. Fossel

History in the Courtroom

Lawyers tussle in a San Francisco court to resolve long-standing historical disputes over such issues as sausages, poetry, and fisticuffs

by Brian McGinty

14-22 These two spreads from *Americana Magazine* show how typography can be appropriate to the character of the magazine and to the subject of the article, while varying considerably in design. (©1983 *Americana* Magazine, Inc., all rights reserved)

Once a design mood is set for an article on its opening page, that mood should be carried through to the article's conclusion. A six-page article that starts out with old-fashioned type dress and 1890 layout style should carry that dress and style throughout all six pages.

It is not necessary, however, for any magazine to carry the same typographical or design mood from cover to cover. There should be some standardization throughout all of its pages, but each article can take on its own personality, especially in a magazine that is trying to present highly varied content. The two parts of Figure 14-22 are from the same magazine; each spread is in harmony with its subject, and they differ from each other quite substantially.

A Word About Special Pages and Problem Pages

Front covers and table-of-contents pages require special layout attention—covers because they are so important; contents pages because they tend to be dull and uninspiring.

The Front Cover

A magazine's front cover is like a store's display window, a building's entrance or an automobile's exterior styling. It should encourage attention and create the desire to go inside.

The functions suggested by these comparisons are vital, and there is the additional need for the instant identification of the magazine as distinct from its competitors, and of its current issue as distinct from its previous issues.

Covers consist of type display alone or of type and illustration combined. The latter is employed most frequently today. The principal identifying characteristic is usually a distinctive name plate, but design or color or both may be used for the same purpose. A name plate must be unique and large enough to merit quick recognition. Design, as an aid to recognition, should be flexible so that necessary variations in the shapes of illustrations can be accommodated from issue to issue. Cover illustrations selected from the interior content can entice a reader into

14-23 Covers designed to get buyers to choose magazines from display racks range from those using only type to those with primary emphasis on illustrations. (Photo by Ralph Kliesch)

the magazine, but type is needed as well to direct the reader to specific articles inside. Reference to page numbers is an added lure.

Issues may be set apart from each other by changes in color and design, and the use of volume and issue numbers. No cover is complete without the latter, but such information is usually so subordinate that instant issue identification must be aided in other ways.

Because some magazines sell their front covers to advertisers at a premium price, the editorial department is compelled to create covers that are so valuable in maintaining readership that the business office will not appropriate this vital part of a magazine to add to income. This pressure, plus the cover's important functions, makes cover designing especially important.

The Contents Page

Any magazine that is large enough for the reader to have logical difficulty in locating material should have a table of contents. Its information may consume only a portion of a page but must have sufficient display to be

14-24   Use of illustrations and rules (lines) help make these table of contents pages interesting and orderly. (Courtesy *East-West Perspectives*, a publication of the East-West Center in Honolulu and *Aide Magazine*, USAA, San Antonio, Texas 78288, ©1981)

found instantly, which usually necessitates being placed well forward in the magazine.

Paid-circulation magazines using second-class mail distribution are required to include certain basic information regarding entry as second-class matter, office of publication and so on, somewhere within the first five pages. Since such masthead data is commonly on the table-of-contents page, the position of the latter is more or less predetermined.

The combination of masthead information and a long list of titles can mean a dull page. Therefore, many magazines now (1) make an effort to use illustrations on the page, (2) give special typographical display to some listings in the contents, and (3) bury the mailing and masthead information where it can be found when necessary but where it does not represent a major element on the page.

Small photographs, taken from important articles in the issue and used adjacent to the listing in the contents table, can help spruce up the layout, point out significant features, and inspire readers to want to turn to certain articles.

Checks, bullets, and other typographical dingbats can be used (perhaps in color) to give variety to the listing of titles and tempt the eye. Whatever the device, monotony caused by a long list of items equal in display should be avoided.

Special display should be reserved for what is new in each issue; material that appears regularly, such as mailing information and titles of content departments, should not be emphasized.

Problem Pages

Advertising on split or fractional pages creates layout difficulty for magazines as well as for newspapers. These pages are not a serious problem if their editorial portions are treated as separate design areas. They can be made attractive and functional by realizing that their shapes may be quite different from the ordinary page shape.

The extreme vertical often left after ads have been placed cannot be laid out like a two-page spread, but its dimensions can be exploited. Titles, illustrations, or other layout elements must simply be made to conform to the area. Two facing verticals can be brought together in the center of a spread by ads located on the outsides. Or, with ads spread across the bottom, the upper portions of two pages can be linked for a horizontal layout field. In such cases, the techniques used for spreads are applicable.

Many fractional pages are used for carryover material, but continuations are being avoided more and more. Most magazine articles can be confined to full pages up front, by adjusting the space for display (titles, and so on) to make the text fit. Fractional pages can then be used attractively for short items of various kinds that have adequate reader interest.

15
Newspaper Design

Of all the printed media of communication, the one that has placed the least emphasis on form throughout history has been the newspaper. The result has been predictable: the development of a medium whose appearance has paled in comparison with magazines, books and other printed literature. Designers of printed media for years have pointed to newspapers as the most awkward, least attractive and least readable of these media.

To place this shortcoming in proper perspective, two points must immediately be understood. The first is that there have been good reasons for the lack of attention to design by newspapers during their history in this country. The second is that current developments have been eliminating these reasons for many newspapers and have consequently been forcing a change in approach to the appearance of newspapers.

Why Newspapers Have Been "Made Up" and Not Designed

Problems of Format

The 1700 or so daily newspapers and about 8000 weeklies in the United States are divided between two basic formats: awkward and less awkward, with only a minority in the latter group. Most newspapers are of a size called *broadsheet,* about 14 inches wide and 22 inches deep. These newspapers are also of considerable bulk, scores of pages and several sections being common. Americans have wrestled with this overly large format and formidable bulk for years. Whether sitting in their comfortable living room chairs or on crowded public transit seats, readers of newspapers have been forced to try to fold their papers by hand into a manageable size. Fortunately for the mass transit rider, there is a less awkward format, the *tabloid,* which is exactly one half of the broadsheet. This size, although it is much more convenient and has gained particular favor for magazine supplements in Sunday editions and for special sections, remains the exception rather than the rule.

These large sizes seem to be the result of historical accidents, and they are still with us because of investment in equipment and tradition. The first several newspapers published in the American colonies were scarcely larger than this book, and not quite as large as typing paper. Later, when British newspapers adopted the broadsheet page size to circumvent a tax based on the number of pages, American newspapers followed suit. The development of the Penny Press in America just before the Civil War resurrected a smaller page size for the papers trying to attract a new audience of factory laborers with their penny price and human interest journalism. At the same time, however, some business or politically oriented newspapers went to extremely large formats. Some of these—in order to brag that they were the biggest papers in town— had pages as large as 3 feet by 5 feet and were called *blanket* papers. However, most steam-powered presses and related machines such as folders that were introduced at that time were designed to accommodate the "standard" broadsheet. The heavy investment that was then required for these new machines made further size experimentation almost impossible.

The tabloid, because it is half the size of the broadsheet, fitted the standard equipment, with one additional fold being the only special requirement for production. Unfortunately for newspaper readers, the use of the tabloid has been limited because it was tarred with a label of sensationalism when it first came into use in this country. The first tabloids of the 1920s sought mass audiences with an editorial product emphasizing sensational news coverage and appearance. Consequently, for many newspaper readers and publishers alike, "tabs" and sensationalism are synonymous. Although there has been some movement toward tab-

15-1   The standard format for American newspapers has become about 14 inches wide and 23 inches deep, a *broadsheet*. The tabloid size of the *Daily News* is about half that size. (Courtesy *Columbus Citizen-Journal* and *Daily News*)

loid format by conservative and respected newspapers (e.g., the *Christian Science Monitor*) the broadsheet size remains a fact of newspaper life that designers must continue to face.

The charge that newspapers have not only been awkward but also less than attractive (or even unattractive) is another aspect of newspaper design that must be understood and accepted. There are several reasons why this is also a fact of life.

For example, the mere size of the broadsheet makes functional, attractive arrangement of elements difficult. And if news coverage policies mandate the display of a score or more stories on a single page, the task becomes still more difficult. The result has been some extreme but necessary design restrictions. In order to maintain a constant personality and give some order to a large design area that includes a score or more elements, *monotypographic* (all from the same family) headlines are often specified. Stringent *headline schedules,* which prescribe limited typographical patterns (e.g., flush left lines only and no more than two lines), have also been the norm. These restrictions, undesirable as they may be from a designer's standpoint, have been accepted as essential by most newspapers. With only a few minutes available for the layout of pages before deadlines, editors are forced to "go with what they have" and, without headline schedules and other aids, their job would become impossible.

Narrow newspaper columns and the resultant *vertical* flow of design elements, both of which have been a characteristic of newspapers for years, have also not been the result of mere whim. Primary newspaper financial support comes from advertising, and *column inches* and *agate lines* have been the basis for space rates to advertisers. Thus practical economics favored narrow columns: narrowing columns results in more agate lines and column inches per page, and widening produces fewer agate lines and column inches per page. A tendency to widen columns for editorial matter to get better readability and to narrow them for ads to increase revenues or to save newsprint added to what has always been a design problem. Adoption of a Standard Advertising Unit (SAU) in 1984 by the American Newspaper Publishing Association and advertising groups should help standardize column widths in the future. The SAU is based on a column inch in a six-column format newspaper with columns $2\frac{1}{16}$ inches wide and $\frac{1}{8}$ inch between columns. Depth of the standard page was set at 21 inches. Most newspapers had accepted the SAU by 1985.

With all of these factors at work, it is no wonder that newspapers have been made up and not designed. But perhaps the most important reason that newspaper designs have tended to be so unimaginative is that newspaper designers have not been forced to do any better. As pointed out earlier, the importance of graphic design varies inversely with the interest of the reader: The greater the interest, the less important the graphics. Football fans wading through scores of large pages to a sports section and from there to a column of scores presented in agate type obviously are not being stopped by a lack of graphic niceties. They are, in fact, pushing aside really formidable graphic obstacles to get information they desperately desire. The desire of readers for the news they offer has kept newspapers in an enviable position: Form of presentation has been almost immaterial. However, current developments would seem to be forcing newspapers to give greater attention to their appearance.

In terms of having their products functional—that they be easily read—newspapers have also been behind other media. Type size, because newspapers have always tried to squeeze as much information into their columns as possible, has always tended to be too small. The same pressure has also kept adequate leading from helping the reader, and the long, narrow vertical columns have made readers struggle through unusually short lines as they have sought out their news. Display type has been crowded into position without adequate white space for it to do its work effectively.

All of these shortcomings are now getting increased attention because of changes both inside and outside the newspaper industry. These changes will force many newspapers to be less awkward, more attractive and more functional in the future.

Times Are Changing—and So Are Newspapers

The impact of television on American society has been felt in every part of life—social, economical, political and cultural. For newspapers, the impact has been especially forceful, both directly and indirectly.

Effects of Television

A direct effect of television is that newspapers have lost some of the national advertising that formerly filled their pages and gave them a solid financial base. Television has been very efficient in selling cereals, cars, toothpastes and other national brand items with the result that advertisers have bought more TV time and less newspaper space. Some reader time has been lost, too, and in the precious evening time period. A decline in the evening newspaper in contrast to its morning counterpart has been caused, in part, by this loss of reader time to television. Another change has been an increasing passiveness toward media—the development of watchers rather than readers. Reading is work; viewing pictures is not. The challenge of luring readers to the printed page and getting them to read what is printed there has become greater than ever before. But perhaps the most important development has been television's capture of one of the newspaper's major roles: being the first with the news. Not only can television reveal major details of news events before newspapers, it often can be on the scene showing details of the event as it occurs.

To reduce television's time advantage in presenting spot news, many newspapers have been responding with greater depth of treatment and additional analysis for appropriate subjects, as well as more specialization and departmentalization. The end result for such changes has been to make these newspapers more like a daily magazine than a traditional newspaper. The more a newspaper tends to resemble a magazine in its content, the more it must consider the magazine as a primary competitor.

Effects of Magazine Competition

A resurgence of magazines, which includes the revival of some general consumer greats of the past but is especially pronounced among the specialized and regional types, also is affecting newspaper design. Magazines have been joining suburban newspapers and free-circulation "shoppers" in competing with metropolitan dailies for local, state and regional advertising dollars. If newspapers are to meet such competition successfully, their appearance must match the high quality of magazines.

Effects of New Production Technology

Another development, the radical change in the technology of newspaper production, has also been providing impetus for change. Offset printing, for example, is the most commonly used reproduction system for all media. For newspapers, offset makes possible a much more attractive product. With offset printing, illustrations can be handled more economically, more efficiently, and with much better results. Arrangement of elements on a page is no longer limited by the unbending right angles of metal type engravings. Cold type, area composition, and, perhaps most spectacularly, pagination by computer and cathode-ray tube typesetters have forced total rethinking of newspaper design and makeup. In developing computer-assisted page layout systems, *templates* (patterns) are evolved. Since rectangles are much simpler to deal with than more complicated shapes, these templates use simple rectangles in building up full pages. One of the templates developed at Massachusetts Institute of Technology in a project funded by the American Newspaper Publishers Association is shown in Figure 15-2. Early attempts at page layout on

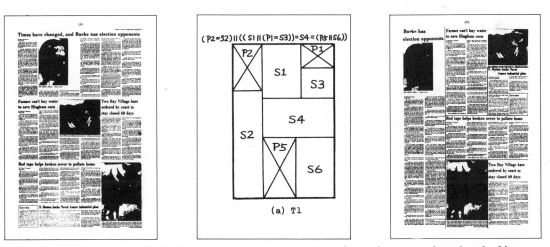

15-2 Experiments in computer-assisted page layout conducted at the Massachusetts Institute of Technology (MIT) have involved formulation of computer-stored templates (patterns). *Left:* a page of the *Boston Globe* laid out by the staff. *Center:* A template used to arrange the same page elements by computer. *Right:* The page produced from the template. (Reprinted by permission from *Computer-Assisted Layout of Newspapers*, J. Francis Reintjes, Donald R. Knudson, and Hsin-Kuo Kan; Massachusetts Institute of Technology, Dec. 1977; under a grant from the American Newspaper Publishers Assn.)

15-3 A page produced for *Newsday* by means of x-y coordinates. The typesetter followed keyboarded instructions to set the headline and the first column of type, then moved the photopaper to set the caption, the next headline and the second column under it, and so on. A screened print of the photograph was then pasted in place. Rectangular modules evolve naturally from electronic pagination systems. (Courtesy *Newsday*)

video terminal screens also tended to force a similar approach to page design because the terminal screens could not show a full page at once. Even when full-page terminal display is possible, the rectangular building-block approach is used; see Figure 15-3.

Changes in Approach to Newspaper Page Design

The impact of television, magazines and new technology has brought about, for many contemporary North American newspapers, a new approach to the packaging of their product. Essentially, the change involves accepting the proposition that newspapers must give more attention to their appearance, and making a strong commitment to accept the changes that would be involved.

For many papers, the first step has been to hire a designer to establish the typographic and layout practices that would result in an appearance that is both pleasing and functional. The second step has been to provide the staff and equipment necessary to produce a more attractive product under the pressure of deadlines.

Results of such redesigning efforts have varied according to the personality the paper's appearance is expected to reveal, policy restraints kept in force by publishers, the talents of the designers involved and the usual constraints of equipment and deadlines. However, three broad categories of newspapers seem to have prevailed. These are:

1. those that have gone to a totally "magazinelike" approach
2. those that have accepted the principles that relate directly to a functional approach to news presentation but have retained some traditional approaches to news display and headlines
3. those that have made a minimum of changes because they want to retain a traditional personality

The first of these categories is designated *contemporary,* whereas the other two are termed *traditional.*

To call either of these categories better than the other is not the purpose of this discussion. For a newspaper, the most valuable asset is a personality that readers like and believe in, and appearance is an essential part, but only a part, of that personality. In the end, content must take precedence in the design of a newspaper. In every instance the goal is to present the news in the most effective fashion. From a study of examples of each category, it will be seen that great newspapers come in many different packages.

Contemporary (Modular) Design

The basic change accepted by newspapers in the contemporary group as necessary to improve their appearance has been to break the large page format into *modules* (mods), each containing various graphic elements that can be independently arranged with a freedom from restraint that has been typical in magazine design. In effect, the page designer is thus reducing a complicated problem into several simpler ones. He or she is acting like the electronics engineer who designs a television set so that it is composed of a small number of modules, each much easier to repair or replace than the multitude of small parts that make it up. Or perhaps a better parallel is newspaper readers on the subway who fold their newspapers into halves, then quarters, and perhaps to one-eighth the normal size so that they can focus their attention on only one item.

Once a page has been broken into rectangular modules, each mod can be designed as effectively as an ad or a magazine page. With perhaps only one item to the mod, design can be simple and striking. Or, in the case where a module is to be made up of many small parts, the overall result is to give the impression of one large element. Each module contributes to a pleasing geometric pattern for the page (see Figure 15-8).

As shown in Figure 15-8, overall page appearance is enhanced by a variety of rectangular shapes ranging from extreme horizontals to extreme verticals; as in advertising and other design, squares are avoided because they lack interest. Lack of variety in shapes produces page patterns that are too obvious and static.

Many modular papers routinely give one mod dominance, and often this module, complete with the largest illustration on the page, is placed near the optical center of the page. At other times they seem to make an

15-4 *Left:* USA Today, with its emphasis on modular design, color, charts and other graphics, has exemplified the contemporary design being adopted by many newspapers. In its first two years of existence, *USA Today* has attracted enough readers to become second in circulation, behind only the *Wall Street Journal.* (Reprinted with permission of *USA Today*)

15-5 *Right:* Along with *USA Today, The Morning Call* of Allentown, Pennsylvania, has been selected by newspaper designers as one of the best-designed papers in the country. Serving a medium-sized community, it presents a very attractive "face" to its readers. Executive policy encourages attention to design, and an excellent graphics staff has carried out that policy successfully. (Courtesy *The Morning Call*)

15-6 *Left:* The *Chicago Tribune*, also named one of the best-designed newspapers, has also emphasized color, modular design, and large photographs to serve its readers. (Courtesy *Chicago Tribune*)

15-7 *Right: The Milwaukee Journal*, another midwestern newspaper known for its excellence of news coverage, has been redesigned to take advantage of all aspects of contemporary design. Here, as in other examples, color usage is striking but, of course, not evident in this reproduction. Process color for the large photo and multi-color reproduction of the graphic elements across the top compel attention. (Courtesy *The Milwaukee Journal*)

15-8 Lines set off the interesting rectangular shapes of the modules of this front page. (Courtesy *The Morning Call*)

effort to grade news for their readers by placing the top story of the day in a module starting in the upper left, the key quadrant for design areas (Figure 15-9).

Making Mods Work for Readers

While keeping the number of mods per page at a minimum, page designers can also perform some desirable reader services. One of the most important of these is the departmentalizing of news items: the grouping of two or more separate items into one mod, each with its own separate heading but jointly carrying a departmental label, such as LABOR, STRIKES or INFLATION. A common example of this technique is the *news brief* module, often carried under a heading giving the day of the week (Figure 15-10).

15-9 Primary emphasis is usually in the upper left and at the optical center, with the major story of the day in the upper left quadrant and a large photo dominating the optical center. (Courtesy *The Sun-Tattler* and *Evansville Courier & Press*)

One of the weaknesses of modular design as compared with a traditional approach is the reduction in the number of separate items on a page, each of which could attract its own share of readers. Efforts to correct this weakness are concentrated on the news brief device and on magazinelike indexes (Figure 15-11). In looking at these indexes, one must be impressed with the similarity of page one indexes to the hard-sell "teasers" that are common to newsstand magazine covers. It is the function of these indexes to get a reader (who might find the story that interests him or her on page one of a *traditional* newspaper) to go to an inside page to a particular story that meets his or her interest.

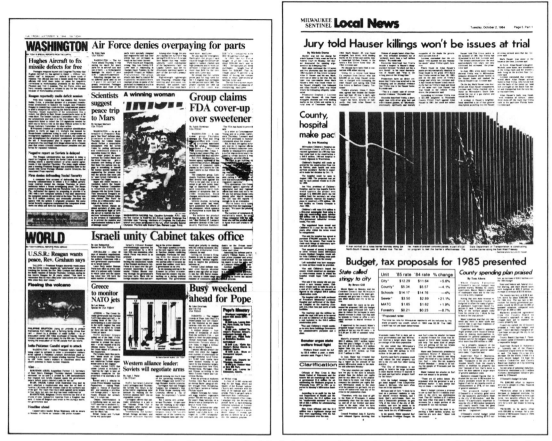

15-10 Grouping of related stories and departmentalizing are helpful to readers. *USA Today* groups stories by several categories, including the WASHINGTON and WORLD, as shown here. The *Milwaukee Sentinel* and many other papers group stories according to geographical units in their circulation area as well as by traditional subjects. (Courtesy *USA Today* and *Milwaukee Sentinel*)

Use of Borders

Modules often have only white space for borders, but many contemporary newspapers are inclined to place printed borders around many of them, often in color. Geometric patterns are enhanced by these borders, but care should be taken to keep the borders from becoming heavy and obtrusive. Display type and illustrations can be totally confined within these borders or permitted to extend beyond them.

15-11 News brief modules and magazine-like indexes are used on the front page to lure readers inside to other items of interest. (Courtesy Dayton *Journal Herald*)

Use of Display Type

A primary characteristic of contemporary newspapers is greater freedom in the use of display type. Headline schedules may still be rather strictly employed with the result that headlines are standardized and perhaps monotypographic when all other characteristics of the page are contemporary (Figure 15-13).

In such cases the most used and most functional headline pattern is the *flush left,* or one of its modifications. Easy to write and set into type, the flush left pattern has become virtually *the* basic pattern for American newspapers. This pattern has been modified to have the lines indented somewhat on the left, thus providing for some added white

15-12   Modules are formed by ruled lines or by white space, as can be seen in the front pages of *The Morning Call* and *Milwaukee Sentinel,* respectively. (Courtesy *The Morning Call* and *Milwaukee Sentinel*)

space around the type. Often accompanying this modification is a short line called a *kicker* above the main grouping. Figures 15-3 to 15-13 show several examples of flush left headings plus their variations.

Many sectional pages now have an even greater variety of headline patterns (Figure 15-14). These same pages often employ other techniques that might be considered more radical for newspapers: variation in placement of headings, incorporation of artwork into headings and varied type fonts in individual headings. A rather standardized pattern for contemporary heading is constructed from a one-word label that is given special emphasis with size and position, followed by smaller type in greater quantity and a different size.

15-13   A recent redesigning of *The Pittsburgh Press* introduced modular design but retained a somewhat traditional approach to headlines and balance of elements on the page. Reader preferences were given strong consideration in the look. (Courtesy *The Pittsburgh Press*)

15-14   A variety of headline patterns, many resembling titles used by magazines, are finding their way into contemporary newspapers. Note also the use of an initial letter to begin articles on this page. (Courtesy *The Morning Call*)

Headline Capitalization and Punctuation

Most contemporary newspapers use standard sentence capitalization for headlines. That is, each heading is treated as a sentence, and the beginning word plus proper nouns are capitalized. Some newspapers, however, capitalize every word in a headline, following a tradition of long duration. Some newspapers capitalize the main words, using lowercase for prepositions and articles. The use of all-capital headlines has virtually been eliminated.

Capitalization differs in that, although most headlines are skeleton-ized sentences, they are not ended with a period. In cases where one line of a headline is a complete sentence to be followed by another, it is ended with a semicolon. Commas are often permitted to substitute for *and,* and sometimes colons are used in the sense that they substitute for "say," e.g., Mayor, Council: Let's Debate.

Use of White Space

A central goal in the use of display type by contemporary papers seems to be the increased use of white space. Skillfully used, white space adds to the impact and potential of any visual display, including newspaper headings. White space between lines makes each line more legible, but then additional white space around the heading becomes essential to bind the lines into a single unit. Along with the willingness to use greater variety of placement and patterns for headlines and larger amounts of white space has come the need for greater appreciation of the effects of white space. It is imperative, for example, that readers know exactly which bit of text or which illustration the type is intended to accompany. Ruled lines can bind these items together, but often white space must do the job. As a general rule, assigning greater amounts of white space to the outside of the heading and lesser amounts between the heading and its related element will do the trick.

Use of Photos and Other Illustrations

Perhaps the most striking of the differences between contemporary and traditional newspaper layouts are those involving the use of photos and other illustrations. Some of these differences are cosmetic and readily apparent to a casual observer, whereas others deeply involve basic atti-tudes regarding the functions of illustrations.

Most readily apparent is the greater size—a dynamic new magni-tude—now commonly given to illustrations, especially photographs. Vir-tually all of the front page examples shown in this chapter illustrate a willingness—an insistence—of editors that illustrations be large and dominant. Full-page illustrations would once have been unthought of, but not today. Dynamic verticals that reach from top to bottom and spread over several columns are commonplace, as are half-page horizontals. The "large" two- and three-column photos of other eras seem to be microscopic in comparison with contemporary dimensions. See Figures 15-12 and 15-13 for some typical examples of contemporary sizes of photographs in newspapers.

Another rather obvious change has been an increased use of "non-photo" illustrations, such as drawings and charts. *USA Today* has been a leader in this development. Except for editorial cartoons and the com-ics, many newspapers historically ignored drawings as a means of illus-

15-15 Artwork in color has become much more common in newspapers, especially those employing modular approach to design. This MONEY page from *USA Today* shows this emphasis. (Courtesy *USA Today*)

trating the news. As Figures 15-14 and 15-15 show, drawings are finding an important place in newspapers, and charts and diagrams such as pictographs, bar graphs and line graphs have joined weather maps and war maps as standard illustrations for many papers. Increased emphasis on diagrams (often called *graphics*) has come from the major news services as well as from *USA Today* and local editors and artists. Writing in *AP Log,* Hal Buell of Associated Press said, "No doubt good graphics improve readability in a visual age. Well done, they show with great clarity exactly what happened. They provide information in easily understandable tabular form or in an instant show how subjects compare, or how they have changed. When well done, they put across the point quickly and with clarity." Note also in these examples that such techniques as combination reproductions, vignettes and mortises are being used with good effect. These production techniques often have been considered legitimate only for ads, magazines and other media, and too involved or gimmicky for newspapers.

These changes are obvious to the eye. They represent, however, some basic changes in attitude about the use of illustrations in newspapers. One of these is the belief that illustrations are the best single means of attracting and seizing reader attention; it is natural that illustrations are increasing in size and usage. Another change relates to the role of the photograph: an appreciation of the artistic and symbolic roles that photos can play. The traditional spot news photo still gets plenty of attention, emphasis, and awards. News photographers who either by planning or by happenstance point their camera in the right direction at the right time to record the split second of an accident or disaster are well rewarded with contest ribbons and prime page position. But they are also winning awards and getting dominant display for their work when they capture a scene of beauty or a moment of emotion not tied directly to a news happening. The pages reproduced in this chapter show many examples of photos that can be called artistic as well as newsworthy.

Use of Body Type

The establishment of column widths for body type is one of the most fundamental and important layout decisions for any newspaper, not because of its effect on appearance but because it does affect income and readability.

As pointed out earlier, newspaper advertising income has depended on column inches and agate lines, and the more columns there are on a page the more inches and lines there will be. Traditionally, the broadsheet was divided into eight columns that were 12 picas wide. As efforts to conserve newsprint by narrowing pages took their toll, columns shrank to 11.5 and 11 picas. Meanwhile, editorial departments were agitating for improvements in type readability that could only come from larger type, more leading, and *especially* wider columns. For many papers the solution has been a 6-9 format—editorial material presented in six columns and ads in nine. Some papers have six columns on page one and eight or nine columns on all other pages. Other papers have retained narrow columns throughout or have made wide columns standard. Some papers use only five columns; others use five, six and nine.

Although the result of experimentation with column widths has been a hodgepodge, there is no doubt that there is a strong trend toward the use of wider columns for news display. Even the *New York Times,* with its traditional character, went to 6-9 in 1976. An increased appreciation of the value of white space has also permitted an increased use of a point of leading between the lines and ample white space between columns. A common practice for gaining extra white space between columns is to spread type horizontally over one extra column, e.g., five columns of type over six columns (Figure 15-16).

15-16 Spreading five columns of type over the width of six columns is a technique used by many newspapers to add white space and draw attention. (Courtesy *The Pittsburgh Press*)

Arrangement of Ads on Pages

So far, our examples of newspaper pages have been restricted to front pages, which usually do not contain advertising. Inside page layout, because of the complications caused by advertising placement, is especially difficult.

The placement of ads is done by the advertising department *before* news is placed on a page. Not only does the advertising department determine how many ads are to be placed on the page but it also determines the number of pages that are feasible for an issue. Thus, on days when there is heavy advertising, there are more pages for news. Newspaper carrier boys are familiar with the heavy midweek issues that are loaded with grocery store ads and the light Saturday issues caused by a diminished desire for advertising in the pre-Sunday issue. Following a

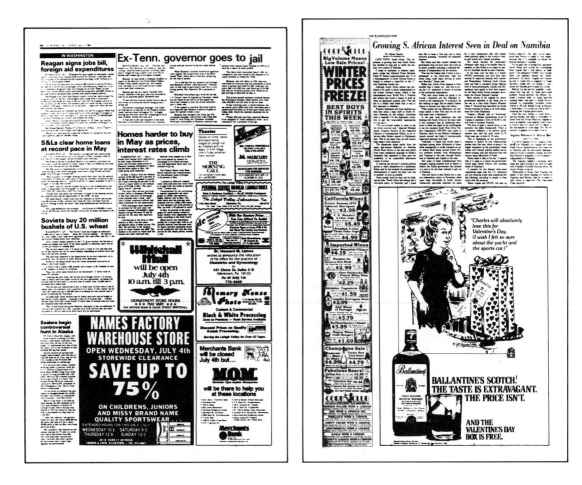

predetermined ratio of advertising to news (e.g., 60 percent/40 percent) the advertising department arranges ads over the required number of pages. In placing the ads, pyramids are formed with larger ads on the bottom and smaller ones on top. The resulting arrangements can be a *pyramid to the right,* with the upper left remaining for news; a *pyramid to the left,* with the upper right as the news hole; or a *double pyramid* with a center news hole. The insistence by advertising departments on these arrangements has been based on the insistence by advertisers that their ads be next to news. Only a pyramid can give all advertisers that desired juxtaposition.

Of these alternatives, news departments have favored the pyramid to the right because it leaves the main optical area (upper left) for news presentation. On some newspapers, notably those that now have art directors, there has been considerable pressure to have ads blocked off to form a horizontal line across the page. Modular inside page layout would be considerably easier if that were done, but there has not been much

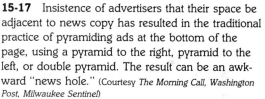

15-17 Insistence of advertisers that their space be adjacent to news copy has resulted in the traditional practice of pyramiding ads at the bottom of the page, using a pyramid to the right, pyramid to the left, or double pyramid. The result can be an awkward "news hole." (Courtesy *The Morning Call, Washington Post, Milwaukee Sentinel*)

success in getting publishers to order the change. Computer-assisted placement of ads has also been developed to retain pyramids.

Figure 15-18 shows excellent modular layout on inside pages that offers a variety of shapes and sizes of news holes, and also shows how departmentalization as an aid for the reader is executed through the modular approach.

Sectional Front Pages

Although contemporary page design is evident on all pages of many newspapers, it may be most evident in the front pages of sections or departments. For obvious reasons, a greater freedom of design has been permitted for these pages, resulting in spectacular visual presentations.

In many instances, the news policies that cause many newspapers to retain traditional makeup procedures are not kept in effect for these

sectional pages. Newspapers that are traditional to the core when it comes to layout of the front page employ many nontraditional devices on the front pages of sections. Figure 15-19 shows sectional front pages of contemporarily designed newspapers, but Figure 15-20 shows sectional front pages from traditional newspapers.

The nontimely character of many of the subjects treated and the ability to display only one or perhaps a few items on these pages contribute to their new look. Large dominant illustrations, extra white space, and other landmarks of contemporary design can therefore prevail for these pages though they may be missing from others.

Editorial pages also can provide excellent examples of contemporary layout (Figure 15-21). Perhaps because they too are less timely—or perhaps because it is known that reader interest is low—the editorial pages of many newspapers show more design experimentation than any

15-18 These three pages show the design advantages of a large open rectangle for news display on inside pages. (Courtesy *The Morning Call*)

others. Wide variation in column widths, drawings, extra amounts of white space and special headings are found on many editorial pages.

The Traditional Approach to Page Layout

For some contemporary layout practices to be accepted, long-followed traditions must be set aside, and for some newspapers the abandonment of these practices is considered to be unwise. For example, the *New York Times* is considered by many professionals and laypersons alike as the model of quality for other newspapers to emulate. For more than a century, the *Times* has built a reputation as the great recorder of all human events, a reputation that is of inestimable value. Reputation is built on character, and character, personality, and appearance are so intertwined that to change any of these could well endanger what has

taken years of excellence to build. That such changes would be made slowly and carefully, if at all, is understandable. The front page of the *Times*, familiar to everyone, represents the facade of an institution that could never be torn down to incorporate changes which might or might not stand the test of time.

The *Washington Post* (Figure 15-22) is also a great American newspaper with a special reputation. The *Times* and the *Post* retain traditional approaches to page appearance. To suggest that either of these great newspapers totally adopt changing contemporary standards might be as unwise as suggesting that Rolls-Royce try to reshape its product to contemporary design standards. It is equally unwise to suggest that, because their front page appearance remains traditional, these newspapers have not changed, have not "progressed." Indeed, these newspapers have changed, but not in areas that are important in retaining the character and reputation they both have achieved. Widening of columns and contemporary design for sectional pages are changes already accepted, even by papers with traditional front pages.

15-19 Some of the most interesting newspaper page designs are found on section pages. The organization of the newspaper into standard subject-matter sections, each with its own front page, has been a strong trend. (Courtesy *Chicago Tribune* and *The Morning Call*)

The list of newspapers that retain some or all of the traditions of layout that they have developed would be a long one, and no attempt is made here to develop such a list. For that matter, there are so many gradations of adherence to traditional practices that it is foolhardy to attach specific labels to specific newspapers. Even the most traditional newspapers employ some contemporary techniques. What is discussed here are the approaches to layout that are based on tradition (and remember, traditions are being made at any time). Examples of these traditional approaches are shown. Because it is especially important for the student, we try to emphasize the "whys" for these traditions just as we try to emphasize the reasons for contemporary changes.

Some Basic Assumptions

Traditional layout practices begin with some important and basic assumptions. Among these are:

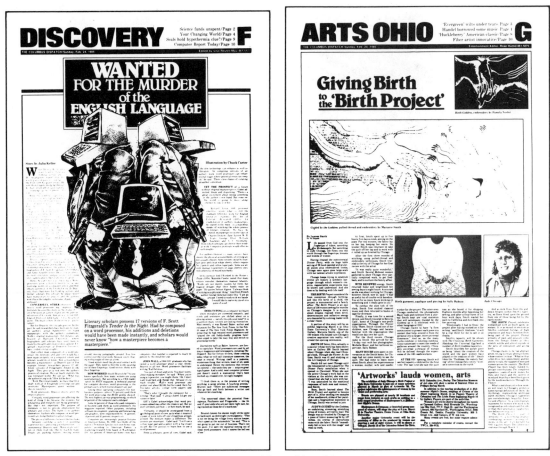

15-20 Newspapers with traditional approaches to page layout are also creating interesting and unusual sectional front pages. (Courtesy *Columbus Dispatch*)

1. News coverage is of overwhelming importance, and appearance must be secondary. This assumption is so strong that it leads to a belief that too much attention to appearance will probably be counterproductive.

2. Spot news is still the heart of a newspaper. Timeliness in presentation is also of such importance that makeup practices that slow the layout process cannot be accepted.

3. Pages must be treated as a complete unit, with all elements contributing to an overall harmony and unity.

4. Headlines serve a useful function of grading the news—telling the reader how important a story is—and their size and placement should help with this function.

5. Headlines must be standardized and restricted in order to obtain har-

15-21 Editorial pages often show special attention to design, with drawings, special headings, and extra white space used in an attempt to increase interest in the page. (Courtesy Dayton (Ohio) *Journal Herald* and Huntington (W. Va.) *Herald-Dispatch*)

mony among them and to permit maximum speed in writing and preparation.

6. The front page each day should be sufficiently similar to those of previous and following days so that they form a recognizable physical personality for the newspaper.

7. Illustrations primarily serve to amplify words.

Depending upon how strictly these assumptions are followed, singly and as a group, there is a great variety of end products as the page reproductions in this section show.

An Editor's Layout Tools

A newspaper layout editor works with three "tools": a *copy schedule*, a *headline schedule* and a *dummy sheet*. The copy schedule lists the inventory of all the stories that have been processed and sent into print,

15-22 Balance and contrast are the main goals in the design of newspapers retaining traditional layout practices. *The Washington Post* and the *Los Angeles Times*, both great newspapers, are excellent examples of newspapers that rely on these elements when displaying the news. Note the symmetrical design of this page from *The Washington Post*. (Courtesy *The Washington Post*)

the headline schedule is the inventory of the headline patterns the editor can use, and the dummysheet is a scaled-down blank newspaper page on which story positioning will be shown.

Entries on the copy schedule (Figure 15-23) are made as stories are assigned to copyreaders. In most cases, headlines are assigned at the same time, so when the copyreader is finished a full entry on the copy schedule can include: a *slug* (a one- or two-word description of the story); headline description; length of the story in column inches; a running total of column inches edited; a notation of any art (pictures) to accompany the story; and any special comments about the story. Some stories are set into type without headlines and are marked HTK (head to come). The headlines are not assigned on these stories because their relative importance will be determined by events still unfolding.

This part of an editor's work is monumental. With several pages under his or her control, the editor must evaluate stories quickly, assign a headline that will work into a page layout that has not yet even been conceived, and speed the flow of copy so that deadlines can be met.

Of special help to the editor is the headline schedule, which usually shows a sample of each headline as it would look in type, and gives the maximum unit count for each line of type. It also labels each headline, usually with a number, a letter, or a combination. By simply assigning and entering a number, such as #1, the editor is specifically identifying the many facets of a headline: type size, number of lines, arrangement of lines, and so on. The headline schedule thus helps make the editor's duties easier to carry out.

The headline schedule also is vital in another way. More than any other device, it sets the paper's appearance and outward personality. Policy judgments have already been made and incorporated into the headline schedule; there is, for example, no need to waste time deciding

		COPY SCHEDULE				
Slug	Headline	Story length (col. in.)	Total (col. in.)	Art	Typesetting	Page
COUNCIL	# 4	6	6	—		1
EXPLOSION	#6-6	18	24	2-COL x 9 INCHES	2 - COL	1
RALLY	#5-6	11	35	1-COL x 3 INCHES		

15-23 A copy schedule and dummy sheet.

whether a 72-point banner (headline over six full columns) can be used; the headline schedule makes it available or it does not. The same is true about typefaces. Under time pressure, an editor cannot decide whether Bodoni or Garamound or Futura or some other face would be best suited for a particular story. All display faces must be carefully selected in advance and then specified in the schedule. A good headline schedule will be complete, providing enough basic news headlines to meet all needs, plus any special purpose headlines. Sports and other departments may have distinctive headlines of their own.

Headline Patterns

Most newspapers rely on *flush left* or *modified flush left*. Other patterns that may be specified in a headline schedule include the *stepline, hanging indention, inverted pryamid* and *flush right*. Two-line steplines are formed by making the top line flush left and the bottom line flush right; if there is to be a middle line, it is centered. A hanging indention is formed with the first line flush left and the remaining lines indented uniformly at the left. The inverted pyramid is formed by centering all lines and having the lines decrease in length from top to bottom. Flush right is formed as the name implies.

Special headline forms may include one in which a rule is placed at the top and on both sides of the type (a *hood*) or one starting with a single subject word in large type followed by some smaller lines elaborating on the subject word (a *label*). Label heads with their secondary lines are reminiscent of earlier headlines that relied on several *decks* to form a single headline. Kickers are also, except for form, much like decks. Although many newspapers still use headlines composed of a top deck plus a second deck, few will include more than two. Special *jump* heads are also usually included in a headline schedule. These are headlines given special typographical form and used over the continued (jumped) portion of a story.

To Jump or Not to Jump

As they swiftly put entries on the copy schedules, approve headlines and do other preliminary chores involved in page layout, newspaper editors must be aware of a policy regarding carrying portions of stories from page one to an inside page. Some newspapers do not tolerate the practice, others encourage it, and some tolerate it but discourage it. Most studies indicate that there is a loss of readership of the jumped portion of a story, but a no-jump policy places restrictions on depth of coverage that many newspapers consider intolerable. At any rate, editors must have a policy in mind as they prepare a dummy. This policy ordinarily should establish standard locations for jumps and standardized typographical labels for the continued portions as well as jump notices at the end of the beginning portion.

Preparing the Dummy

With a completed copy schedule in hand, the layout editor is ready to put the pages together. If the preliminary work has gone well, there will be enough copy to fill the news holes (but not too much *overset*, wasted type). There will also be a sufficient variety of headlines assigned to stories so that a reasonably functional and attractive page can be created.

As layout editors position stories, they have two dominant considerations in mind. The first and most important of these is the importance of each story. They want the page to grade the news for the readers, to let them know what is most important. The other consideration involves appearance; the editors want each item to have *contrast*, but they also want the elements to *balance* (create a state of equilibrium), and they want the final result to be a *harmonious* unit.

Grading the News

In positioning the most important story of the day, an editor is likely to place it in the upper right-hand corner, a position that is contrary to design principles. This practice is a holdover from the early uses of banner headlines when editors thought it would be best to place stories in the right-hand column in such situations. It seemed unwise to start readers in column one with a headline, take them across the full width of the page, and then bring them back to column one to read the story.

More and more newspapers are shifting away from this tradition, especially in situations that do not involve headlines spreading over all or most of the columns. In such situations, the number one story is placed in the upper left quadrant of the page.

In any event, the top of the page is accepted as preferred for the most important stories, and the two or three most important ones are assigned to that area. In order to get contrast in the bottom area of a page, some strong display items, often of an *interesting* as opposed to *important* nature, are placed there.

The *nameplate* or *flag* (a newspaper's name as set in distinctive fashion) usually goes at the top of page one above all headings or art, but sometimes is moved to other positions. If the nameplate is placed at the top it often will have *ears* placed on each side. These are small display items, such as Scripps-Howard's lighthouse symbol, a weather box, or a symbol indicating the edition.

Achieving Desirable Contrast

As they place each story according to importance and interest, editors are also eager to have each story stand out, each trying to lure as many readers as possible. To accomplish this goal, the editors try to achieve contrast. As pointed out in earlier chapters, contrast comes from opposites: light and dark; large and small; tall and short; fat and thin; straight and crooked. It is the element that makes graphic communication possible; contrast between lightness and darkness makes type and illustrations visible.

Because we start with a field of white, it is easy to fall into the trap of thinking that contrast automatically comes from dropping large dark areas onto this field. It is true that the first of these will give maximum contrast, but with consecutive additions, contrast is steadily reduced.

Contrast Among Headlines

With this in mind, two rules of contrast apply to headlines.

1. *Headlines should be separated by white space, gray matter or illustrations.* Some newspaper makeup persons put teeth into this rule by insisting that two headlines never be placed together on a page. There are a number of ways to separate them. Spread leads provide gray matter between spread headlines and the headlines of stories below. Photographs, illustrations and boxes serve likewise. Most makeup persons treat boxes as if they were illustrations because they perform the same functions in layout.

    Separation of headlines on a horizontal plane is especially important. If two headlines of like size and style are next to each other horizontally, they form a so-called *tombstone*. Tombstones reduce the contrast for each headline so much that the reader can be tricked into reading the two headlines as one. Obviously they should be avoided.

2. *If headlines must be together, they must be individually distinctive so as to retain some contrast.* Their difference can be in type size, type style or the typographical pattern of the headline.

    Two-spread heads in large type can be separated by a single-column head in smaller type. An italic head may be placed next to a roman, or a lightface next to a boldface. Boxed heads or feature heads can stand out from adjacent heads by white space and size-difference. Spread heads with a broad horizontal sweep are distinct from single-column heads in a vertical shape, but again difference in type size or style helps.

Contrast in Body Areas

The practice of changing the line measure for editorials is a good example of contrast in body areas. With lines in single-column measure on the rest of the page, editorials that are two columns wide get special visual attention.

Change of measure for contrast is not restricted to the editorial page, of course. Front-page feature stories and major interpretative efforts displayed under a *skyline* (a banner on a story above the nameplate) or a spread head at the bottom of the page are frequently given the additional eye appeal of wider columns.

The technique of spreading type over one more column than required (i.e., the 5 on 6) as discussed earlier has become increasingly popular for many traditional newspapers.

Special typographical devices—such as setting some paragraphs in boldface or italic, beginning paragraphs with a word or two in boldface, and inserting boldface lines (subheads) are also used to give some contrast in body type areas.

A Word of Warning

Contrast is essential to good design, but it can have undesirable aspects. Imagine a page with every headline set in a different face, and body copy varying widely among stories. There would be plenty of contrast, but the overall result would be distasteful. Effective contrast makes each component stand out on its own without destroying the equilibrium, harmony and unity that are necessary for good design.

Newspaper makeup that concentrates so much on contrast that it neglects other parts of good design is called "circus makeup." It is characterized by spread headlines, often in excessively large type, all over a page with little or no thought being given to the total picture. Circus makeup creates an impression of action and noise—but so much from so many directions that the reader can barely see or hear any of it.

Balance is primary in the makeup of some newspapers and purely secondary for others. Newspapers trying to project a conservative, steady and reliable personality are inclined to make balance dominant in their page design. "Shouters" may deliberately try to subordinate balance lest their readers think the day's news a trifle dull. Most newspapers try for a middle ground.

Balance on a newspaper page is acquired by placing relatively equal weights on both sides of an imaginary line splitting the page into vertical halves. Balancing opposite corners is also considered. When these weights are virtually identical, the makeup is in *formal balance,* or *symmetrical* (see Figure 15-22). When they are only relatively alike, the balance is *informal.*

Headlines and illustrations have the most inherent contrast, which means they exercise the strongest influence on equilibrium; therefore, their placement is especially important. A formally balanced newspaper page has every headline and illustration on one side of the page perfectly matched in weight and position by others on the opposite side.

But because makeup acts to grade the news for readers, formal balance demands that news stories develop in importance by pairs. Naturally, this is rare, and as a result formal balance is relatively uncommon in newspapers.

Functionally, in newspaper makeup, headlines are balanced by pictures, headlines of one pattern by those of another, and lighter elements by heavier elements placed closer to the center, like the heavier child sitting closer to the center of a seesaw.

Harmony in Newspaper Makeup

The makeup person is concerned with three kinds of harmony when laying out newspaper pages:

1. the general appearance of the pages must harmonize with the character or personality of the newspaper
2. types must harmonize with each other
3. special pages must harmonize with their subjects and readers

Harmony of Appearance and Character

Because harmony in a paper's personality concerns the paper's basic character, it is usually controlled by specific management policies. Only minor decisions on detail are made in this respect from day to day.

The range of headlines, the emphasis on illustration, and the preferred makeup patterns are a matter of policy. The makeup person must simply translate his or her news judgments into assigning headlines, display for photographs, and page arrangements that do not depart from the predetermined paths.

Typographic Harmony

Newspapers have more difficulty achieving typographic harmony than the other printed media do. The large size of the pages and the great number of individual units of type display almost require that the selection of display be *monotypographic* within any *section* of a newspaper. Some newspapers still have headlines in two, or at the most three, type families, but their ranks are steadily decreasing. Restricting the use of display type to one family assures harmony, and the numerous variations within any type family offer many ways to avoid monotony.

Type families can and should change from department to department. One family may be used for basic news pages, another for the sports pages, and yet another for the editorial page.

Harmony with Subject and Reader

Type families can be changed in different sections because subjects and readers differ. The heavy sans serifs of a sports page may be inappropriate for an editorial page. Compare the typography of the sports and editorial pages of several newspapers; these pages have display faces that are completely different, but each is harmonious with subject and reader.

Changing Traditions

The makeup practices described as traditional in this section are constantly being sharpened and revised to improve the final product. Without totally discarding tradition and adopting complete new faces, most newspapers are integrating changes in their appearance.

These changes, many of which blur the distinction between what we have chosen to call contemporary and traditional practices, are

1. Reduction of the number of columns per page to six or five, thus permitting greater readability because of improvements in type size and line length. One-column headlines can be much more descriptive and are easier to write. Wider columns also offer mechanical and cost advantages. Hyphenation, the curse of typesetting, is reduced sharply. Fewer, longer lines means fewer justification problems and faster typesetting. Pasteup of pages is also easier.
2. Horizontalism—the tendency to arrange stories and headlines so they form horizontal masses. Fewer decks and fewer lines in headlines that are spread over more columns produce these horizontal shapes.
3. More and larger illustrations, with greater appreciation for their artistic appeal.
4. Legible headline patterns based on the flush left pattern and its variations.
5. More and better use of white space.

As one can readily see from this listing—and by looking at the reproductions of contemporary and traditional pages in this chapter—the major differences between the two groups are diminishing. There remain, of course, small or subtle differences, not only between these two groups but among the thousands of papers published in this country. Each newspaper in its own way is using graphic elements to get the most news into the mind of its readers in the best possible fashion. And that's the name of the game.

16
Design of Pamphlets and Brochures

Although production and design work in newspapers, magazines and books can be challenging, equal challenges also can be found in the design and production of *direct literature* such as pamphlets and brochures. These materials go directly to readers either by mail or hand distribution. They promote products, sell services, announce special events and report proceedings. They are an indispensable part of the world of business.

In producing these pamphlets and brochures, the professional communicator makes the fullest use of the principles of graphic communications. He or she must consider

1. the appropriate printing process
2. the creative and cost-effective use of color
3. the paper stock needed
4. how the publication will be folded
5. the size and shape of the product

This is, of course, in addition to the myriad other content and design considerations that affect mass communications.

338

Kinds of Direct Literature

These printed pieces take many forms, too many to be covered in this text. In broadest terms these pieces can be divided into two groups:

1. booklets
2. flat or folded sheets

Booklets

Generally, the printed piece of direct literature comes from the printing press as flat sheets of paper, which may be folded and trimmed to become booklets. For example, Figure 16-1 shows a flat sheet with the folios (page numbers) as they would fall on one side. Take a sheet of paper, write the folios on it as shown, and fold it in the two directions indicated by the dotted lines. Folded properly, the paper should look like Figure 16-2. You can now carefully lift the leaves and place the folios 2, 3, 6, and 7 on the proper pages.

Now refold the sheet and imagine staples driven through the "backbone" at the points indicated by the arrows in Figure 16-2. The staples should clinch parallel with and on top of the fold between pages 4 and 5. Next, imagine that the entire unit is compressed and that knives trim on the dotted lines as shown on the top and bottom edges and the fore edge in Figure 16-2. You can do this on your folded sheet, using two staples that you force through the backbone with your fingers and then taking scissors to the edges. You will wind up with what is shown in Figure 16-3, a folded and trimmed eight-page booklet.

What you have just produced is a *self-cover booklet.* A four-page cover can be printed (usually on a heavier paper) and the eight-page unit can be inserted before stapling and trimming. Then you have a *separate-cover booklet.* If the cover stock is so heavy that it makes folding difficult, it may first be processed with a scoring rule on special equipment.

Booklets are sometimes called *brochures.* Essentially the booklet is a small book and is made up of eight or more pages bound together and usually stapled. The booklet ranges in number of pages up to 36 or 40 and the number of pages must be divisible by four. The format itself may be either vertical or horizontal.

Books usually have more pages and are bound with more permanent covers. Books, moreover, are of a literary or scientific nature, whereas the content of booklets is more likely to reflect promotional interests.

Book format, which is traditionally standardized, has roughly three main divisions:

1. the preliminaries, or front matter
2. the text
3. the references, or back matter

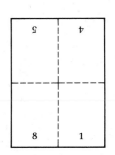

16-1 Flat sheet ready to fold to make eight-page booklet.

The preliminaries include the *half title,* the book's first printed page, on which appears only the book's title; the *title page,* which includes the

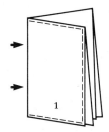

16-2 Folded sheet that will be trimmed and "bound" to make an eight-page booklet (brochure).

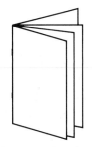

16-3 Folded and trimmed eight-page booklet.

title and the names of the author and the publisher and the place of publication; the *copyright page;* the *preface;* the acknowledgments; the *contents;* the *introduction* when it is not a part of the text proper; and, often, a second half title. Tradition governs the order of these pages and whether they fall on a left- or right-hand page. *Folios,* or page numbers, are in lowercase or small cap roman numerals, appearing first on the opening preface page, although the actual numbering starts from the half title.

The text section contains the chapters; the reference section consists of appendixes, bibliography, glossary and index. In text and reference sections the folios are in arabic, and may be either at the top or at the bottom of the page. *Running heads* usually appear at the top of each page, and the content is often different on the right- and left-hand pages.

Throughout, the progressive margins remain consistent although text on facing pages may run a line or two long or short depending upon makeup.

This description of book design refers to traditional formatting. However, as we saw in Chapter 4, book design may be altered considerably in the New Typography.

In the design of booklets, tradition and formality may also be applied in varying degrees (see Figures 16-4 and 16-5). Because of their usual promotional nature, booklets are more often of an informal design. Because a message unfolds through succeeding pages, as in a book, a continuity of style must be maintained by the designer, who works with

16-4 Formal design in a brochure. Note observation of margins and internal white space. (Courtesy Specialty Advertising Association International)

calendars to obtain wider and more consistent display of his business announcements. In 1869 George Coburn of Hartford, Connecticut, began printing calendars which carried advertising, and in 1879 a newspaper editor in Coshocton, Ohio, produced advertising specialties in the form of candy boxes and school bags. These may very well have been the first advertising specialties other than calendars to be made and distributed in the United States. However, without library files, in contrast to newspapers and magazines, and with the records of many old businesses long lost or destroyed, there exists little possibility of establishing an exact and undisputed date or place of origin for this method of advertising. However, this is of small consequence since it is the present position of specialty advertising and its potential for future development that are important both to businessmen who sell and use it and to students planning careers in advertising.

SPECIALTY ADVERTISING OF TODAY

Specialty advertising industry sources estimated 1970 sales at $871 million. The industry employs some 250,000 people in its many phases. Of the approximately 4,400 companies in the field, some 900 are suppliers, 3,200 are distributors, 10 are direct selling houses. Also associated with the industry are a number of firms and individuals engaged in the manufacture and/or sale of machinery, equipment, materials, services or supplies to other members of the industry.

Within the industry itself, the terms **supplier, distributor** (often referred to as a specialty advertising "counselor" or "agency") and **direct selling house** are defined as follows:

"A **supplier** manufactures, imports, converts, imprints, or otherwise processes advertising specialties, calendars or business gifts for sale through specialty advertising distributors."

"A **distributor** develops ideas for the use of specialty advertising products, buys these products from suppliers and sells them to advertisers under his own company name."

"A **direct selling house** combines the functions of supplier and distributor within one organization. It primarily manufactures its own products and sells them directly to advertisers through its own sales force."

The industry is served by Specialty Advertising Association International which was formed in 1964 by the consolidation of two existing trade associations. SAAI and its predecessor organizations have served the field since 1903. It publishes a monthly newsletter, conducts two trade shows each year, and works in general to advance and promote the welfare of the industry as well as its member firms. SAAI also performs a number of special services for its members which include, in part, a comprehensive public relations program, annual Executive Development Seminars, Management Practices Conferences, a Sales Training Manual and fact sheets on various types of advertisers, and an annual

Estelle Carpey, "The History of the Ad Specialty Industry," **The Advertising Specialty Counselor,** May 1954 (Philadelphia, Pa.: The Advertising Specialty Institute, Inc.)

8

Awards Competition for outstanding use of specialty advertising in business promotion. The Association maintains a Washington-based counsel.

Also serving the industry is The Advertising Specialty Institute, a privately owned business organization, which operates as a central source of information for many industry firms. It publishes **The Advertising Specialty Register** and the semi-annual **Market and Credit Report,** the standard directories of specialty advertising suppliers and distributors, respectively. **The Counselor,** a monthly trade journal devoted to the industry, also is published by the Institute.

For most of its history, the specialty advertising industry was concerned primarily with products, and its sales tended to be highly seasonal. But operations and orientation have changed greatly during the past two decades. Although there is still some seasonal peaking toward year's end because of the calendar business and the use of other types of advertising specialties and gifts as Christmas remembrances, on the whole sales are spread more evenly throughout the year than they once were. This has been due in large part to a marked change in the level of selling in the industry and type of sales representatives engaged in this function. The "peddler," whose interest never went beyond making a sale when making a sale meant little more than displaying a variety of merchandise and letting it sell itself, is being replaced among the more progressive distributors by the specialty advertising counselor. These counselors are trained to sell an advertising or sales promotion idea rather than selling merchandise. They are consultants and advisors to their clients, helping them with their individual advertising problems and fitting the advertising specialty to the specific job that confronts each client.

SAAI's annual Executive Development Seminars contribute to the advancement of this trend toward improved and more scientific procedure with the specialty advertising industry. The Seminars run for eight days and include, among other things, courses in marketing problems, advertising media, employee selection and training, and written and oral communications. These Seminars, conducted by midwestern universities, are more than refresher courses and permit those attending to earn the title of Certified Advertising Specialist (C.A.S.) upon successful completion of the program.

9

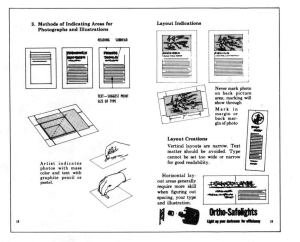

units of individual pages or units of facing pages. The arrangement of elements in a booklet can differ from page to page. Cuts can bleed; copy block widths and margins can be varied; and display and color can be used with a free hand.

The front cover, often referred to as the *OFC* (outside front cover), will receive one of two types of treatment. In the case of an informative or literary booklet, it will be more conservatively handled with only a title set in type and placed formally or informally (see Figure 16-6). If the nature of the booklet is more promotional, display treatment of the cover may be more extensive, incorporating both visual and verbal elements (see Figure 16-7).

Folders

The printed flat sheets delivered from the press do not always take the form of books or booklets. Many printed jobs are known as *flat pieces* or *pamphlets*. Several may be printed together on a large press sheet and then trimmed (cut) from it. Such flat pieces take many forms, such as letterheads, cards, announcements, posters, fliers, business forms, instruction sheets, envelope stuffers and so on. These are often printed on one side only. The principles of design that were previously discussed apply to planning the message they carry.

We are, however, more interested here in those printed messages that are not finished flat but are, instead, folded. Such pieces are known as *folders.* The subject of folding is given a comprehensive treatment in Chapter 13, but certain implications in the folder have a direct bearing on information processing. This is primarily the result of the fact that, like booklets, folders consist of pages. The serial ordering of these pages is not so rigid as it is with booklets. Thus the design of folders presents special problems.

16-6   Conservative treatment of a front cover.
(Courtesy of Edwards Brothers, Inc., Ann Arbor, Michigan, Bruce Nathan, Account Executive)

16-7   More promotional, display-oriented front cover. (©Copyright 1986 by nuArc Co., Inc., Niles, Ill., U.S.A.)

Human information processing is basically serial. When we present a message on one flat area, we hope that we can control information intake by guiding the eye through the message by means of visual syntax. Nonetheless, the reader may still look at any part of the total message at any time he or she wishes (but not when he or she reads a booklet). However, the problem arises again when we consider the folder.

Broadly speaking, the folder piece can be given any of several kinds of the so-called *letter fold.* Such pieces are usually about 8½ by 11, 9 by 12, or 8½ by 14 inches. A letter fold takes such pieces down to a size that will be the No. 10 envelope, which is 4⅛ inches deep by 9½ inches wide. In addition to these more common-size folders there is the *broadside,* which is a jumbo folder, usually 19 by 25 inches up to 25 by 38 inches when it is flat (before folding). It unfolds to a smashing spread concentrated on one idea.

Figure 16-8 shows some common letter-fold pieces, which result in 4-, 6-, 8-, and 10-page folders. Only a few of the many possible treatments are presented, with particular concern to their effect in information processing. Try making these folds yourself with pieces of paper. The

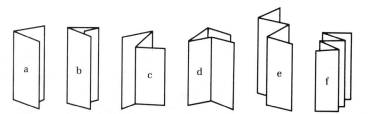

16-8 **Common letter folds. a:** 4-page single fold; **b:** 6-page standard or wrap-around; **c:** 6-page accordion; **d:** 8-page standard, double parallel fold or fold within a fold; **e:** 8-page accordion; **f:** 10-page accordion.

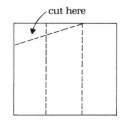

16-9 Angle-cut accordion fold.

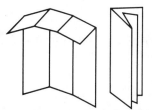

16-10 *Left:* Shortfold, 12 pages. *Right:* Off-center double parallel fold, 8 pages.

drawings indicate vertical formats, but the folder could also have a horizontal format.

Folder (a) presents no particular problems. Page 1 could be treated as a separate page, pages 2 and 3 separately or as a spread, and page 4 as a single unit. But folders (b), (c), (d), (e), and (f) offer more interesting possibilities. Consider, for example, (d). Take the folder you have made. Close it by swinging the left half to the right. When the reader opens it, he or she comes to a two-page spread; another opening reveals a four-page spread. The design of the same folder could be treated in other ways. Turn it back for front. Now consider what was the back as the front. Now it unfolds in a different manner. The order of the message and the designs given the pages may call for different treatments from folder to folder.

These considerations do not exhaust the possibilities. Look at Figure 16-9. Take a piece of paper. Fold it as a six-page accordion. Before doing so, cut off a piece diagonally as shown. Note the step-effect that allows portions of page 3 and page 5 to be seen from the front.

Folds do not have to be equal as seen in Figure 16-8. Figure 16-10 shows what are known as a *short fold* and an *off-center fold.* To do the latter, lay a sheet in front of you. Bring the left edge toward the right but let it fall short, then crease; repeat and crease. As with the diagonal-cut accordion fold, an interesting tab or index step is visible.

What Kind of Printed Piece?

An important creative decision is the kind of printed piece to be produced. The following factors favor the use of a booklet:

1. lengthy copy requiring continuity of presentation
2. need for a number of illustrative examples
3. highly technical material
4. catalog material
5. high quality production that may want to be retained for a longer

period of time than a folded pamphlet (e.g., a corporation's annual report)

The folder, on the other hand, lends itself when these conditions exist:

1. A series of illustrations is to be presented, as the number of different models of a product.
2. Short but crisp text is offered.
3. The unfolding naturally builds a climactic impression.
4. Production speed and *economy* are required. Booklet production means time-consuming, extra folding-and-binding operations, whereas folders can be *self-mailers*. With the latter, one section is left open for addressing and for the printing of postal *indicia*, an indication that the sender has a permit to pay postage at time of mailing in lieu of affixing stamps. Booklets are usually mailed in envelopes, thereby entailing the dual expense of envelopes and insertion.
5. *Imprinting* of various dealer names is called for. Such work can be done economically on the flat sheets before folding.

Standard Unit Sizes

An early step in planning the printed piece is the preparation of the dummy. At this point the designer must remember that the size of the piece has a significant effect on final production cost because manufacturers, in the interest of economy, produce certain standard sizes of paper, available through printers. Thus, only certain-sized pamphlets and other forms of direct literature can be cut advantageously from these stock sheets. These standard sizes are

Bond: 17 by 22 (basis), 17 by 28, 19 by 24, 22 by 34, 28 by 34, 34 by 44 inches.
Book: 25 by 38 (basis), 28 by 42, 28 by 44, 32 by 45, 35 by 45, 38 by 50, 19 by 25, 23 by 29, 23 by 35, 36 by 48, 41 by 61, 44 by 66, 45 by 68, 50 by 76, 52 by 76 inches.
Cover: 20 by 26 (basis), 23 by 35, 26 by 40, 35 by 46 inches.

(Note that the basic size—basis—of cover stock, *20 by 26 inches,* is slightly larger than 19 by 25 inches, which is one-half the basis size of book paper. This is to allow for *overhang covers,* that is, covers with dimensions larger than the inside of the booklet.)

Suppose an 8-page booklet, $4\frac{1}{2}$ by 6 inches, is being planned. What size stock can be used? Remember these points before solving this problem:

1. One-half inch should be subtracted from the short dimension of the stock to allow for press grippers, which hold the paper as it goes through the press. This is three-eighths of an inch on some presses. Printing can extend to, but not beyond, the grippers.

16-11 How 32 pages (each 4½ by 6 inches) are imposed on one side of a 25-by-38-inch sheet. No pages at the head (gripper edge) can bleed. If head bleeds were necessary, 28 by 42 sheets would be used. (Refer to the table below, "Common Sheet Sizes," for sheet selection for trim and bleeds.)

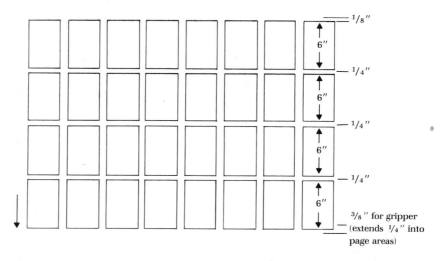

1/8″
6″
1/4″
6″
1/4″
6″
1/4″
6″
3/8″ for gripper (extends 1/4″ into page areas)

2. One-eighth inch should be allowed for bleed trim on every edge of the piece.

Thus, we can determine that 64 pages can be printed on a 25-by-38-inch sheet, 32 on each side, as shown in Figure 16-11. This means a total of *eight* 8-page booklets per sheet of paper.

The finished booklet should be $4\frac{5}{8}$ by $6\frac{1}{4}$ inches to allow trim of $\frac{1}{8}$ inch on top, bottom and outside to open the pages. The fractions along the right side of the sheet in Figure 16-11 indicate trim allowances. As long as the print area falls at least $\frac{1}{2}$ inch below the top of the sheet, 25 by 38 inches is adequate.

But when bleed pages are in the design, the printed booklet should be $4\frac{3}{4}$ by $6\frac{1}{2}$ inches. When trimming is done, the cut to make the finished $4\frac{1}{2}$ by 6 inches is then deep enough to ensure inclusion of the bleed art. The piece should be printed on a 28-by-42-inch sheet for bleeds.

Common Sheet Sizes

Size of piece (in inches)	Sheet size for trim	Sheet size for bleeds	Number of pages
$3\frac{3}{8}$ by $6\frac{1}{4}$	28 by 42	28 by 44	96
$3\frac{3}{4}$ by $5\frac{1}{8}$	32 by 44	35 by 45	128
$4\frac{1}{4}$ by $5\frac{3}{8}$	35 by 45	38 by 50	128
$4\frac{1}{2}$ by 6	25 by 38	28 by 42	64
4 by $9\frac{1}{8}$	25 by 38	28 by 42	48
$5\frac{1}{4}$ by $7\frac{5}{8}$	32 by 44	35 by 45	64
$5\frac{1}{2}$ by $8\frac{1}{4}$	35 by 45	38 by 50	64
$8\frac{1}{2}$ by $5\frac{1}{2}$ (oblong)	23 by 35	25 by 38	32
6 by $9\frac{1}{8}$	25 by 38	28 by 42	32
$7\frac{3}{4}$ by $10\frac{5}{8}$	32 by 44	35 by 45	32
$8\frac{1}{2}$ by 11	35 by 45	38 by 50	32
$9\frac{1}{4}$ by $12\frac{1}{8}$	25 by 38	28 by 42	16

A piece can be printed from other than standard-sized paper. Manufacturers make paper in special sizes, and quantities in excess of 5000 pounds can be purchased economically. For small amounts, extra costs usually dictate fitting the design to a standard size.

Presses and envelopes are made to accommodate all of the standard-sized pieces. Special envelopes can be made to order. Both standard-sized letter and *booklet envelopes* are available through the printer.

Special Paper Considerations

In addition to size, certain other aspects of paper need the attention of the designer. These are (1) kind, (2) color, and (3) weight.

Kind of Paper

Bond lends itself well to folders because of its good folding quality. It is also strong and durable. Offset prints well on its hard surface, but bond should be avoided for most letterpress work. Common weights of bond that are in use are 20- and 24-pound, equivalent to the book paper weights of 50- and 60-pounds. Weight means the *basis weight*, the weight in pounds of a ream (500 sheets) of paper cut to its basic size.

Equivalent Basis Weights of Stock

Book paper Basis: 25 × 38	Cover paper Basis: 20 × 26	Bond paper Basis: 17 × 22
30	—	—
35	—	13
40	—	16
45	25	—
50	—	20
60	35	24
70	40	28
80	45	32
90	50	36
100	55	40
120	65	—
150	80	—

Note that paper is not usually made above the 150-pound weight. Most presses, especially offset ones, have difficulty with book weights above 130. Here are some key points to remember in paper selection:

1. Coated book stocks are expensive and tend to crack in folding. Uncoated stocks may seem less distinctive, but they reflect less light and can provide substantial cost savings.

2. Book papers, especially those for offset use, fold excellently, especially in the 60- 80-pound range.
3. Cover stock must be scored (creased for folding) above weights of 65 pounds.
4. Special attention should be given to the grain (fiber pattern) of the paper stock you select. It has important implications for how the paper can be successfully scored.
5. It is wise to ask your printer to show examples of printing, especially color processes on various paper stocks. These results will help your decision making.

Color

White has been the traditional color for paper since the earliest days of printing, and black ink on white paper will probably continue to be most popular in the future. But for some time interest in color stocks has grown. There are several reasons for this:

1. The contrast of color stock to white. With the bulk of printing done on white paper, messages on color stock attract attention.
2. Increased understanding of the psychological effects of color. As discussed, color stimulates positively and negatively. Skillfully used, color stock creates atmosphere and builds retention. Because black and white are in a sense the absence of color, they lack the psychological impact of printing in color ink on color stock.
3. Research in developing compatible inks and papers. Paper and ink manufacturers, with the assistance of psychologists, ophthalmologists, and lighting engineers, have uncovered pleasing combinations of color ink on colored paper. Four-color process printed on a color stock has proved startlingly effective when the key color black is substituted by a dark color ink that is compatible with the paper.

The reading task is simplified when the message is printed color-on-color. There is less reflection than in black-on-white. Many experts contend that this reduction in contrast is a welcome relief for the reader. Because the cost of color-on-color is not much greater, the continued improvements in paper and ink manufacture will no doubt mean an expanded use of color-on-color printing.

It is possible to match the color of some text stocks with cover stocks when this is desired. If a perfect match cannot be made, the designer would do well to consider a definite contrast between the two.

If a color stock is used for folders, all pages must, of course, be of that color. In the case of booklets, however, it is possible to use color stock for some of the pages, the number of such pages being divisible by four.

Even when a stock of one color is used throughout a booklet, it is possible to give some pages a different color by laying the color on the pages with ink. Offset printing is particularly adaptable to this technique. This applies to the printing of folder pages as well.

Weight

The weight of the stock used must be considered primarily because of its effect on mailing costs. This factor alone cannot, however, determine the weight. The nature of the message and the effect of the paper on the reader may require a stock of such substance that higher mailing costs can be justified. If a booklet carries a self-cover, consideration must be given to durability, which means that a substantial stock may be called for. Self-mailer folders likewise call for heavier paper.

Other Design Considerations

If the decision is made to maintain margins from page to page in a folder, the two side margins and the top should be about the same and the foot margin should be slightly larger. Such a decision is likely when the message is primarily verbal, as in Figure 16-12. Incidentally, on the four pages on the opposite side of those shown were the Income Statement and the Balance Sheet, each spread across two pages. What letter fold

TO OUR SHAREHOLDERS

We are pleased to enclose a check representing the quarterly dividend on shares of stock which you owned of record March 11, 1974. For those of you who have elected to participate in our dividend reinvestment plan, you will receive a statement of the amount of the dividends being reinvested for you into additional shares of common stock of the Company.

For the quarter ending March 31, 1974, the Board of Directors has declared a dividend of 37 cents per common share and the regular dividend on all of the outstanding series of preferred stock. The dividend on common stock represents an increase of 1¼ cents per share in the quarterly dividend rate, and raises the annual dividend rate from $1.43 to $1.48 per share.

For the 12 months ended February 28, 1974, earnings per average common share were $1.72, compared with $1.94, for the same period last year. Earnings for the two months of 1974 were 30 cents per average share, compared with 33 cents for last year.

Unusually mild weather experienced in the Company's service area during January and February, 1974, together with conservation measures of our customers, kept revenues for the two-month period below anticipated levels.

The Board of Directors, at the January, 1974, meeting, approved a construction budget of $144 Million for 1974, approximately $80 Million more than 1973's construction expenditures.

During January, the Company sold—at private placement—150,000 shares of 6⅞% Five-year Cumulative Preferred Stock, $100 Par Value. The proceeds from the sale were used to reduce the Company's short-term indebtedness resulting from construction expenditures. Indications are that the next permanent financing—probably consisting of debt securities—will be about mid-year.

The Company continues to collect revenues, subject to refund, on rate increases applicable to retail customers, pending final decision from the South Carolina Public Service Commission. As stated in the Notes to Financial Statements of the 1973 Annual Report to Stockholders, the Company's right to place its retail rates in effect under bond was contested in Federal Court. A three-judge court upheld the constitutionality of the State statute and allowed the Company to continue its rates under bond. This ruling was appealed by the contestants to the United States Supreme Court. The Company has received notice that the Supreme Court has upheld the constitutionality of the South Carolina law by adopting the ruling of the three-judge panel.

The Annual Report for 1973 is to be mailed to all stockholders on or about March 22, 1974.

S. C. McMeekin
Chm. of the Board

Arthur M. Williams
President

March 21, 1974

This report is issued solely for the purpose of providing information. It is not intended for use in connection with any sale or purchase of, or any offer or solicitation of offers, to buy or sell, any securities.

SOUTH CAROLINA
ELECTRIC & GAS COMPANY
328 Main Street, Columbia, S. C. 29218

SOUTH CAROLINA ELECTRIC & GAS COMPANY

INTERIM REPORT
February 28, 1974

16-12 Margins on standard folder pages. (Courtesy South Carolina Electric & Gas Company)

do you think was given the piece? The treatment of three equal margins and a larger foot margin may be given to booklets of 8 or 12 pages. If the booklet contains more pages, progressive margins are often followed throughout.

Folios are rarely placed on folder pages, and unless they are an aid to the reader, they are not used in booklets. If folios are used, a table of contents is generally included.

The decision of whether or not to print on the *IFC, IBC* or *OBC* (inside front cover, inside back cover, outside back cover) of booklets is often determined by the nature of the contents. If the content is informative and the layout formal, these covers are often left blank, particularly if the piece carries a separate cover. If the booklet is promotional and the design less formal, the covers are often printed, particularly if the piece carries a self-cover.

Whether the folder or booklet is vertical or horizontal is a matter of option. Nonpromotional booklets that are formally designed are usually vertical in the tradition of the book. Promotional materials may be presented in either format. A particular advantage of the folder is that vertical and horizontal layouts are possible within the same piece. Consider the wraparound, six-page folder, for example. Page 1 may be a vertical. Upon opening it, the reader may see a horizontal spread over pages 2, 3 and 4.

By bridging the gutter in a vertical format book, the designer can also present horizontal designs. Some of the techniques for doing this were shown in Chapter 14. Figure 16-13 shows a spread from a booklet in which some of these techniques are applied.

16-13 Creating horizontal designs over vertical pages by bridging folds.

Meredith Wiley
has a record of
accomplishment

*** Founder & chairman of the Oregon Downtown Revitalization Coalition for economic development of small cities.
*** Defended Calapooia property owners' rights in a dispute with the State Division of Lands over the river's navigability.
*** 1982 Vice President of Linn County Bar Association.
*** Named "Outstanding Young Woman of America" twice, 1974 and 1980 by National Federation of Womens Groups.
*** Founding member and state public relations director of Women for Agriculture.
*** Legislative advocate 1969-1976 on behalf of Women for Agriculture, Albany Planning Commission, Albany Museum commission.
*** 1972-1976, Albany Planning Commission.
*** Organized a group of Albany citizens in 1974 to establish historic districts in downtown Albany, continues today to be a viable and active group that has gained support of local and state officials and the National Trust for Historic Preservation.
*** Board member for Albany Boys and Girls Club.
*** Board member for Children's Farm Home.

The Wiley family, (left to right) Caroline, 14, Gretchen, 18, Meredith, Bill, 16, and Kent

Meredith understands the issues: jobs.

*** Jobs through economic development. . . Reduce governmental regulation, encourage existing businesses to expand, attract new business, boost small business.
*** Jobs through changes in the tax policy . . .Oregon tax policy restricts business

growth, places unfair burdens on property owners and businesses. Lifting the tax burden creates new jobs.
*** Jobs through effective use of natural resources. Agriculture and forest lands in Oregon should be under more local control. Without a better balance, Oregonians will continue to lose jobs.

Checking Press Sheets

Once a message is released to a medium, the opportunity for controlling the printed result fades. In the case of direct literature, however, there is a chance to check the printed piece as it comes from the press. At this point it is possible to find and correct *fill-in* or *plugging* of halftones and fine lines; streaks, slurs and other blemishes; and improper makeready and inking.

Press sheets, or *press proofs,* are marked by an arrow that indicates change of position. The arrow is drawn to point out where type or art is to be moved. A circle is drawn around areas where makeready is faulty or where some other imperfection is spotted, and the proofreader's delete symbol draws attention to the circle.

One cannot be too careful in searching for errors in either verbal or visual copy before releasing it for publication. Information processing theory tells why. Things that we look at are usually within a familiar context which aids us in perception. Sometimes we see things that are not there; at other times we do not see things that are there, simply because of our expectations, which are guided by the context. Thus it is easy to misperceive.

One interesting study of proofreading confirms this interpretation. Subjects were asked to cross out each letter *e* in passages of prose. Analysis of results showed that the subjects were more likely to miss the silent *e* than the pronounced one. Further, the *e* in the word "the" was more likely to be missed than other pronounced *e*'s. It was also found that the absence of an *e* that would have been silent is less likely to be discovered than the absence of an *e* that would have been pronounced.[1] It would seem that there is an interrelationship between visual symbols and acoustic coding. In any event, proofreading requires close attention.

[1] D. W. J. Corcoran, "Acoustic Factors in Proofreading," *Nature* 214 (1967):851–852.

17

New Horizons: Technology's Breathless March

Consider the fate of the printer's job case. It was the voice box of the print shop. In its shallow, wooden drawers lay well-worn but distinctive pieces of metal type that became articulate as line after line of it was set by hand. It held the successors of Gutenberg's 15th-century movable type. Still in use in the middle of the 20th century, the job case's only dramatic change took place when a single case consolidated a system that had separated capital and lower case letters.

Today, these cases are museum pieces or showcase items in antique stores. A favorite use is to insert family memorabilia into them and hang them on living room walls. Now small pictures, pressed flowers, special announcements, crafts and other family remembrances occupy the tiny wooden rooms that once housed the families of Bodoni and Cheltenham.

On a larger scale, museums of science and industry showcase our past technology in printing and its allied arts. There we see the early presses of William Caxton; the first linecaster driven by perforated tape; the first photograph transmitted by radio signals; and the then-futuristic

351

phototypesetter. The museums have always had time to consider and catalog their collections. However, the traditional distance between past and present is narrowing because of emerging and potential technology. In other words, the future has shown up for dinner tonight when we were expecting it for breakfast next month.

The purpose of this chapter is to examine some of the rapid changes that have taken place in graphic arts technology and to forecast some future directions this technology will take. Continuing education is important for minds and professions; if this chapter alerts you to changes in the field and helps you to foster an attitude of preparation and training, then its purpose will be well-met.

Two Centuries of Rapid Change

A brief look at almost 200 years of printing practices shows us that a march toward speed, greater cost efficiency and less dependence on human labor has been a single-minded notion of the graphic arts field.

In the 19th century, printing was done by hand-setting of type by skilled hands and by hand-feeding of paper to presses that operated by human pressure. That laborious process soon gave way to steam-powered, rotary presses that more than matched the increase in typesetting speed that new linecasting machines provided. Add to that the inventions of the telegraph and halftone screens for photographic reproduction, and by 1890 our printing technology seemed so advanced that further developments could only be pipe dreams.

But in the 20th century, which gave us movies, radio and television in quick succession, there was more to showcase in the world of printing: automated typesetting systems, which were first driven by perforated tape and then operated through computer memory; transmission of photographs by radio signals and then by satellite relay; elimination of many craft units of employment with the introduction of offset printing; creation of an effective system of phototypesetting that blended well with offset systems; satellite transmission of printing plates to remote printing sites; the beginnings of computer-generated typesetting systems; development of digital printing systems; and a strong direction toward a complete system of pagination (an electronic production system that eliminates manual dummying and pasteup of text and graphics in order to move directly from the computer to the printing press).

With the 21st century rapidly approaching, the face of the new technology is already quite familiar. We saw it in 1983, when *Time* magazine abandoned its traditional "Man of the Year" cover and replaced it with a "Machine of the Year"—the computer. The face becomes even more clear when we understand the relationship of the computer in printing technology to the radio, telephone and satellite. Indeed, the look of "new" printing is electronic. Job-case type, with its worn, uneven faces has been replaced with cool, "high tech" silicon wafers that contain *megabytes* of information. These wafers now carry libraries once characterized by handsomely bound volumes of hand-dipped paper pressed with the rich ink held by handset type. Even our proof presses are vanishing, replaced by glowing screens.

Let's examine some of the changes taking place in the graphic arts industry, paying particular attention to how these changes will affect both work organization and the pursuit of style and creativity. Specifically, we will look at the development of complete pagination systems, plateless printing, computer generation of type, computer graphics, electronic applications for photography, and all-electronic publishing.

Pagination Systems

Pagination is an "electronic collection" process that brings text, graphics and design together on a computer terminal for layout and finished page production. In a newspaper and magazine configuration, a reporter/writer/editor is not only a typesetter in this system but a pasteup artist and process camera operator as well. All work is done through keyboard input and digital scanning, with the "proof" of work showing up on the screen of a terminal, which can order the completed page as a photo positive, film negative or plate (Figure 17-1).

The speed and labor savings available with such a system are readily apparent. However, the conflict that naturally arises when human labor is displaced from the workplace has been one of the main stumbling blocks to the widespread use of pagination systems. Although several U.S. newspapers and many magazines are using systems that take them—electronically—from text input to platemaking, most others are using only partial systems because of labor problems, difficulty in justifying costs or incompatibility with a firm's existing equipment.

For many publications, the biggest problem in using pagination is that while text and makeup can be done electronically by terminal, most line art and photography still have to be handled manually because the computers lack the storage capacity (memory) needed for graphic information. In response, several U.S. firms that manufacture pagination systems say they now have computers that can scan and store photographic information as easily as textual matter. A second problem has been the conversion of digital signals from the computer to platemaking machines. The newest platemakers use laser etching, and their speed and storage capacity have increased tremendously in recent years. So the problem for many publications becomes how much new equipment to buy at once. Can the cost be justified? When the *Pasadena Star-News* became the first U.S. newspaper to achieve total pagination with suc-

17-1 The future is here. Although only a handful of publications were working with basic pagination systems a few years ago, these *text/graphic input to press* systems are gaining more widespread use. These pictures show the page lay-out on a screen display and its photographic output, ready for platemaking. (Courtesy *Pasadena Star-News*)

cessful storage of graphics, its production manager claimed that the system would "pay for itself" in less than five years.

An "ideal" system of computer-to-plate pagination is sketched in Figure 17-2. With improvements in graphics scanning and storage (and forecasting the elimination of silver-based photography), we are drawing ever closer to all-electronic publishing.

For many graphic arts firms, even a partial system will be attractive. Their paste pots, pica rules and hot wax can be replaced by keyboards and "mouses" (tracers that give commands to the computer as they point to various places on the screen). Although a pagination system may produce only film, the prospect of handling all art manually and creating plates remains palatable. Speed and cost advantages have already been obtained; it is only a matter of time before the typesetter is a complete platemaker, too.

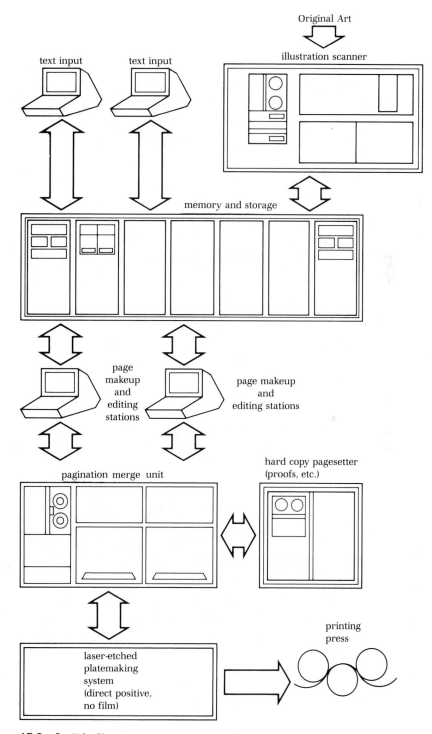

17-2 An "ideal" pagination system that eliminates manual production steps.

Plateless Printing

Ever since the manufacturers were able to move machine-set metal type into the memories of computers and onto screens for display, their short-cutting of production steps has focused on another goal: the elimination of all manual production steps between keyboarding of type and the actual printing of the product. What has been envisioned is a computer-to-press process without the use of plates.

A plateless printing system depends on *non-impact* printers, which could be driven by ink jets or lasers. Actually, these systems are better called *computer-directed digital printers.* When you consider that laser and ink-jet printers now successfully print such small jobs as address labels *without* plates, it is not unreasonable to foresee a time when all impact printing (e.g., offset, gravure) will be replaced by larger-capacity systems of plateless printing.

Such a change will result in the ultimate use of a pagination system—total control of all aspects of printing and production with a *keyboard.* However, while the conversion from hot to cold type has gone relatively smoothly, the transition to digital printing will take longer, require greater planning and demand higher investment. It is one thing for a digital printer to handle relatively simple width and depth measurements and commands to produce four lines of an address on a label. It is quite a quantum leap to have these laser or ink-jet systems print a 96-page newspaper on instructions from a keyboard alone, with a computer that controls press speed and paper tension and has the memory to tell the digital printer what to "set" for the 100 lines of a story—and does this for 60,000 "impressions."

When such a system is perfected, the "presses" we use with it will be a far cry from the hefty frameworks that contain high-speed cylinders. Like the newsroom of today that only contains the humming and beeping of word processors and editing terminals, the "noise factory" of the pressroom will soon be overwhelmed by its new silence.

Computer Generation of Type

As computer memory expands, so does its ability to store more sophisticated information. In the area of typography, computer systems are creating startling new developments in "character generation." One such machine now in use is a *digigraphic typesetter,* which stores master fonts and symbols as digitized information. These are high-quality characters; it has been reported that thousands of families of type can be stored in these machines, with output (actual printed type) etched by a high-resolution laser that creates type with a definition exceeding 5000 scanning lines per inch.

The amazing aspect of digitized typesetting is that once additional memory can be obtained, the typesetter can also become a typographic designer. With stored digital information for each type family as a base or matrix, the computer operator can redesign existing type by changing strokes and slants, elongating other portions, and perhaps even borrowing "information" from another family to bring something different to a new face. Drawing on the computer screen with a stylus or "mouse" can also give the operator greater design capabilities.

The implications for such developments are profound. Such a typesetter, with all its creative functions, could easily be tied into any master word-processing unit. As the text is stored on a disk, the operator could also call up a variety of fonts carried in the system. He or she would "set" a few to help visualize how that typeface would look in the desired design and how it would relate to the actual content. A final face could be selected, and with the computer set up for a pagination process, all type specifications, column widths and headline positioning could be ordered. In effect, the keyboard operator would *bypass* all the traditional functions of the typesetting shop. It would seem that large type and print shops would be wise to start creating special software programs to allow users of their previous services to do all word processing and type selection in-house and then transmit their digital information to the print shop for film and platemaking before printing. These tie-in systems, channeled by a simple telephone modem (a hookup that lets computers receive and transmit their digital information over phone lines), are actually in use in some print shops today.

Developments such as this show the effect of what is called "technological push and cultural pull." Are people ready to use such advanced technology? Will craftsmanship be sorely affected as machines take over the proud work of typographers? What is the best way to plan and train for these new technologies? Such questions reveal both the excitement and anxiety about future developments.

Computer Graphics

In much the same way that type can be designed by computer, so too has line art, photography and animation been influenced by computer systems. It is estimated that expenditures for computer graphics will hit $6 billion annually by 1990.

Computer graphics move art from the canvas and sketch pad to the video screen. They offer sophisticated capabilities that give new looks to corporate logos, page designs and line art. Through the use of the considerable memory of the computer and the responsiveness to an operator's stylus, a new generation of art has been born. This so-called *computer art* gives greater dimensional value to graphics. It will help designers visualize their color schemes more quickly. And with the aid of more sophisticated plotters (devices that print out, in color, all designs made on the screen), the designer has an instant proofing system.

Today, the computerized graphic systems present art at a highly defined level (see Figure 17-3). Some of the laser-driven plotters are capable of producing images that contain more than 600 dots to the inch. With improvements that most certainly will come in the near future, these systems will be able to do more enhancement of existing images, which in the past only professional airbrushing artists could do. Electronic enhancement of images from other media can sharpen focus, add new elements, create composite images and combine type and other matter that previously could only be done by elaborate hand-stripping and double-burning of plates. *U.S. News and World Report,* a weekly magazine that was the first publication to use a partial pagination system successfully, now has a computerized layout system that makes extensive use of computer graphics.

As these improvements become more cost-effective, more publications will be using them and incorporating electronic layout and computer graphics to their in-house work plan.

Electronic Applications for Photography

Unlike printing, photography is relatively young—it won't even be 200 years old until the year 2035. Incredible effort and heartache went into the development of a stable, silver-based process that gave us the era of the "wet" darkroom. Yet here is just a brief list of some recent changes that have taken photography into the computer age:

—creation of an electronic "still" camera that stores continuous-tone images on a magnetic disk, allows viewing on a monitor, and transmits its images electronically to other sites

—an electronic "darkroom" that stores continuous-tone images in a computer bank for evaluation, cropping, printing and transmission

—laser-controlled color separation and platemaking machines that have extensive color correction capabilities

—scanning devices that can separate and transmit color transparencies via satellite systems

—photo transmitters that can scan a black-and-white *negative* and send a finished, cropped *print* to another site (Figure 17-4)

Because so much of photography is going "on-line" (being tied into a computer system), there is greater capability for integration of text and graphic components of production on an in-house basis. These new systems will grow in sophistication. One sure direction is the elimination of any type of wet darkroom and silver-based systems. Film and paper will surely be relegated to museums and to institutions of fine arts.

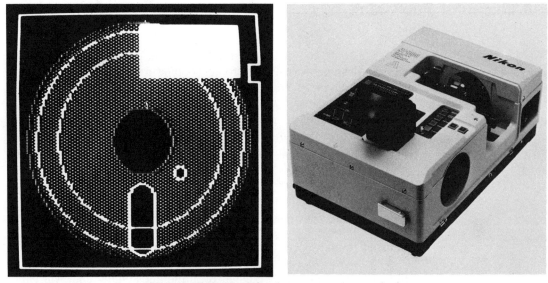

17-3 *Left:* Highly defined computer-generated art.
(Courtesy Ken O'Connell, University of Oregon)

17-4 *Right:* High-speed photographic negative scanner and transmitter. This device can send a completed, cropped print to a remote site using only the negative. (Courtesy Nikon Corp.)

Once they understand the programming techniques, in-house staff will be able to "enhance" the photographic product. Experiments with laser-scanning and image storage devices have already shown their ability to alter photographs and create composites of them with no signs of manipulation visible to the unaided eye. It soon will be possible to store large quantities of photographic images easily and cheaply in computer banks and have a laser scanner match a segment of one photograph to another on the basis of density and tone and then transfer elements within those pictures. Of course, this has serious ethical implications. It is somewhat reminiscent of the overt, detectable manipulations of photographs done in the 20s and 30s by some sensational tabloids. One such paper, the New York *Graphic,* used their vaunted "composographs" to boost circulation. A high point in the paper's brief success came in 1926, when it displayed an "exclusive" picture of opera star Enrico Caruso meeting the recently deceased actor Rudolph Valentino in Heaven.

While such pictures were not taken too seriously, the potential for more subtle, undetectable manipulation of images should cause some concern. It shows another example of "cultural pull": What will be the ethical guidelines for the use of these systems?

All-Electronic Publishing

If you consider the potential capabilities of processes we have described in this chapter, you can easily understand that production for *all* publication will soon be totally electronic. Looking at what is already available today, we can be assured that future developments will continue to spin our cluttered heads.

For example, the printing and transmission system of such newspapers as the *Wall Street Journal* and *USA Today* shows us just how electronic publishing has become. *USA Today* produces all of its pages in Rosslyn, Virginia. However, in order to cover the country quickly with its early morning distribution system, it transmits all the digitized information of this production to a satellite 22,300 miles above the equator. The satellite retransmits this information to 17 U.S. printing sites, which pick up the signal through facsimile receivers. As of now, the page is transmitted and received in negative form in three minutes.

Soon we will see faster transmission times and the elimination of film. The process, totally paginated on the transmitting end, will either allow transmission directly to plate, or it will feed information to a digital inking system that sprays or laser-etches the paper as it speeds through the press. Figure 17-5 shows a schematic of such a system.

On a smaller scale of production, we will see print shops turning into *computerized receiving centers* for text and graphic production from assorted publishers all over the country. Because capability exists today for doing a large amount of electronic typesetting, layout and design by the publisher, print shops have had to face the fact that they must become "software brokerages"—that is, they must offer special computer services to receive the floppy disks and digitized information from publishers and have that matter converted into plates for printing without any re-keyboarding, proofing or design work. This "composition by telecommunication" means that traditional typesetting, proofreading, design, and preparation of mechanicals soon will be eliminated. In its place, the print shop of tomorrow will receive information by telephone or satellite systems, receiving an already-paginated product that simply needs to be printed, bound, and perhaps labeled and mailed. So instead of typesetting, the print shop will translate production codes from a publisher. Offering ease of translation and quick turnaround of transmitted information is a key to the future survival of print shops.

All of this means that people working at the *source* end of the production process must become familiar with computer systems that are encompassing so much of our traditional craft. In addition to learning the language of these systems, production personnel must learn more about typography, readability, design elements, graphic storage, pagination processes and transmission. It is no easy task, and the "old way—new way" battle will rage for some time.

It is indeed a far cry from the days of Gutenberg, when German monks must have been devastated to learn that a new process would

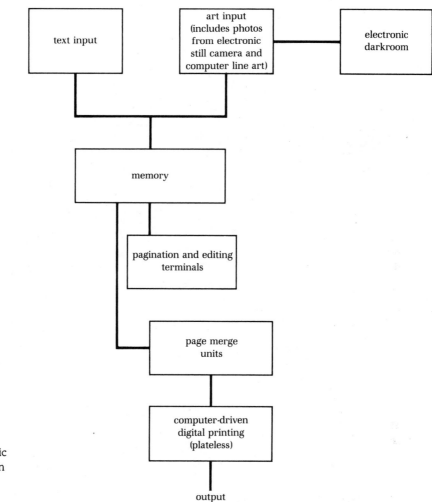

17-5 The all-electronic age of printing, as seen in this input-to-inking schematic.

eliminate the centuries-old dependence on their laboriously hand-copied manuscripts. Just as the printer's job case has found its way to the wall of the living room, so, too, will many of our current printing and production devices find themselves speeding toward obsolescence. What replaces them must be studied and mastered, for ease of use and speed of transmission will hardly guarantee quality and effectiveness.

How we use our new systems, and *what* we create with them, most assuredly will capture the critical eye of the historian. As technology marches ahead, *we* must be the drummer.

APPENDIX

Some Commonly Used Typefaces

Typefaces shown in this section are designs commonly used for body and/or display in all forms of printed matter. They are set in moderate sizes to show their suitability for various purposes. By analyzing the characteristics of these typefaces, students soon will recognize these common designs.

Some of the faces below also will have a listing of character counts next to them. These counts, expressed as characters per pica (CPP), are given for four commonly used text sizes.

Avant Garde Medium

ABCDEFGHIJKLMNOPQRSTUVWXYZ
abcdefghijklmnopqrstuvwxyz
1234567890

Baskerville

ABCDEFGHIJKLMNOPQR STUVWXYZ&
abcdefghijklmnopqrstuvwxyz
$1234567890

	6 pt.	8 pt.	9 pt.	10 pt.
CPP	4.8	3.5	3.2	2.9

Baskerville Italic

ABCDEFGHIJKLMNOPQR STUVWXYZ&
abcdefghijklmnopqrstuvwxyz
$1234567890

	6 pt.	8 pt.	9 pt.	10 pt.
CPP	5.4	3.9	3.6	3.3

Bembo

A B C D E F G H I J K L M N O P Q R S T U V W X Y Z
a b c d e f g h i j k l m n o p q r s t u v w x y z
1 2 3 4 5 6 7 8 9 0

	6 pt.	8 pt.	9 pt.	10 pt.
CPP	4.4	3.3	2.9	2.6

Benguiat Book

A B C D E F G H I J K L M N O P Q R S T U V W X Y Z
a b c d e f g h i j k l m n o p q r s t u v w x y z
1 2 3 4 5 6 7 8 9 0

	6 pt.	8 pt.	9 pt.	10 pt.
CPP	4.2	3.1	2.8	2.5

Bernhard Gothic Medium

A B C D E F G H I J K L M N O P Q R S T U V W X Y Z &
a b c d e f g h i j k l m n o p q r s t u v w x y z
$ 1 2 3 4 5 6 7 8 9 0

Bernhard Modern Bold

A B C D E F G H I J K L M N O P Q R S T U V W X Y Z &
a b c d e f g h i j k l m n o p q r s t u v w x y z
$ 1 2 3 4 5 6 7 8 9 0 ¢

Bodoni

A B C D E F G H I J K L M N O P Q R S T U V W X Y Z &
a b c d e f g h i j k l m n o p q r s t u v w x y z
$ 1 2 3 4 5 6 7 8 9 0

	6 pt.	8 pt.	9 pt.	10 pt.
CPP	5.2	3.9	3.5	3.2

Bodoni Italic _____

A B C D E F G H I J K L M N O P Q R S T U V W X Y Z &
a b c d e f g h i j k l m n o p q r s t u v w x y z
$ 1 2 3 4 5 6 7 8 9 0

	6 pt.	8 pt.	9 pt.	10 pt.
CPP	5.6	4.2	3.8	3.5

Bookman _____

ABCDEFGHIJKLMNOPQRSTUVWXYZ&
abcdefghijklmnopqrstuvwxyz
$1234567890

	6 pt.	8 pt.	9 pt.	10 pt.
CPP	4.2	3.2	2.8	2.5

Caledonia _____

ABCDEFGHIJKLMNOPQRSTUVWXYZ&
abcdefghijklmnopqrstuvwxyz
$1234567890

	6 pt.	8 pt.	9 pt.	10 pt.
CPP	4.6	3.5	3.1	2.7

Carousel _____

A B C D E F G H I J K L M N O P Q R S T U V W X Y Z
a b c d e f g h i j k l m n o p q r s t u v w x y z
1 2 3 4 5 6 7 8 9 0

Caslon _____

A B C D E F G H I J K L M N O P Q R S T U V W X Y Z &
a b c d e f g h i j k l m n o p q r s t u v w x y z
$ 1 2 3 4 5 6 7 8 9 0

	6 pt.	8 pt.	9 pt.	10 pt.
CPP	5.3	4.0	3.6	3.2

Caslon Italic _____

A B C D E F G H I J K L M N O P Q R S T U V W X Y Z &
a b c d e f g h i j k l m n o p q r s t u v w x y z
$ 1 2 3 4 5 6 7 8 9 0

	6 pt.	8 pt.	9 pt.	10 pt.
CPP	5.4	4.1	3.7	3.3

Century Schoolbook

A B C D E F G H I J K L M N O P Q R S T U V W X Y Z &
a b c d e f g h i j k l m n o p q r s t u v w x y z
$ 1 2 3 4 5 6 7 8 9 0

	6 pt.	8 pt.	9 pt.	10 pt.
CPP	4.7	3.5	3.2	2.8

Cheltenham Medium

ABCDEFGHIJKLMNOPQRSTUVWXYZ&
abcdefghijklmnopqrstuvwxyz
$1234567890

Clarendon Semi-Bold

A B C D E F G H I J K L M N O P Q R S T U V W X Y Z
a b c d e f g h i j k l m n o p q r s t u v w x y z
$ 1 2 3 4 5 6 7 8 9 0

Cooper Black

A B C D E F G H I J K L M N O P Q R S T U V W X Y Z &
a b c d e f g h i j k l m n o p q r s t u v w x y z
$ 1 2 3 4 5 6 7 8 9 0

Dom Casual

A B C D E F G H I J K L M N O P Q R S T U V W X Y Z &
a b c d e f g h i j k l m n o p q r s t u v w x y z
$ 1 2 3 4 5 6 7 8 9 0 $

Egmont Light Italic

A B C D E F G H I J K L M N O P Q R S T U V W X Y Z
a b c d e f g h i j k l m n o p q r s t u v w x y z
$ 1 2 3 4 5 6 7 8 9 0

	6 pt.	8 pt.	9 pt.	10 pt.
CPP	4.2	3.1	2.7	2.5

Electra

ABCDEFGHIJKLMNOPQRSTUVWXYZ&
abcdefghijklmnopqrstuvwxyz
$1234567890

	6 pt.	8 pt.	9 pt.	10 pt.
CPP	5.3	4.0	3.6	3.2

Eurostyle

ABCDEFGHIJKLMNOPQRSTUVWXYZ
abcdefghijklmnopqrstuvwxyz
1234567890

Franklin Gothic

ABCDEFGHIJKLMNOPQRSTUVWXYZ&
abcdefghijklmnopqrstuvwxyz
$1234567890

Franklin Gothic Italic

ABCDEFGHIJKLMNOPQRSTUVWXYZ&
abcdefghijklmnopqrstuvwxyz
$1234567890.,-:;!?'

Futura Medium

ABCDEFGHIJKLMNOPQRSTUVWXYZ&
abcdefghijklmnopqrstuvwxyz
$1234567890

	6 pt.	8 pt.	9 pt.	10 pt.
CPP	4.8	3.6	3.2	2.9

Garamond

ABCDEFGHIJKLMNOPQRSTUVWXYZ&
abcdefghijklmnopqrstuvwxyz
$ 1 2 3 4 5 6 7 8 9 0

	6 pt.	8 pt.	9 pt.	10 pt.
CPP	4.7	3.5	3.2	2.8

Goudy

ABCDEFGHIJKLMNOPQRSTUVWXYZ&
abcdefghijklmnopqrstuvwxyz
$1234567890

	6 pt.	8 pt.	9 pt.	10 pt.
CPP	5.0	3.7	3.4	3.0

Helvetica

ABCDEFGHIJKLMNOPQRSTUVWXYZ&
abcdefghijklmnopqrstuvwxyz
$1234567890

	6 pt.	8 pt.	9 pt.	10 pt.
CPP	4.9	3.6	3.2	2.9

Helvetica Italic

ABCDEFGHIJKLMNOPQRSTUVWXYZ&
abcdefghijklmnopqrstuvwxyz
$1234567890

	6 pt.	8 pt.	9 pt.	10 pt.
CPP	5.1	3.7	3.3	3.1

Korinna

ABCDEFGHIJKLMNOPQRSTUVWXYZ
abcdefghijklmnopqrstuvwxyz
1234567890

	6 pt.	8 pt.	9 pt.	10 pt.
CPP	5.1	3.8	3.4	3.1

Lightline Gothic

ABCDEFGHIJKLMNOPQRSTUVWXYZ&
abcdefghijklmnopqrstuvwxyz
$1234567890

	6 pt.	8 pt.	9 pt.	10 pt.
CPP	5.1	3.8	3.4	3.1

Lubalin Graph Book

ABCDEFGHIJKLMNOPQRSTUVWXYZ
abcdefghijklmnopqrstuvwxyz
1234567890

Madison

A B C D E F G H I J K L M N O P Q R S T U V W X Y Z
a b c d e f g h i j k l m n o p q r s t u v w x y z
1 2 3 4 5 6 7 8 9 0

Melior

A B C D E F G H I J K L M N O P Q R S T U V W X Y Z &
a b c d e f g h i j k l m n o p q r s t u v w x y z
$ 1 2 3 4 5 6 7 8 9 0

	6 pt.	8 pt.	9 pt.	10 pt.
CPP	4.6	3.4	3.1	2.7

Melior Italic

A B C D E F G H I J K L M N O P Q R S T U V W X Y Z &
a b c d e f g h i j k l m n o p q r s t u v w x y z
$ 1 2 3 4 5 6 7 8 9 0

	6 pt.	8 pt.	9 pt.	10 pt.
CPP	4.9	3.5	3.3	3.0

Memphis Medium

A B C D E F G H I J K L M N O P Q R S T U V W X Y Z
a b c d e f g h i j k l m n o p q r s t u v w x y z
1 2 3 4 5 6 7 8 9 0

	6 pt.	8 pt.	9 pt.	10 pt.
CPP	4.1	3.1	2.7	2.5

Newtext Book

A B C D E F G H I J K L M N O P Q R S T U V W X Y Z
a b c d e f g h i j k l m n o p q r s t u v w x y z
1 2 3 4 5 6 7 8 9 0

	6 pt.	8 pt.	9 pt.	10 pt.
CPP	3.9	2.9	2.6	2.3

Optima

A B C D E F G H I J K L M N O P Q R S T U V W X Y Z
a b c d e f g h i j k l m n o p q r s t u v w x y z
$ 1 2 3 4 5 6 7 8 9 0

	6 pt.	8 pt.	9 pt.	10 pt.
CPP	4.2	3.3	3.0	2.7

Palatino

A B C D E F G H I J K L M N O P Q R S T U V W X Y Z
a b c d e f g h i j k l m n o p q r s t u v w x y z
$1234567890

	6 pt.	8 pt.	9 pt.	10 pt.
CPP	4.0	3.2	2.8	2.5

Palatino Semi-Bold

A B C D E F G H I J K L M N O P Q R S T U V W X Y Z
a b c d e f g h i j k l m n o p q r s t u v w x y z
1234567890

Serif Gothic

ABCDEFGHIJKLMNOPQRSTUVWXYZ
abcdefghijklmnopqrstuvwxyz
1234567890

	6 pt.	8 pt.	9 pt.	10 pt.
CPP	4.1	3.3	3.0	2.7

Souvenir Bold

A B C D E F G H I J K L M N O P Q R S T U V W X Y Z
a b c d e f g h i j k l m n o p q r s t u v w x y z
1 2 3 4 5 6 7 8 9 0

Stymie Bold

A B C D E F G H I J K L M N O P Q R S T U V W X Y Z &
a b c d e f g h i j k l m n o p q r s t u v w x y z
$ 1 2 3 4 5 6 7 8 9 0

Times Roman

ABCDEFGHIJKLMNOPQRSTUVWXYZ&
abcdefghijklmnopqrstuvwxyz
$1234567890

	6 pt.	8 pt.	9 pt.	10 pt.
CPP	4.5	3.5	3.2	2.9

Univers

ABCDEFGHIJKLMNOPQRSTUVWXYZ
abcdefghijklmnopqrstuvwxyz
1234567890

	6 pt.	8 pt.	9 pt.	10 pt.
CPP	3.9	3.1	2.8	2.5

Univers Italic

ABCDEFGHIJKLMNOPQRSTUVWXYZ
abcdefghijklmnopqrstuvwxyz
1234567890

	6 pt.	8 pt.	9 pt.	10 pt.
CPP	3.9	3.1	2.7	2.5

Wedding Text

ABCDEFGHIJKLMNOPQR
STUVWXYZ&
abcdefghijklmnopqrstuvwxyz
$1234567890

Windsor

ABCDEFGHIJKLMNOPQRSTUVWXYZ&
abcdefghijklmnopqrstuvwxyz
$1234567890

Zapf Book Light

ABCDEFGHIJKLMNOPQRSTUVWXYZ
abcdefghijklmnopqrstuvwxyz
1234567890

	6 pt.	8 pt.	9 pt.	10 pt.
CPP	4.1	3.2	2.8	2.6

Glossary

Cross references are indicated by **boldface** within entries.

acetate Plastic sheet placed over mechanicals; copy that is to overlay copy on the pasteup or mechanical is affixed to the acetate.

agate Name for $5\frac{1}{2}$-point type; agate line is unit of advertising space measurement, $\frac{1}{14}$ inch deep, one column wide.

alignment *See* **baseline.**

ampersand The symbol &, meaning "and."

area composition Output of a photocomposing or cathode-ray tube composing machine that is greater than a single column in width.

art Photographs, drawings, and hand lettering. Also pasteup of materials for camera copy, as in offset and rotogravure.

ASCII The American Standard Code for Information Interchange. The most common 8-level code used in computer word processing.

astonisher Name sometimes used for headlines that include a short line above and/or below the main lines. Also printers' slang for exclamation point.

author's alterations Abbreviated "AAs," refers to changes in proofs not caused by compositor's or printer's error. The publisher or author pays the charges.

author's proof Proof the author reads and marks "OK" or "OK with changes" and then initials.

backbone Portion of book binding between the front and back covers; the *spine.*

back lead The ability of a photocomposing or cathode-ray tube machine to roll exposed photopaper back to a starting point for added exposures.

back slant   The opposite of italic type stance; available through some cathode-ray tube or photocomposing machines.

backup   Duplicate hardware in electronic systems that can be used in case of breakdown.

banner   Newspaper headline crossing the full width of the page. Also called *streamer* or *ribbon.*

bar graph   A graph using varying lengths of bars to show relative quantities.

baseline (or *base*)   Line on which center body rests; phototypesetter type families and sizes can be mixed since they all have common alignment or the same baseline. (See also **x-height.**)

basic weight   The weight of a ream of paper at standard size (book 25 by 38; cover 20 by 26; index 25½ by 30½), also called "substance."

Benday process   A method of applying shading and tinting (lines or dots) to line artwork.

binary digit   The amount of information needed to resolve uncertainty between two alternatives. The number of alternatives determines the binary digits needed.

binding   In a broad sense, any further treatment of stock after printing; includes cutting, folding, trimming, gathering, stitching, gluing, and casing.

bit   Contraction for binary digit.

bleed   An illustration filling one or more margins and running off the edge of the page.

blind keyboard machine   A tape-perforating machine that does not display the copy.

blowup   Enlarged type or picture materials.

blueprint (or *blue* or *blueline*)   A fast proof on paper from an offset flat or negative; all printing is blue.

body type   Type for main message; generally under 12-point size. Also called *text type.* Opposite of **display type.**

boldface (bf)   A variation of a typeface that is heavier and darker than the fullface or lightface versions (as in all the **entry words** here).

bond paper   A paper stock suitable for business purposes, such as letterheads and forms.

book   Trade slang for magazine.

booklet   Small book with either a self-cover or a soft cover.

book paper   A paper stock for periodical printing as well as books and direct literature (promotion and so on).

box   Printed matter enclosed in rules.

braces   Symbols to embrace two or more lines: { }.

brackets   Symbols to enclose words or other symbols: [ ].

branch   Variations within a family of type, such as condensed or italicized versions of the type design.

break-of-the-book   Allocation of space in a magazine.

broadsheet   A full-size newspaper page format.

brownline or **Vandyke**   Same as blueprint except printing is brown.

buildup   An excess of ink sufficient to cause smudging or filling-in of letters.

bulk   Thickness of paper, without reference to its weight.

bullet   Large dot used as an attention-getter and sometimes as a divider.

burn   To expose a photomechanical to a sensitized printing plate.

butted slugs   Two or more linecaster slugs placed together to form a single line of type. Slugs must be butted when the printed line is to be longer than the machine can set.

byte   A series of bits used to identify symbols—a series of 8 bits will identify 256 symbols; a series of 6 bits will identify 64 symbols.

calendering   A rolling operation during papermaking that produces smoothness of surface. Super-calendered paper is rolled between polished steel cylinders to create an especially smooth surface.

callout   Instructions to the printer written on mechanicals or other layouts.

caps and small caps   CAPITALS (uppercase) and SMALL CAPITALS. Small capitals are the same height as lowercase letters in any typeface (the **x-height**) but have uppercase formation.

caption   Text accompanying illustrations. Also used to describe the overlines or "heads" above newspaper illustrations.

carding   A command in type composition by photocomposing machines and CRT machines, whereby spacing is provided between lines to enlarge the type area to a desired depth.

case   A tray holding foundry type that is hand-set. (See also **job case.**)

casebound   A book with a hard cover.

case fraction A fraction that is a font character. (See also **piece fraction.**)

casting off Determining space required for the composition of typewritten manuscript.

cathode-ray tube (CRT) A TV-like electronic tube used to create and then transmit images (words and pictures) onto paper, film, or printing plates.

channel The medium through which a message is transmitted in the communication process.

chase Metal frame to contain type and plates for printing or for molding duplicates.

clc or **c.l.c.** Abbreviation for caps and lower case. The most common way to set textual matter.

clean proof A proof with error-free composition.

clean tape Tape containing only the necessary codes for operating linecasting, photocomposing, or electronic type-generating equipment with all errors and extraneous codes having been removed by an editor or a computer.

closure Process of completing recognition and comprehension of a concept or symbols. Has application in language, psychology and design.

coated paper Paper to which a surface coating has been applied for a smooth finish.

cold type Type composed by other than traditional methods (**hot type** or **foundry**)—namely, photocomposition, pastedown, or "typewriter methods." The latter type is printlike in varying degrees.

collage A combination of several distinct pictures into a composite picture. (See also **montage.**)

collotype *See* **photogelatin.**

colophon Symbol or trademark identifying a printer or publisher.

color print Color photograph viewed by reflected light as compared with a transparency, which is viewed by transmitted light.

color separation In the color reproduction process, a method of "disassembling" a color transparency of print into its three primary colors and black in order to make press plates. This is done either with a process camera or laser-scanning device. (See also **register.**)

column inch One inch of depth in one column of a publication.

combination Line and halftone combined into a single illustration. Also a run of several different jobs at one time on one press.

command In electronic systems a communication from one part of the system to another—e.g., a keyboard stroke to put material in storage or to forward it through the system.

composing stick A device in which foundry type is assembled by hand and justified into lines.

comprehensive A hand-drawn layout or dummy, carefully prepared and finished to approximate the piece in print. May also be a hand-painted presentation of a cover.

computer graphics An electronic, computer-driven system of creating line drawings, designs and other art. These developing systems help forecast an exciting future for type design, image enhancement, and complete pagination systems.

contact print A print on photo paper from negative or positive in contact, as opposed to enlargement or reduction.

continuous tone Refers to a black-and-white photograph with its complete range of contrast and density, from deep black to textureless white. Such prints are screened (halftoned) for mechanical reproduction.

contrast The range of tonality, from black to white, or deep colors to bright ones, in a photograph or drawing. For example, a photograph with only middle grey tones is said to be low in contrast or flat.

copy Text or art to be printed or reproduced.

copy editing Correcting, improving, and marking copy to be printed.

copyfitting Determining (1) space required for copy, (2) amount of copy to be written for allotted space, (3) size of type to accommodate an amount of copy in an allotted space.

copyreading Reading copy for errors and marking copy for printer.

copy schedule An inventory sheet kept by copy desk chief of a newspaper; contains sufficient information about each item for a dummy to be made.

core memory The computer memory that holds program and type-element information that is being processed.

coquille board A textured board used to produce shading in drawings.

counting keyboard machine A tape-perforating machine that signals the operator when hyphenation and justification directions must be punched into the tape.

cover stock Special paper suitable for covers of booklets.

crash A breakdown in computerized electronic systems.

crop To mark artwork or photographs indicating which portions are to be reproduced.

CRT Cathode-ray tube.

cursor On VDT screens a small block of light that locates on the screen the character(s) being affected by the keyboard.

cut A **photoengraving** (line or halftone) for letterpress printing.

cutlines Text accompanying illustrations. (See also **caption.**)

cutoff rule A rule that prints a line used horizontally across columns in newspapers to separate items and guide the reader.

cylinder press A press on which paper is held to a cylinder that revolves, rolling the paper across a flat, inked letterpress form to receive impressions.

Datanews The high-speed digital news service of United Press International.

Datastream The high-speed digital news service of Associated Press.

dead matter Printing materials (type and illustrations) no longer needed (foul matter).

deep etch Special offset technique for long runs in which plates are made from film positives instead of negatives.

dial-in To indicate to a hard-wired logic photocomposition or cathode-ray tube machine the format specifications by setting the controls.

die-cut A printed piece cut into special shape by dies made by shaping steel blades into the desired form.

digital Information in binary digit (0 and 1) form.

digital printing A plateless method of printing that uses either ink-jet sprays or laser-etching to create an image. Controlled by computer memory.

dingbat Typographic decorative device such as a bullet or star.

direct image master Short-run offset plate, usually of paper or plastic, and made without photographic negatives or positives.

directory In electronic systems a listing of all files stored in memory.

diskette In electronic systems a storage medium resembling a 45-rpm recording. (Also called *floppy.*)

display type Type larger than body.

doctor blade The blade on a gravure press that wipes excess ink from the plate before the impression.

double-burn The exposure of light in succession through two separate **flats** or **mechanicals** onto the same **plate;** in many cases one flat contains halftones and the other contains line copy.

doubleprint A surprint, for example, a black line appearing on a tone area.

downtime Unproductive time caused by failure of electronic equipment.

dropout A halftone without dots in unwanted areas; produced by a number of photomechanical means.

dummy Proofs of text, illustrations, captions (or measured holes for each element), and display pasted into position on sheets in specific page arrangement for compositor's guidance in making up pages. In newspapers and magazines the elements may be sketched in place.

dump To release copy from a video display terminal's screen to the perforator or to computer storage. Also a term used to "kill" all stored copy.

duotone A two-color reproduction of a halftone from separate plates. When two plates are made from a single black-and-white photo (one high-key carries color, the other normally carries black) it may be called a *duograph.*

ear Small amounts of type, illustration, or both on either side of a newspaper nameplate. Also refers to the hook on the letters *r* and *g.*

electrostatic printing A technique of affixing a printed image in powder form on paper by means of electrostatic charges.

electrotype A metal plate cast from a wax mold of the original type page.

ellipses Three dots signifying omission as in a quote.

em (short for **em quad**) Nonprinting square of a metal type of any size; designates a square white space of any point size in phototypesetting. Also measure of amount of type composition.

embossing Pressing a relief pattern of type, art, or both into paper or cover materials.

en A metal quad half the width of a mutton (em quad). Also refers to white space half as wide as an em of white space.

end papers Paper glued to the inside covers of a book; often left blank but may contain printing.

engraving A printing plate etched by acid from photographic or other copy; a copper plate into which letters are hand-etched in reverse for printing invitations, calling cards, and so forth. Also a synonym for a cut or photoengraving.

ephemera Printed material of a transitory nature, generally materials other than books.

exception dictionary A computer memory store of hyphenation codes for words not amenable to the logic algorithm for breaking.

face The printing surface of type or plate. Also the name for a specified type.

factoid A *USA Today* technique of overprinting color blocks with tabulated information.

facsimile transmission Scanning and conversion of text and graphic material into electromagnetic signals for transmission to distant printing sites.

fake process color Full-color reproduction from a black-and-white photo, effected by the engraver's manipulation of four separate negatives so that they represent the respective primaries and black. (See **process color.**)

family All related designs within a particular set of type, such as Bodoni or Cheltenham.

file management A computer program that organizes input within memory so that it may be retrieved for further use.

filling in Building up of excess ink to a point where letters plug or close up.

first revise A proof of type with corrections made after first proofreading.

fit Space between characters; can be altered to tight or loose in phototypesetting.

flag Nameplate of a newspaper.

flat A vehicle for holding film positives or negatives in position for exposing onto **plates.** Offset flats are usually **goldenrod** paper; photoengraving and gravure flats are usually glass.

flatbed press A direct-from-type (or engraving) press using either platen or cylinder to print from a flat, as opposed to curved, type form.

flat color Simplest form of spot color; each color stands alone, solid or screened—colors do not overlay each other to form additional colors.

flat piece A printed sheet delivered to a customer unfolded.

flexography A relief printing method using liquid fast-dry ink on rubber plates.

flop To reverse art laterally—image, when printed, is opposite from original.

floppy *See* **diskette.**

flush In typesetting terminology, an extreme direction. Flush left means setting the type to the extreme left of the measured column. Flush left and right is another term for fully justified copy.

folder A printed piece with one or more folds; also a machine that folds printed flat sheets.

folio A page number.

folo head Headline over a small story related to, and placed directly following, the main story.

font All the letters and characters in one size of a typeface.

form Metal type and photoengravings locked in a chase ready for printing or preparing a duplicate, either a mat or a metal or plastic plate.

format The shape, size, and style of a publication; also the typographic requirements for composition, such as line length, typeface, size, and so on.

formatting In electronic systems the capability of specifying typographic composition requirements with terminal keystrokes.

foundry type Hand-set type.

fullface The standard or normal weight and width of a typeface.

furniture Metal or wooden material used to fill in large nonprint areas of a letterpress form.

galley A metal tray for storing metal type. Also a term for a galley proof.

galley proof Proof from type in a galley; also refers to a proof from phototypesetting of type matter not made into pages.

gang To run several jobs on one press at a time. Also, to make several engravings—all at same enlargement or reduction—at one time.

gauge See **line gauge.**

goldenrod Opaque golden-orange paper that serves as the vehicle for an offset **flat.** (See also **mask.**)

gothic type Those faces with, generally, monotonal (noncontrast) strokes and no serifs; also called **sans serif,** *contemporary,* or *block letter.*

Greek golden mean An elegant and universal ratio manifested in natural growth and development and applicable to graphic design.

grid A division of design space into orderly and

regular rectangular areas that serve to contain printed elements, thereby establishing a structural relationship among them. Also, a ruled pasteup sheet.

gripper edge The edge of a sheet held by the gripper on the impression cylinder press or sheetfed rotary; it represents an unprintable $\frac{3}{8}$ to $\frac{1}{2}$ inch.

gutter The inside margin of a page at the binding.

halftone A reproduction made from a photograph, wash drawing, and so forth. Gradation of tone is reproduced by a pattern of dots produced by the interposition of a screen during exposure.

h&j Hyphenation and justification; codes for hyphenation and justification incorporated into perforated tape produced by a computer that has been fed idiot tape or produced from a counting-keyboard perforator; such codes may also be **on-line.**

hanging indention A typesetting style; the first line is full measure with succeeding lines indented from the left.

hanging punctuation Typesetting style in which smaller punctuation is to the right of the right-hand margin of lines of type.

hard copy A printed, usually typewritten, record produced (1) simultaneously when the message is perforated onto tape, or (2) as printout from a computer that has prepared composition tape. Used for editing purposes.

hardware The actual computer and its other "hard-to-the-touch" components. (See also **software.**)

hard-wired logic Wired-in capability of an automated phototypesetter or CRT to perform certain mathematical and logical functions. Such machines are not programmable and can perform only their wired-in functions.

hed sked A headline schedule, the newspaper inventory sheet showing all headlines the newspaper normally uses.

highlight The lightest portion of a photo or other art or reproduction of same. To highlight a halftone is to remove mechanically or photographically the dots in certain areas. Such a halftone is called a highlight or dropout halftone.

hot metal See **hot type.**

hot type Type composed by machine from molten metal; sometimes includes **foundry type.**

IBC Inside back cover.

idiot tape Perforated tape without h&j codes. (Also called *raw tape.*)

IFC Inside front cover.

image (verb) To expose a type element photographically.

image conversion Any of several techniques for adapting hot metal composition to film negative images for making offset or roto plates.

imposition The location of pages in a form or on a sheet so that when the printed sheet of the signature is folded, the pages will fall in proper order.

impression The pressure of type or plate against paper in printing. Also, "impressions per hour" refers to the number of sheets being delivered.

imprint To run a printed piece through another press to add information such as a name or address.

indent To set one or more lines in from left or right margin; one em indent from left of first line signifies a paragraph start.

information graphics Charts, diagrams and other drawings used to convey and explain information. They are receiving increased use as accompaniment to newspaper and magazine stories.

in-house Printing production systems located in, and part of, an editorial operation.

initial A large letter used to start a copy area.

ink-jet printing Plateless printing system using fast-moving, computer-driven ink jets to put an image on paper.

insert A separately printed piece placed in a publication at the time of binding.

intaglio Process of printing from depressed areas carrying ink. (See also **rotogravure.**)

interface To hook various text-processing devices directly via hard wire in lieu of using perforated tape for intermachine communication.

IPS Information processing system; a biological or man-made system capable of accepting information, interpreting (processing) it, and reacting after making a decision.

italic Type that *slants right;* counterpart to roman posture, which is upright.

jig A customized ruled pasteup sheet marked for columns, margins, and so on. (See also **dummy.**)

jim dash A short dash (about three ems long)

used between headline decks in some newspapers.

job case In the hand-set, letterpress process, a drawer holding a font of type.

jump To carry over a portion of a story from one page to another. Also the continued portion of the story.

justify To space or quad out a line of type to make it full to the right margin.

K A designation of computer capacity, each K representing 1024 bytes.

kerning Reducing space between letters so that one extends over another, i.e., placing an *i* under a *T*. Sometimes used as a general term for tight letterspacing.

keyline A **pasteup** or **mechanical** on which lines are drawn to show where art, tint blocks, and so on should be stripped into the **flat.**

key plate The printing plate in color printing that is laid first and to which others must register.

kicker A short line of type above and/or below the main part of a headline; used mainly for feature story headlines.

laser Light beams used to scan photographs, full pages, and symbols and send the scanned results in digital form to cameras, to typesetting equipment, and to platemaking equipment and from point to point, as with AP laser photographs.

layout Often used as a synonym for **dummy.** A pattern, roughly or carefully drawn, to show the placement of elements on a printed piece.

leaders A row of dots used to guide vision across open areas of tabular material.

leads (pronounced "leds") Thin metalic strips used to provide extra space between type lines. (See also **linespacing.**)

legibility That degree of visibility which makes printed matter read easily and rapidly. (See also **readability.**)

letterfold The basic fold given to business letters and to most direct literature.

letterpress The traditional system of printing from raised (relief) areas.

letterset A printing process similar to offset but without the use of water.

letterspacing Adding or subtracting units of space between characters in phototypesetting.

ligature Two or more letters joined together as a single unit, such as *ffl, fi, ff, ffi, œ,* or *œ.*

line In *advertising*, an agate line; in illustrations, artwork and plates composed only of extreme tones as opposed to halftone illustrations. In *design*, a guide to the viewer to show movement, direction, and emphasis. Also a line of type.

linecaster A machine, such as Linotype, which casts type in line units.

line conversion A relatively new technique of converting photographs to line illustrations for special effects.

linecut An engraving, usually on zinc, containing no gradation of tone unless applied by Benday or similar means.

line gauge Printer's ruler marked off in picas and other printing units of measure. Also called a "pica pole."

line printer A high-speed impact printer that produces hard copy of computer-stored information.

linespacing Adding extra space between lines of type; reduction of space is possible in **photocomposition.** (See also **wordspacing.**)

lithographic conversion Lithographic printing of plates originally made for letterpress. Plates can be chalked and photographed directly or proofs can be pulled and photographed.

lithography A system of printing from a flat surface using the principle that grease and water do not mix. (See also **offset.**)

lockup The securing of type, engraving, and furniture in a form before plating.

logotype Originally a hot-type term for two or more images, especially letters, on one type body; today refers to any brand, corporate or store name consistently appearing in a certain typeface; the logotype, or logo; may also include art, such as a trademark or a trade character, or a particular design.

long-term memory (LTM) Human "permanent" memory of vast storage capacity and very long duration, perhaps a lifetime.

lowercase Small letter, as distinguished from a capital.

lower rail In type composition, the normal weight and posture of the size in use.

Ludlow Typograph A typecasting machine usually used for display type; molds are hand set in lines and then the line is cast as a single slug.

makeready Preparation of page forms or plates in letterpress printing to make certain that impression is even and light when paper is impressed against the inked forms or plates.

makeup Arrangement according to design of type, illustrations, and other elements into pages.

mark up To put composition instructions on copy or layout. As a noun, refers to ad layouts so marked. Also, to give command codes to a photocomposition machine or computer indicating typographic formats.

mask A sheet of opaque paper used to prevent light from striking the **plate** while making offset or engraving plates; areas are cut from the mask so that the desired images will be positioned in windows and thus exposed on the plate. Masks may also be made photographically on film. (See also **flat, goldenrod.**)

matrix A mold of a typesetting machine from which a type character or other element is cast. Also the sheet of papier-mâché or composition material used as a mold in stereotyping.

measure Page, line or column width expressed in picas.

mechanical Camera-ready copy with type and pictures positioned on illustration board or heavy paper, keylines drawn to show positioning of other elements, trim marks drawn, and instructions written in margins. One or more overlays may carry additional copy and art with instructions for positioning to the keylines. (Also called **pasteup.**)

mechanical binding Type of binding using plastic, metal spirals, or rings instead of traditional sewing or stapling.

merge On dual screen VDTs, the ability to select the best from two stories to form one story.

mezzotint An illustration that has been given a textured impression through the use of a special halftone screen.

microprocessor A single chip computing device, having the capacity of a minicomputer.

miniature A small **layout** prepared as a preliminary to executing a full-scale layout.

mixing Placing two or more typefaces, type styles, or type sizes within a line, matched to common alignment.

modular design An approach to page design that emphasizes geometric shapes (modules) for text and graphics.

moiré A pronounced screen pattern that results from the clash of dot patterns when two or more screens are used; corrected in full-color and duotone work by changing screen angles.

monitor printer *See* **line printer.**

Monotype A typecasting machine; casts single letters rather than lines and uses both a tape-punching unit and a casting unit to do this.

montage A combination of several distinct pictures into a composite picture; usually called a **collage** unless the edges of the component pictures are made to blend into each other.

mortise A cutout area in a halftone that permits the insertion of type or other matter; if the cutout is from outside edges, it is usually called a **notch.**

nameplate The name of a newspaper, usually at the top of page one.

negative In photography, engraving, and photographic printing processes, the film containing a reversed (in tone) image.

nonpareil A size of type, 6-point.

notch A portion cut out from one or more edges of an illustration.

numerals Numbers within a font, either lining (or Modern), that do not extend below the baseline (1234567890), or Old Style (or nonlining) that extend below the baseline (1234567890).

OBC Outside back cover.

OCR **Optical character recognition.**

OFC Outside front cover.

Offset A lithographic printing method in which the inked image transfers from plate to rubber blanket to paper. Often called indirect or photo-offset **lithography.**

on-line Electronic text processing machines that are directly connected via hard wire.

optical alignment The projection of certain letters beyond the left margin to give a more aesthetic appearance, for example, the stem of a capital T aligned with the left stem of an N in the succeeding line, with the T cross stroke left of the margin.

optical character recognition (OCR) Scanning of typewritten or printed characters, followed by the conversion of the message to magnetic or perforated tape or electronic signals.

overhang cover A cover that, after trimming, projects beyond the dimensions of the inside pages.

overlay Transparent paper or acetate flap placed over a **mechanical** or art to protect it; or to give **photomechanical** instructions; or to carry images to be combined on the same plate with images on the key mechanical.

overset Type that is set but not used.

page proof Proof of type matter in page form together with illustrations or with holes left for them. Also called blueprint or brownprint depending on image color.

pagination An electronic system of text and graphics assembly that allows all layout and design to be done on a video display screen. In its most complete form, pagination is a direct screen-to-printing-plate process without any manual "intervention."

parameters Specifications for photocomposition or CRT composition; the details of formatting.

pasteup A layout board with visual elements (proofs from hot metal or cold-type composition) pasted on it (and often also on one or more overlays) in exact positions; the pasteup is then photographed to make printing plates. (Also called **mechanical**.)

patch To correct photocomposition by pasting in reset matter on the paper or stripping it into the film; also reset material to be pasted in or cut in.

patent base A frame locked up in a letterpress form and to which duplicate plates less than type-high may be attached by hooks.

perfect binding A method of binding books with paper in lieu of case and flexible glue instead of stitching.

perfecting press A press capable of printing on both sides of a sheet or web at the same time.

photocomposition Type composed of exposing negatives of the characters on film or paper.

photoengraving Letterpress plate used to reproduce line or halftone materials.

photogelatin process A screenless printing process using gelatin plates, especially suitable for reproducing tone illustrations. (Also called *collotype*.)

photomechanical Film positives of type, line art,

and halftones positioned on transparent film base from which a single film negative is made.

photostat A photocopy, either positive or negative (reversed in tone), same size, enlarged, or reduced (usually called *stat*).

pica Standard unit of linear measurement (12 points); approximately $\frac{1}{6}$ of an inch.

pi characters Special characters or symbols not found in most type fonts.

pictograph A graph using pictures of objects to show relative amounts of data.

piece fraction A fraction made on a phototypesetter by using numerals plus a slash or a hyphen between superior and inferior numerals. (See also **case fraction;** piece and case fractions should not be used together in composition.)

pie chart An illustration showing a circle divided into segments to show relative quantities of statistical data.

pixel A picture element in computer storage and available on command for use as part of an information graphic.

plate An image carrier, usually metal, which transfers ink to paper or other printing surface.

platen press A flat-surfaced relief press. Paper is supported on one surface, type on the other. The two are brought together for impression.

PMT (photomechanical transfer); a processor for automatically making enlarged or reduced photoprints from line copy, including type, or screened photoprints (**Veloxes**) from continuous-tone copy such as photos. The photoprints are placed on the **pasteup.**

point Printer's unit of measuring size of type and rules, border, spacing material; there are 12 points to a pica and approximately 72 points to an inch. As unit of measurement for thickness of cardboard, equals $\frac{1}{1000}$ inch. Also, a position in the space of a design that is the viewer's primary area of attention.

posterization A special technique for reproducing halftone illustrations in which the two absolute tones (white and black) are combined with only one middle tone.

press proof One of the first copies off the press; it offers a final opportunity to make changes in the job.

process color The reproduction of continuous-tone color originals by separating out each color and recording it on film; plates are made from these films to carry the respective colors to paper.

program In electronic systems, the "thinking" or decision-making processes of which equipment is capable. (See also **software.**)

progressive proofs Proofs of process color plates; each color is shown separately, then in combination with each other. For four-color process a set of *progs* would show seven printings.

proof A trial printing of type, negatives, or plates, to be checked for possible errors.

quad In hand composition a less-than-type-high spacing material used within lines; an em quad is the square of the type size. In electronic composition spacing created by moving the escapement system without exposure of type elements. In automated composition, quad left is the same as flush left and quad right is the same as flush right. Quad center is centered.

queue In electronic systems a listing similar to a directory or a lineup of material held in memory for processing.

quick print Efficient, automated printing based on electrostatic platemaking and offset printing.

quire Usually 25 (sometimes 24) sheets of paper of the same size and quality.

quoin A wedge-shaped device used in locking up letterpress forms.

ragged left Opposite of ragged right.

ragged right Composition in which all lines of type are aligned at the left but are of different lengths and thus uneven or ragged on the right.

rated speed The capacity of a photocomposition or CRT typesetting device expressed in lines per minute, usually based on 8-point, 11 picas (approximately 30 characters and spaces per line).

raw tape *See* **idiot tape.**

readability That degree of visibility that makes printed matter read easily and rapidly.
printed matter read easily and rapidly.

ream Usually 500 (sometimes 480) sheets of paper of the same size and quality.

redundance Excess of information needed to make a decision.

register Placement of forms, plates, or negatives so that they will print in precise relation to or over other forms, plates, or negatives, as in color printing.

reproduction proof A proof on special paper of exceptional cleanness and sharpness to be used as camera copy for offset, rotogravure, or relief plates (usually called *repro*).

reverse Reproducing the whites in an original as black and the blacks as white.

reverse lead *See* **back lead.**

roman A type characterized by serifs; also refers to vertical type commonly used for typesetting as distinguished from *italic.*

rotary press A press that prints as paper passes between a cylindrical impression surface and a curved printing surface.

rotogravure Printing and printing presses using the rotary and gravure principles; **intaglio** process.

rough A preliminary layout not in finished form.

routing Cutting away of excess metal from non-printing areas of engravings or duplicates.

rule A strip of type-high metal that produces a line on paper; rules vary in width. Also the printed line itself (phototypesetters, CRT typesetters, and strike-on machines can create such lines). Also, the black adhesive-backed tape pasted on mechanicals to photograph and print as a black line.

run The number of copies to come off the press.

running heads Titles or heads repeated at the top of book and publication pages, usually followed by or preceded by folio. (When at the bottoms of pages they are *running feet.*)

saddle-stitch To fasten a booklet together by stitching or stapling through the middle fold of the sheets.

sans serif Type having no serifs. (See **gothic type.**)

scale To find any unknown dimension when enlarging or reducing original art for reproduction to size.

scanner An electronic machine that "reads" visual images and produces by means of electrical impulses reproduction materials. Some scanners can produce black-and-white negatives (or positives) from black-and-white photos or composed characters; others can produce screened or unscreened color separation negatives (or positives) from color photos (prints or transparencies); some can read mechanicals or paste-ups and produce printing plates for offset or letterpress. There are also scanners that read materials and send them via wire or radio waves to other locations. (See also **optical character recognition.**)

score To crease paper or cover stock to facilitate folding without breaking.

screen Cross-ruled glass or film used in cameras to break continuous-tone copy into halftone dots. The number of lines per linear inch on the screen governs the fineness of engraving or reproduction. Also a tint block or flat tone.

script Types that simulate handwriting in which letters appear to join.

scroll On video display terminals, to roll the text material up across the face of the video tube for reading; permits seeing previous input that has gone off the screen. (Similar to rolling paper up or down in an ordinary typewriter.)

second generation In **photocomposition,** used to describe electro-mechanical units incorporating rotatable lenses. (See also **third generation.**)

self-cover A cover that is part of one of the signatures of a booklet and of the same paper.

separation *See* **color separation.**

series The range in sizes of a typeface.

serif The finishing cross stroke at the end of a main stroke in a type letter.

set width The width of a character plus the small amount on either side to keep it separate from other characters in composition; measured in units; can be increased or decreased in phototypesetting.

sheetfed Referring to presses that accept sheets, not rolls (webs).

sheetwise An imposition calling for printing half the pages in a signature on one side of the sheet, the other half on the other side.

short-term memory (STM) Human memory of short duration and limited capacity; information quickly forgotten unless moved to **LTM.**

side-stitch To fasten sheets together sideways through the fold.

signature A number of pages printed on one sheet of paper; when folded and trimmed, the pages fall in numerical order. A book signature may contain 8, 16, 32 or 64 pages.

silhouette Reproduction of art or photo with background removed.

silk-screen process A process of printing by which ink or paint is "squeegeed" through a stencil-bearing silk screen to the paper beneath.

slave terminal A terminal with no storage and processing capability of its own.

slug A line of type from a linecasting machine. Also, between-line spacing material of metal 6 points or greater in thickness. Also, the word or two to identify a story.

small caps *See* **caps and small caps.**

soft copy Copy seen on a video display device.

software The programs that direct the operation of a computer as it performs mathematical and logical functions. (See also **hardware.**)

split-fountain printing In printing, the ink receptacle (fountain) can be separated into compartments corresponding to segments of the ink roller, which has also been split. By putting different colors in each fountain segment, more than one color can be printed from a form during one press run.

split page A magazine page that is part advertising and part editorial.

split-roller *See* **split fountain printing.**

split screen The feature on some VDTs that permits display of two stories in side-by-side columns.

spot color Any color printing other than process printing.

square indention A newspaper headline pattern in which all lines are uniformly indented from the left; a modification of the flush left headline.

square serif Types basically **gothic** in nature but having monotonal serifs.

stand-alone Electronic text processing machine that is not on-line.

stereotype A letterpress duplicate metal plate (flat or curved) made from a mold similar to cardboard.

STM Short term memory.

stock Paper or cardboard.

straight matter Text copy composed in normal paragraph form; contrast with tabular matter.

strike on Cold-type composition produced on machine that resembles a typewriter.

strip The computer function of removing **h&j** codes from wire-service tape and inserting new h&j codes in a second tape.

stripped slug A type slug that is shaved underneath; it can then be mounted at any angle on base material that brings it type high.

stripping   Affixing film negatives or positives to a **flat.** Also, cutting linecast slugs to less than type height. (See **stripped slug.**)

substance   A term for the basis weight of paper.

surprint   A combination **plate** made by exposing line and halftone negatives in succession on the same plate.

syntax   The relationship of verbal (sometimes visual) elements arranged so that they impart information clearly.

tabbing   Composing copy in even columns within a specified line measure.

tabloid   A format that is half the size of a **broadsheet.**

teletypesetter   An attachment that automatically operates a mat-circulating linecasting machine from perforated tape.

text   A typeface with an "Old English" look. Also any body type. Also the body of a book excluding front and back matter.

text-processing system   Combination of various electronic composition gear that puts author's original copy into type on photo paper or film.

thermography   A printing process that produces a raised impression simulating an **intaglio** engraving. An image is put on paper in the usual way; it is powdered while wet, then heated so that powder and ink fuse to a raised image.

third generation   In **photocomposition,** used to describe totally electronic units that utilize **CRT** technology. (See also **second generation.**)

thumbnail   A miniature **layout.** Also a half-column photoengraving.

tint block   A photoengraving used to print tints of any percentage of color. Also refers to the panel printed from a block.

tip-in   A single sheet or partial signature glued into a book or magazine. It is often of smooth stock used for halftone printing whereas remainder of publication may be printed on a cheaper stock of paper.

tombstone   The typographical effect that results from side-by-side placement of two or more headlines too similar in size and face to stand as separate units.

transfer type   Type carried on a waxy, acetate sheet that can be rubbed (transferred) onto another surface. Excellent for "setting" small amounts of special display type.

transparency   A color photograph that may be viewed by transmitted light. (See also **color print.**)

trim mark   Right angle marks on a mechanical to show the four corners of the printed sheet after it has been trimmed; the marks are cut off when the piece is trimmed.

TTS code   A six-level digital code used for teletypewriters and in many computerized typesetting systems.

type high   In letterpress printing, .918 inches, the desired height for all elements in a form.

typo   A typographical error.

unit   A measurement of set width, usually 18 per em of the type size.

uppercase   Capital letter.

upper rail   In type composition the **boldface** or *italic* alternative that is available for the size in use.

value   Relates to relative brightness of light, color and tone.

VDT   Video display terminal.

vellum   Originally a calfskin or lambskin prepared as a writing surface; now used to label a paper stock with a good writing surface.

Velox   A screened photographic print similar to a **photostat** positive, but usually sharper in definition.

video display terminal (VDT)   A cathode-ray tube keyboard-operated device for viewing material as it is keyboarded into or drawn from computer storage.

video layout system (VLS)   A video-screen, keyboard-control unit-system for area composition of advertisements up to $\frac{1}{2}$ newspaper page width and full-page depth.

vignette   The treatment given a photograph or halftone so that edges fade away into the background without breaking sharply.

visualization   An important step in design. Refers to ability to see or forecast the "look" of a proposed design.

watermark   A faint design or lettering pressed into paper during its manufacture that can be seen when the sheet is held up to light.

webfed   A press that prints on paper fed from a roll.

white print   A photocopy (contact print or enlargement) from a negative (halftone or line).

widow   A short line at the end of a paragraph; always to be avoided at the top of newspaper or magazine columns or book pages, but its presence elsewhere may or may not be disliked.

wire strip   Elimination of typesetting codes from stories transmitted by a wire service such as AP or UPI.

wordspacing   Adding or reducing units of space between words in **photocomposition.** (See also **linespacing.**)

word wrap   The capability of a VDT to end each line with a full word. Adding a word to any line will push as many words forward as necessary to make room, perhaps involving several lines. The change of characters is instantaneous.

work-and-tumble   A system resembling **work-and-turn** except that the sheet is turned so that a new edge is grabbed by the grippers.

work-and-turn   A system of printing both sides of a printing piece on one side of a sheet, then turning the sheet so that its gripper edge remains constant and the sheet is printed on the reverse side.

work-up   A fault in relief printing that causes a spot to be printed because spacing materials or blank portions of type slugs have risen high enough to gather ink.

wrap   An insert into a magazine or book. Unlike a tip-in, it is wrapped around a signature.

wraparound press   A relief press (sheet- or webfed) that utilizes a shallow-etch curved plate made from a **flat** similar to that used in offset.

wrong font (wf)   A letter or character that is of different size or face from the type that was specified.

xerography   A dry system of printing based on electrostatic principles.

x-height   The height of the center body of lowercase letters, excluding ascenders and descenders. The bottom of the x-height is on the **baseline.**

zinc   A photoengraving, line or halftone, made of zinc.

Suggested Readings

Arnheim, Rudolph. *Art and Visual Perception,* 2d ed. Berkeley, Cal.: University of California Press, 1974.

Arnheim, Rudolph. *Visual Thinking.* Berkeley, Cal.: University of California Press, 1980.

Bain, Eric K. *The Theory and Practice of Typographic Design.* New York: Hastings House, 1970.

Biggs, John R. *Basic Typography.* New York: Watson-Guptill, 1968.

Burt, Sir Cyril. *A Psychological Study of Typography.* London: Cambridge University Press, 1959.

Campbell, Alastair. *The Graphic Designer's Handbook.* Philadelphia: Running Press, 1984.

Click, J. W., and R. N. Baird. *Magazine Editing and Production,* 4th ed. Dubuque, Iowa: William C. Brown Co., 1986.

Corcoran, D. W. J. "Acoustic Factors in Proofreading." *Nature* 214 (1967): 851–52.

Craig, James. *Designing with Type.* New York: Watson-Guptill, 1980.

Dondis, Donis A. *A Primer of Visual Literacy.* Cambridge, Mass.: M.I.T. Press, 1973.

Garcia, Mario. *Contemporary Newspaper Design.* Englewood Cliffs, N.J.: Prentice-Hall, 1981.

Gregory, D. L. *Eye and Brain*, 2d ed. London: World University Library, 1973.

Haber, R. N. "How We Remember What We See." *Scientific American* 222(5) (1970): 104–12.

Hurlburt, Allen. *Layout*. New York: Watson-Guptill, 1977.

Hurlburt, Allen. *Publication Design*. New York: Van Nostrand Reinhold Co., 1979.

Hurley, Gerald D., and Angus McDougall. *Visual Impact in Print*. Chicago: Visual Impact, Inc., 1979.

International Paper, ed. *Pocket Pal*. New York: International Paper Co.

Lewis, John. *The 20th Century Book*, 2d ed. New York: Van Nostrand Reinhold, 1984.

Lieberman, J. Ben. *Type and Typefaces*. New Rochelle, N.Y.: Myriade Press, 1978.

Lindsay, Peter H. and Donald A. Norman. *Human Information Processing*, 2d ed. New York: Academic Press, 1977.

Nelson, Roy Paul. *Publication Design*, 3d ed. Dubuque, Iowa: William C. Brown Co., 1983.

Paterson, D. G., and M. A. Tinker. *How to Make Type Readable*. New York: Harper and Row, 1940.

Smith, Frank. *Comprehension and Learning*. New York: Holt, Rinehart and Winston, 1975.

Smith, Stan, and H. F. Ten Holt, eds. *The Designer's Handbook*. New York: Gallery Books, 1984.

Tinker, M. A. "Recent Studies of Eye Movements in Reading." *Psychological Bulletin* 54 (1958): 215–231.

Tufte, Edward R. *The Visual Display of Quantitative Information*. New Haven: Graphics Press, 1983.

White, Jan. *Designing for Magazines*. New York: R. R. Bowker Co., 1982.

Zettl, Herbert. *Sight, Sound, Motion: Applied Media Aesthetics*. Belmont, Cal.: Wadsworth Publishing Co., 1973.

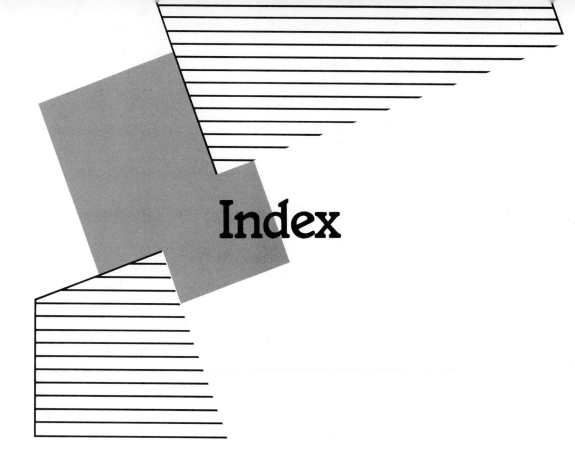

Index